IoT Architectures, Models, and Platforms for Smart City Applications

Bhawani Shankar Chowdhry
Mehran University of Engineering and Technology, Pakistan

Faisal Karim Shaikh
Mehran University of Engineering and Technology, Pakistan

Naeem Ahmed Mahoto
Mehran University of Engineering and Technology, Pakistan

A volume in the Advances in Computer and
Electrical Engineering (ACEE) Book Series

Published in the United States of America by
IGI Global
Engineering Science Reference (an imprint of IGI Global)
701 E. Chocolate Avenue
Hershey PA, USA 17033
Tel: 717-533-8845
Fax: 717-533-8661
E-mail: cust@igi-global.com
Web site: http://www.igi-global.com

Library of Congress Cataloging-in-Publication Data

Names: Chowdhry, Bhawani Shankar, editor. | Shaikh, Faisal Karim, editor. |
   Mahoto, Naeem Ahmed, 1983- editor.
Title: IoT architectures, models, and platforms for smart city applications
   / Bhawani Shankar Chowdhry, Faisal Karim Shaikh, Naeem Ahmed Mahoto,
   editors.
Description: Hershey, PA : Engineering Science Reference, an imprint of IGI
   Global, 2019. | Includes bibliographical references and index. |
   Summary: "This book examines the major aspects of the internet of things
   and how this platform can enhance smart cities by securing innovative
   solutions for their challenges rather than using basic off-the-shelf
   solutions"-- Provided by publisher.
Identifiers: LCCN 2019026570 (print) | LCCN 2019026571 (ebook) | ISBN
   9781799812531 (hardcover) | ISBN 9781799812548 (paperback) | ISBN
   9781799812555 (ebook)
Subjects: LCSH: Smart cities. | Internet of things.
Classification: LCC TD159.4 .I68 2019 (print) | LCC TD159.4 (ebook) | DDC
   307.760285/4678--dc23
LC record available at https://lccn.loc.gov/2019026570
LC ebook record available at https://lccn.loc.gov/2019026571

This book is published in the IGI Global book series Advances in Computer and Electrical Engineering (ACEE) (ISSN: 2327-039X; eISSN: 2327-0403)

British Cataloguing in Publication Data
A Cataloguing in Publication record for this book is available from the British Library.

All work contributed to this book is new, previously-unpublished material. The views expressed in this book are those of the authors, but not necessarily of the publisher.

For electronic access to this publication, please contact: eresources@igi-global.com.

Advances in Computer and Electrical Engineering (ACEE) Book Series

Srikanta Patnaik
SOA University, India

ISSN:2327-039X
EISSN:2327-0403

MISSION

The fields of computer engineering and electrical engineering encompass a broad range of interdisciplinary topics allowing for expansive research developments across multiple fields. Research in these areas continues to develop and become increasingly important as computer and electrical systems have become an integral part of everyday life.

The **Advances in Computer and Electrical Engineering (ACEE) Book Series** aims to publish research on diverse topics pertaining to computer engineering and electrical engineering. **ACEE** encourages scholarly discourse on the latest applications, tools, and methodologies being implemented in the field for the design and development of computer and electrical systems.

COVERAGE

- Circuit Analysis
- Sensor Technologies
- Qualitative Methods
- Algorithms
- Analog Electronics
- Programming
- Digital Electronics
- VLSI Design
- Computer Architecture
- Electrical Power Conversion

Titles in this Series

For a list of additional titles in this series, please visit:
https://www.igi-global.com/book-series/advances-computer-electrical-engineering/73675

Handbook of Research on Emerging Applications of Fuzzy Algebraic Structures
Chiranjibe Jana (Vidyasagar University, India) Tapan Senapati (Padima Janakalyan Banipith (H.S.), India) and
Madhumangal Pal (Vidyasagar University, India)
Engineering Science Reference • © 2020 • 300pp • H/C (ISBN: 9781799801900) • US $285.00

Electrical Insulation Breakdown and Its Theory, Process, and Prevention Emerging Research and Opportunities
Boxue Du (Tianjin University, China)
Engineering Science Reference • © 2020 • 230pp • H/C (ISBN: 9781522588856) • US $215.00

Challenges and Applications for Implementing Machine Learning in Computer Vision
Ramgopal Kashyap (Amity University, Raipur, India) and A.V. Senthil Kumar (Hindusthan College of Arts and
Science, India)
Engineering Science Reference • © 2020 • 293pp • H/C (ISBN: 9781799801825) • US $195.00

Handbook of Research on Recent Developments in Electrical and Mechanical Engineering
Jamal Zbitou (University of Hassan 1st, Morocco) Catalin Iulian Pruncu (Imperial College London, UK) and
Ahmed Errkik (University of Hassan 1st, Morocco)
Engineering Science Reference • © 2020 • 553pp • H/C (ISBN: 9781799801177) • US $255.00

Architecture and Security Issues in Fog Computing Applications
Sam Goundar (The University of the South Pacific, Fiji) S. Bharath Bhushan (Sree Vidyanikethan Engineering
College, India) and Praveen Kumar Rayani (National Institute of Technology, Durgapur, India)
Engineering Science Reference • © 2020 • 205pp • H/C (ISBN: 9781799801948) • US $215.00

Handbook of Research on Advanced Applications of Graph Theory in Modern Society
Madhumangal Pal (Vidyasagar University, India) Sovan Samanta (Tamralipta Mahavidyalaya, India) and Anita
Pal (National Institute of Technology Durgapur, India)
Engineering Science Reference • © 2020 • 591pp • H/C (ISBN: 9781522593805) • US $245.00

Novel Practices and Trends in Grid and Cloud Computing
Pethuru Raj (Reliance Jio Infocomm Ltd. (RJIL), India) and S. Koteeswaran (Vel Tech, India)
Engineering Science Reference • © 2019 • 374pp • H/C (ISBN: 9781522590231) • US $255.00

701 East Chocolate Avenue, Hershey, PA 17033, USA
Tel: 717-533-8845 x100 • Fax: 717-533-8661
E-Mail: cust@igi-global.com • www.igi-global.com

Editorial Advisory Board

Table of Contents

Detailed Table of Contents

Chapter 1

  Seema Ansari, Institute of Business Management, Pakistan
  Tahniyat Aslam, Institute of Business Management, Pakistan
  Javier Poncela, University of Malaga, Spain
  Pablo Otero, University of Malaga, Spain
  Adeel Ansari, Shaheed Zulfiqar Ali Bhutto Institute of Science and Technology, Pakistan

The demand for global healthcare systems for human health improvement is ever growing. Internet of things (IoT) has influenced every industry in the market. IoT-based healthcare monitoring systems have emerged using smart gateways between sensor networks and the internet. This chapter aims at focusing on the impact of IoT on healthcare and explores the difference that IoT has made in the recent years. IoT applications in healthcare have helped people keep track of their medical requirements such as reminding them of appointments, keeping a check on calorie count, variations in blood pressure, a check on exercises, and many more. In this chapter, studies of IoT-based healthcare applications are presented. The chapter begins with the introduction and history of IoT in healthcare, sharing state of the art, architecture, applications of IoT in healthcare, advantages, future concerns and challenges, and future of IoT in healthcare, followed by conclusion.

Chapter 2

  Saeed Ahmed Khan, Sukkur IBA University, Pakistan
  Shamsuddin Lakho, Sukkur IBA University, Pakistan
  Ahmed Ali, Sukkur IBA University, Pakistan
  Abdul Qadir Rahimoon, Sukkur IBA University, Pakistan
  Izhar Hussain Memon, Benazir Bhutto Shaheed University of Technology and Skill
    Development Khairpure Mirs, Pakistan
  Ahsanullah Abro, Sukkur IBA University, Pakistan

Most of the emerging electronic devices are wearable in nature. However, the frequent changing or charging the battery of all wearable devices is the big challenge. Interestingly, with those wearable devices that are directly associated with the human body, the body can be used in transferring or generating energy in a number of techniques. One technique is triboelectric nanogenerators (TENG). This chapter covers different applications where the human body is used as a triboelectric layer and as a sensor. Wearable TENG has been discussed in detail based on four basic modes that could be used to monitor the human health. In all the discussions, the main focus is to power the wearable healthcare internet of things (IoT) sensor through human body motion based on self-powered TENG. The IoT sensors-based wearable devices related to human body can be used to develop smart body temperature sensors, pressure sensors, smart textiles, and fitness tracking sensors.

Chapter 3

Lubna Luxmi Dhirani, University of Limerick, Ireland
Thomas Newe, University of Limerick, Ireland
Shahzad Nizamani, Mehran University of Engineering and Technology, Pakistan

Cloud computing migrations are increasing rapidly. The main influencing factor being IT management costs. IoT-based enterprises that started their cloud journey by setting up small private clouds within their enterprise have often found that as the applications and services they use broaden. Then the shift towards incorporating public clouds becomes inevitable. The current problem that many of these firms are encountering is the difficulty of managing multiple clouds that reside within different vendors running on different platforms, computational requirements, and vendor SLAs. Lack of support for a single standard for an overall multi-cloud hybrid model exposes the hybrid IT-management to further threats. This makes it difficult for an adopting enterprise to manage and maintain its cloud-based systems during peak performance hours, which often leads to system downtime. This chapter discusses various SLA issues specific to a hybrid multi-cloud environment and suggests possible solutions to help adopting firms in their management.

Chapter 4

Christopher Teh Jun Qian, Universiti Teknologi PETRONAS, Malaysia
Micheal Drieberg, Universiti Teknologi PETRONAS, Malaysia
Patrick Sebastian, Universiti Teknologi PETRONAS, Malaysia
Azrina Abd Aziz, Universiti Teknologi PETRONAS, Malaysia
Hai Hiung Lo, Universiti Teknologi PETRONAS, Malaysia
Abu Bakar Sayuti H. M. Saman, Universiti Teknologi PETRONAS, Malaysia

Currently, there is lack of implementation of practical power-saving schemes in most of the batteries powered by IoT smart city applications available in the market that can extend the battery lifetime, even though numerous researches have been carried to reduce the average power consumption. This is because electronics consume similar amounts of power during the idling state as compared to the active state, resulting in low power efficiency of the application. Thus, power consumption is affected by the modes of the electronic operations. Different electronics also have their own types of settings that can be configured to reduce the power consumption, and this will be further investigated in this study. This chapter will address the issue of how to create a power-saving IoT application by applying power-saving schemes and creating an accurate model to predict the battery lifetime of the IoT application.

Chapter 5

Bishwajeet Kumar Pandey, Gyancity Research Consultancy Pvt Ltd, India
D. M. Akbar Hussain, Aalborg University, Denmark
Jason Levy, University of Hawaii, USA

Anything that has an IP address is IoT-enabled. In this chapter, the authors have surveyed nine different IoT-enabled designs from IoT-based water management cyber-physical system (IoT-WMCPS) to IoT-based random access memory (IoT-RAM). They have also surveyed a platform called Quickscript. The Quickscript platform is used to develop natural language based IoT system. The nine different IoT-enabled designs discussed in this chapter are IoT-enabled bicycle called Mo-Bike, IoT-enabled house, IoT-enabled water utility, IoT-enabled mining, IoT-enabled healthcare, IoT-enabled frame buffer, IoT-enabled RAM, IoT-enabled key generator, and IoT-enabled wi-fi encoder. In cyber physical systems for water supply, researchers are able to integrate IPv6 addresses into sensors, actuators, and controllers used in water supply systems. The IPv6 address is integrating into every object available in the city so that researchers may track any object when need occurs. We may locate freely available IoT-enabled bicycles if we need to go anywhere, and we may also trace bicycles in case of theft by criminals.

Chapter 6

Navuday Sharma, Tallinn University of Technology, Estonia
Maurizio Magarini, Politecnico di Milano, Italy
Muhammad Mahtab Alam, Tallinn University of Technology, Estonia

Unmanned aerial vehicles (UAVs) are expected to provide data service to users as aerial base stations, as gateways to collect the data from various sensors, and as sensor-mounted aerial platforms deployed in smart cities. The study in this chapter initially starts with the air-to-ground (A2G) channel model. Due to the unavailability of channel parameters for UAVs at low altitudes, measurements were performed using a radio propagation simulator for generalized environments developed using ITU-R parameters. Further, cell coverage analysis is shown with simulation results obtained from the ray tracing. Later, an optimal replacement to UDNs was proposed to support the flash crowds and smart cites known as ultra-dense cloud drone network. This system is advantageous as it offers reduction in total cost of ownership due to its on-demand capability. Further, work is shown on implementing parameters for 5G physical layer with generalized frequency division multiplexing modulation over A2G channel on the UAV network to provide reliable and faster connectivity for ground users and sensors.

Chapter 7

Uferah Shafi, National University of Sciences and Technology, Pakistan
Rafia Mumtaz, National University of Sciences and Technology, Pakistan
Syed Ali Hassan, National University of Sciences and Technology, Pakistan
Syed Ali Raza Zaidi, University of Leeds, UK
Awais Akhtar, National University of Sciences and Technology, Pakistan
Muhammad Moeez Malik, National University of Sciences and Technology, Pakistan

Agriculture holds paramount significance in Pakistan due to its high impact on gross domestic product (GDP). However, there is huge gap between actual production and estimated production in agriculture due to manual farming system, which is time-consuming, inefficient, and labor-intensive. As of today, ultra-modern technology such as Internet of Things (IoT) can assist in acquiring timely and accurate crop information essential for the success of precision agriculture technology. Towards such ends, the authors propose an IoT-based crop health monitoring system comprised of different sensors used in agricultural fields. Additionally, low altitude remote sensing platforms, such as drones, are used to capture the spectral imagery of the entire crop field of the study region. The development of such a system can be instrumental for crop status monitoring and localizing the areas under stress to maximize the agricultural output by leveraging the IoT technology.

Chapter 8

Bhawana Rudra, National Institute of Technology, Karnataka, India
Thanmayee S., National Institute of Technology, Karnataka, India

The internet of things is a new paradigm where smart embedded devices are connected to the internet. In this context, wireless sensor networks (WSN) are becoming an important alternative for sensing and actuating critical applications like industrial automation, healthcare, etc. 6LoWPAN provides a means of carrying packet in the form of IPv6 over IEEE 802.15.4 and other networks. It provides end-to-end IPv6, and as such, it is able to provide direct connectivity to a huge variety of networks and to the internet. It uses an adaptation layer for fragmenting and reassembling of the IPv6 packets. Due to its low-cost communication network, it allows IoT connectivity with limited power and throughput. It can be used to overcome the challenges that are faced during the integration of WSN and IP protocols. This chapter briefly discusses IoT followed by an introduction to IPv6 and 6LoWPAN in detail along with architecture that suits IoT, 6LoWPAN mote design features and functions. It also focus on the advantages of LoWPAN with respect to IoT and its security along with smart city case studies.

Chapter 9

Badar Muneer, Mehran University of Engineering and Technology, Pakistan
Faisal Karim Shaikh, Mehran University of Engineering and Technology, Pakistan
Qi Zhu, University of Science and Technology of China, China

Under the umbrella of 5G there are many technology projects (e.g., internet of things, in-vehicle communication, smart cities, e-health systems, etc.). To understand the concept of IoT, the authors first understand the revolution of technological networks and later discuss what IoT is, the importance of antennas, and future vision.

Chapter 10

Jayapandian N., Faculty of Engineering, Christ University, Bangalore, India

The main objectives of this chapter are to discuss the basics of IoT and its applications and to solve data security and privacy issues in Industry 4.0. Industry 4.0 is mainly focus on IoT technology. The IIoT is generating digital data, and that data is stored in cloud server. There are two major issues in this IIoT. The first one is data storage, and the second one is data security. Industry 4.0 is not only involved in the manufacturing industry. It is also in the transportation and automobile industries. Electrical, electronic, mechanical, and computer technology fields are involved in Industry 4.0. This chapter enhances the hybrid security protocol in Industrial IoT. This hybrid mechanism combines lightweight protocol and the probabilistic encryption (LPP) algorithm.

Chapter 11

Muhammad Rehan Yahya, Nanjing University of Aeronautics and Astronautics, China
Ning Wu, Nanjing University of Aeronautics and Astronautics, China
Zain Anwar Ali, Sir Syed University of Engineering and Technology (SSUET), Pakistan

The evolution of internet of things (IoT) applications, cloud computing, smart cities, and 4G/5G wireless communication systems have significantly increased the demands for on chip processing. Network on chip (NoC) is a viable alternative that can provide higher processing and bandwidth for increasing demands. NoC offers better performance and more flexibility with lower communication latency and higher throughput. However, use of NoC-based IoT devices have raised concerns on security and reliability of integrated chips (IC), which is used in almost every application. IoT devices share data that becomes vulnerable to attack and can be compromised during the data transfer. Keeping in view these security challenges, a detailed survey is presented that covers the security issues and challenges focusing on NoCs along with proposed countermeasures to secure on-chip communication. This study includes on-chip security issues for electrical as well as optical on-chip interconnects.

Foreword

Today we live in the digital era surrounded by smart devices. As emerging technologies become more powerful and cost-effective, they are making it possible to design smart buildings, transform traditional methods into smarter and more efficient techniques in a wide range of application domains such as education, health, agriculture, transportation, power consumption and resource management. As smart cities continue to grow and evolve, smart and innovative solutions have become vital for improving productivity, increasing operational efficiencies and reducing management costs. Smart infrastructures, devices, and services along with the users are the major components of a smart city, where Internet of Things (IoT) technologies enable strong connectivity among them. The number of smart devices connecting to the Internet keep growing every day and it is expected that by 2025, more than 50 billion devices will be connected together through the IoT ecosystem. This timely book presents several aspects of IoT technologies that will play a fundamental role in the evolution of smart cities.

Various authors have contributed to this book and they have presented a wide range of smart city applications in various areas including health, agriculture, transportation, communication protocols, resource and power management, privacy and reliability. The authors have also discussed IoT-enabled architectures, models and platforms for smart city applications.

Smart cities and IoT technologies will continue to play an important role in our daily lives in the future and this timely book will serve as a valuable reference for various stakeholders dealing with these technologies. I hope you will enjoy reading this book as much as I did!

Sherali Zeadally
University of Kentucky, Lexington, USA

Preface

Scientific research and technological innovation have reshaped our routine activities. Today, we live in a dynamic, fast spaced world that is entrenched in technological innovation – becoming integrated part of our lifestyle. The term smart city is globally well-established concept, which has reshaped the lifestyle of inhabitants of urban cities. Smart city uses information and communication technologies to increase operational efficiency, share data with the public and enhance both the citizen enrolment and quality of government. It provides sustainable development to nations and contribute towards knowledge economy. With the passage of time people equip their homes with IoT (Internet of Things) devices such as smart TVs, smart locks and smart voice assistants. Moreover, health, treatment, education, safety, security and waste management are the fundamental needs of inhabitants of the cities. Smart healthcare system uses innovative technologies to bring advancements in e-Health, where the sensors communicate with medical devices using different technologies. Such advancement drives growth of intelligent and connected medical devices. Thus, technological shift has changed the traditional concept of healthcare services to smart healthcare to ensure well-being of citizens. Likewise, safety and security solutions turn the traditional ways into smarter ways to cope with the new and emerging cyber challenges. With the growing inhabitants and urbanization solid waste is also becoming a major issue and the technological evolution has provided solutions to overcome it and to provide true scenarios of smart cities.

This book seeks to bring together theoretical and practical research from variety of disciplines, which build our cities with novel and innovative technological solutions, especially, attempts taken towards building smart cities. It aims at covering fundamental units of cities that how these basic needs are embedded with IoT technologies. For instance, in order to properly maintain the health of crops, it is required to continuously monitor and identify the affected areas. As the involvement of IoT increases, security concerns are on the top priority thus a practical solution must find the trade-offs between effectiveness and privacy risks. A sophisticated attacker could, for example, take control of various intelligent devices such as lights, cameras, traffic lights, connected cars and many other smart devices in cities.

Cities sustainability and development is the growing field where every developing country is looking for efficient and cost effective tools to transform their state to the smart city idea. It is need of the time to change the traditional ways into technological smart solutions for the betterment of societies. Energy crises are increasing in developing countries like Pakistan due to dearth of awareness and proper utilization of smart technologies. With the increasing utilization of technology there is also a focus on low power consumption IoT enabled technologies. Further, smart cities also emphasis on intelligent decision making using Artificial Intelligence. Thus, it's need of the hour to address the challenges, issues and sustainable innovative solutions that help in revamping smart city applications.

This book covers essential aspects of IoT based architectures, models and platforms for smart city applications such as health, optimized energy consumption of IoT devices, agriculture, transportation and privacy, reliability of IoT based communication protocols. The structure of the book is as follows:

Chapter 1 introduces IoT based healthcare applications. The development of global health care systems for human health improvement is an ever-growing field and has a lot of demand in every industry in the market. IoT based healthcare monitoring systems that are mostly used in telemedicine have established smart gateways between sensor networks and the Internet. This chapter focuses on the influence of IoT on healthcare and the advancement in the healthcare monitoring systems because of IoT such as: keeping track of the medical requirements like reminding the checkup appointments, keeping record of the calorie count, blood pressure, exercise, etc. Numerous IoT based healthcare applications are presented in this chapter, the detailed discussion on the origin of the IoT in healthcare and its architecture along with its advantages and disadvantages have also been reported. At the end of the chapter, the future concerns and challenges are discussed of IoT in healthcare, followed by conclusion.

Chapter 2 presents energy harvesting techniques for powering IoT enabled healthcare. Various electronics devices are emerging that are wearable in nature and the frequent changing or charging the batteries of the wearable devices is the big challenge by itself. However, some wearable devices are associated with the human body and they can use the human body for generating the electricity that can charge them. This task can be done by various techniques. One of those techniques is triboelectric nanogenerators (TENG). This chapter covers on the multiple applications through which the human body can be used as a triboelectric layer and as a sensor. A detailed overview of the wearable TENG is discussed in the four basic modules, which can be used to monitor the human health using various parameters.

Chapter 3 focuses on hybrid multi-cloud SLAs for smart city enterprises. In the recent years there is a rapid increase in the cloud computing migrations. The major effecting factor is the IoT management costs. IoT based enterprises, which have initiated as the private clouds on a small scale have figured out that the applications and the services they use broaden, then to completely transfer to proper incorporating public clouds - becoming inevitable. The challenge in the current scenario is the management of multiple clouds, which reside over different vendor machines and are running over multiple platforms and also require different computational resources. The cloud-based systems often face shutdown or system failures due to the lack of the support of a single standard for an overall multi-cloud hybrid model. This chapter discusses the SLA issues that the hybrid multi cloud environment faces and suggests possible solutions to help adopting firms in their management.

Chapter 4 introduces power saving schemes for IoT enabled smart city applications. Despite of the numerous researches that had been carried for reducing the average power consumption and improving the battery lifetime in the IoT smart city applications, there is still lack of implementation of power saving schemes. This happens because the electronic devices consume similar amount of power during the idling state as compared to the active state resulting in the low power efficiency of the smart city application. This chapter addresses the issue of how to create a power saving IoT application by applying power saving schemes and creating an accurate model that can predict the battery lifetime of the IoT applications.

Chapter 5 brings together artificial intelligence and FPGA based IoT architectures, models and platforms for smart city applications. IoT enable design has a requirement of IP address. This chapter covers nine different IoT enable design from IoT based Water Management Cyber-Physical System (IoT-WMCPS) to IoT based Random Access Memory (IoT-RAM) along with the detailed discussion on Quickscript. The nine different IoT enable design discussed in this chapter are: IoT enable Bicycle called Mo-Bike,

IoT enable House, IoT enable Water Utility, IoT enable Mining, IoT enable Healthcare, IoT enable Frame Buffer, IoT enable RAM, IoT enable Key Generator, and IoT enable Wi-Fi Encoder.

Chapter 6 foresees smart cities, which are enabled with Internet of drones. In near future Unmanned Aerial Vehicles (UAVs) are expected to serve as aerial base station for providing the data services to the users, collecting the data from various sensors and as a sensor mounted aerial platforms deployed in the smart cities. This chapter focuses on Air-to-Ground (A2G) Channel Model, ITU-R parameters, optimal replacement to UDNs, Ultra-Dense Cloud Drone Network and implementing parameters for 5G physical layers.

Chapter 7 discusses about precision agriculture and crop health monitoring using IoT. There is huge gap between actual production and estimated production in agriculture due to manual farming system especially in the developing countries. To assist an algorithm for acquiring time and accurate crop information essentials, this chapter proposes an IoT-based crop health monitoring system, which comprised of different sensors used in agricultural fields to maximize the agricultural output by leveraging the IoT technology.

Chapter 8 addresses IPv6 functionality for low power nodes to enable smart cities. Wireless Sensor Networks (WSN) are an important alternative for sensing and actuating critical applications like industrial automation, health care and many more. 6LoWPAN provides a means of carrying packet in the form of IPv6 over IEEE 802.15.4 and can be used to overcome the challenges that are faced during the integration of WSN and IP Protocols. This chapter previews a detailed discussion on IPv6 and 6LoWPAN along with the architecture that suits IoT and focus on the advantages of 6LoWPAN with respect to IoT and its security along with smart city case studies.

Chapter 9 focuses on RF and microwave aspect of IoT and presents designs of antennas for IoT. This chapter focuses on the modern wireless communication systems and their role in IoT, millimeter wave that is broadly used in 5G, revolution of technological networks, importance of antennas and future vision of 5G in IoT based application.

Chapter 10 covers privacy and security issues in IoT. This chapter discusses the basic of IoT and its applications for solving data security and privacy issues in Industry 4.0. The industry 4.0 is mainly focused on IoT technology and all the industry machines that are interlinked with the IoT technology. This chapter is dedicated to methodologies on enhancing hybrid security protocol in industrial IoT. This hybrid mechanism is combining lightweight protocol and Probabilistic encryption (LPP) algorithm.

Chapter 11 describes reliability and security challenges in IoT Applications. The use of Network on Chip (NoC) based IoT devices have security threats and reliability of the Integrated Chips (IC) is vulnerable (which is used in every IoT based device). Keeping these security challenges in mind, a detailed survey is presented in this chapter that covers the security issues and challenges focusing on NoCs. The countermeasures are also proposed in this chapter to secure on chip communication and to overcome security issues for electrical as well as optical on-chip interconnects.

With the emerging urbanization scenarios, it is vital to develop smart cities. Indeed, US, China or UAE launched smart city projects e.g., Malmo, Fujisawa, Santander etc. IoT enables the basic architecture for a smart city. Certainly, IoT can be foreseen in many smart city scenarios such as infrastructure monitoring, environmental monitoring, waste management, smart parking, or autonomous driving. In order to achieve such goals, a great number of connected objects are needed. The number of connected objects is growing exponentially and it is estimated that more than 50 billion connected objects will be deployed in smart cities by 2025. However, the high number of connected objects will open up numerous challenges. The book covers major aspects of IoT corresponding to smart city paradigms and provide audience at a glance how a smart city will look alike and what are the fundamental challenges. It provides knowledge about IoT enabled health care and how energy harvesting can benefit in healthcare domain. It also explores precision agriculture and energy saving schemes to provide energy efficient smart city services. An insight about integration of drones to facilitate the smart city is also a way forward for future applications. Audience will also learn how to enable popular Internet Protocol for low power devices to support smart city applications. Finally, the impact of security, privacy and reliability on IoT protocols is focused to observe their effectiveness in various smart city scenarios.

Acknowledgment

This book, *IoT Architectures, Models, and Platforms for Smart City Applications,* is the result of continuous support and struggle of several people. Specially, we are grateful for our friends and colleagues in encouraging us to start the work and to finally publish it.

We want to thank Ali Akbar Shah, Sehrish Memon and our fellow colleagues from Department of Electronics Engineering, Mehran University of Engineering and Technology (Jamshoro-Pakistan) for their academic support and friendship.

We would also like to thank our international friends, Thomas Newe from University of Limerick (Ireland) and Abzetdin Adamov from School of IT and Engineering (Azerbaijan), who supported, assisted and helped us to shape our ideas into this book.

Chapter 1
Internet of Things–Based Healthcare Applications

Seema Ansari

https://orcid.org/0000-0002-0108-7481

Institute of Business Management, Pakistan

Tahniyat Aslam

Institute of Business Management, Pakistan

Javier Poncela

University of Malaga, Spain

Pablo Otero

University of Malaga, Spain

Adeel Ansari

Shaheed Zulfiqar Ali Bhutto Institute of Science and Technology, Pakistan

ABSTRACT

The demand for global healthcare systems for human health improvement is ever growing. Internet of things (IoT) has influenced every industry in the market. IoT-based healthcare monitoring systems have emerged using smart gateways between sensor networks and the internet. This chapter aims at focusing on the impact of IoT on healthcare and explores the difference that IoT has made in the recent years. IoT applications in healthcare have helped people keep track of their medical requirements such as reminding them of appointments, keeping a check on calorie count, variations in blood pressure, a check on exercises, and many more. In this chapter, studies of IoT-based healthcare applications are presented. The chapter begins with the introduction and history of IoT in healthcare, sharing state of the art, architecture, applications of IoT in healthcare, advantages, future concerns and challenges, and future of IoT in healthcare, followed by conclusion.

DOI: 10.4018/978-1-7998-1253-1.ch001

INTRODUCTION

In 1999, Kevin Ashton invented the term 'Internet of Things' (IoT). It is referred to electrical equipment of any size or competence that are linked to the Internet for sharing information (Miraz, Ali, Excell, & Picking, 2015). The main concern of IoT is to focus on physical devices that are communicating with each other. 'Internet of Everything' (IoE) is considered as a superset of IoT. The term IoE has been used by both CISCO and Qualcomm. (Weissberger, 2014). Qualcomm replaced this term with the IoT.

The IoE is transforming the communication between human beings and devices, and establishing the way that all of them work cooperatively to accessing the services. IoE is based on four pillars of people, data, process and things as shown in Figure 1. Cisco, which first invented IoT, considers that the process gets people, data, and things collectively to create interacted connections more pertinent and valuable. The IoE is assisted by the growth of Cloud Computing, aiding to link "everything" online (Bradley, Loucks, Macaulay, & Noronha, 2013). In 2013, a study by CISCO predicted that in coming next ten years, $14.4 trillion may be utilized by employing IoE with M2M, M2P and P2P.

IoT based healthcare applications connect devices anywhere, with anybody at any time, using a network and services that lead to smart healthcare (Bardram, et al., 2011). A world where the actual and the virtual are uniting to build "smart environments" that creates many domains besides health, such as transportation, energy, living, buildings, cities and industries.

When worn on the body these network sensors collect data about the patients' health. This information can bring an affirmative change in the healthcare sector, related to medicine, treatment options, reducing the cost with better results. The aim of the Internet of Things is to allow communicating devices to be linked at all times, anywhere with whatever e-device using any network and services. IoT is a novel innovation of the Internet (Vermesan & Friess, 2013). Now, the Internet is not only the computer networks, but it has advanced into a network of several devices of different types and sizes, that are linked and communicated continuously all the time.

As defined by the International Telecommunication Union (ITU), (ITU-T /Y.2060) report, IoT comprises a universal framework for connecting physical and virtual devices or things on current and evolving

Figure 1. Internet of everything (Cisco)

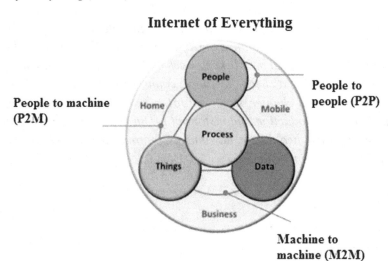

communication technologies. IoT offers facilities including identifications, processing and capturing of data by ensuring the requirement of confidentiality and security.

Vision of IoT is to facilitate the healthcare sector, by developing a link to provide a novel service of life changing and improving. It has brought financial and societal advantages to the individuals, inhabitants, governments, and business with cutting-edge and enhanced services. IoT can be recognized as a vision with complete implementation of social and technological implications.

Regardless of the advancements, IoT in the Healthcare sector has paved the way for numerous possibilities to leverage from and challenges to be focused. According to forecast of the market, the IoT Healthcare Market is worth of $158.07 billion with 50 billion associated equipment's and devices by 2020. The expected IoT development in healthcare affords the capability to respond with speed and influences the entire community or a nation. (Rao, 2018)

IoT European Research Cluster (IERC) and International Telecommunication Union (ITU) defined, IoT as a worldwide architectural network of communicating devices with different identities, specifications, standards, interfaces and communication protocols integrated into a common infrastructure (Internet of Things - IERC, 2014).

The increase in health issues and aging of population is one of the major problems that have caused excessive pressure to healthcare systems around the world. IoT offer promising solutions for the improvement of human health. So, the usage of technologies for providing healthcare to the common people has been naturally highlighted. In near future, the model of healthcare will convert from the existing centric hospitals to many distributed healthcare networks. (Koop CE, 2008)

The healthcare market is rising fast, posing novel prospects and threats for businesses in the healthcare segment in addition to the companies that function in the bigger healthcare esteem chain. These aspects and challenges related with retrieval to healthcare continue to show the complete functioning of healthcare systems. Nowadays, the healthcare business is at an overturning point, due to which leading prominent market players are now associating with finest class market research companies to discover novel opportunities and markets for progression.

An IoT based Healthcare scenario explained by (Pang, 2013) is illustrated in Figure 2. In this scenario all medical instruments are embedded with sensors and actuators that gather and transmit real time information about the patient's (Bertholdo, et al., 2012). All medical equipment's, medicine and patients can be followed and observed continuously by wearable WSN devices (Ersoy & Alemdar, 2010).

This framework extends the healthcare services from hospitals and communities to home. It delivered Healthcare and medical services including emergency services, nutrition and medicine management, telemedicine services, health related social interacting through the internet (Ludwig, et al., 2012).

All the healthcare record can be gathered and stored continuously (Domingo, 2012). The medical record collected from these devices can then be examined by doctors and physicians at remote location. IoT primarily changes the healthcare equation by improving the patients care, offering efficient and enhanced care delivery and make hospitals networks smarter.

Internet of Things (IoT) explained by (Vermesan & Friess, 2013) as model and a paradigm that considers wide range of objects/ devices that are linked together via wired or wireless connections and in order to communicate with each and every other devices/ networks to originate novel applications and services. IoT-based enterprise systems have been developed for various applications such as in healthcare domain, smart environment domain, transportation domain etc. (Atzor, Iera, & Morabito, 2010). The objective of this chapter is to highlight the impact of IoT on healthcare, and explore the difference it has made in the field of medicine in the recent years.

Figure 2. Internet of Things Based Healthcare Scenario (Pang, 2013)

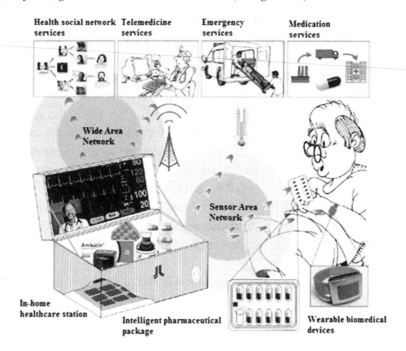

CHRONICLE OF IOT IN HEALTHCARE

A decade ago, patients were introduced to internet-connected devices various forms. In the past years, the Internet of Things began to merge into healthcare on both the physician and patient fronts. Whether data comes from ultrasounds, thermometers, glucose monitors, electrocardiograms etc, tracing health data is important for certain patients, though several of these process required further appointments with the doctors.

Electronic Health Records (EHR) focused on health record of patients. That record was only available to authorized users (The History of Healthcare Technology and the Evolution of EHR, 2019). The first medical record emerged in 1920s. The health information management (HIM) industry started to set the methods by which medicinal reports were exploited and recorded. After 40 Years, computer started new methodologies to HIM for the regularization and sharing of health documentations. Physician allowed accessing a medical history of patient's to confirm the diagnoses. A voice recognition prototype Dragon system was invented in 1982, to cheers the medical officers everywhere. In the late 1980s, computers were used for billing and planning rather than EHR. The World Health Organization approved the ICD-10 coding standards in 1994, for medical records. The Institute of Medicine (IOM) projected that more than 99,000 hospitalized Americans expire every year due to avoidable medical inaccuracies."

In near future patients, physicians, hospital managements want the total portability of health data. Physician wants more in-built EHR interfaces to enter patient's record that takes less time.

SMART HEALTH

Smart health has emerged from the technology that guides to improved diagnostic devices, superior therapy for patients and tools that enhance the value of life for all (Source: Bluestream: Smart Healthcare, 2017). Smart Health can be applied to a wide range, including pediatric care and aged patients care, the monitoring and supervision of prolonged diseases, and the management of health and fitness etc. The objective of smart health is to enhance the quality of life by providing rapid and right medical support. An IoT platform that can focus the healthcare of elderly and disabled person is called ambient assisted living (AAL). The aim of AAL is to deliver a safe, convenient and independent life to incapacitated patient's, by providing them human servant-like aid during the emergency case (Islam, Kwak, Hossain, & Kwak, 2015). So, the healthcare quality is enhanced through continuous attention and care which in turn decreases the budget of healthcare. An IoT based healthcare system classified into two important categories:

1. Individual and Remote Patient Monitoring

Remote patient monitoring is one of the most vital applications of the IoT. The tiny wireless sensors linked through the IoT, making it possible for distant patient observing who is far away from home and hospital. Due to the lack of immediate response many lives are suffering from risk. The safety of an individual, elderly and infant patient can be controlled remotely by alarm systems. Figure 3, presents the monitoring of a remote patient, where medical sensors are attached with patients body for real time observations. The patient's health record is then transmitted through internet to the doctor for proper medical assistance (Sukanya, 2015).

2. Clinical Patient Monitoring

IoT provides an innovative solution to the doctors and hospitals to handle the bedside and critical care patients with a secure and reliable system as shown in Figure 4. This system is used for hospitalized patients whose physiological conditions are not stable and they need constant attention. An IoT based clinical patient monitoring systems uses different sensors to gather biological information which is

Figure 3. Individual and Remote Patient monitoring (Sukanya, 2015)

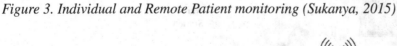
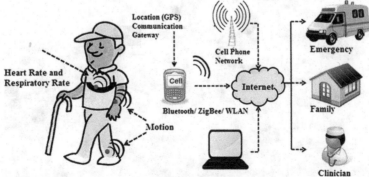

examined and saved by using the cloud. This record is then referred to doctors for further examination (Sukanya, 2015).

Early applications of IoT in healthcare also included smart beds, which can automatically sense the patient and adjust them with correct angle and provide proper support without the manual interaction of nurses. The IoT could also provide benefit to the home-based patient. Some of the patients don't take their medication at correct times or appropriate doses. When patients at home forget to take their medicine, smart medication dispensers could automatically upload the information to the cloud and alert physicians.

ENABLING TECHNOLOGIES OF IOT NETWORKS

According to (Atzori, Iera, & Morabito, 2010), the IoT has become the novel model of information and communication technology (ICT). The enabling technologies of IoT networks are sensors and wearable devices, Wireless Sensor Network (WSN), mobile internet access, cloud computing, Radio Frequency IDentification (RFID), Bluetooth, ZigBee, Wi-Fi, 6LoWPAN and cellular network as shown in Figure 5.The Enabling technologies used in IoT networks are discussed below:

1. Wireless Sensor Networks (WSN)

A huge amount of sensors gather raw data and generate information by processing and examining. WSN is a network of sensors or smart devices which are used to monitor the patients' health, observing the medicine effects and informing the doctor or care taker.

WSN are efficient, low cost, low power devices used in distant tracking applications (Chorost, 2016).

2.   Radio-Frequency Identification (RFID)

Figure 4. Clinical Patient Monitoring (Sukanya, 2015)

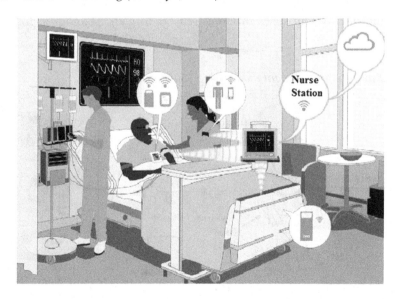

Figure 5. Enabling Technologies (Sukanya, 2015)

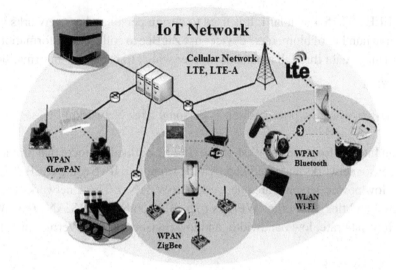

RFID is from the class of technologies called Automatic Identification and Data Capture (AIDC). An AIDC technique automatically enables objects identification, their data collection and forwarding the data to computers systems directly without human intervention. Radio waves are used to accomplish this.

RFID plays an essential role in IoT applications. RFID chip holds the information of devices or people and transfer the data to the reader. RFID allows effective management, tracing, and observing processes (Singh, Bhattacharya, Chowdhary, & Jat, 2017).

3. Wearable Devices

"Wearable Devices" are electronic gadgets that are integrated into wearable objects and can be worn comfortably. Wearable devices (e.g., shoes, watch, glasses, belt, etc.) can be used to sense biometric information. A wearable gadget gathers the data and transfers it to the medical center through the Internet (Lakshay G., Abhishek B., Meetu G., 2015).

4. Bluetooth

Bluetooth is a WPAN (Wireless Personal Area Network) protocol created for wireless data transmission. It is used to connect devices within short range. It can be used as wireless body area network (WBAN) to observe patient's health (Patel & Wang, 2010).

5. Wi-Fi

Wi-Fi is a WLAN (Wireless Local Area Network) technology based on the IEEE 802.11 standards. Wi-Fi Devices includes cellphones, smart devices, Computers, etc. Wi-Fi devices have a wireless communication range of about 30 meters indoors (Sukanya Mandal, 2016).

6.   ZigBee

ZigBee is an IEEE 802.15.4 standard. It is used to design personal Area networks with Low power digital radios. A large number of biomedical devices use ZigBee to collect the information. These devices can observe and manage data through a database center which transfers the information to the doctors (Ullah, et al., 2012).

7.   6LoWPAN: (IPv6 over Low power Wireless Personal Area Networks)

6LoWPAN is an Internet Engineering Task Force (IETF), defined protocol that provides connectivity between wireless sensor networks and internet providing support to IPv6 using IEEE 802.15.4. It denotes a wireless link for low power personal area networks (LoWPANs). These networks are categorized by their more restricted abilities than other WPANs (e.g. Bluetooth) and WLANs (e.g.WiFi), they have small frame size, low data rate, low bandwidth, and low transmit power. (Vermesan & Friess, 2013)

8.   IEEE 802.15.4 Standard

IEEE 802.15.4 is a recommended standards that define a range of wireless personal area networks (WPANs) for different purposes. It is a low-cost, low-speed, low-power WPAN (Wireless Personal Area Network) protocol for ubiquitous communication between devices. Its operative frequency range comprises the 2.4 GHz industrial, scientific and medical band providing global accessibility (Howitt & Gutierrez, 2003).

9.   Cellular Network

Cellular network is a mode of communication technology that allows the use of cell phones. A mobile phone is a transceiver that permits instantaneous transmission and reception of radio waves.

10.   Long Term Evolution (LTE)

It is a standard for 4G wireless broadband technology that suggests improved network capacity and speed to cell phone users. (LTE A) stands for Long Term Evolution Advanced. It is a cellular standard which adds major capabilities to the basic LTE standard. LTE establishes the latest step for 4G wireless broadband technology that suggests improved network capacity and speed of mobile communication. The 3GPP Release LTE-A (Long Term Evolution Advanced) has proven to be the fastest emerging cellular technologies in the world. (Kanchi, et al., 2013)

STATE-OF-THE-ART

There have been remarkable advancement in the area of Internet of Things (IoT) based healthcare systems. (Rahmani, gia, Thanigaivelan, & Granados, 2015) proposed a Smart e-Health Gateway and demonstrated an IoT-based healthcare observing device with improved performance, interoperability, security and reliability. Various difficulties like energy efficacy, scalability and dependability issues in healthcare systems can be overcome by Smart e-Health Gateway.

The function of gateways is to provide a link among the sensors and clinical apparatus to the cloud computing platform and IP based systems. In a smart healthcare system, the gateway provides a path connecting both the Body Area Network (BAN) /PAN/Local Area network (LAN) and the wide area network (WAN). IoT based health observing system is illustrated in Figure 6. It is used in smart clinics and home. Different sensors, actuators and medical apparatus can attach to the systems to gather patient health record and to transmit the collected information to concern medical supervisors. The architecture comprises of following sections:

1. **Medical Sensor Network**: It is used for sensing and transmitting biomedical signals to the gateway through communication protocols such as Serial, SPI, Bluetooth, Wi-Fi or IEEE 802.15.4.
2. **Smart e-Health Gateway**: Smart e-Health gateway assists various communication protocols and provide a bridging between a network of sensors and the Internet.
3. **Back End System:** It consist of a platform comprising a local swich and cloud computing facility that supports broadcasting, data warehousing and Big Data analytic servers along with a graphical user interface for web clients.

According to the report of ITU-T (Ubiquitous Sensor Networks (USN), 2008), an essential enabling technology of IoT includes Wireless Sensor Network (WSN). It integrates different autonomous spatial distributed sensors into a network and passes the data through wireless transmission links. These networks can be linked to other systems through a gateway network. WSN is constructed with several hundreds or even thousands of sensor or actuator nodes, where every node is usually transportable, inexpensive and simply deployable. When WSN is incorporated into a system of IoT, a network is formed called Ubiquitous Sensor Networks (USN).

Healthcare Architectures: Elhayatmy, Dey, & Ashour, 2018, proposed a healthcare architecture based on Wireless Body Area Network (WBAN). This architecture comprises of three tiers as shown in Figure. 7.

Figure 7, shows several sensor nodes or tiny patches placed on the patient's body. They are either wearable sensors or implanted patches beneath the skin that work within the wireless network. Constantly, these sensors collect and transfer essential signs such as blood pressure, temperature, sugar level, humidity and heart activity. However, health record may require preceding on-tag handling of the nodes.

Figure 6. Health observing system (Rahmani, gia, Thanigaivelan, & Granados, 2015)

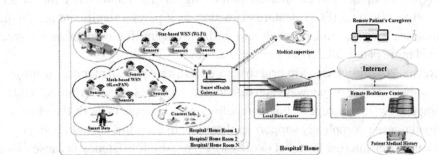

Figure 7. Wireless Body Area Network for healthcare architecture (Elhayatmy, Dey, & Ashour, 2018)

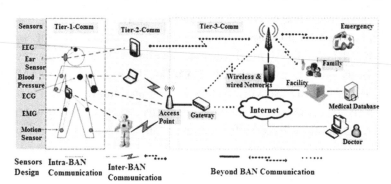

Later, the gathered health record either linked to a central controller attached with the body or directly transferred through Bluetooth or ZigBee to the close personal server (PS), for continuously diagnosing through a WLAN (wireless local area network) connection for emergency alert or to a medical record.

- Tier-1 network is Intra-BAN Communications, which denotes about 2m radio communications close to the human body, which provides connections with the body sensors or between portable PS. (Chen, Valenzuela, Leung, & Vasilakos, 2011).
- Tier-2 network is Inter-BAN Communication that generally works as autonomous systems. The (Access point) APs are the central parts of the dynamic environment's infrastructure for handling serious incident. All the communication among the APs and PS is exploited in the inter-BAN communications. Consistently, this network is engaged to communicate the BANs with several accessible networks, for example the cellular network and Internet.
- Tier-3 network indicates the Beyond–BAN Communication network. The inter-BAN and beyond-BAN communication network are connected with Gateway device.

The beyond-BAN tier communication allows the authorized physicians for distant accessing to the patients' healthcare record via the Internet or any cellular network. The beyond-BAN communication strategy is adapted for the user specific services, as it not only records the medical history of the patient's but automatically informed the health information to the patient's family through several communication resources.

Gia, et al., 2015, proposed an IoT based healthcare system architecture that is based on the model of fog computing. The author demonstrated the efficiency of fog computing in term of bandwidth utilization, quality of service (QoS) assurance and continuous monitoring. In this architecture a model is presented in Figure 8, for Electrocardiogram (ECG) feature extraction, as it plays a significant part in diagnosing several cardiac diseases. The experiment result shows that by using fog computing architecture low latency response and more bandwidth efficiency were achieved.

Mohapatra & Rekha, 2012, discussed a hybrid structure for distant patient monitoring through a cloud sensor. A central computing layer of gateways and distributed databases is placed between different sensors and cloud computing. The concept of Fog computing is the advancement of the cloud computing model, because cloud doesn't completely support applications in real-time including video conference applications, and Voice over Internet Protocol (VoIP) which require low latency because of significant

Figure 8. Internet of Things based Fog Computing (Gia, et al., 2015)

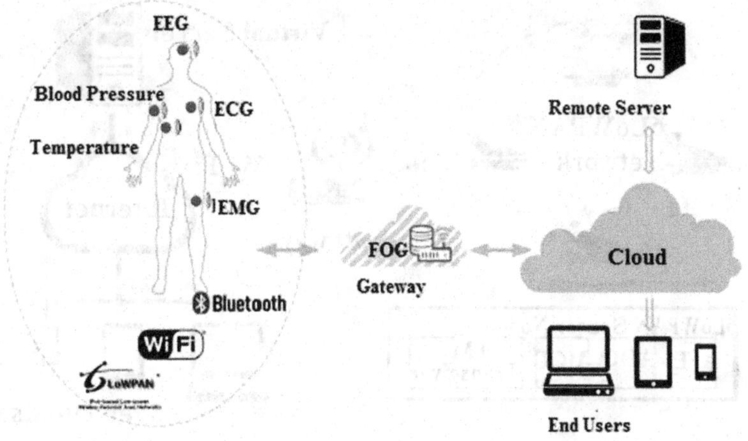

delays may causes decreasing QoS. A very high bandwidth is needed to transmit a large amount of data over the networks (Bonomi, Milito, Natarajan, & Zhu, 2014). An uninterrupted data monitoring is required between monitoring system and the cloud in case of connectivity loss (Bessis & Dobre, 2014).

Jara et al., 2011 proposed an IoT based Ambient Assisted Living (AAL) structural design to aid blood glucose management and insulin therapy. The idea is to deliver a diabetic patient with an apparatus that will save the readings of blood glucose and provide the guidance about the next dosage of insulin injection. This architecture contains various enhanced technologies for identification and security purposes, communication through Internet; including 6LoWPAN and RFID technologies that establish an origin of personal services based on Internet of things. 6LoWPAN connectivity allows direct linking of a person to diabetes management system.

Gia, et al., 2014 suggested IoT based system that delivers a simple and cost efficient method to examine both distantly and continuously health information such as Electrocardiogram (ECG) and Electromyography (EMG) data.

The architectural design of IoT based system is presented in Figure 9. The proposed structure consists of medical sensor nodes, a gateway, a cloud server and web clients. A medical sensor node collects health information which is then transmitted to a server through a gateway. The virtual server saves and processes the collected data. A doctor can observe the processed data through web client including smart phone or a laptop. Sensor nodes comprise the following four sub modules:

- Analog front end (AFE) devices are used to collects bio-signals.
- Analog-to-Digital Converter (ADC) transforms the analog signals into digital format.
- Microcontroller Unit (MCU) control and packetizing the information to 6LoWPAN packets.
- RF transceiver unit transfers the information to the gateway.
- Gateway transferred the information to the distant server. It delivers tunneling in 6LoWPAN and IPv4/IPv6 protocols. The Web clients are responsible for storing data.

The structural services 6LoWPAN for a healthcare system from the perspective of continuous monitoring, reliable transmission and cost efficacy are elaborated.

Figure 9. Architectural design (Gia, et al, 2014)

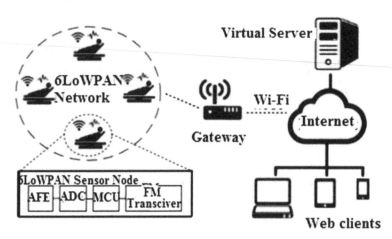

Figure 10, presented the medical sensor node which is used to transmit bio-signals. Various bio-signals such as Electrocardiogram (ECG), Electromyography (EMG), body temperature, Peripheral capillary oxygen saturation (SpO2), blood pressure, respiration, glucose and contextual data are identified and transferred to a network through interfaces. These data are distantly observed by different medical specialists and delivered suitable feedbacks. Hence, health record are very essential in healthcare environments and it must satisfy the requirements defined by (ISO/IEEE, 1996), presented in Table 1.

IoT Healthcare architectures use various technologies such as ZigBee, Wi-Fi and RFID. Wu & Huang, 2012 suggested a platform of healthcare management, implemented on ZigBee. Another contribution by Tsibas et al., 2010, presented a scenario of RFID-IPv6 based healthcare setting. The RFID technology

Figure 10. Medical sensor node (Gia, et al, 2014)

Table 1. Data rate of and Latency of bio-medical signals (ISO/IEEE, 1996)

Bio-medical Signal	Latency	Data Rate
Blood pressure	< 3 s	80-800 bps
Pulse / Heart Rate	< 3 s	80-800 bps
Glucose	< 3 s	80-800 bps
Temperature	< 3 s	80-800 bps
Respiration	< 300 ms	50-120 bps
SpO2	< 300 ms	50-120 bps
ECG	< 300 ms	3-lead (2.4 kbps), 5-lead (10 kbps), 12-lead (72 kbps)

and IPv6 with Virtual MAC address Generator policy is utilized but none of the policies reflect the kind of data such as real-time monitoring of ECG and EMG data.

Kirbas & bayilmis, 2012, illustrated a healthcare systems created on web based interface. Without any requirements for web-browsers health face can be recovered through IP based devices. Various architectural works is present based on 6LoWPAN. A mobile healthcare structure to assist network based mobility of 6LoWPAN sensor nodes was recommended by (Kim, Haw, & Hong, 2010).

Jara, et al, 2010, discussed intra mobility for hospital based on 6LoWPAN. Though, this network is only depending upon flexibility without taking into account for continuous monitoring and lifetime of sensors battery. Touati, et al., 2013, suggested an indoor 6LoWPAN based healthcare architecture for continuous observing, confirmed by an ECG simulator and Labview for user interface.

There are many limitations on existing platform:

1.   ECG record are not collected from actual analog front-end device
2.   Gateway needs to be linked with 6LoWPAN network.
3.   User requires a computer with Labview software.

Smart Toilet and Washrooms: People still have to go to the hospital laboratory for a hands-on sampling process to analyze their urine. Conventional process of taking urine sample can feel awkward and unhygienic for the patients. This results into the discomfort due to manual collection. Several healthcare devices have been invented to diagnose health conditions of an individual at their home. Smart Toilet has resolved this issue by collecting and monitoring a patient's urine to indicate health condition instantly. Sensor based toilets have been introduced that separate the faeces and urine, analyze the components of urine and transmit the information to the user in real time.

BAE & LEE, 2018, tested some routine test to diagnose various diseases. The examination includes diagnosis of proteins, glucose, ketones, haemoglobin, bilirubin, urobilinogen, acetone, nitrite, and leucocytes, in addition to the analysis of pH, specific gravity and infection by examining various pathogens. The significant features for testing urine is analysis of sugar levels, that indicates the patient's health condition related to diabetics. After separating the urine from faeces, the component analyzer for urine analyzes the component by using urine reagent strips.

Smart bathroom contains advanced technologies to care about user's health and provide medical utilities. IoT is a novel concept for home bathroom. Various parts of the bathroom, like the commode seat, bath rug, floorboards, can be fitted with wireless sensors to detect abnormalities and aid users to track their health. Skin color variation can be detected from a camera fitted with the bathroom mirror. Bathtub with sensors would be able to sense blood pressure and perform echo test. All the valuable collected data is sent to doctors. (Kooa, Lea, Sebastiania, & Kimb, 2016).

Neonatal Infant Monitoring: Neonatal Intensive Care Unit (NICU) is for weak, ill and premature babies who need special care and attention from the specialists and pediatric staffs. A newborn baby of 28 days of life is defined as neonatal by World Health Organization (WHO) (Quinn, et al., 2016). Newborn babies need special care and constant monitoring because some babies are born with health issues. So it is necessary to examine the infant's condition such as temperature and pulse rate continuously. This is the crucial time for infant as there is high probability of death because of many complications. Thus, a smart neonatal observing system must be a beneficial solution in order to monitor newborn consistently.

Najib, Hassan, Shair, Rahim, & Wahab, 2019, proposed a system that transmits the vital signs of the newborn babies such as body temperature and pulse rate can be constantly monitored through the Internet of Things (IoT) termed as Thing Speak. A mobile application is created for doctors and pediatric staff to observe a neonatal health condition frequently.

Monitoring of Aged Population: Japan is the one of the most "super aged" country in the world. According to the World Health Organization (WHO) if 14% of the inhabitants are of age 65 and older are defined as "aged" and 21% of the inhabitants in the same age group come under "super aged" society. Statistics issued by Japanese government in 2018, shows that 35.57 million populations was at the age of 65 and older, with more than 2.19 million populations was at the age of 90 and older. The increase in aging populations affects the healthcare issue, now Japan is using IoT to support aging inhabitants. In late 2017, Shintomi adopted smart devices that are used in homes and other nursing amenities to aid family members or caregiver's staff to lift, move and monitor aged persons. Home-based robots are used as companions for seniors at Shintomi. A robotic baby equipped with an artificial intelligence that is proficient of replying when spoken to. (Zhang, 2019)

Aged family members who are living alone are the major concern of their families. Now days, IoT based monitoring or watch over system for aged citizen have been developed. Hideo Suzuki, Mogi, Matsushita, Hanada, Suzuki, & Niijima, 2018, proposed a system based on Raspberry Pi, with different wireless sensors that are placed within the home. The first feature was based on sensors instead of using cameras or microphone in order to secure the privacy of the aged people. Second feature was to transmit the message in case of emergency or unhealthy conditions to the designated family members like an infrequently long time in bathing or sleeping, too high temperature in home, dementia or Alzheimer loitering etc.

Sreekanth & Niktha, 2016, reviewed the models, applications and several existing services and technologies for healthcare. The Table 2, presents the comparison of current healthcare systems for the services and patients' observation.

Architecture of Internet of Things (IoT): (Dey, Ashour, & Bhatt, 2017)

The IoT architecture consists of several layers, namely:

- The Sensor Layer
- Gateways and network Layers
- Management Service Layer
- Application layer

Table 2. Comparison of current Healthcare systems (sreekanth & niktha, 2016)

Methodology	Type of Sensor	Provision of Services and Technology
Architecture based on IoT, for Smart healthcare Techniques	Temperature and ECG sensor.	Distant examining in emergency situation
IoT based curative observing cloud service system	Body environment sensor	Medical monitoring in clinics.
Healthcare In Smart Homes	Room temperature, body temperature s light sensor	IoT technique for e- homes, modular method
Intelligent Wallet for Healthcare	Motion sensors, environment sensors	Intelligent wallet for supervised observing of persons
The Internet Of Things based Healthcare Applications	Pill camera, wrist band, fitness tracker	Clinical care, remote monitoring
A Wearable Multi parameter System	ECG sensor, blood pressure acceleration and temperature sensor	Wearable device, observing and alert systems for heart patients.
Body Sensor Networks For Health Monitoring	ECG, accelerometer, blood pressure monitor, pulse oximeter, weight scale and GPS	Cardiac pulse monitoring, cardiac rehabilitation, monitoring of discharged patients
WSN based Healthcare Monitoring System	Blood pressure sensor, heart rate monitor.	Increases medical services
IoT in healthcare systems	RFID tags	Curative products with Electronic Product Code (EPC), tagged patients

The healthcare trust on IoT is increasing day by day, to improve accessibility to care and augment the quality of care with reduced cost (Frederix, 2009). The IoT architecture is illustrated into layers using various technologies as shown in Figure 11.

1.   Sensor Connectivity and Network Layer

This is the lowest layer comprising of integrated smart devices along with the sensors and RFID. These sensors and RFID allow the real world to interconnect with the physical measurements for real-time information process. Sensors can have a memory. They are used to measure and record a physical

Figure 11. IoT Architecture (Sukanya, 2015)

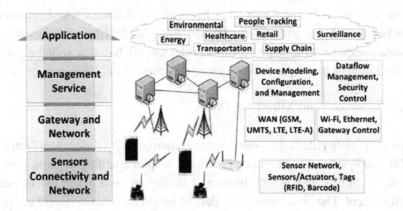

property such as quality of air, temperature and movement (Abdelwahab, Hamdaoui, Guizani, & Rayes, 2014), Miorandi, Sicari, Pellegrini, & Chlamtac, 2012), (Haller, Karnouskos, & Schroth, 2008).

2.   Gateways and Networks Layer

Gateways are used for routing the data received from the sensor layer and transmit it to the Management Service Layer. It is a layer in which huge amount of data is created by different sensors, that involves a better implementation and robust of wired or wireless network structure. Many networks are interlinked through several communication protocols and technologies to incorporate in a hybrid structure.

3.   Management Service Layer

It is responsible for organizing the IoT service. This layer involves data processing through the control of security, analytics, and devices management. Several methods are engaged for extraction of actual record from massive amount of raw data. The data can be retrieved, measured and integrated through data management service.

4.   Application Layer

This layer consists of the several applications of the IoT based systems such as in home, industries, environment, health, agriculture, transportation and energy etc.

Advantages of IOT in Healthcare

Internet of Things (IoT) has a wide range of advantages in several fields related to healthcare. The complete usage of the model in healthcare field is a great prospect as it permits clinical hubs to operate more proficiently and provide better cure to the patients. With this healthcare technology, there are incomparable advantages which could enhance the quality and efficacy of cures and hence improving the patient's wellbeing. The advantages of IoT in Healthcare are discussed below (Patel, 2017):

1.   Concurrently Informing and Observing:

Real time observing with IoT Based devices can protect many people in the case of a medical emergency. The IoT device gathers medical and other necessary health data. The health record is saved in the cloud and can be forwarded to an authorized contributing health firm or a consultant, to observe the gathered health data irrespective of the place, time, or device. IoT based healthcare device observes and transport health data such as blood pressure, oxygen, sugar levels in blood, weight and ECGs.

2.   End-to-End Connections and Affordable Cost:

IoT enables interoperability; device-to-device data exchanging that makes healthcare service delivery more effective. IoT can systematize patient care with the help of enabling technologies. Many lives can be protected through real time monitoring in case of medicinal crises. The IoT device gathers health data for medical treatment. The cloud stores this data of health and shares it with the permitted personnel which could be a doctor, a consultant or a health organization. It permits them to inspect the data collected irrespective of location, device and time.

The protocols used in the connectivity could be Bluetooth LE, Wi-Fi, Z-wave, ZigBee, and new latest protocols. Subsequently, IoT based system lowers the price, by reducing number of appointments, using improved means, and refining the allocation and scheduling.

3.   Data Collection and Assessment:

A healthcare device transfers massive amount of data very fast. Collection of real-time data is difficult to gather and control if the access to cloud is unapproachable. Manual analysis of data collected from various sources and devices is not an easy task even for the healthcare personnel.

IoT based healthcare devices can gather, inform and examine the health record continuously and decrease the requirement to save the unprocessed information. All process happens over cloud and only the final reports with graphs are accessible to the healthcare providers. Moreover, healthcare processes permit establishments to acquire essential healthcare analytics and data-driven perceptions which accelerate decisiveness and are less susceptible to mistakes.

4.   Alerts and Tracking:

A tracking and on-time alert helps the healthcare service providers to assess the patient's situation, and take timely action, irrespective of the time and place. It aids in on-time treatment. With the help of IoT, devices not only gather the important health data but transfer the record to the concerned doctors for real-time tracking, whereas notifying the persons about serious health issues with the help of mobile apps.

The alerts help the doctors to know the patients conditions and make decisions to provide on-time treatment, regardless of location and time. Thus, IoT enables real-time alerts, tracing, and keeping an eye on patients, thus providing hands-on cures, superior precision and appropriate involvement by specialists and improve patient treatment.

5.   Remote Medical Help:

During emergency, a person can directly communicate with a smart mobile app to the physician who is far away. Through mobility assistance in healthcare, the physicians can immediately examine the patient's records and discover the cause sicknesses.

Furthermore, several healthcare firms are predicting to make apparatuses that can issue medicines according to patient's health record and data related to illness, accessible through connected devices. IoT aims to improve the patient's care in hospital and cut down people's expenses on healthcare.

UTILIZATION OF IOT IN HEALTHCARE

In the past many people have lost their lives due to unavailability of timely help and medicinal aid. Advancement in WSN technology and emergence of IoT has made it possible to achieve timely assistance in the remote areas. IoT in healthcare has made it attainable by fitting required gadgets with sensors to the patients. The doctors receive alerts in case a change occurs in the patient's condition. Due to provision of help by distant monitoring, there can be a notable decrease in the duration of stay at the hospitals. This form of novelty created by IoT is a blessing to manhood, especially for old persons. (Infiniti Research, 2018). The Internet of Things (IoT) has unlocked the many possibilities in medical sector. Smart medical devices were introduced to collect valuable health record to provide care and treatment remotely. Following are the major services and applications of IoT in healthcare (Internet of Things in healthcare, 2019):

1.   Cancer Treatment

The medical trial of head and neck cancer patients was conducted by smart cuff embedded with an indicator tracing app, to direct the health record to the doctors and provides a quick response to treatment every week. According to the report of American Society of Clinical Oncology (ASCO), the patients who used this smart technology experienced less serve symptoms than to the patients who carried on with monthly doctor visits.

2.   Smart Device for Glucose Monitoring

Diabetes is a disease in which blood glucose levels are too high. Diabetes requires frequent checking of blood glucose levels and management of insulin dose. Smart devices like continuous glucose monitoring (CGM) and insulin pens improve the condition of diabetic patients. In this technique, an IoT based blood glucose collector is linked with the relevant doctor through IPv6 connectivity. They send blood glucose levels data to an app on iPhone, Android or Apple Watch. These devices have ability to record the information related to the injected dose of insulin and recommend the right insulin dose. Glucose level monitoring reveals the changing patterns of blood glucose and providing aids in the planning of meals, activities, and medication times.

3.   Closed-Loop Insulin Delivery

The automatic delivery of insulin changes the lives of diabetics. This system differs from a CGM because it doesn't only measure the amount of glucose but also delivers insulin. OpenAPS observes the patient blood glucose levels and retain the insulin dose supplied into the system. It supports to maintain the blood glucose within a safe range, avoiding maximum highs and lows glucose levels.

4.   Connected Inhalers

Asthma is a severe disease and can kill if it is not treated the right way. The largest manufacturer of smart inhaler technology is Propeller Health. An inhaler is attached with a sensor that connects with an app and allows patients to identifying the cause of symptoms and shared the report to the doctor that shows whether they are using it as frequently as is recommended.

Automated Device for Asthma Monitoring and Management (ADAMM) Asthma Monitor, is a smart device that monitors the indications of an asthma attack before its beginning and lets the patient to cope with it before the attack gets severe.

5.   Ingestible Sensing Capsules

Ingestible sensing capsules are fast prominent technology in healthcare industry. It has the ability to telecommunicate for disease diagnosing and monitoring. Ingestible sensors are roughly the size of a medicine capsule, composed of biocompatible materials, which monitor the medication in patient's body and notifies, if it detects any irregularities in the body. Example includes Proteus Digital Health.

According to the report of World Health Organization (WHO), many patients forget to take medicines as prescribed by the doctors. Ingestible sensors are smart tablets; generate a small signal that is picked by wearable sensor. The record is then transferred to the app, ensuring that the patient has taken their prescribed medicine.

6.   Connected Contact Lenses

Google Life Sciences developed a connected contact lens that could sense tear glucose and provides an alert for diabetic patients about their rising and dropping blood glucose level.

7.   The Apple Watch App for Depression Monitoring

Now a days, mental health and mood measurement are the most popular digital health platforms. An Apple Watch app is created for observing and assessing patients with Major Depressive Disorder (MDD) throughout their daily lives. This app also gives informative conversation to the patients about care.

Moodable Devices: Moodable devices are soon to be manhood's best friend. They are mood enhancing devices that can help the person with stress disorders and provide relaxation. They are head mounted wearable device that can send low-intensity current to the brain which elevates the mood.

8.   Coagulation Testing

A Bluetooth based coagulation system permits patients to examine how rapidly their blood clots. It helps the patients to remain within their beneficial range and reduces the possibility of stroke or bleeding.

9.   Apple's Watches and Parkinson's Disease

Apple Watches are developed to observe Parkinson's disease symptoms. This Apple's watches have been used in different health issues, like an arthritis study and an epilepsy study.

10.   Inspecting Hand Hygiene

Inspecting hygiene and cleanliness of hands is now a requirement and reality with the latest applications of IoT in healthcare. The hygiene of any healthcare laborer can be checked by using IoT gadgets. Recent research has shown that out of every 20 patients, one is infected due to unhygienic and uncleanness conditions in the hospitals for common public. This results in infecting patients developing severe fatal diseases. IoT applications enable collection of all data related to workers and saved in databases for evaluation and assessment by the relevant personnel.

11.   Hearable Technology

Hearable technology is new-era aids which have completely changed the world of those people who suffered hearing loss. A hearable device is designed like a standard hearing aid and is placed into a patient's ear. Currently, Hearable are compatible with Bluetooth which synchronize with the smartphone. This technology not only filters and equalizes the sound but it can add layered features to the sounds of real world. One of the most appropriate example is Doppler Labs.

12.   Robotic Machine Vision Technology

Robotic machine vision technology has given rise to drone technology whose purpose is to mimic visual perception and making decision depends on the situation. Drones like Skydio use this technology to sense obstacles and to navigate around them.

13.   Healthcare Charting

IoT devices such as Audemix ease much manual work which a consultant has to do during patient monitoring. It is powered by voice commands and saves the patient's record. It can easily accessible for review. It saves the time of doctors.

14.   Electrocardiogram (ECG) Heartbeat Monitoring Information

The electrocardiogram (ECG) is used for monitoring of heart electrical activity during each cycle. An IoT-based ECG heartbeat monitoring system comprises of a compact wireless transmitter and a receiver. The system is used for automation method to detect abnormal data on a real-time basis.

15.   Blood Pressure Monitoring

The blood pressure monitor is used to measure signal of pressure and pulsation. An IoT based electronic blood pressure is linked with WLAN or Bluetooth to the Internet. It can not only transmit the real-time measured pulse wave to the doctors for suggestions but it can store and record the data to the processing center.

16.   Smart Wheelchair

Intel has revealed the IoT connected Smart Wheelchair. This wheelchair is a smart appliance solving the real-world problems. It observes all the healthcare related problems of the patient seated on the wheelchair such as heart rate, blood pressure, and body temperature.

FUTURE CONCERNS AND CHALLENGES OF IOT IN HEALTHCARE

IoT has the ability to provide doctors with valuable health record that can improve patient's health, but there are several challenges ranging from data security to legacy infrastructure may delay the IoT healthcare initiatives. Although, various devices uses secure procedures and techniques to communicate to the cloud, but they are still susceptible to the hackers. Islam, et al., 2015, explained following challenges:

1. Security and Privacy of Health Record

One of the most significant concerns for regulatory bodies is the safety of patient's health information, collected and transferred through connected devices. IoT based health monitoring devices capture and transmit data in continuously. However various healthcare companies make sure that the confidential data is saved in a protected and encrypted manner, but they do not have command over the privacy of the access points being used to send the health data. All these issues create the health record extremely susceptible to hackers, who can hack the system and comprise personal health data of both patient's as well as physicians.

Hackers can exploit patient's health information to make duplicate cards to purchase medicines and apparatus which they can sell in future. Also they can case a fake Insurance entitlement in patient's name. These significant security and privacy threat increases gradually as more devices connected to the network.

2. Integration: Multiple Devices and Protocol

There are several vendors that manufacture a wide range of medical devices and equipment's. Integrating multiple devices is a major obstacle for successfully employment of IoT in healthcare. The reason behind the interruption is that the companies have not followed standard rules and regulations for compatible interface and protocol among the all medical devices. So multiple devices are linked to the network for collection of health data, the difference in protocol make difficult and delays in the process of accumulation of data. Therefore the lack of uniformity of connected medical devices protocols and standards reduces the scope and stability in IoT in healthcare sector.

3. Cost

Unfortunately, IoT based healthcare facilities are not reasonable to the general public yet. The rise in the healthcare sector prices is a disturbing symbols for everyone specifically the developed countries. IoT is an interesting and promising idea of healthcare sector.

Now a days, patients with serious illnesses access healthcare facilities of the developing nations which charges them as less as one-tenth. Though, it hasn't resolved the cost considerations. For successful implementation of IoT, the stakeholders need to check its cost effectiveness else common public will not be able to take advantage of this facility. Only the rich class will be able to afford it.

4. Data Overload and Accuracy

The procedure of collecting and data aggregating is difficult due to different set of protocols and standards. But, still IoT medical devices saved a lot of information. The health data gathered by IoT devices are developed to gain essential visions. Though, the significant quantity of data is quite challenging and becomes extremely difficult for doctors. Classifying valuable and important data is decisive as most of the doctors and physicians find it challenging to conclude with the growth of data. The decision making process with rapidly increasing health record ultimately affects the quality. Furthermore, the concerns are rising as more devices are linked that continuously collect more data and generate a big health record.

5.   Quality of Service (QoS)

Healthcare facilities are extremely requiring QoS. Continuous system availability is vital in medical situation; due to lack of QoS can put many lives in danger especially in case of emergency and disaster.

6.   Transition of Technology

Healthcare sectors can update their existing devices and instruments for providing better resources by merging IoT methodologies into the existing healthcare network. So, a continuous evolution to IoT based healthcare network is a main challenge.

7.   New Diseases and Syndromes

Cellphones are the most important device in IoT healthcare sector. Though there are several new healthcare apps are being added to the list regularly, but the development has been restricted to limited kinds of illness and diseases. So the Research & Development activities for novel kinds of diseases and syndromes are crucial.

CRITICAL ANALYSIS OF THE TECHNIQUES AND TECHNOLOGIES

Sensors or actuators and devices have enabled enormous growth in interconnection of devices. In IoT, the communication between devices is via internet, while the data is collected and analyzed by the cloud. The devices connected are producing huge data that needs to be processed, governed examined and stored at cloud. According to Virgin Atlantic (Computerworld UK, (2019)), Boeing 787 generates 0.5 Terabyte of data per flight. In 2008, the analysis showed that there were more things than people linked to the internet. Currently 4.9 billion objects connected. By 2020, the number is expected to increase by 50 billion (Dave, E., (2011)). According to (The many faces of IoT in Healthcare (2014), 30.7% devices in IoT are related to healthcare, while 69.7% of of IoT devices are related to other fields like Business, transport, manufacturing etc. The data loads are constantly growing.

Due to constant generation of data by IoT devices, a rapid analysis is required. Large volumes, diversity and speed of IoT data necessitate a requirement of new computing model that ensures (Evolution of Cloud to Fog Computing, (2019).): Minimum latency, network Bandwidth conservation, data security and reliability. In IoT, the data generated requires protection both during transfer and at rest. Thus there is a requirement of constant checking and automated response across the entire attack range: in advance, during, and afterwards. Since IoT data in healthcare is used for decisions affecting patients' treatment the reliability and accessibility of the infrastructure and data cannot be questioned. The data must be placed at a location closer to the devices for extremely time-sensitive decisions. Considering the transmission of high volumes of data using lesser bandwidth, Fog computing can be more meaningful as it provides feasible architectural solutions to fulfill the demand. It can accommodate devices like wireless routers, IP video cameras, switches, and computer chips which are making advancement with technology, compared to cloud, to generate data close to the device.

The above requirements are not fulfilled by conventional cloud computing architectures. The traffic from numerous IoT devices eats up the bandwidth. Fog computing can be used which acts as a bridge to connect IoT devices with far-off data centers. It improves processing by using the computing devices at the edge (Chandra, S. N., & Haeng-Kon K., (2016).

FUTURE PROSPECTS OF IOT IN HEALTHCARE

The IoT has unlocked a realm of opportunities in the field of medicine. The connection of IoT to internet enables collection of valuable data via the conventional health equipment's, provide additional information of symptoms and facilitate distant care giving patients control over their illness treatment.

The presences of different apps have assisted the healthcare market in making the hardware devices accessibility possible and enhance the healthcare market. As per the report provided by Heather Landi in March 2, 2017, the majority of the hospitals (87%) will adopt IoT technology by 2019. According to the study 73% IoT applications in healthcare will be exploited for monitoring distant patients and upkeep. 50% for distant processes and control, and 47% for locality-based services. Healthcare personnel see an enormous potential and many advantages from the IoT based healthcare technology. (Healthcare Innovation, 2019).

In future, patients, physicians, hospital managements would want the total portability of health data. Physician would want more in-built EHR interfaces to enter patient's record that takes less time.

CONCLUSION

The aim of this chapter is to evaluate the effectiveness of IoT in healthcare. IoT is benefitting both doctors and patients and providing them medical facilities from remote locations. The future of IoT in the field of healthcare is very optimistic inspite of the security challenges. Today, IoT has become a reality that has made life comfortable for healthcare providers and patients alike. There are apprehensions about slow development of IoT based healthcare medicines, however, it can be seen that from adherence to diagnosis, the applications are multifarious. From the analysis discussed above, we conclude that fog computing can perform better than cloud computing meeting the emerging demands of faster processing and lesser delay. With the implication of fog computing the services of IoT can be further enhanced. The two technologies serve two different sectors but complement each other where needed.

REFERENCES

Abdelwahab, S., Hamdaoui, B., Guizani, M., & Rayes, A. (2014). Enabling Smart Cloud Services Through Remote Sensing: An Internet of Everything Enabler. IEEE Internet of Things Journal, 1(3).

Ashton, K. (2009). That "Internet of Things" Thing. *RFiD Journal, 22*, 97–114.

Atzor, L., Iera, A., & Morabito, G. (2010). The Internet of Things: A survey. *Computer Networks, The International Journal of Computer and Telecommunications Networking.*

Bae, J.-H., & Lee, H.-K. (2018). *User Health Information Analysis With a Urine and Feces Separable Smart Toilet System.* Special Section on Healthcare Information Technology for the Extreme and Remote Environments.

Bardram, J., Doryab, A., Jensen, R., Lange, P., Nielsen, K., & Petersen, S. (2011). Phase recognition during surgical procedures using embedded and body-worn sensors. *IEEE International Conference on Pervasive Computing and Communications (PerCom)*, 45–53. 10.1109/PERCOM.2011.5767594

Bertholdo, L., Granville, L., Tarouco, L., Arbiza, L., Carbone, F., & Marotta, M. (2012). Internet of things in healthcare: interoperati-bility and security issues. *IEEE International Conference Communications (ICC, IEEE)*, 6121-6125.

Bessis, N., & Dobre, C. (2014). *Big Data and Internet of Things: A Roadmap for Smart Environments.* Springer. doi:10.1007/978-3-319-05029-4

Bluestream: Smart Healthcare. (2017). Retrieved from http://www.bluestream.sg/smart-healthcare

Bonomi, F., Milito, R. A., Natarajan, P., & Zhu, J. (2014). *Fog Computing: A Platform for Internet of Things and Analytics.* Springer.

Bradley, J., Loucks, J., Macaulay, J., & Noronha, A. (2013). *Joseph Internet of Everything (IoE) Value Index: How Much Value Are Private-Sector Firms Capturing from IoE in 2013? Cisco Internet Business Solutions Group (IBSG).* Cisco Systems, Inc.

Brock, D. L. (2001). *The Electronic Product Code (EPC), A Naming Scheme for Physical Objects.* MIT Auto-ID Center, MIT-AU-TOID-WH-002.

Chandra, S. N., & Haeng-Kon, K. (2016). From Cloud to Fog and IoT-Based Real-Time U-Healthcare Monitoring for Smart Homes and Hospitals. *International Journal of Smart Home*, *10*(2), 187–196. doi:10.14257/ijsh.2016.10.2.18

Chen, M., Valenzuela, S. G., Leung, V. C., & Vasilakos, A. V. (2011). Body area networks: A survey. Mobile Networks and Applications. *ACM/Springer MONET, 16*, 171–193.

Chorost, M. (2016). *The Networked Pill.* MIT Technology Review.

Cisco. (n.d.). Retrieved from Internet of Things (IoT): https://www.cisco.com/c/en/us/solutions/internet-of-things/overview.html

ComputerworldUK. (2019). Retrieved from: http://www.computerworlduk.com/news/data/boeing-787s-create-half-terabyte-of-data-per-flight-saysvirgin-atlantic-3433595/

Dey, N., Ashour, A. S., & Bhatt, C. (2017). *Internet of Things Driven Connected Healthcare. Internet of Things and Big Data Technologies for Next Generation Healthcare.* Springer.

Domingo, M. C. (2012). An overview of the Internet of Things for people with disabilities. *Journal of Network and Computer Applications*, *35*(2), 584–596. doi:10.1016/j.jnca.2011.10.015

Elhayatmy, G., Dey, N., & Ashour, A. S. (2018). Internet of Things Based Wireless Body. Springer International Publishing AG.

Ersoy, C., & Alemdar, H. O. (2010). Wireless sensor networks for healthcare: A survey. Computer Networks. *The International Journal of Computer and Telecommunications Networking, 54*(15), 2688–2710.

Evolution of Cloud to Fog Computing. (2019). Retrieved from: http://rankwatch.com/blog/evolution-of-cloud-to-fog-computing/

Frederix, I. (2009). Internet of things and radio frequency identification in care taking, facts and privacy challenges. In *Wireless Communication, Vehicular Technology, Information Theory and aerospace and Electronic Systems Technology. IEEE 1st International Conference on Wireless VITAE*, (pp. 319-323). IEEE. 10.1109/WIRELESSVITAE.2009.5172467

Gia, T. N., Jiang, M., Rahmani, A. M., Westerlund, T., Liljeberg, P., & Tenhunen, H. (2015). Fog Computing in Healthcare Internet of Things. *2015 IEEE International Conference on Computer and Information Technology; Ubiquitous Computing and Communications.*

Gia, T. N., Thanigaivelan, N. K., Rahmani, A. M., Westerlund, T., Liljeberg, P., & Tenhunen, H. (2014). *Customizing 6LoWPAN Networks towards Internetof-Things Based Ubiquitous Healthcare Systems.* IEEE.

Haller, S., Karnouskos, S., & Schroth, C. (2008). The Internet of Things in an Enterprise Context. In *FIS 2008: Future Internet.* Springer.

Healthcare Innovation. (2019). Retrieved from: https://www.hcinnovationgroup.com/cybersecurity/news/13028203/study-87-percent-of-healthcare-organizations-will-adopt-iot-technology-by-2019

Hideo Suzuki, Y. K., Mogi, T., Matsushita, K., Hanada, M., Suzuki, R., & Niijima, N. (2018). *An Updated Watch-over System Using an IoT Device, for Elderly People Living by Themselves. In 3rd International Conferernce on System Reliabilty and Safety.* ICSRS.

Howitt, I., & Gutierrez, J. A. (2003). IEEE 802.15.4 low rate - Wireless personal area network coexistence issues. In *Wireless Communications and Networking. WCNC 2003.* IEEE.

Infiniti Research. (2018). *Retrieved from Six Innovative Applications of IoT in Healthcare.* Retrieved from Business Wire site: https://www.businesswire.com/news/home/20180828005288/en/Innovative-Applications-IoT-Healthcare-Infiniti-Research

Internet of Things - IERC. (2014). Retrieved from IERC-European Research Cluster on the Internet of Things: http://www.internet-of-things-research.eu/about_iot.htm

Internet of Things in healthcare. (2019). Retrieved from 10 examples of the Internet of Things in healthcare, Econsultancy: https://econsultancy.com/internet-of-things-healthcare/

Islam, S. R., Kwak, D., Hossain, M., & Kwak, K. S. (2015). *Survey, The Internet of Things for Health Care: A Comprehensive.* IEEE.

ISO/IEEE. (1996). *IEEE Standard for Medical Device Communication, Overview and Framework.* ISO/IEEE.

ISO/IEEE 11073 Committee (ITU-T /Y.2060). (n.d.). Retrieved from ITU-T Recommendations: https://www.itu.int/ITU-T/recommendations/rec.aspx?rec=y.2060

Jara, J., Zamora, M. a., & Skarmeta, A. (2010). Intra-mobility for Hospital Wireless Sensor Networks Based on 6LoWPAN. *Intra-mobility for Hospital Wireless Se 6th International Conference on Wireless and Mobile Communications*. doi:10.1109/ICWMC.2010.54

Kanchi, S., Sandilya, S., Bhosale, D., & Pitkar, A. (2013). Overview of LTE-A technology. *IEEE Global High Tech Congress on Electronics*. 10.1109/GHTCE.2013.6767272

Kim, J. H., Haw, R., & Hong, C. S. (2010). Development of a framework to support network-based mobility of 6LoWPAN sensor device for mobile healthcare system. *Digest of Technical Papers International Conference on Consumer Electronics (ICCE)*. doi:10.1109/ICCE.5418817

Kirbas, I., & Bayilmis, C. (2012). A web-based remote monitoring interface for medical healthcare. *Turk J Elec Eng & Comp Sci, 20*(4). doi:10.3906/elk-1011-934

Kooa, D. D., Lea, J. J., Sebastiania, A., & Kimb, J. (2016). An Internet-of-Things (IoT) System Development and Implementation for Bathroom Safety Enhancement. In *International Conference on Sustainable Design, Engineering and Construction*. Elsevier. 10.1016/j.proeng.2016.04.004

Koop, C. E., Mosher, R., Kun, L., Geiling, J., Grigg, E., Long, S., ... Rosen, J. (2008). Future delivery of health care: Cybercare. *IEEE Engineering in Medicine and Biology Magazine, 27*(6), 29–38. doi:10.1109/MEMB.2008.929888 PMID:19004693

Lakshay, G., Abhishek, B., & Meetu, G. (2015). Wearable Devices: Google Glass & Smart Watch. *International Journal of Computer Science and Information Technologies, 6*(2), 1872–1873.

Ludwig, W. (2012). Health-enabling technologies for the elderly--an overview of services based on a literature review. Computer Methods and Programs in Biomedicine.

Miorandi, D., Sicari, S., Pellegrini, F. D., & Chlamtac, I. (2012). Internet of things: Vision, applications and research challenges. *Ad Hoc Networks, 10*(7), 1497–1516. doi:10.1016/j.adhoc.2012.02.016

Miraz, M. H., Ali, M., Excell, P. S., & Picking, R. (2015). *A Review on Internet of Things (IoT), Internet of Everything (IoE) and Internet of Nano Things (IoNT). Conference: Internet Technologies and Applications*. ITA.

Mohapatra, S., & Rekha,, K. S. (2012). Sensor-Cloud: A Hybrid Framework for Remote. *International Journal of Computer Applications, 55*(2).

Najib, S. M., Hassan, N. B., Shair, N. T., Rahim, N., & Wahab, N. A. (2019). Intelligent Neonatal Monitoring System Based on Android Application using Multi Sensors. *Computer Applications and Industrial Electronics (ICCAIE), International Conference on*. 10.1109/ISCAIE.2019.8743867

Pang, Z. (2013). *Technologies and Architectures of the Internet-of-Things (IoT) for Health and Wellbeing* (PhD thesis). Kista Sweden: KTH Royal Institute of Technology.

Patel, M., & Wang, J. (2010). Applications, Challenges, and Prospective in Emerging Body Area Networking Technologies. *IEEE Wireless Communications, 17*(1), 80–88. doi:10.1109/MWC.2010.5416354

Patel, N. (2017). *Internet of things in healthcare: applications, benefits, and challenges*. Retrieved from Peerbits: https://www.peerbits.com/blog/internet-of-things-healthcare-applications-benefits-and-challenges.html

Quinn, J.-A., Munoz, F. M., Gonik, B., Frau, L., Cutland, C., Mallett-Moore, T., ... Buttery, J. (2016). Preterm birth: Case definition & guidelines for data collection, analysis, and presentation of immunisation safety data. *Vaccine*, *34*(49), 6047–6056. doi:10.1016/j.vaccine.2016.03.045 PMID:27743648

Rahmani, A. M., Gia, T. N., Thanigaivelan, N. K., & Granados, J. (2015). Smart e-Health Gateway: Bringing Intelligence to Internet-of-Things Based. *12th Annual IEEE Consumer Communications and Networking Conference (CCNC)*.

Rao, R. (2018). *Internet of Things (IoT) Healthcare Benefits*. Retrieved from The IoT Magazine: https://theiotmagazine.com/internet-of-things-iot-healthcare-benefits-2aae663c5c79

Singh, B., Bhattacharya, S., Chowdhary, C., & Jat, D. (2017). A review on internet of things and its applications in healthcare. *Journal of Chemical and Pharmaceutical Sciences*.

Sreekanth, K., & Niktha, K. (2016). A Study on Health Care in Internet of Things. *International Journal on Recent and Innovation Trends in Computing and Communication*, *4*(2).

Sukanya. (2015). *Internet of things world, Europe*. Retrieved from opentechdiary: https://opentechdiary.wordpress.com/tag/internet-of-things/

Sukayna Mandal. (2016). *Internet of Things (IoT) - Part 4 (Network Protocols and Architecture)*. Retrieved from: https://www.c-sharpcorner.com/UploadFile/f88748/internet-of-thingsiot-part-4-network-protocols-and-arc/

The History of Healthcare Technology and the Evolution of EHR. (2019). Retrieved from vertitechit: https://www.vertitechit.com/history-healthcare-technology/

The Internet of Things. (2005). ITU Internet Reports.

The many faces of IoT in Healthcare. (2014). Retrieved from: http://www.slideshare.net/stockerpartnership/the-many-faces-of-internet-of-things-iot-in-healthcare/11

Touati, F., Mnaouer, A. B., & Tabsih, R. (2013). Towards u-Health: An indoor 6LoWPAN Based Platform for Real-Time Healthcare Monitoring. *Conference: Wireless and Mobile Networking Conference (WMNC), 6th Joint IFIP*.

Tsibas, H., Giokas, K., & Koutsouris, D. (2010). "Internet of Things", an RFID - IPv6 Scenario in a Healthcare Environment. In *XII Mediterranean Conference on Medical and Biological Engineering and Computing*, (pp. 808-811). Academic Press.

Ubiquitous Sensor Networks (USN). (2008). ITU-T Technology Watch Briefing Report Series, No. 4.

Ullah, S., Higgins, H., Braem, B., Latré, B., Blondia, C., Moerman, I., ... Kwak, K. S. (2012). A Comprehensive Survey of Wireless Body Area Networks on PHY, MAC, and Network Layers Solutions. *Journal of Medical Systems*, *36*(3), 1065–1094. doi:10.100710916-010-9571-3 PMID:20721685

Vermesan, O., & Fries, P. (2013). *Internet of Things - Converging Technologies for Smart Environments and Integrated Ecosystems*. River Publishers.

Weissberger, A. (2014). *TiECon 2014 Summary-Part 1: Qualcomm Keynote & IoT Track Overview*. IEEE ComSoc.

Wu, M., & Huang, W. (2012). WSN-based Health Care Management Platform for Long-Term Care Institutions. *J. Converg. Inform. Technol., 7*(7).

Zhang, K. (2019). *Countries adopting a new high-tech approach to aging care*. Retrieved from China Daily: http://www.chinadaily.com.cn/a/201905/21/WS5ce35403a3104842260bcd21.html

KEY TERMS AND DEFINITIONS

Ambient assisted living (AAL): AAL is capable of providing assistance services to the aged and handicapped patients by continuous activity monitoring and getting access to medical support.

Machine to Machine (M2M) Communication: It is defined as a direct communication between devices. The communication channels can either be wired or wireless.

Patients Surveillance: Continuous monitoring of a patient's condition.

Protocols: Protocols are a set of rules and regulations that governs the communications between computers or communicating devices on a network.

Security: Security refers to all actions that are taken to protect a person or place from a danger or threat.

Smart Devices: It is refer to electronic devices, connected with other devices and networks by different wireless protocol. The term smart devices also denotes to a ubiquitous computing devices.

Tracking: The act or process of following something or someone continuously is known as tracking.

6LoWPAN (IPv6 low power personal area networks): It is an Internet Engineering Task Force (IETF), defined protocol that provides connectivity between wireless sensor networks and internet providing support to IPv6 using IEEE 802.15.4. It denotes a wireless link for low power personal area networks (LoWPANs). These networks are categorized by their more restricted abilities than other WPANs (e.g. Bluetooth) and WLANs (e.g.WiFi), they have small frame size, low data rate, low bandwidth, and low transmit power.

Chapter 2
Powering Healthcare IoT Sensors–Based Triboelectric Nanogenerator

Saeed Ahmed Khan

Sukkur IBA University, Pakistan

Shamsuddin Lakho

Sukkur IBA University, Pakistan

Ahmed Ali

Sukkur IBA University, Pakistan

Abdul Qadir Rahimoon

Sukkur IBA University, Pakistan

Izhar Hussain Memon

Benazir Bhutto Shaheed University of Technology and Skill Development Khairpure Mirs, Pakistan

Ahsanullah Abro

Sukkur IBA University, Pakistan

ABSTRACT

Most of the emerging electronic devices are wearable in nature. However, the frequent changing or charging the battery of all wearable devices is the big challenge. Interestingly, with those wearable devices that are directly associated with the human body, the body can be used in transferring or generating energy in a number of techniques. One technique is triboelectric nanogenerators (TENG). This chapter covers different applications where the human body is used as a triboelectric layer and as a sensor. Wearable TENG has been discussed in detail based on four basic modes that could be used to monitor the human health. In all the discussions, the main focus is to power the wearable healthcare internet of things (IoT) sensor through human body motion based on self-powered TENG. The IoT sensors-based

DOI: 10.4018/978-1-7998-1253-1.ch002

wearable devices related to human body can be used to develop smart body temperature sensors, pressure sensors, smart textiles, and fitness tracking sensors.

INTRODUCTION

The current major issues of the world are related to energy transportation, generation, and conservation; moreover, the serious life threating environmental issues are also caused by standard energy resources like nuclear, biomass, and fossil fuels (coal, oil, and natural gas), etc. Implementing stable, enduring and innovative energy policies are crucial for economic and social development globally. Renewable energy technologies such as solar, geothermal and wind energies have an important role in lowering Carbon dioxide CO_2 emissions which is the major cause of increased global warming. Therefore, these technologies also known as clean and green energy sources. (Panwar, Kaushik, & Kothari, 2011) On the other hand, with the ever-growing development of nanotechnology-based devices, power consumption is the major issue in these devices(Hussein, 2015; S. Wang, Lin, & Wang, 2015). Moreover, self-powered and sustainable devices are more popular than systems with standard batteries. At the smaller scale, energy is required to power small electronics that should be self-powered, wireless, and maintenance-free for the small sensor networks, that is known as the Internet of Things (IoT) (Gope & Hwang, 2016; Saravanakumar et al., 2015; Sodhro, Pirbhulal, Luo, & de Albuquerque, 2019). Reduction in the size of microprocessor, sensor, and even portable/wearable personal small electronic devices are the main reason for the self-powered systems(A. Ali, Hwang, Choo, & Lim, 2018a). In the near future, these devices can modify the method tend to control the air/water quality, environmental conditions, organic structure, and structural health. However, because sensors and devices are increasing day by day, there is a huge challenge of powering these devices and sensors. (Lara & Labrador, 2013). Figure 1 shows an overview of wearable and flexible health-monitoring sensors to detect physical activity and a variety of biosignals from the human body as well as user interaction and communication systems for practical applications. (Ha, Lim, & Ko, 2018). The human body generates different types of signals they are categorized here in main three signals i-e Physical signals (pressure, motion, tactile and vibration), thermal signals which are (fever and hypothermia) and Electrophysiological signals (Brain wave, cardiac activity, and muscle movement). Figure 1 illustrates the different sensors are attached to the human body like a smartwatch, smart textile, smart band, thermometer, electroencephalogram (EEG), electromyography (EMG), and electrocardiogram ECG. These all sensors are connected to the user interactive system via wireless communication systems like Bluetooth, near-field communication (NFC) and radio-frequency identification (RFID). The user interactive system contains remote medical services, self-diagnosis, and healthcare. Over the years, great developments have been made in nanofabrication with different functionalization and integration, in addition to that great cutting edge materials have been prepared with skin-like properties like, flexibility/elasticity and stretchability for empowering wearable devices (A. Ali, Hwang, Choo, & Lim, 2018b; Rogers, Someya, & Huang, 2010). Therefore, together with the Internet of Things (IoT), and Artificial Intelligence, wearable devices have been growing day by day. The worldwide market of wearable devices innovation is expected to grow over $150 billion by 2026 and predicted to develop at a yearly rate of 23% from 2019 to 2023(X.-S. Zhang et al., 2018). Broadly speaking wearable devices are practically applicable to every field of life, from individual wellbeing to versatile correspondence, personalized medicines, security, safety, and numerous other areas. However, there are some challenges that need to be addressed for any practical application. The first major challenge is how to power the wearable device for a long period of time, the other issues are related to biocompatibility and ergonomics(Miotto, Wang, Wang, Jiang, & Dudley, 2017; Sodhro, Li, & Shah, 2016). For power batteries are the classical choice, however, they suffer from many problems such as, constantly recharging, limited life and the replacement with the time.

There is one challenge to generate power from the living body, especially form the Human body. From where many watts can be produced by physical movement or warmth emanation(M.-K. Kim, Kim, Lee, Kim, & Kim, 2014). Over the past few years, many methods have been reported to generate power from the body, based on: photovoltaic, thermoelectric, electromagnetic, piezoelectric, and triboelectric effect. Generating power from a living being is a promising method to fulfill the power requirements of wearable devices that can be used for Internet-of-Things. This method has shown great potential for the development of self-powered gadgets that do not require batteries and long wires. From above all mentioned types of generating power the Triboelectric Nanogenerator (TENG)(Zhong et al., 2013), is reported to be a promising method, Triboelectric Nano-generator is the generator which converts the natural/environmental energy into electrical energy through the process of the triboelectrification and electrostatic induction. Now a day's mostly electronic devices are related to the human motion for the sake of communication, safety, and health monitoring. The most sufficient energy which is related to human is the mechanical energy in the form of body motion. Electrostatic-charges are formed upon the surfaces of triboelectric materials when the two triboelectric materials are brought in contact with each other(Niu et al., 2013). But when the mechanical-force enforced upon the two triboelectric materials, they become separated from each other, induced charges which can create the potential drop, and the electron flow can be driven between two electrodes mounted over the bottom and top surfaces on those triboelectric materials. Wang's group is the pioneer of the Triboelectric Nano-generator. In 2012 they invented the first triboelectric nanogenerator (TENG). The aim was to harvest the small scale environment/mechanical energy and convert it into electrical energy, to drive the low voltage electronic devices(Z. L. Wang, Zhu, Yang, Wang, & Pan, 2012). Recently authors have reported TENG operating under complex deformation like twisting, stretching and bending, based on shape adaptive material. The reported TENG harvested energy through subject under test deformation motions, thereby obtaining self-powering ability as well as monitoring abilities for different health challenges. The TENG was composed of copper acetate-II and Ecoflex. The reported TENG was very flexible (200%.) with VOC of 70V and ISC of 11µA and provided the power of 55µW to the maximum load resistance of 80MΩ. (Shamsuddin, 2019).

In this chapter authors have worked on the reviews of nearly all reported wearable devices, and the developments in healthcare wearable and flexible triboelectric nanogenerators devices that can be directly attached to the human body to sense the different kinds of human body motions, that can be employed to generate electricity, Moreover, we have given insights about how the IoT healthcare sensor can be powered up through triboelectric nanogenerator vie human body motion.

Figure 1. Human body phycial biosignals and analogous healthcare monitoring detectors including user interactive systems on the left side. Illustrative physiological bio-signals and kinds of wearable healthcare detectors to detect the thermal (thermometer), physical (smartwatch, smarttextile smartband,), and electrophysiological (ECG, EEG, EMG) energetic signs on the right side. Wireless communication based user-interactive, healthcare systems (RFID, NFC, Bluetooth) and response system for the omnipresent healthcare. Reproduced with the permission (Ha, Lim, & Ko, 2018).

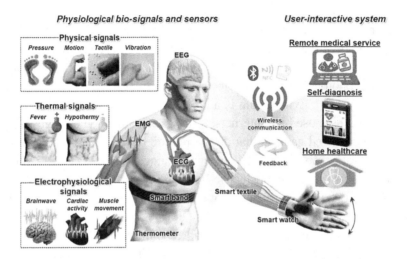

BACKGROUND

Body Movement Activities

Tracing body actions and routines movements cater valuable clue to guarantee health and right position. Regular examination of body movements permits diagnosis of certain posture and abrupt trembling fingers that are the sign of life threating ailments like Parkinsonism(Guan et al., 2016), Alzheimer's(Sheridan, Solomont, Kowall, & Hausdorff, 2003), Parkinsonism(Guan et al., 2016) and can enables initial tracing and cure of such ailments. The development in movement tracking sensors has opened new avenues research in of dermatoplasty, ergonomics, athletics, and rehabilitation engineering. Mostly these movement tracking sensors are composed of flexible material, such as paper, fibers rubbers (Z. Liu et al., 2018). and nanocomposite(Gui, He, Gao, Tao, & Wang, 2017; Hussein, 2015), that could be simply placed on the curvy skin and other areas, which enables the tracing of various body movements such as, twisting at joints of finger and feet, and shrinkage and swelling of various muscle of body. Resistive strain sensors based on microbeads fibers have been reported to record a variety of athletic movements, these strain sensors were directly laced at the clothes (Figure 2a)(Ma et al., 2017). The 120% stretchability was achieved by using CNT-Au decorated Polydimethylsiloxane PDMS threads. The gauge factor (GF) of these strain sensors was found to be hundred, the value of GF is excellent as compared to other fiber-based stain sensors, mainly due to rearrangement and focusing of repeatedly formed fiber geometry. 2D Ti_3C_2_MXene based extremely elastic and resistive sensors were reported with GF of 179 and rapid response time less 29 ms(Gui et al., 2017). The distinctive geometry of Ti_3C_2 coupled with MXene depicted excellent sensitivity with extreme thinness and compressibility facilitated the tailoring the attachment to body and tracing of body movements (Figure 2b). J. Zhao et al. prepared wearable ionic sensors that were able to detect tiny pressure, the voltage was generated with the application of pressure, due to pressure trigger ion movement (J. Zhao et al., 2017). Likewise, handbags prepared using the same pressure trigger ion movement were able to sense signal produced by finger motions (Figure 2c).

User-Interactive and Skin-Connective Health Monitoring Systems

Although extensive studies have been carried out for the fabrication of effective wearable health monitoring systems, still there is a lot of room for the improvement, particularly for sustainability, deformability flexibility, deformability, and user-friendliness. All these mentioned factors are crucial for efficient and successful wearable health monitoring system. Over the past few years, several advancements have been reported for the development of wearable health monitoring system. The most important aspect of the wearable device is its conductive stretchability, the sensor should maintain all its attributes even after it is bent or folded, especially electrical components and connections should not be changed even under strain. Moreover, multiplex sensors that can trace a variety of physiological signals in a single unit have shown to be promising for the development of miniaturized smart wearable systems especially for fitness and health monitoring (A. Ali; Ha et al., 2018). Cordless systems that are free from any wires could also make wearable health monitoring system simple and user-friendly, such systems have more communication and networking potential than wired systems, last but not the least effective energy management with self-energy harvesting could enhance and substitute the present widely used heavy batteries based

Figure 2. Wearable and Flexible pressure/strain sensors to monitor different Human body movements (a) by the deviation of the resistance sports activities can be monitored by directly wearing the microbeads on fiber based on wearable cloths. Reproduced with the permission (Zhiyuan Liu et al., 2018) Copyright 2018, Wiley-VCH. (b) A flexible and comprisal pressure sensor based on 2D Ti$_3$C$_2$-Mxene, can be easily attached with human skin and can sense the eye blink insignificant strain (scale bar: 20 nm). Reproduced with the permission (Ma et al., 2017) Copyright 2017, Nature Publishing Group. (c) Gloves based on the wearable ionic sensor that can observe the different motion that follow the sign languages. Reproduced with the permission (Zhao et al., 2017) Copyright 2017, American Chemical Society.

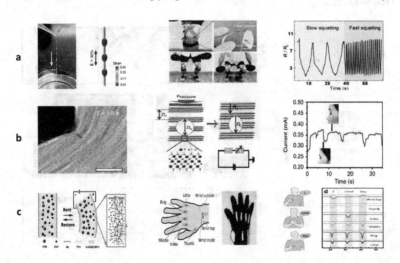

system. Moreover, effective energy handling would make the wearable health monitoring systems more sustainable, user-friendly and, inexpensive.

Wireless System

Commercially feasible wearable user-friendly fitness tracking systems that can cater valuable knowledge about various body physiological signal would probably be closed loop and wireless system. To achieve this extensive studies have been carried to integrate wearable devices to flexible platforms and widely used wireless communication plugin such as RFID, Bluetooth, and NFC (Choi et al., 2016; Honda, Harada, Arie, Akita, & Takei, 2014; Kang et al., 2011; Y. Khan et al., 2016; J. Kim et al., 2015; J. Kim et al., 2016; Park et al., 2017). The bending angle was near 5mm that made the system to be easily placed at body curvy surfaces such as fingers, teeth, and other human skin. The proof of concept was also depicted by the wireless working of light emitting diodes LEDs. The also extended the study by developing chemical and temperature monitoring systems based on same NFC system Three modes pyro resistive, piezoresistive and piezoelectric were integrated to develop flexible wireless system equipped with reprogrammable display integrated circuits ICs that can be placed at any location on the human body(Zhang, Wang, & Yang, 2017). This three-mode system was not able to detect pressure and temperature change but also was also able to communicate with mobile phone vie Bluetooth technology. Moreover, the extended version of the system was also able to detect human physiological signals, such as movements, breathing, and temperature change and exhibition of mentioned physiological signals on the mobile phone screen in real time. (Figure 3b). Apart from the function of signal communication, wireless devices have been used to charge batteries unites in a wearable system. The advancement in wireless battery charging systems would increase the lifetime of batteries, supporting the long duration

Figure 3. User interactive wireless systems for healthcare gadgets. (a) Human Body connective near field communication (NFC) gadgets for the wireless communication. Reproduced with the permission (Kim et al., 2015) Copyright 2015, Wiley-VCH. (b) Flexible wireless gadgets with skin connective sensor having triple mode. Reproduced with the permission (Kang et al., 2011) Copyright 2018, MDPI. (c) Ni plated CNT-PDMS wireless charging system. Reproduced with the permission (Hong et al., 2017) Copyright 2017, Wiley-VCH.

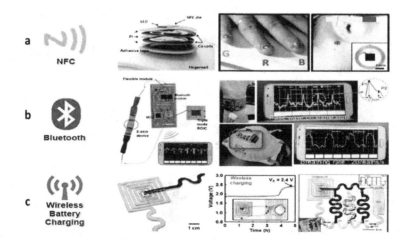

examination and detecting and predicting any wrong sign, without going through the troublesome battery changing/replacing process. Likewise, Nickel coated carbon nanotube- PDMS nanostructure was studied for the development of efficient flexible electrodes which can be employed at twisting flexible wireless energy transportation coil, lithium-ion cells and triboelectric generators (Figure 3c)(Hong et al., 2017). These nanostructures based system combined all the constituent into an individual wearable device which also enabled the wireless charging of batteries. Inkjet printing based polyimide substrates were used to prepare stretchable microcircuits, these substrates were further used for the preparation of photodetectors, wireless charging coil, and supercapacitors(S. A. Khan, Gao, Zhu, Yan, & Lin, 2017). The extended study combined the photodetector system, supercapacitors and wireless charging system, that not only delivered energy to photodetectors but was also powered the batteries wirelessly (Yue et al., 2016). Battery-free and flexible epidermal devices that equipped with photodiodes, LEDs and NFC module for tracking of tissue blood pressure, heart rate, and cardiogenic shock (J. Kim et al., 2016). The NFC served dual purpose information transmission and wireless energy transmission which permitted the batter free function. The system was also integrated with a cell phone for real-time recording of useful information

SELF-POWERED SENSORS AND DEVICES

The operation of various sensors and remote flag handsets in wearable gadgets need a small amount of energy (Raghunathan, Schurgers, Park, & Srivastava, 2002; Q. Wang, Hempstead, & Yang, 2006). Present energy systems are stiff, big in size and weight, need frequent charging, and replacement and can catch fire at higher temperature (Stoppa & Chiolerio, 2014; S. Wang, Lin, & Wang, 2012). To develop feasible body-wearable, skin-connectable, and fitness data logger systems, energy requirements should be scaled down, they should be stretchable and robust. Modern energy harvester system can produce energy by itself, based on surrounding resources, like strain, pressure, force, temperature change and photo variations (Lee et al., 2016). These modern energy harvesters have the potential to solve the above-mentioned issues. (M.-K. Kim et al., 2014). Over the past few years, many methods have been reported to generate power from body, based on: photovoltaic, thermoelectric, electromagnetic, piezoelectric, and triboelectric effect Zhang at et. reported a self-powered smart patch sensor with the ability of wireless transmission for monitoring the motion and the temperature of the human body (Figure 4). The electrostatic charges are the main reason for making the system self-powered. The device transmitted signals and energy wirelessly to the receiver by the electrostatic induction. Device wireless transmission efficiency was at the distance of 1cm with a receiver 16cm^2 reached 26.6% that represents the outstanding ability of the wireless transmission in the near-field. The current of the receiver remained identical to the current source at the various loads ranging in between 1 Ω to 1 MΩ. The designed smart patch not only gather energy for driving the commercial sensors, but it can also behave as an active sensor to monitor the human motion.

Integration With Batteries for Self-Charging Power Systems (SCPSs)

The battery is superior to supercapacitor in charge storing capacity, and its essential parameter for useful applications. Numerous forms of batteries have been designed and widely used in PDAs, tablets devices, and battery-controlled automobiles(Dunn, Kamath, & Tarascon, 2011; Y. Tang, Zhang, Li, Ma, & Chen,

Figure 4. Smart patch self-powered wireless structure. (a) Smart patch self-powered wireless Schematic diagram contains the Generator made up of two pieces of cloth and CNT pasted over cloth 2 the generator transmit to the receiver through a wireless signal. Reproduced with the permission (Zhang et al., 2018)

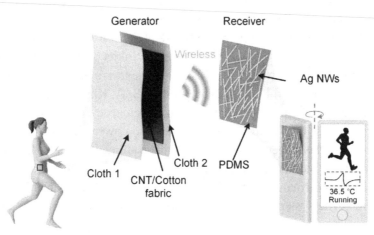

2015). In this part of the book chapter, we will discuss recent developments in the self-charging power system (SCPS) vie combining batteries with TENGs. Wang et al. initial fabricated a flexible (SCPS) by combining (TENG) and the Lithium-cell in 2013(S. Wang et al., 2013). As shown in (Figure 5a), the combination was implemented vie preparing a stretchable lithium cell above the curvy TENG geometry. When mechanical motion is applied onto the SCPS, the TENG part can efficiently generate electricity, and the rectified energy can be stored in the Lithuim Ion Battery LIB part. A novel operation mode called "sustainable mode" was developed. The SCP can deliver 1.9 µA current and 1.56 v in this mode for nearly two days and constantly energize the ultra-violate UV transducer. This performance is far superior to LIB that has a value of 4h. TENG as a power generator and stretchable lithium cell as power storing device is depicted in (Figure 5b)(Xiong Pu et al., 2015). The sensitive polyester surface was chosen as the substrate and successively covered with parylene sheet and conductive Nickel Ni sheet. Ni-sheet was used as a current collector, and LiFPO$_4$ was used as an electrode of lithium-cell. The power generated from human movements vie TENG structure was shown to be able to charge lithium cell, which then was employed to energize a sensor that can also communicate to the mobile device. When continuous force is applied lithium cell store the energy, whereas when recurring force is applied the structure act as TENG to transfer human movement into electrical energy, other than human movements any kind of movements can be used to generate electrical energy.(X. Liu, Zhao, Wang, & Yang, 2017).. Gao et al. developed an SCPS that could concurrently hunt and stock tidal force into chemical energy (Gao, Zhao, Liu, & Yang, 2017). A stretchable lithium cell positioned in the center of a dielectric sheet of air operated TENG so that lithium cell and TENG are integrated as one device. Under windy conditions of 25 m/s, the lithium cell can be charged from around 4 volts with excellent storage. Moreover, a number of other tidal energy based SCPs with analogous geometry was also studied (Jiang, Chen, Zhang, & Yang, 2017; Zhao, Yang, Liu, & Wang, 2017). Apart from that, the choice of suitable energy storage systems or electrode structures is also crucial for SCPs based TENG. Energy storage capacity, repeatability, reproducibility, and simplicity are the basic parameters of interest. Zhang et al. examined the effects of the vibrated output of TENG on dynamic performance and polarization of lithium cell and dynamic behaviors (X. Zhang et al., 2018). It has been reported that lithium cell-based chemical reaction have enhanced energy storage performance and increased coulombic performance especially for TENGs applications. Moreover, the vibrating current has a constructive role in enhancing the repeatability and lowering the charge transmission impedance (Hou et al., 2017). A number of other reports have used various energy storage devices the details are given here (S. Wang et al., 2015; Z. L. Wang, 2013; X. Zhang et al., 2018). Nevertheless, they have a number of disadvantages like bulky in size, heavy weight, low reproducibility, and cost. Therefore, lithium cells based TENGs are promising for future advancements (M.-C. Lin et al., 2015; Son et al., 2018; M. Wang et al., 2018).

WEARABLE HEALTHCARE SENSORS BASED ON TRIBOELECTRIC NANOGENERATOR TO MONITOR THE BIOSIGNALS

Wearable healthcare monitoring is considered as one of the most important and largest applications of the IoT. It got attention and motivation by the increasing costs of healthcare, these devices have been used for multiple reasons from the simple pulse monitoring to motion/activity monitoring and in implantable detectors. Time by time sensing capabilities of these sensors has drastically improved. In the year 2001 IBM's Watch Pad having a single sensor to sense the movements of the hand, it was supplied power by the lithium polymer battery having a capacity of 60mAh and 3.7V. At the same time, there were available larger batteries with same footprints and the capacity up to 200mAh. The reason behind using the 60mAh battery was only the less cost. During operation, this device requires an average 27mA(Talari et al., 2017), so this electronic device lasted many hours before to be recharged. Since the power consumption has been reduced automatically for the data processing, and sensors now are able to detect/

Figure 5. A picture flexible self-charging power unit which contains the lithium-ion battery and a triboelectric nanogenerator and the schematic diagram. Reproduced with the permission (Wang et al., 2013) Copyright 2013, American Chemical Society Equivalent circuit and the photograph of the self-charging power system which contains the flexible lithium-ion battery belt and a textile triboelectric nanogenerator Reproduced with the permission (Pu et al., 2015) Copyright 2015, John Wiley and Sons.

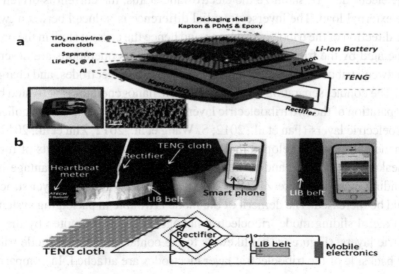

monitor the sleep quality, heart rate, activity movements, body motions, body temperatures and many more. Especially reduction in the cost of batteries has made possible these devices to use the 200mAh lithium-Ion cells. Wearable smartwatches are accomplished of heart rate monitoring, body temperatures monitoring, sleep quality and many exercises related to body motion. (Shamsuddin, 2019).

Working Mechanism of Triboelectric Nanogenerator

The fundamental working system of the triboelectric nanogenerators includes the combination of electrostatic enlistment and the triboelectrification amid the transformation of mechanical energy into electrical energy(S. Wang et al., 2012; Z. L. Wang, Jiang, & Xu, 2017). The triboelectric impact is regularly viewed as irritating or even unsafe in everyday life since it might offer ascent to start, dust ingestion and harm to hardware(W. Tang, Meng, & Zhang, 2013; Z. L. Wang et al., 2017). In the examination, the energy collection of the triboelectric nanogenerator from the environment relies on the combined impacts of electrostatic induction and triboelectrification(Hussain et al., 2019; Zhou et al., 2013). In this way, factors affecting those two physical procedures sway the electric energy execution of the triboelectric nanogenerators, particularly inherent properties of the material, for example, the electron partiality, work capacity, and contact. The TENG has numerous points of interest including minimal effort, auxiliary decent variety, stable electric yield, high vitality transformation productivity, shape-versatile capacity, and eco-friendly, etc(Liang et al., 2017; Saravanakumar et al., 2015).There are four fundamental modes of TENGs with their exceptional merits, features, and applications, which includes vertical lateral-sliding mode, contact-separation mode, and freestanding triboelectric-layer mode, single electrode mode(Saravanakumar et al., 2015). There are initially one pair of the triboelectric surfaces contact together for all the basic modes of the triboelectric nanogenerator (Normally there are two pair of the triboelectric surface for the Free Standing mode) as shown in (Figure 6a (iv)). Likewise at least two electrodes are used that are protected from each other very carefully. The ground is supposed to be the second electrode in a single electrode mode(S. Wang, Niu, Yang, Lin, & Wang, 2014). The electrostatic charges are transferred from one surface to another surface due to the specific capabilities to attract the electrons of two triboelectric surfaces. Original electrostatic status is broken by the flow of the electrostatic charges as the displacement is applied on the triboelectric layer, and a potential difference is created there between the electrodes. To stabilize the electrostatic status, the current is driven by the potential difference by the external load. The inverse potential difference is induced between two the electrodes due to the inverse direction of the triboelectric layer, and hence the current flow in the opposite direction. AC output is generated by the triboelectric nanogenerator and its operations are described by relative displacement x between triboelectric layers the voltage V between electrodes, and charge transfer Q between electrodes. The contact separation mode triboelectric nanogenerator is activated by the process of the contact and separation of the two triboelectric layers. (Figure 6a(i)). The charge collector/electrode is pasted on the triboelectric layers'(Fan et al., 2012; S. Wang et al., 2012; Zhu et al., 2012) backside. This is a very basic mode and firstly developed mode, this mode contains the merits of robustness, simple structure, high peak output current, and facial fabrication. The structural advantage is comparatively higher than the sliding mode structure(Zi et al., 2015). By stacking the multilayer structures the output performance could be increased. The demerit of the mode is trouble in packaging system because of the diverse volume. Lateral sliding mode triboelectric nanogenerator is prompted by the sliding between the two triboelectric layers. (Figure 6a(ii)) likewise to the contact separation mode triboelectric nanogenerator, on the backside of the triboelectric layer electrodes are attached. In comparison through the contact-separation mode, the sliding-mode results in the lower structural advantage. Though Charge creation is most effectual than by the contact, through the highest charge density formed(M. Ali et al., 2019; Zhu et al., 2013). The main edge of this mode of triboelectric nanogenerator is that through the scraping structure the output performance of the current can be improved. The lateral sliding structured mode triboelectric nanogenerator can be reshaped into the rotational grating cylindrical structure (Bai et al., 2013; L. Lin et al., 2013; Zhu, Chen, Zhang, Jing, & Wang, 2014). Both contact separation and lateral sliding mode have the same demerit, that there should be a wire connected with the moving the triboelectric layers by the back electrode. The application of the triboelectric nanogenerator might be limited by such configuration in the wider area for the energy scavenging by the free movement of the objectives. To fix the issue, one back electrode may be removed, to form the single electrode mode triboelectric nanogenerator (Figure 6(iii)). This mode of triboelectric nanogenerator has a simple design and very easy to design. The performance of this mode is limited with the small voltage and the small charge transfer. This mode is used in the application of self-powered sensing devices(Y. Yang, Zhang, et al., 2013; Y. Yang, Zhou, et al., 2013). Freestanding mode triboelectric nanogenerator is operated by the triboelectric layer freely moving between the two electrodes. The triboelectric layer not attached with the electrode in this mode moves with or without contact through the two electrodes which are static, so this is the outstanding robust(S. Wang, Xie, Niu, Lin, & Wang, 2014). A high output performance is also determined at the same time with the structural advantage accomplished. Based on the merits of the higher output, integration, and facile fabrication this mode has the different outputs triboelectric nanogenerators with the records both in the energy conversion efficiency and maximum power output(Xie et al., 2014; Zhu et al., 2014). Figure 6b shows the triboelectric series, there are two types of materials in this series i-e positive and negative which is used in the fabrication of the triboelectric nanogenerator.

TENG as an Active Sensor for Detection of the Different Body Movements

Triboelectric nanogenerator application located on ears was shown by Guo et al. the vertical contact-separation mode was adopted for this wearable triboelectric nanogenerator(Ouyang et al., 2017) (Figure

Figure 6. (a)The basic four modes of triboelectric nanogenerator (i) Vertical Contact separation mode (ii) lateral sliding mode (iii) Single Electrode mode (iv) Free standing triboelectric nanogenerator (b) Triboelectric series of the materials.

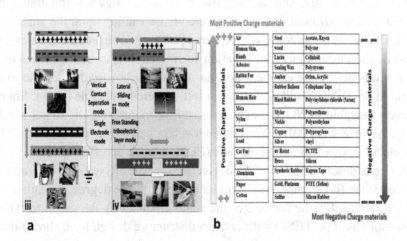

7a). Researchers fabricated a wearable triboelectric nanogenerator based self-powered triboelectric auditory-sensor (TAS) with the merits of the single-channel design, easy fabrication, and circular type. For assembling the circular device, the Kapton, fluorinated ethylene propylene (FEP), Au, acrylic and the spacer for the gap-creating were used. For realizing the greater surface charge to boost the sensitivity of the triboelectric auditory sensor (TAS), then of nanostructure was created on the surface of FEP. A triboelectric auditory sensor (TAS) was obtained with higher sensitivity about $\approx 110 \text{mV dB}^{-1}$ and revealed the huge variety of frequency (100-5000Hz) based on the recently designed triboelectric nanogenerator method. For the hearing aids and the social robotics, this can be put on their ears directly. Yang at al. designed a self-powered bionic membrane sensor (BMS) based on the electrification effect (Figure 7b) (J. Yang et al., 2015). BMS which is based upon the triboelectric nanogenerator works with the contact separation mode. To fabricate a device like oval shape indium tin oxide (ITO), polyethylene terephthalate (PET), and polytetrafluoroethylene (PTFE), and Nylon was utilized. PTFE and nylon were used as triboelectric layers and the ITO behaved as the electrode layer. To act like human being's eardrum, the PET was strongly attached to the nylon and PTFE, the conical cavity was created between the nylon and PTFE an air spacer were utilized that gave the output in the form of formation and the deportation of the charges. For enhancing the output performance, PTFE surface has the nano-surface modification. BMS working principle could be defined as follows, the layer of PTFE generates the electricity in the reaction to the mechanical vibration by the process of the contact electrification. For revealing the cardiovascular system's condition, the author exhibited, the BMS can be utilized as a self-powered sensor. Additionally, fabricated device/sensor that could be affixed on the human neck which can act as the microphone and it does not need any external power. The BMS is Mini, low-cost, wearable, eye-catching and self-powered sensor, it has the possibility for the different applications in biometric authentication and wearable healthcare. Ouyang et al. designed a self-powered pulse sensor (SUPS) with the wearable triboelectric nanogenerator with high sensitivity for the wrist (Figure 7c)(Ouyang et al., 2017). This working mode of SUPS based on TENG is contact-separation mode. The device contained with Copper Cu and Kapton as the triboelectric layers. After the encapsulation dimensions of the SUPS becomes (20mmx10mmx0.1mm). The output results were typically $\approx$voltage 109V, current 2.97µA, and transferred charge 7.6nC. On the radial arteria, SUPS can generate the nominal output voltage 1.52V, current 5.4nA and transferred charges 1.08nC. The physiological information can be reflected by the radial artery electrical signal electrical signals through the SUPS regarding the atrial fibrillation, atrial septal absence, and coronary heart disease. The ant diastole and cardiovascular diseases were diagnosed by applying the SUPS successfully. Additionally, Bluetooth technology was integrated into SUPS. This device also detected the cardiovascular diseases wirelessly depending upon the small pulse-signal. By the combination of Bluetooth technology, self-powered pulse sensor executed wireless, precise and the actual observation of the physiological information for the cardiovascular diseases depend upon the small pulse-signal. Considering the efficient analysis of the cardiovascular disease in the future, this wearable SUPS based on TENG could perform as a self-powered wearable sensor. Shi et al. suggested a free-standing mode wearable TENG as an active sensor for monitoring the finger bending in the year of 2016(Shi, Wang, Wang, & Lee, 2016). The device was fabricated from the deionized (DI) water, multiple copper (Cu) electrodes, polydimethylsiloxane (PDMS) layer, and flexible PET film. The working principle of the device is described below. The device/sensor was affixed on the human finger, a water chamber center fixed at the finger joint. As the finger angled at some degree, it resulted in various pressure. Water flow was induced in the passage of the water chamber by the pressure. The output results of this wearable sensor based on TENG with enhanced structure design have shown the enormous applications for monitoring the complicated body movements. Pu suggested the joint motion triboelectric quantization senor (jmTOS) in 2018, which relies on the finger wearable triboelectric nanogenerator with the merits of speed, direction, and the detection of high sensitivity finger joint extension degree (Figure 7d)(Xianjie Pu et al., 2018). This system can restrain the robotic hand through the different gestures of human. Contribution of this work is to drive the natural real-time interface and high precision. Yi et al. suggested a flexible rubber-based triboelectric nanogenerator on the stomach having the sliding mode that can work like an active sensor (Figure 7e)(Yi et al., 2015). Two triboelectric layers were utilized to fabricate the device i-e first was aluminum film and the second was the elastic rubber. By stretching and the releasing the rubber the distribution on the surface of the rubber and charge density can be varied. For the detection of the diaphragm breathing and joint moment, the fabricated device was affixed on the human body.

TENG as a Power Sources

Yi et al. fabricated the stretchable self-charging power system (SSCPS) which confined on the wearable triboelectric nanogenerator having the supercapacitor and working mode of the contact separation (Figure 8a)(Yi et al., 2016). Various body motion can be converted into electrical energy by the wear-

Figure 7. Representation of the wearable triboelectric nanogenerators used as the active sensors a) TENG affixed on ears as the social robot and hearing care. Reproduced with the permission (Zhuo Liu et al., 2019) Copyright 2018, the American Association for the Advancement of Science. b) Observing the different kinds of human position and the signals on the throat. Reproduced with the permission (Yang et al., 2015) Copyright 2015, Wiley VCH. c) Cardiovascular sickness detection for the wrist. Reproduced with the permission (Ouyang et al., 2017) Copyright 2017, Wiley VCH d) oversighting finger gesture. Copyright 2018, Elsevier e) observation of the stomach diaphragm inhaling Copyright 2015, Wiley-VCH.

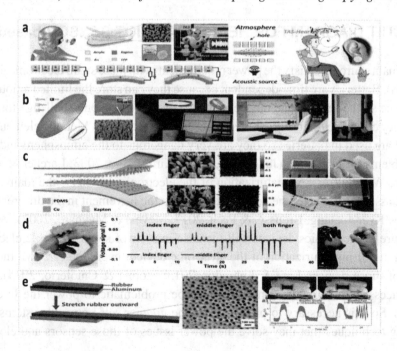

able triboelectric nanogenerator, and that energy was reserved in the supercapacitors. Combination of silicon rubber and the black carbon was utilized for the electrode and the grating layer, for the other grating layer silicon rubber was utilized(J. Wang et al., 2015; Wen et al., 2016). For enhancement in the electrical output of the triboelectric nanogenerator, a micro/nanostructure was formed on the grating layer surface by a method called a sandpaper polishing method. The generated output of the triboelectric nanogenerator was stored in the stretchable supercapacitor having dimensions (5mmx5mm). The authors showed a charging rate about to 178mV/min and reliable performance of the charging of the SSCPS that is proving that the device is waterproofed. The SSCPS can drive the electronic wearable watch about 16sec, as the SSCPS device is touched for 8min at the frequency 1.3Hz. This discovery showed that this SSCPS can power the wearable electronic devices by scavenging the biomechanical energy through the different human movements, from this work a new direction is found for the fabrication of the different triboelectric nanogenerators with higher stretchability for the wearable electronic devices. Lai et al. fabricated the electric eel skin-inspired TENG to power up the wearable electronics devices with the merits of the stretchability and the durability (Figure 8b)(Li, Wu, & Lee, 2016). The working mode of the eel skin-inspired triboelectric nanogenerator is single-electrode. The electrode layer of the device was made up of the silver Ag nanowires because of their stretchability and the fine electrical conductivity. For the enclosed material and stretchable grating layer the silicon rubber (Ecoflex-00-10) was used. Having the structure of the single electrode, when the skin touches the triboelectric layer the transformation of the charges take place. The device has the dimensions (2.5x2.5cm2), under the force of 10N, the open circuit voltage obtained the 70V and the charge density obtained $100\mu C\ m-2$. Hence it is proved from this demonstration that the smartwatch can be powered up through this device/sensor by wearing on the forearm with hand touching. These types of outcomes will boost the advancement in flexible wearable electronics. In this work, the author has also shown that this system empowers biomechanical energy assortment and the wearable electronic watch can also be powered. In the future, according to the author, this development will edge in encouraging advancement in the field of wearable self-powered electronics

MODEL CIRCUIT DIAGRAM FOR HEALTHCARE IOT SENSOR based on TENG

Batteries are the main source to satisfy the power requirement of all these small electronic devices(Armand & Tarascon, 2008). Batteries are time-dependent because they can store the limited amount of the charge for the limited time so the sensors and device may be driven. The second challenge for the batteries is dumping when they complete their lifespan(Osibanjo & Nnorom, 2007). Metallic elements like mercury, lithium, and lead are used in batteries so they are very dangerous to the atmosphere and they create the many health problems for human life(Jung, Park, Yoon, Kim, & Joo, 2003; Larcher & Tarascon, 2015; Zheng, Shi, Li, & Wang, 2017). Miniaturization of the electronic devices is the main reason which is driving down the assembly value of the devices resulting in the increment in the different kinds of small electronic devices(Kyeremateng, Brousse, & Pech, 2017; Meyers & Maynard, 2002). With the passage of time huge figure of electronics devices will increase in sorts of small wearable electronics and the sensors, in this trend of miniaturization of the electronic devices everyone can own these devices and use the variety of those devices(Lara & Labrador, 2013; Stoppa & Chiolerio, 2014). Managing the power of all devices could be challenging and it can be problematic to power the Internet of Things through batteries. So it is necessary to proceed onto the greener self-powered systems and the newer energy harvesting techniques that may solve the power issues of those sensors and electronic devices

Figure 8. Wearable triboelectric nanogenerator demonstrated as the power sources a) black carbon and silicon rubber TENG based on contact-separation mode.(Yi et al., 2016) Copyright 2016, American Chemical Society b,c) silicon silca gel and silver Ag nanowires TENG based on single electrode mode. b)(Lai et al., 2016) Copyright 2016, Wiley-VCH. c).(Guo et al., 2016) Copyright 2016, American Chemical Society

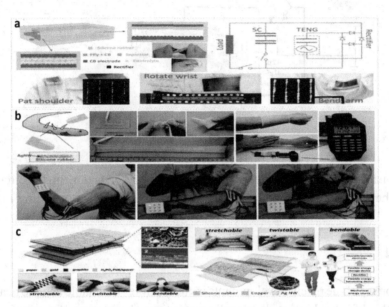

empowered through the Internet of Things (IoT)(Ku, Li, Chen, & Liu, 2015; Tan, 2013; Zheng et al., 2017). The author proposed a model for the healthcare IoT sensors, shown in Figure 9. The triboelectric nanogenerator TENG generates AC voltages with low frequency, so to convert these AC voltages into DC, a rectifier is used with TENG to drive the electronic devices. The DC voltages are stored in the storage device i-e capacitor which is directly connected to the data acquisition system (DAQ) in order to supply the required power to the sensor. The wearable sensor sends data to the smartphone, which communicate to the network.

FUTURE RESEARCH DIRECTIONS

Before presenting a potential product/technology in a sophisticated form, it passes through the different steps of evolution and iterations in order to impact human lives. Improvements in the technology of triboelectric nanogenerator harvesting and the future research directions have been discussed as follows: The development and the improvements in the technology of triboelectrification and self-powered sensors have come a long way. The output voltage and current have enhanced since then in the form magnitude, but the big challenge is the low current from the triboelectric nanogenerator based devices. The high impedance of the triboelectric nanogenerator based device is the main reason behind the low current. For the improvements of the TENG output in the form of current and to reduce the impedance of the device the structure of the device and the materials need to be enhanced. For the efficient utilization of

Figure 9. Circuit Diagram of the TENG with rectifier, storage device data acquisition system, healthcare IoT sensor, smartphone, and the Network

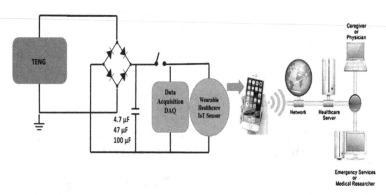

the converted mechanical energy into an electrical energy power management, the circuit can be used to fix the output of the triboelectric nanogenerator to power the low current operating IoT devices.

CONCLUSION

This chapter comprises of the recent developments in the flexible stretchable and the healthcare wearable devices to detect the different biosignals as well as real-time observation of the body activities, which brings the convenient information for managing the health condition of the human being. Diversified access for the detection of the human different kinds of the movements such as respiratory and cardio-vascular condition, motion, tactile sensation, electrophysiological signals in a not interfering aspect, body temperature have been consolidated by the various designs of the micro/nanomaterials. Additionally, the demand for the fast development in flexible wireless sensor, multimodal sensors, self-powered system, and the stretchable conductors. Which empowers the insignificant, miniaturized and imposing integrated system based on constructive healthcare devices. Although the enormous development in the flexible healthcare wearable devices, one cannot use these devices for personal healthcare which is still confronted in the form of comfortable fit, reliability, and sustainability. The wider applications of the wearable triboelectric nanogenerators significantly brunt future of public life from the savvy electronic devices to healthcare surveillance. The technology called the Internet of things (IoT) though is in initial phases, to brunt the human healthcare and correlated the market an extensive scale. Due to the recently developed sensor and high-speed internet access, it is very easy to trial human and so many different objects.

ACKNOWLEDGMENT

This research was supported by the Start-up Research Grant Program (SRGP) of the Higher Education Commission (HEC) of Pakistan [Grant No: Ref. No. (SRGP# 1751)].

REFERENCES

Ali, A., Hwang, E. Y., Choo, J., & Lim, D. W. (2018a). Nanoscale graphene oxide-induced metallic nanoparticle clustering for surface-enhanced Raman scattering-based IgG detection. *Sensors and Actuators. B, Chemical, 255,* 183–192. doi:10.1016/j.snb.2017.07.140

Ali, A., Hwang, E. Y., Choo, J., & Lim, D. W. (2018b). PEGylated nanographene-mediated metallic nanoparticle clusters for surface enhanced Raman scattering-based biosensing. *Analyst (London), 143*(11), 2604–2615. doi:10.1039/C8AN00329G PMID:29741172

Ali, M., Khan, S. A., Rahimoon, A. Q., Hussain, F., Abro, S. A., & Hussain, I. (2019). *Triboelectric Nanogenerator Scavenging Sliding Motion Energy.* Paper presented at the 2019 2nd International Conference on Computing, Mathematics and Engineering Technologies (iCoMET).

Armand, M., & Tarascon, J.-M. (2008). Building better batteries. *Nature, 451*(7179), 652–657. doi:10.1038/451652a PMID:18256660

Bai, P., Zhu, G., Liu, Y., Chen, J., Jing, Q., Yang, W., ... Wang, Z. L. (2013). Cylindrical rotating triboelectric nanogenerator. *ACS Nano, 7*(7), 6361–6366. doi:10.1021/nn402491y PMID:23799926

Choi, M. K., Park, O. K., Choi, C., Qiao, S., Ghaffari, R., Kim, J., ... Kim, S. J. (2016). Cephalopod-Inspired Miniaturized Suction Cups for Smart Medical Skin. *Advanced Healthcare Materials, 5*(1), 80–87. doi:10.1002/adhm.201500285 PMID:25989744

Dunn, B., Kamath, H., & Tarascon, J.-M. (2011). Electrical energy storage for the grid: a battery of choices. *Science, 334*(6058), 928-935.

Fan, F.-R., Lin, L., Zhu, G., Wu, W., Zhang, R., & Wang, Z. L. (2012). Transparent triboelectric nanogenerators and self-powered pressure sensors based on micropatterned plastic films. *Nano Letters, 12*(6), 3109–3114. doi:10.1021/nl300988z PMID:22577731

Gao, T., Zhao, K., Liu, X., & Yang, Y. (2017). Implanting a solid Li-ion battery into a triboelectric nanogenerator for simultaneously scavenging and storing wind energy. *Nano Energy, 41,* 210–216. doi:10.1016/j.nanoen.2017.09.037

Gope, P., & Hwang, T. (2016). BSN-Care: A secure IoT-based modern healthcare system using body sensor network. *IEEE Sensors Journal, 16*(5), 1368–1376. doi:10.1109/JSEN.2015.2502401

Guan, L., Nilghaz, A., Su, B., Jiang, L., Cheng, W., & Shen, W. (2016). Stretchable-Fiber-Confined Wetting Conductive Liquids as Wearable Human Health Monitors. *Advanced Functional Materials, 26*(25), 4511–4517. doi:10.1002/adfm.201600443

Gui, Q., He, Y., Gao, N., Tao, X., & Wang, Y. (2017). A Skin-Inspired Integrated Sensor for Synchronous Monitoring of Multiparameter Signals. *Advanced Functional Materials, 27*(36), 1702050. doi:10.1002/adfm.201702050

Ha, M., Lim, S., & Ko, H. (2018). Wearable and flexible sensors for user-interactive health-monitoring devices. *Journal of Materials Chemistry. B, Materials for Biology and Medicine, 6*(24), 4043–4064. doi:10.1039/C8TB01063C

Honda, W., Harada, S., Arie, T., Akita, S., & Takei, K. (2014). Wearable, human-interactive, health-monitoring, wireless devices fabricated by macroscale printing techniques. *Advanced Functional Materials*, *24*(22), 3299–3304. doi:10.1002/adfm.201303874

Hong, S., Lee, J., Do, K., Lee, M., Kim, J. H., Lee, S., & Kim, D. H. (2017). Stretchable electrode based on laterally combed carbon nanotubes for wearable energy harvesting and storage devices. *Advanced Functional Materials*, *27*(48), 1704353. doi:10.1002/adfm.201704353

Hou, H., Xu, Q., Pang, Y., Li, L., Wang, J., Zhang, C., & Sun, C. (2017). Efficient Storing Energy Harvested by Triboelectric Nanogenerators Using a Safe and Durable All-Solid-State Sodium-Ion Battery. *Advancement of Science*, *4*(8), 1700072. PMID:28852625

Hussain, I., Khan, S. A., Rahimoon, A. Q., Abro, A., Hussain, F. S., & Ali, M. (2019). *Flexible Triboelectric Nanogenerator Based on Paper, PET and Aluminum.* Paper presented at the 2019 2nd International Conference on Computing, Mathematics and Engineering Technologies (iCoMET).

Hussein, A. K. (2015). Applications of nanotechnology in renewable energies—A comprehensive overview and understanding. *Renewable & Sustainable Energy Reviews*, *42*, 460–476. doi:10.1016/j.rser.2014.10.027

Jiang, Q., Chen, B., Zhang, K., & Yang, Y. (2017). Ag nanoparticle-based triboelectric nanogenerator to scavenge wind energy for a self-charging power unit. *ACS Applied Materials & Interfaces*, *9*(50), 43716–43723. doi:10.1021/acsami.7b14618 PMID:29182240

Jung, H., Park, M., Yoon, Y.-G., Kim, G.-B., & Joo, S.-K. (2003). Amorphous silicon anode for lithium-ion rechargeable batteries. *Journal of Power Sources*, *115*(2), 346–351. doi:10.1016/S0378-7753(02)00707-3

Kang, S.-J., Mintz, G. S., Park, D.-W., Lee, S.-W., Kim, Y.-H., Whan Lee, C., ... Park, S.-J. (2011). Mechanisms of in-stent restenosis after drug-eluting stent implantation: Intravascular ultrasound analysis. *Circulation: Cardiovascular Interventions*, *4*(1), 9–14. doi:10.1161/CIRCINTERVENTIONS.110.940320 PMID:21266707

Khan, S. A., Gao, M., Zhu, Y., Yan, Z., & Lin, Y. (2017). MWCNTs based flexible and stretchable strain sensors. *Journal of Semiconductors*, *38*(5), 053003. doi:10.1088/1674-4926/38/5/053003

Khan, Y., Garg, M., Gui, Q., Schadt, M., Gaikwad, A., Han, D., ... Wilson, W. (2016). Flexible hybrid electronics: Direct interfacing of soft and hard electronics for wearable health monitoring. *Advanced Functional Materials*, *26*(47), 8764–8775. doi:10.1002/adfm.201603763

Kim, J., Banks, A., Xie, Z., Heo, S. Y., Gutruf, P., Lee, J. W., ... Brown, G. (2015). Miniaturized Flexible Electronic Systems With Wireless Power and Near-Field Communication Capabilities. *Advanced Functional Materials*, *25*(30), 4761–4767. doi:10.1002/adfm.201501590

Kim, J., Salvatore, G. A., Araki, H., Chiarelli, A. M., Xie, Z., Banks, A., ... Jang, K.-I. (2016). Battery-free, stretchable optoelectronic systems for wireless optical characterization of the skin. *Science Advances*, *2*(8), e1600418. doi:10.1126ciadv.1600418 PMID:27493994

Kim, M.-K., Kim, M.-S., Lee, S., Kim, C., & Kim, Y.-J. (2014). Wearable thermoelectric generator for harvesting human body heat energy. *Smart Materials and Structures, 23*(10), 105002. doi:10.1088/0964-1726/23/10/105002

Ku, M.-L., Li, W., Chen, Y., & Liu, K. R. (2015). Advances in energy harvesting communications: Past, present, and future challenges. *IEEE Communications Surveys and Tutorials, 18*(2), 1384–1412. doi:10.1109/COMST.2015.2497324

Kyeremateng, N. A., Brousse, T., & Pech, D. (2017). Microsupercapacitors as miniaturized energy-storage components for on-chip electronics. *Nature Nanotechnology, 12*(1), 7–15. doi:10.1038/nnano.2016.196 PMID:27819693

Lara, O. D., & Labrador, M. A. (2013). A survey on human activity recognition using wearable sensors. *IEEE Communications Surveys and Tutorials, 15*(3), 1192–1209. doi:10.1109/SURV.2012.110112.00192

Larcher, D., & Tarascon, J.-M. (2015). Towards greener and more sustainable batteries for electrical energy storage. *Nature Chemistry, 7*(1), 19–29. doi:10.1038/nchem.2085 PMID:25515886

Lee, J.-H., Kim, J., Kim, T. Y., Al Hossain, M. S., Kim, S.-W., & Kim, J. H. (2016). All-in-one energy harvesting and storage devices. *Journal of Materials Chemistry. A, Materials for Energy and Sustainability, 4*(21), 7983–7999. doi:10.1039/C6TA01229A

Li, G., Wu, X., & Lee, D.-W. (2016). A galinstan-based inkjet printing system for highly stretchable electronics with self-healing capability. *Lab on a Chip, 16*(8), 1366–1373. doi:10.1039/C6LC00046K PMID:26987310

Liang, Q., Zhang, Q., Yan, X., Liao, X., Han, L., Yi, F., ... Zhang, Y. (2017). Recyclable and green triboelectric nanogenerator. *Advanced Materials, 29*(5), 1604961. doi:10.1002/adma.201604961 PMID:27885725

Lin, L., Wang, S., Xie, Y., Jing, Q., Niu, S., Hu, Y., & Wang, Z. L. (2013). Segmentally structured disk triboelectric nanogenerator for harvesting rotational mechanical energy. *Nano Letters, 13*(6), 2916–2923. doi:10.1021/nl4013002 PMID:23656350

Lin, M.-C., Gong, M., Lu, B., Wu, Y., Wang, D.-Y., Guan, M., ... Hwang, B.-J. (2015). An ultrafast rechargeable aluminium-ion battery. *Nature, 520*(7547), 324–328. doi:10.1038/nature14340 PMID:25849777

Liu, X., Zhao, K., Wang, Z. L., & Yang, Y. (2017). Unity convoluted design of solid Li-ion battery and triboelectric nanogenerator for self-powered wearable electronics. *Advanced Energy Materials, 7*(22), 1701629. doi:10.1002/aenm.201701629

Liu, Z., Qi, D., Hu, G., Wang, H., Jiang, Y., Chen, G., ... Chen, X. (2018). Surface Strain Redistribution on Structured Microfibers to Enhance Sensitivity of Fiber-Shaped Stretchable Strain Sensors. *Advanced Materials, 30*(5), 1704229. doi:10.1002/adma.201704229 PMID:29226515

Ma, Y., Liu, N., Li, L., Hu, X., Zou, Z., Wang, J., ... Gao, Y. (2017). A highly flexible and sensitive piezoresistive sensor based on MXene with greatly changed interlayer distances. *Nature Communications, 8*(1), 1207. doi:10.103841467-017-01136-9 PMID:29089488

Meyers, J. P., & Maynard, H. L. (2002). Design considerations for miniaturized PEM fuel cells. *Journal of Power Sources, 109*(1), 76–88. doi:10.1016/S0378-7753(02)00066-6

Miotto, R., Wang, F., Wang, S., Jiang, X., & Dudley, J. T. (2017). Deep learning for healthcare: Review, opportunities and challenges. *Briefings in Bioinformatics*, *19*(6), 1236–1246. doi:10.1093/bib/bbx044 PMID:28481991

Niu, S., Wang, S., Lin, L., Liu, Y., Zhou, Y. S., Hu, Y., & Wang, Z. L. (2013). Theoretical study of contact-mode triboelectric nanogenerators as an effective power source. *Energy & Environmental Science*, *6*(12), 3576–3583. doi:10.1039/c3ee42571a

Osibanjo, O., & Nnorom, I. (2007). The challenge of electronic waste (e-waste) management in developing countries. *Waste Management & Research*, *25*(6), 489–501. doi:10.1177/0734242X07082028 PMID:18229743

Ouyang, H., Tian, J., Sun, G., Zou, Y., Liu, Z., Li, H., ... Fan, Y. (2017). Self-Powered Pulse Sensor for Antidiastole of Cardiovascular Disease. *Advanced Materials*, *29*(40), 1703456. doi:10.1002/adma.201703456 PMID:28863247

Panwar, N., Kaushik, S., & Kothari, S. (2011). Role of renewable energy sources in environmental protection: A review. *Renewable & Sustainable Energy Reviews*, *15*(3), 1513–1524. doi:10.1016/j.rser.2010.11.037

Park, D. Y., Joe, D. J., Kim, D. H., Park, H., Han, J. H., Jeong, C. K., ... Lee, K. J. (2017). Self-Powered Real-Time Arterial Pulse Monitoring Using Ultrathin Epidermal Piezoelectric Sensors. *Advanced Materials*, *29*(37), 1702308. doi:10.1002/adma.201702308 PMID:28714239

Pu, X., Guo, H., Tang, Q., Chen, J., Feng, L., Liu, G., ... Wang, Z. L. (2018). Rotation sensing and gesture control of a robot joint via triboelectric quantization sensor. *Nano Energy*, *54*, 453–460. doi:10.1016/j.nanoen.2018.10.044

Pu, X., Li, L., Song, H., Du, C., Zhao, Z., Jiang, C., ... Wang, Z. L. (2015). A self-charging power unit by integration of a textile triboelectric nanogenerator and a flexible lithium-ion battery for wearable electronics. *Advanced Materials*, *27*(15), 2472–2478. doi:10.1002/adma.201500311 PMID:25736078

Raghunathan, V., Schurgers, C., Park, S., & Srivastava, M. B. (2002). Energy-aware wireless microsensor networks. *IEEE Signal Processing Magazine*, *19*(2), 40–50. doi:10.1109/79.985679

Rogers, J. A., Someya, T., & Huang, Y. (2010). Materials and mechanics for stretchable electronics. *Science, 327*(5973), 1603-1607.

Saravanakumar, B., Thiyagarajan, K., Alluri, N. R., SoYoon, S., Taehyun, K., Lin, Z.-H., & Kim, S.-J. (2015). Fabrication of an eco-friendly composite nanogenerator for self-powered photosensor applications. *Carbon*, *84*, 56–65. doi:10.1016/j.carbon.2014.11.041

Shamsuddin, S. A. K., Khan, S. A., Ali, A., Rahimoon, A. Q., & Jalalzai, P. (2019). Harvesting Energy of Body Motion Through Single Electrode Based Self-Powered Triboelectric Nanogenerator. *Journal Nanoelectronics and Optoelectronics*, *14*(11), 1–9. doi:10.1166/jno.2019.2580

Sheridan, P. L., Solomont, J., Kowall, N., & Hausdorff, J. M. (2003). Influence of executive function on locomotor function: Divided attention increases gait variability in Alzheimer's disease. *Journal of the American Geriatrics Society*, *51*(11), 1633–1637. doi:10.1046/j.1532-5415.2003.51516.x PMID:14687395

Shi, Q., Wang, H., Wang, T., & Lee, C. (2016). Self-powered liquid triboelectric microfluidic sensor for pressure sensing and finger motion monitoring applications. *Nano Energy*, *30*, 450–459. doi:10.1016/j.nanoen.2016.10.046

Sodhro, A. H., Li, Y., & Shah, M. A. (2016). Energy-efficient adaptive transmission power control for wireless body area networks. *IET Communications*, *10*(1), 81–90. doi:10.1049/iet-com.2015.0368

Sodhro, A. H., Pirbhulal, S., Luo, Z., & de Albuquerque, V. H. C. (2019). Towards an optimal resource management for IoT based Green and sustainable smart cities. *Journal of Cleaner Production*, *220*, 1167–1179. doi:10.1016/j.jclepro.2019.01.188

Son, S.-B., Gao, T., Harvey, S. P., Steirer, K. X., Stokes, A., Norman, A., ... Ban, C. (2018). An artificial interphase enables reversible magnesium chemistry in carbonate electrolytes. *Nature Chemistry*, *10*(5), 532–539. doi:10.103841557-018-0019-6 PMID:29610460

Stoppa, M., & Chiolerio, A. (2014). Wearable electronics and smart textiles: a critical review. *Sensors, 14*(7), 11957-11992.

Talari, S., Shafie-Khah, M., Siano, P., Loia, V., Tommasetti, A., & Catalão, J. (2017). A review of smart cities based on the internet of things concept. *Energies*, *10*(4), 421. doi:10.3390/en10040421

Tan, Y. K. (2013). *Energy harvesting autonomous sensor systems: design, analysis, and practical implementation*. CRC Press.

Tang, W., Meng, B., & Zhang, H. (2013). Investigation of power generation based on stacked triboelectric nanogenerator. *Nano Energy*, *2*(6), 1164–1171. doi:10.1016/j.nanoen.2013.04.009

Tang, Y., Zhang, Y., Li, W., Ma, B., & Chen, X. (2015). Rational material design for ultrafast rechargeable lithium-ion batteries. *Chemical Society Reviews*, *44*(17), 5926–5940. doi:10.1039/C4CS00442F PMID:25857819

Wang, J., Li, X., Zi, Y., Wang, S., Li, Z., Zheng, L., ... Wang, Z. L. (2015). A Flexible Fiber-Based Supercapacitor–Triboelectric-Nanogenerator Power System for Wearable Electronics. *Advanced Materials*, *27*(33), 4830–4836. doi:10.1002/adma.201501934 PMID:26175123

Wang, M., Jiang, C., Zhang, S., Song, X., Tang, Y., & Cheng, H.-M. (2018). Reversible calcium alloying enables a practical room-temperature rechargeable calcium-ion battery with a high discharge voltage. *Nature Chemistry*, *10*(6), 667–672. doi:10.103841557-018-0045-4 PMID:29686378

Wang, Q., Hempstead, M., & Yang, W. (2006). *A realistic power consumption model for wireless sensor network devices*. Paper presented at the 2006 3rd annual IEEE communications society on sensor and ad hoc communications and networks. 10.1109/SAHCN.2006.288433

Wang, S., Lin, L., & Wang, Z. L. (2012). Nanoscale triboelectric-effect-enabled energy conversion for sustainably powering portable electronics. *Nano Letters*, *12*(12), 6339–6346. doi:10.1021/nl303573d PMID:23130843

Wang, S., Lin, L., & Wang, Z. L. (2015). Triboelectric nanogenerators as self-powered active sensors. *Nano Energy*, *11*, 436–462. doi:10.1016/j.nanoen.2014.10.034

Wang, S., Lin, Z.-H., Niu, S., Lin, L., Xie, Y., Pradel, K. C., & Wang, Z. L. (2013). Motion charged battery as sustainable flexible-power-unit. *ACS Nano, 7*(12), 11263–11271. doi:10.1021/nn4050408 PMID:24266595

Wang, S., Niu, S., Yang, J., Lin, L., & Wang, Z. L. (2014). Quantitative measurements of vibration amplitude using a contact-mode freestanding triboelectric nanogenerator. *ACS Nano, 8*(12), 12004–12013. doi:10.1021/nn5054365 PMID:25386799

Wang, S., Xie, Y., Niu, S., Lin, L., & Wang, Z. L. (2014). Freestanding triboelectric-layer-based nanogenerators for harvesting energy from a moving object or human motion in contact and non-contact modes. *Advanced Materials, 26*(18), 2818–2824. doi:10.1002/adma.201305303 PMID:24449058

Wang, Z. L. (2013). Triboelectric nanogenerators as new energy technology for self-powered systems and as active mechanical and chemical sensors. *ACS Nano, 7*(11), 9533–9557. doi:10.1021/nn404614z PMID:24079963

Wang, Z. L., Jiang, T., & Xu, L. (2017). Toward the blue energy dream by triboelectric nanogenerator networks. *Nano Energy, 39*, 9–23. doi:10.1016/j.nanoen.2017.06.035

Wang, Z. L., Zhu, G., Yang, Y., Wang, S., & Pan, C. (2012). Progress in nanogenerators for portable electronics. *Materials Today, 15*(12), 532–543. doi:10.1016/S1369-7021(13)70011-7

Wen, Z., Yeh, M.-H., Guo, H., Wang, J., Zi, Y., Xu, W., ... Hu, C. (2016). Self-powered textile for wearable electronics by hybridizing fiber-shaped nanogenerators, solar cells, and supercapacitors. *Science Advances, 2*(10), e1600097. doi:10.1126ciadv.1600097 PMID:27819039

Xie, Y., Wang, S., Niu, S., Lin, L., Jing, Q., Yang, J., ... Wang, Z. L. (2014). Grating-structured free-standing triboelectric-layer nanogenerator for harvesting mechanical energy at 85% total conversion efficiency. *Advanced Materials, 26*(38), 6599–6607. doi:10.1002/adma.201402428 PMID:25156128

Yang, J., Chen, J., Su, Y., Jing, Q., Li, Z., Yi, F., ... Wang, Z. L. (2015). Eardrum-inspired active sensors for self-powered cardiovascular system characterization and throat-attached anti-interference voice recognition. *Advanced Materials, 27*(8), 1316–1326. doi:10.1002/adma.201404794 PMID:25640534

Yang, Y., Zhang, H., Chen, J., Jing, Q., Zhou, Y. S., Wen, X., & Wang, Z. L. (2013). Single-electrode-based sliding triboelectric nanogenerator for self-powered displacement vector sensor system. *ACS Nano, 7*(8), 7342–7351. doi:10.1021/nn403021m PMID:23883397

Yang, Y., Zhou, Y. S., Zhang, H., Liu, Y., Lee, S., & Wang, Z. L. (2013). A single-electrode based triboelectric nanogenerator as self-powered tracking system. *Advanced Materials, 25*(45), 6594–6601. doi:10.1002/adma.201302453 PMID:24166972

Yi, F., Lin, L., Niu, S., Yang, P. K., Wang, Z., Chen, J., ... Liao, Q. (2015). Stretchable-rubber-based triboelectric nanogenerator and its application as self-powered body motion sensors. *Advanced Functional Materials, 25*(24), 3688–3696. doi:10.1002/adfm.201500428

Yi, F., Wang, J., Wang, X., Niu, S., Li, S., Liao, Q., ... Wang, Z. L. (2016). Stretchable and waterproof self-charging power system for harvesting energy from diverse deformation and powering wearable electronics. *ACS Nano, 10*(7), 6519–6525. doi:10.1021/acsnano.6b03007 PMID:27351212

Yue, Y., Yang, Z., Liu, N., Liu, W., Zhang, H., Ma, Y., ... Long, F. (2016). A flexible integrated system containing a microsupercapacitor, a photodetector, and a wireless charging coil. *ACS Nano*, *10*(12), 11249–11257. doi:10.1021/acsnano.6b06326 PMID:28024378

Zhang, K., Wang, S., & Yang, Y. (2017). A One-Structure-Based Piezo-Tribo-Pyro-Photoelectric Effects Coupled Nanogenerator for Simultaneously Scavenging Mechanical, Thermal, and Solar Energies. *Advanced Energy Materials*, *7*(6), 1601852. doi:10.1002/aenm.201601852

Zhang, X., Du, X., Yin, Y., Li, N.-W., Fan, W., Cao, R., ... Li, C. (2018). Lithium-Ion Batteries: Charged by Triboelectric Nanogenerators with Pulsed Output Based on the Enhanced Cycling Stability. *ACS Applied Materials & Interfaces*, *10*(10), 8676–8684. doi:10.1021/acsami.7b18736 PMID:29446611

Zhang, X.-S., Han, M., Kim, B., Bao, J.-F., Brugger, J., & Zhang, H. (2018). All-in-one self-powered flexible microsystems based on triboelectric nanogenerators. *Nano Energy*, *47*, 410–426. doi:10.1016/j.nanoen.2018.02.046

Zhao, J., Han, S., Yang, Y., Fu, R., Ming, Y., Lu, C., ... Chen, W. (2017). Passive and Space-Discriminative Ionic Sensors Based on Durable Nanocomposite Electrodes toward Sign Language Recognition. *ACS Nano*, *11*(9), 8590–8599. doi:10.1021/acsnano.7b02767 PMID:28759198

Zhao, K., Yang, Y., Liu, X., & Wang, Z. L. (2017). Triboelectrification-Enabled Self-Charging Lithium-Ion Batteries. *Advanced Energy Materials*, *7*(21), 1700103. doi:10.1002/aenm.201700103

Zheng, Q., Shi, B., Li, Z., & Wang, Z. L. (2017). Recent progress on piezoelectric and triboelectric energy harvesters in biomedical systems. *Advancement of Science*, *4*(7), 1700029. PMID:28725529

Zhong, J., Zhong, Q., Fan, F., Zhang, Y., Wang, S., Hu, B., ... Zhou, J. (2013). Finger typing driven triboelectric nanogenerator and its use for instantaneously lighting up LEDs. *Nano Energy*, *2*(4), 491–497. doi:10.1016/j.nanoen.2012.11.015

Zhou, Y. S., Liu, Y., Zhu, G., Lin, Z.-H., Pan, C., Jing, Q., & Wang, Z. L. (2013). In situ quantitative study of nanoscale triboelectrification and patterning. *Nano Letters*, *13*(6), 2771–2776. doi:10.1021/nl401006x PMID:23627668

Zhu, G., Chen, J., Liu, Y., Bai, P., Zhou, Y. S., Jing, Q., ... Wang, Z. L. (2013). Linear-grating triboelectric generator based on sliding electrification. *Nano Letters*, *13*(5), 2282–2289. doi:10.1021/nl4008985 PMID:23577639

Zhu, G., Chen, J., Zhang, T., Jing, Q., & Wang, Z. L. (2014). Radial-arrayed rotary electrification for high performance triboelectric generator. *Nature Communications*, *5*(1), 3426. doi:10.1038/ncomms4426 PMID:24594501

Zhu, G., Pan, C., Guo, W., Chen, C.-Y., Zhou, Y., Yu, R., & Wang, Z. L. (2012). Triboelectric-generator-driven pulse electrodeposition for micropatterning. *Nano Letters*, *12*(9), 4960–4965. doi:10.1021/nl302560k PMID:22889363

Zi, Y., Niu, S., Wang, J., Wen, Z., Tang, W., & Wang, Z. L. (2015). Standards and figure-of-merits for quantifying the performance of triboelectric nanogenerators. *Nature Communications*, *6*(1), 8376. doi:10.1038/ncomms9376 PMID:26406279

Chapter 3
Hybrid Multi–Cloud Demystifying SLAs for Smart City Enterprises Using IoT Applications

Lubna Luxmi Dhirani
University of Limerick, Ireland

Thomas Newe
ⓘ https://orcid.org/0000-0002-3375-8200
University of Limerick, Ireland

Shahzad Nizamani
Mehran University of Engineering and Technology, Pakistan

ABSTRACT

Cloud computing migrations are increasing rapidly. The main influencing factor being IT management costs. IoT-based enterprises that started their cloud journey by setting up small private clouds within their enterprise have often found that as the applications and services they use broaden. Then the shift towards incorporating public clouds becomes inevitable. The current problem that many of these firms are encountering is the difficulty of managing multiple clouds that reside within different vendors running on different platforms, computational requirements, and vendor SLAs. Lack of support for a single standard for an overall multi-cloud hybrid model exposes the hybrid IT-management to further threats. This makes it difficult for an adopting enterprise to manage and maintain its cloud-based systems during peak performance hours, which often leads to system downtime. This chapter discusses various SLA issues specific to a hybrid multi-cloud environment and suggests possible solutions to help adopting firms in their management.

DOI: 10.4018/978-1-7998-1253-1.ch003

HYBRID CLOUD COMPUTING

Hybrid cloud computing is a widely accepted and implemented cloud model in both business and education sectors. Generally, enterprises use the hybrid model when they do not wish to completely outsource their entire IT infrastructure or processing to a remote location as this can increases the level of risk associated with data privacy, governance and control. Hybrid cloud offers various benefits to the Internet of Things (IoT) industry by overcoming the real-time data processing, storage, capacity, availability and storage. It is estimated that the number of IoT connected devices would increase to 50.1 billion by 2020, which may not allow the existing IT based architecture to function to its full capacity (Dhirani, Newe, & Nizamani, 2018a). IoT based tenants resisting cloud migrations may limit their applications reachability, availability and usability.

Cloud Classification

Cloud Computing can be categorized based on the architecture of models (Public cloud, Private cloud, Hybrid Cloud and Community Cloud), services (Infrastructure as a Service, Platform as a Service, Software as a Service, etc.) and applications provided by the cloud vendor on the cloud management portfolio. These models can also be categorized further such as: Lone Hybrid Cloud and Multi-Cloud Hybrid model.

Lone Hybrid Cloud

This model demonstrates a company outsourcing a part of its application and data processing with a single vendor at peak processing times. The relationship between the user and vendors can be formed in the following possible ways:

- 1:1 (single tenant: single vendor)
- M:1 (multiple tenants: single vendor)
- M:1:M (multiple tenants: single vendor: multiple third-party subcontractors)

Multi-Cloud Hybrid Model

This model suits companies who develop multiple small private clouds and enter the hybrid environment with multiple vendors based on the vendors expertise and services. The relationship between the user and vendors can be formed in the following possible ways:

- 1:M:M (single tenant: multiple private clouds: multiple public cloud vendors)
- M:M:M (multiple tenants, multiple private clouds: multiple public cloud vendors)
- M:M:M:M (multiple tenants, multiple private clouds: multiple public cloud vendors: multiple third-party subcontractors)

CLOUD SLA ISSUES

Some of the Hybrid Cloud IaaS model extended combinations are already in practice by giant cloud vendors such as Amazon Web Service and IBM. However, cloud tenants should note that as the model usage increases, the level of complexity, visibility, control and proximity of risk increases as well. Various issues associated to Hybrid, Federated and multi-cloud SLAs (i.e. unplanned downtime, outage, loss of data, Denial of Service (DoS), privacy breach, etc.) have been discussed by (Dhirani, Newe & Nizamani, 2018b). This chapter precisely focuses on the SLA Operations Management (OM) and areas which play a vital role in cloud SLA QoS such as: cloud federation SLAs, Hybrid SLA Management, commercial IT operational management tools, SLA standardization and vendor SLAs, viable solutions followed by the last Section which concludes the chapter.

FINTECH (USE-CASE EXAMPLE)

Hybrid cloud issues are majorly identified post-implementation. The authors introduce a use-case example (FinTech) to explain the complexity of the heterogeneous cloud model throughout this chapter. FinTech is a banking firm using IoT-based applications (i.e. Telematics, Machine to Machine solutions and beacons) to increase its core competence and hybrid cloud to support its IT Infrastructure and data processing. FinTech (F1, F2 and F3) operates in three countries (i.e. C1, C2 and C3) with each region having its data processed within its own geographic boundaries. The firm used the same IoT-based applications in all regions but its recent merger (F1-C1) with another bank (B1) has created IT-Operational issues and complexity, since both banks (F1-C1 and B1) used different applications and cloud platforms. Fintech is susceptible to SLA Operational Management, SLA Standardization and multi-cloud issues.

MOTIVATION

Lack of standardization and uniformity in Cloud Computing environment leads cloud tenants to vendor lock-in, privacy and security breaches. The commercial solutions (Microsoft OMS, IBM Tivoli, etc.) designed to mitigate these risks also come with number of limitations. The distinct XML-dialects (RB-SLA, PBSLA, GXLA, etc.) and schemas were designed to overcome this limitation however, they have not been implemented by public cloud vendors due to the dynamic and scalable nature of the cloud.

HYBRID SLA MANAGEMENT

The SLA Management (SLAM) system is accountable for obtaining SLA information from the SLA monitoring model, to attain cloud service availability guarantees during and after the cloud service has been repositioned (Keller & Ludwig, 2002). FinTech requires an SLA Management tool to monitor and administrator its cloud quality of service attributes (i.e. availability, usage, scalability, etc.), auditing, verifying, authenticating and keeping a track of its applications and services. Since each application running on a hybrid cloud environment may have a distinct set of SLAs, it is important to have a systematic way to enable insights and visibility via a SLAM (Dhirani et al., 2018b).

CLOUD FEDERATION SLAS

Cloud vendors based in different geographical locations form a federation based on provided better services to cloud tenants. Federation needs to be systematic, as it may involve QoS based metric such as: down-time, cost, billing method, scalability, computing needs, duration, credit claims, etc. Cloud vendors in the federation must be capable of provisioning tenant's demand without failure (Dhirani et al., 2018b). Hence a generic cloud federation SLA model contains a Service Model, Contract Repository, SLA Manager and contract verification interfaces connecting the federated domains in diverse regions (Dhirani et al., 2018b). The key role of this model is to maintain the service specifics, inter-dependencies, measures, verification, validation and details (Bhoj, Singhal, & Chutani, 2001).

As mentioned before, different clouds may have different standards and QoS based parameters to assess the services, in such a situation it is compulsory for hybrid multi-clouds to deploy an SLA management tool since each running application and service may be subject to a separate set of SLAs. Figure 1. represents the complexity of federated hybrid multi-cloud model in which applications and services are running on different vendor clouds based in geographic locations comprising application sharing and data dependencies with other clouds.

Service level agreements involve SLA management and monitoring systems to conduct audits, usage, failover and control (Keller & Ludwig, 2002). SLA monitoring is always performed by the vendors to keep a track of resource provisioning in a multi-tenancy environment, but it may also be done at the tenant end to monitor the service performance levels, threshold, redundancy and violations. Various tools such as: Melodic, AWS CloudWatch, Google Slackdriver, IBM Trivoli monitoring etc. are commercially provided by vendors for monitoring cloud metrics and performance levels. The core features they are required to provide are: actively identifying and notifying of cloud resource failures and provide recovery patterns. This Chapter focuses on the Cloud SLA Operational Management (OM) IaaS tools.

CLOUD COMPUTING TOOLS FOR OPERATIONAL MANAGEMENT

Enterprises highly depend on IT applications and support for sustainability and growth. Enterprises may use different applications to support their business processes but each one of them deal with huge volumes of data and information which may be processed in private or public datacenters. To securely manage their business, it is crucial that all applications are aligned and support the organizational goals. IT operational management tools assist in reducing the overhead costs and application management issues such as: system configurations, resource provisioning, logs, alerts, capacity planning, node failures, etc. It also provides insights and visibility of the overall IT systems and may assist organizations in building their backup systems and service level management. The complexity arises when computational needs are outsourced partially or fully into public or hybrid cloud environments. Managing outsourced applications and services in cloud are susceptible to risks such as: outages, availability, scalability, processing time, throughput, etc.

As discussed before FinTech is susceptible to IT Operational Management (OM) issues since applications running on F1-C1 and B1 both operate on different platforms with different SLAs which leads to vendor lock-in situations. The application SLAs vary in terms of functionality and QoS attributes. FinTech requires a uniform OMS tool to overcome this limitation. The authors discuss various IT Op-

Figure 1. Complexity of federated hybrid multi-cloud model

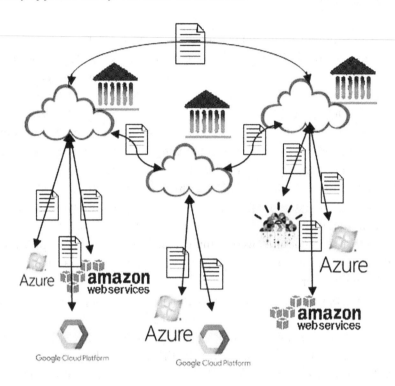

erational Management (IT-OM) and cloud monitoring tools in the sub-section, however the focus lies on Microsoft Hybrid IT Operation Management Suite.

Melodic

Melodic is an open source cross-cloud operational management and security-based tool enabling data-intensive applications to run securely within well-defined QoS parameters on geographic distributed/ federated cloud setups ("MELODIC: Multi-cloud Execution-ware for Large-scale Optimized Data-Intensive Computing," 2017). This OM tool is well-suited for the cross-cloud federated environment and big data applications and claims to counter the vendor lock-in situations in a public cloud environment. Melodic is actively being used by European research projects but the commercial use of the software tool is yet to be announced.

ManageEngine

ManageEngine is an agentless applications manager tool designed to assist SLA monitoring for applications processed in a cloud environment. It assists in managing, monitoring and supporting applications, databases, corporate IT Services, etc. reducing the time to respond to failovers and outages ("ManageEngine Homepage," 2019). It also provides comprehensive performance metrics assisting cloud application performance, monitoring and visibility. This tool is capable of functioning with Amazon Elastic Cloud Compute (EC2) (Erl, Cope, & Naserpour, 2015) and Elastic Block Storage (EBS) volumes attached and continuously checks them for errors ("AWS," 2019). ManageEngine provides visibility and insights enhancing performance and resource utilization of EC2 instances and the applications running on these instances ("ManageEngine Homepage," 2019). Some of the metrics provided by Applications Manager for EC2 instances include: hardware, software and network resource provisioning, metrics of attached EBS volumes ("AWS," 2019) and performance reports. Other benefits may include: gaining insights on tenant's performance and diagnosis on AWS EC2 environment, capacity planning, single platform for monitoring the tenant's cloud ecosystem and monitoring applications simultaneously on the public and private clouds. Limitations associated with ManageEngine include: hard implementations, lack of administration documentation, high cost and some features do not work.

HP Operations Manager

HP offers an IT operational management tool for infrastructure monitoring which proactively performs root cause analysis reducing the time to restore failures and the cost of operations management ("HPE Operations bridge," 2017) this tool detects errors and QoS events using a blend of agent-based and agentless monitoring, and alerts from Hewlett Packard Enterprise (HPE) and third-party managers. Like other OMS, HP Operations Manager (OM) also provides an integrated console, comprehensive ecosystem for improved performance, availability and scalability features. The HPE OM acts as a log manager and gathers QoS metrics using agent-based and agentless monitoring. Agents are installed on explicit nodes to collect information for pre-emptive decisions (i.e. mean-time to respond to failures, capacity planning, monitoring clusters, policies, application configurations) and utilizing HTTPS communication with the HPE OM server.

"Infrastructure Smart Plug-Ins (SPIs) assist agents by collecting data at the infrastructure or managed systems level. The system and cluster SPIs are incorporated with the agent. Voluntary SPIs can also be added to the agent (i.e. Virtual Infrastructure SPI). The system SPI determines operating system and platform resources, prompts warnings on problem-solving measures, monitors system services, processes and resource usage. The cluster SPI detects and characterizes cluster nodes and configured resource groups, monitors cluster-based services and processes, allowing visibility of applications shifting amid cluster servers. The virtualization SPI is assisted by virtualization hypervisors, it finds and analyses virtualization platforms and produces resource consumption detail reports ("HPE Operations bridge," 2017)".

Agentless data collection is performed with monitoring probes. It assists the former method in gathering information and providing elasticity to the HPE OMS. HPE SiteScope assists in monitoring through a lightweight highly customizable web-based architecture for a wide range of IT infrastructure targets. Agentless examinations evaluate both physical and virtual systems. Agentless data assortment is efficient and helps in gathering performance metrics, monitoring proactive tests, customized tools and highlight critical systems which may lead to failures.

Figure 2. depicts HPs operations management architecture. The key benefits of implementing this OMS are: automatic detection and diagnostics of IT problems for faster incident resolution and reduced costs for monitoring and outage resolution ("HPE Operations bridge," 2017).

Ansible

Ansible is an open source tool for IT Configuration Management, Distribution and Orchestration facilitating automation of complex IT applications in a cloud environment. Figure 3 depicts the Ansible architecture and key features. Ansible aims to provide core competence to automation-based tasks in complex environment. It is simple and powerful enough to automate complex multi-tier IT application environments. Hiring technical staff round the clock for managing the computing needs and failovers contributes to major IT based costs in a cloud-free environment. Installing, upgrading, administrating and configuring applications manually is a time consuming and tedious job and this is where Ansible comes handy while provisioning, configuring and scaling the systems. Ansible is agentless, flexible, secure and efficient making it a prime choice for cloud tenant's implementation ("Why Ansible?," 2019).

IBM IT Operations Management

IBM IT Operations Management (ITOM) ("IT Operations Management," 2017) is an OMS used for hybrid cloud environments enhancing visibility and IT infrastructure efficiency. Alike other OMS discussed before IBM ITOM also comprises of features to automate, orchestrate and reduces the mean-time of recovering from a failure. However, details regarding the tool being agentless has not been provided. IBM ATOM and Microsoft's Hybrid OMS share similarities in terms of insights, visibility, tracking and control features. Like Microsoft Hybrid, IBM ITOM also provides real-time analysis via IBM Netcool Operations Insights, the Runbook Automation feature creates and executes runbooks for faster, more repeatable and consistent problem resolution, alert notifications and operations analytics which process huge volume of operational data into understandable insights reducing the time to respond to problems and enhancing services. ITOM provides visibility, monitoring, automation and control-based features making it easier for managing hybrid clouds. Considering a multi-cloud hybrid environment, implementing the tool on a single layer for operations management and control may not be possible as the capacity of IBM ITOM has not been used in such a complex environment yet. IBM also offers a sister tool called IBM Tivoli which particularly focuses on reinforcing policies in terms of authentication, authorization,

Figure 2. HPE Operations Manager ("HPE Operations bridge," 2017)

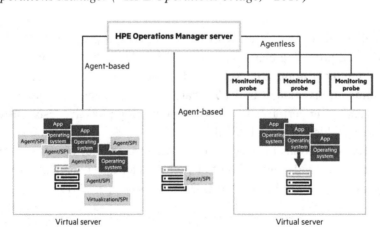

Figure 3. Ansible OMS Architecture ("Why Ansible?", 2019)

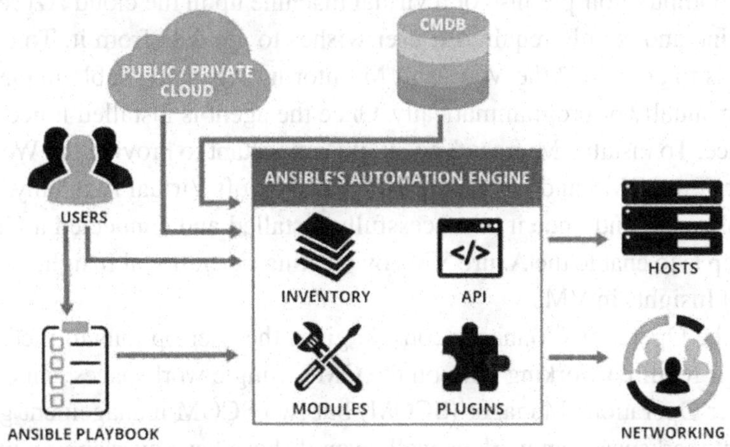

identity and access management in a distributed environment (Kajor, 2003) but lacks features in terms of complete IT operational management.

Microsoft Hybrid IT Management

Microsoft offers an Operations Management Suite (OMS) to gain visibility, infrastructure control and efficiently manage the hybrid clouds ("Microsoft Virtual Academy", 2016). The OMS provide support for heterogeneous environments can be utilized on premises or on the Azure public cloud. The strategic goal of the OMS is to create a unified management support across different platforms in terms of infrastructure and services, which has not been achieved yet. The OMS support agile development and Management-as-a-Service (MaaS), which are prepackages services developed within the cloud but can manage the tenant's on-premise cloud as well. Figure 4 depicts Microsoft OMS graphical user interface. Microsoft offers the combination of System Center and Operations management Suite as a complete package of hybrid cloud IT Management for having near real-time visibility, IT automation, cloud-enabled protection and robust threat analysis (RBA). RBA covers the security aspects of auditing the system, ensuring the total health checkups and breach analysis. The role of comprehensive security and threat analysis is to protect the tenant's servers and workloads. The machines are processing massive data every hour. To control and monitor the logs and to make sense out of it the cloud requires a system to manage the operations. On the other hand, the visibility enhances the security of the overall IaaS environment. The OMS make it easier to control the overall environment ("Microsoft Virtual Academy," 2016).

The OMS dashboard gives live details on the user cloud status as shown in Figure 4. Each tile is capable of pinning down the details in terms of data used in the last few days/weeks/months and the actual number of servers utilized, attacks from malicious IPs, level of threat and Country origin of the attacks, log management, system alerts for upgrades, wire data, capacity planning, the percentage of service level agreement with an average batch processing time, etc. Massive improvement and visibility can be achieved using the OMS, but there is no evidence to support OMS performance in a multi-cloud environment.

OMS is an agent-based deployment which requires a physical computer to install the agent on, or it can be on a physical computer on-premise or a virtual machine up in the cloud Azure. The agent works to monitor the machine and is only required if user wishes to get data from it. To connect the servers directly the user needs to download the Microsoft Monitoring Agent available in OMS settings within the portal. Install it manually or programmatically. Once the agent is installed it needs to be connected to the OMS workspace. To install a Microsoft agent, it is important to provide the Workspace ID, which is created at the start of the OMS and workspace Key ("Microsoft Virtual Academy," 2016). The agent resides in the control panel, and once it is successfully installed and connected a Green tick is shown inside it. The next step is to enable the Azure VMs by creating Operational Insights workspace and then enabling Operational Insights in VMs.

Integrating with the Operations Manager console gives the user options to pick as many numbers of machines or groups required working with on the OMS. Single workspaces can only be used with a single Systems Center Operations Manager (SCOM) but two SCOM management groups created and redirected to different workspace can work as well, even if those have overlapping machines. The only point to note is that the user is being charged for every single workspace that the machine send data to.

Implementing Microsoft OMS can help the multiple clouds in FinTech to uniformly share data with different workspaces. Microsoft may access users log data, analyze it and provide OMS recommended settings based on it. Knowledge Base (KB) reports are provided within the OMS for configuration and recommendations. The Security Analytics helps to mine large sets of security data, detect suspicious activity, perform forensic analysis and analyze unique patterns of attack as shown in Figure 4.

Figure 4. Microsoft Operations Management Suite ("Microsoft Virtual Academy", 2016)

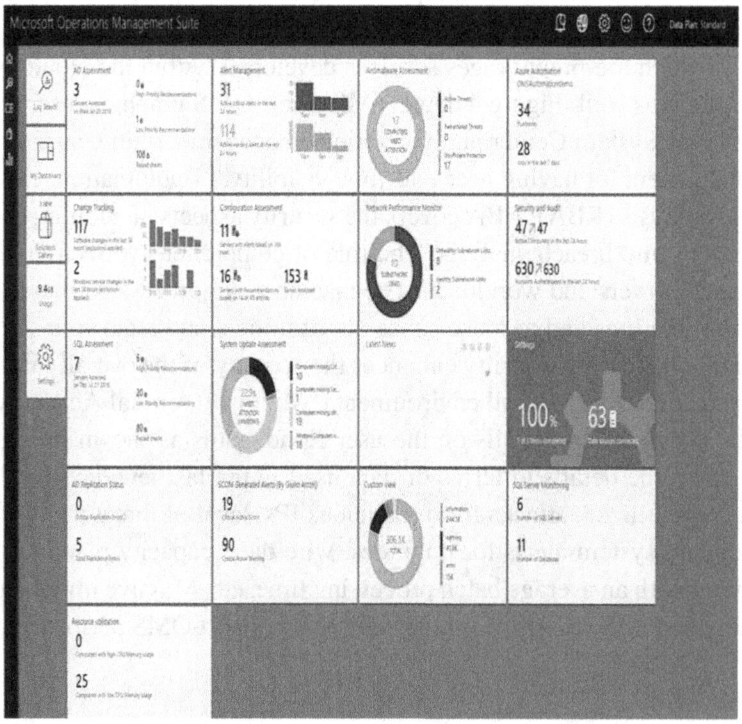

Table 1. below depicts a comparison between Microsoft OMS and Local Hybrid IT Management which may help cloud tenants in making wise decisions for deploying the right tool.

SLA STANDARDIZATION

Migrating a tenant cloud from one platform to another consists of both technical (i.e. platform dependencies, migration, application support, services, etc.) and legal challenges (Dhirani et al., 2018b), which Fintech is already facing. Deploying an OMS may not assist on the federated cloud/multi-cloud ecosystem service level aspects, as the OMS user interface provides support for hybrid cloud tenant's only. So, the principal issue of evaluating and assessing different SLAs remains unsolved. Dissimilarities among different vendors SLAs have been discussed in (Dhirani et al., 2018b). Every single cloud request being run within the homogenous cloud environment by vendors (i.e. AWS, Microsoft Azure) has an explicit SLA ("AWS," 2019) ("Microsoft Virtual Academy," 2016). In these cases, it is impossible to track/manage a multi-cloud offered by different vendors in a unified manner and in such situations, a tool is required which is compatible and platform independent to understand different SLAs and platforms and manages it in a systematic way.

Challenge of Working With Different Vendors With Exactly Same SLAs

Each vendor follows different QoS attributes (i.e. uptime/downtime, availability, credit returns, service provisioning, compute, scheduled upgrades, etc.) (Dhirani et al., 2018b). These attributes contribute towards operational management complexity when different vendor services are deployed for the same enterprises Operational Management. The cross-functional IT and business processes lead to technical complexity, data duplication, redundancy and operational management issues.

POSSIBLE SOLUTIONS

In House Tool for ITOM

The first possible solution is that the enterprise/Fintech itself develops a tool for managing its IT operations with different vendors but will end up in very high costs as customizing the tools in context of multiple vendors will be totally impractical.

Standard SLA Template Incorporated

Any operational management (OM) tool will fail in a multi-cloud hybrid environment to fulfill the business need until and unless a standard framework is incorporated within the software suite.

1. It should be compatible with both former and new IT based systems and must be capable of analyzing and managing different SLAs based on the performance metrics (i.e. monthly uptime percentage, services provided, claims, service credits, unavailability, scalability, etc.).

Table 1. Comparison OMS Versus Local Hybrid IT Management

	OMS ("Microsoft Virtual Academy", 2016)	Local Hybrid IT Management
Minify	Summarize thousands of results into very concise list	Such a task will take longer processing times.
Equipment	Azure Subscription	Rack servers, high end network connectivity within the infrastructure, backups, in-house and third-party software's, anti-malware, anti-virus, threat analysis tools.
Estimate Cost Billing and SLA Compliance	Based on usage, estimation can be generated. It indicates information on the volume of batches sent to the cloud for processing in time which may depend on the types of solutions.	Prices may vary as all three multi-cloud are outsourced and each of the vendors have different pricing schemes.
Pricing	The pricing depends on amount of data transferred via the OMS each day and duration of retaining it. The pricing scheme also depends on the type of package subscribed (i.e. Stand-Alone, OMS subscription, OMS Add-on, etc.) ("Microsoft Virtual Academy", 2016). The services within OMS are billed separately.	Hard to estimate, cost will vary as per usage and may increase in case of system failure or sudden high processing hours.
Resources	KB reports for configuration and recommendations	Need to contact vendors if problem is not resolved
Specifications	Server 2008 SP1 and 32-bit agent. Support for clients and point of sale	Server specifications may vary
Usage	No. of servers utilized, and amount of data transferred to the cloud for processing logs. the usage/solution mentions the usage utilized/solution.	Independent servers will need to be checked for performance and updates.
Log Search	Search over the logs and make sense out of those logs	
Alert Management	Everything is backed up by search	Syslog Server used to generate admin alerts
Change Tracking	Searching changes, takes the tenant back to the database where changes within the last 7 days, every change is being saved at the vendor side as well	Filtering tool required to filter out the high priority messages from huge amount of log data to track the changes.
Malicious IP detection	Detects and highlights malicious IPs and grades the intensity of the threat on a scale of 0-5 (min-max) based on the frequency and types of attacks made on which machines.	Anti-malware software required
Search API	Searchable Application Programming Interface (API) through console and programmatically	API limited to the applications developed in past or currently working on
Wire Data	Wire data depicts network data, information about network loads.	Network traffic monitoring tool
Anti-malware assessment	Malicious activities found are immediately reported to the tenant via the OMS. The system's database is automatically upgraded to the latest threats.	Need to keep the tool updated for the latest threats and keep a close eye on the core machines.
Near real-time performance logs	These counters are a type of metrics which keep track of the system in real-time. The default near real time is 10s, so every 10s the OMS sends data to Microsoft. There are several types of logs (i.e. event logs, performance logs, etc.).	Syslog messages lack authentication, creating possibilities for one machine to impersonate other machines and send bogus log events. It is also susceptible to replay attacks. Log messages can also be lost due to network congestion (Leskiw, 2017)
Syslog	Collect Sys log ingestion on Azure Linux VMs and using diagnostics to collect Sys logs from that.	Syslog Servers
Cost	Log Analytics, back up, Site recovery to customer owned sites and Azure, process automation, desired state configuration, system center (i.e. configuration manager, OM, orchestration, data protection manager, virtual machine manager, service manager, etc.)	Syslog Servers, backup Servers and databases. Monitoring, filtering and management tools. Process automation tools to be bought explicitly. Anti-malware, Anti-virus, Network traffic monitoring tools, OS IT-Management costs incurred due to manual system heath checks, data center power, cooling costs and processing.

2. The OM software should be capable to work across different platforms, operating systems and applications eliminating the vendor lock-in situation.

3. It should be licensed by the vendor on contract basis, without installing any agent or eavesdropping tool on the user's IT environment for secretly monitoring the systems.

4. Mechanism for Access Governance. The software should be capable of providing system security in terms of visibility, control, insights and eliminating the need of buying third-party software packages. It should also provide information on the cloud/workspaces authorized for which type of applications and maintain logs for it.

5. It should keep all the vendors separate. The user can only view the applications and services provided by different vendors and the SLA details. The vendors must be kept private regarding all different contracts to avoid intrusion and privacy breach.

6. Third-party subcontractors should be obligatory of following the same standards to ensure data security, governance, risk and control.

7. It should generate a standard SLA out of the multiple SLAs formed with multiple vendors/cloud service providers. It will be impossible to manage the hybrid multi-cloud operations efficiently otherwise.

An OMS mentioned with the above qualities will benefit both the vendor and user in terms of multi-cloud operational management, privacy and control. Since majority of the companies are shifting towards this trend, it is practical to incorporate a generic operational tool which eliminates technical and legal problems for both users and vendors in the longer run.

Policy Based SLA Management (PBSLM)

Many on-going cloud projects are aiming to reinforce systematic approaches and existing Web-Service policies (WS-Policy, Policy RuleML,WSML, etc.) for building an effective and standardized SLA deployment model across the cloud industry (Paschke, 2005).

Rule Based SLA Language (RBSLA)

RBSLA is a declarative, high-level Rule Based SLA language (RBSLA) extending RuleML to address interoperability with other rule languages (i.e. Semantic Web Rule Language (SWRL), Metalog, International Organization for Standardization (ISO) Common Logic, International Organization for Standardization (ISO) Prolog, etc.) (Paschke, 2005).

Rule Based SLA Management (RBSLM)

The RBSLM tool is divided into two sections such as: Contact Manager (CM) and Service Dashboard (SD). The CM is responsible for managing the language rules whereas the SD deals with projecting the monitoring and implementation process.

Automated Rule-Based SLA/Chaining SLA

Each QoS parameter is related to multiple sub-parameters, and if one parameter is triggered, the other may respond based on the core parameter. For example: Service Quality Metrics may depend on: availability, reliability, performance, scalability and resilience. The Service Availability Metrics may rely on the availability rate and outage metrics, in the same way the rest of the 4 metrics rely of multiple sub-metrics and all these metrics need to be linked with each other, processed automatically and bound by rules for performance assurances.

SLA Related Language Approaches

WS Description Language (WSDL) (Dan, et al., 2004) and WS Level Agreement (WSLA) (Verlaine, et al., 2010) and Ontology Web Language for Services (OWL-S) (Le, Nguyen, & Goh, 2009).

Dynamic SLA

SLAs need to be dynamic in nature with changing cloud requirements ("Rule-based IT Service Management," 2007), many vendors support this feature although the complexity arises in hybrid multi-cloud environment. A possible way to overcome this may be: if the SLA management system supports a standardized logic or rule-based SLA framework.

Real-Time SLA Management

Real-time or transactional SLA management may only be achieved with the logical and conceptual model which is capable of translating, understanding and managing different dialects of SLAs dynamically without confusing the hybrid clouds.

FUTURE RESEARCH DIRECTIONS

Enterprises adaption for Cloud-IoT based applications has been doubled in the last few years which may further increase with fifth generation (5G) technology. The viable solutions discussed above may assist the enterprises in demystifying the hybrid/multi-cloud SLA issues but limit in terms of SLA QoS assessment. The authors future research is based on evaluating Enterprise tenant's hybrid cloud QoS (i.e. assessing the expected and actual service delivered) which leads to hidden costs, re-work and service breaches.

CONCLUSION

Coming to a uniform standardized model in hybrid cloud computing is highly debatable but as enterprises with small private multi-clouds are heading towards the hybrid cloud. The successful outcome of this will only be possible with a standard uniform solution. The authors designed use-case hybrid multi-cloud model for a bank (Fintech) implementing IoT applications depicts various SLA-based issues leading to the vendor lock-ins and non-conformance. The authors do not suggest for the same SLA percentage uptime, pricing or credit claims, but for implementing a template which is understandable by the in-house cloud and easy to manage, monitor and control services across multiple vendors.

SLA and SLM tools such as: IBM Tivoli, Microsoft OMS etc. permit the QoS parameters ("IT Operations Management," 2017) to be defined with high or low limits ("Microsoft Virtual Academy," 2016). These constraints are programmed at the application or database tier which develops complexity when efforts are made to dynamically extend the SLA logic (Keller & Ludwig, 2002). Such tools are restricted and bound with static rules and limited parameters. Commercial tools also lack in terms of specifications, variables and rule chaining which limits their SLAs from functioning dynamically ("Rule-based IT Service Management," 2007).

Despite of Microsoft's OMS wide range of offerings, the biggest limitation with Azure is its Azure Subscription, as majority of the services (IT Automation, back-up and site recovery, performance logs) are not available for the free tier users. Installing an agent on every single machine the IoT enterprise wishes to retrieve data from for increasing the visibility and control poses a security threat as all the logs are being processed on the cloud, which means the vendor silently knows all the limitations and confidential data of tenants. It will be better if Microsoft designs a software package and releases it as a software package for operations management, rather than creating another vendor lock-in situation for the user. HP Openview and IBMs ITOM also limit in terms of being agent-based and which may lead tenants susceptible to security-based limitations.

As discussed, vendors differ based on billing cycles, uptimes, scheduled upgrades and unavailability zones, SLA Exclusions, notice period for changes in services, etc. These vendors also differ based on API and architecture compatibility [12], as a result both migrations from one public cloud to another or moving to an OMS will not solve the IoT based enterprises existing problem, until and unless the vendors agree to a standardized SLA template. The authors also discuss various viable solutions to overcome commercial tools limitations. A wide number of IoT-based tenants end up in a vendor lock in situation due to lack of knowledge about the hybrid cloud computing tools, their functionalities and scope.

ACKNOWLEDGMENT

This project is funded by Erasmus Mundus LEADERS program and is part supported by Science Foundation Ireland grant 13/RC/2094 and co-funded under the European Regional Development Fund through the Southern & Eastern Regional Operational Programme to Lero – the Irish Software Research Centre (www.lero.ie).

REFERENCES

Ansible. (2019). *Why Ansible?* Retrieved January 10, 2019, from https://www.ansible.com/it-automation

AWS. (2019). *Amazon Compute Service Level Agreement.* Retrieved April 10, 2019, from https://aws.amazon.com/compute/sla/

Bhoj, P., Singhal, S., & Chutani, S. (2001). SLA management in federated environments. *Computer Networks*, *35*(1), 5–24. doi:10.1016/S1389-1286(00)00149-3

Dan, A., Davis, D., Kearney, R., Keller, A., King, R., Kuebler, D., ... Youssef, A. (2004). Web services on demand: WSLA-driven automated management. *IBM Systems Journal*, *43*(1), 136–158. doi:10.1147j.431.0136

Dhirani, L. L., Newe, T., & Nizamani, S. (2018a) Can IoT escape Cloud QoS and Cost Pitfalls. *2018 12th International Conference on Sensing Technology (ICST)*.

Dhirani, L. L., Newe, T., & Nizamani, S. (2018b). Federated Hybrid Clouds: Service Level Agreements and Legal Issues. In *Third International Congress on Information and Communication Technology*. Springer.

ΕΠΙΣΕΥ. (2017). *MELODIC: Multi-cloud Execution-ware for Large-scale Optimized Data-Intensive Computing*. Retrieved August 20, 2018, from https://www.iccs.gr/blog/2017/01/18/melodic-multi-cloud-execution-ware-for-large-scale-optimized-data-intensive-computing/

Erl, T., Cope, R., & Naserpour, A. (2015). *Cloud computing design patterns*. Prentice-Hall.

HPE. (2017). *Operations bridge*. Retrieved December 30, 2017, from https://saas.hpe.com/en-us/software/operations-manager

Karjoth, G. (2003). Access control with IBM Tivoli access manager. *ACM Transactions on Information and System Security*, *6*(2), 232–257. doi:10.1145/762476.762479

Keller, A., & Ludwig, H. (2002). Defining and Monitoring Service Level Agreements for dynamic e-Business. *Proceedings of the 16th System Administration Conference*.

Le, D., Nguyen, V., & Goh, A. (2009). Matching WSDL and OWL-S Web Services. *IEEE International Conference on Semantic Computing*, 197-202.

Leskiw, A. (2017). *Understanding Syslog: Servers, Messages & Security*. Retrieved April 30, 2018, from http://www.networkmanagementsoftware.com/what-is-syslog/

ManageEngine. (2019). *Homepage*. Retrieved January, 2019, from https://www.manageengine.com

Microsoft Virtual Academy. (2016). *Homepage*. Retrieved December 15, 2016, from https://mva.microsoft.com

Operations Management, I. T. (2017). *IT Operations Management*. Retrieved December 30, 2017, from https://www.ibm.com/cloud-computing/products/devops/it-operations-management/

Paschke, A. (2005). RBSLA A declarative Rule-based Service Level Agreement Language based on RuleML. In *proceeding of International Conference on Computational Intelligence for Modelling, Control and Automation and International Conference on Intelligent Agents, Web Technologies and Internet Commerce (CIMCA-IAWTIC '06)* (vol. 2, pp. 308-314). 10.1109/CIMCA.2005.1631486

Randy, B. (2013). *Cloudscaling*. Retrieved July 8, 2018, from http://cloudscaling.com/blog/cloud-computing/missing-the-point-on-private-public-and-hybrid-cloud-apis/

Rhoton, J. (2011). *Cloud Computing Explained* (2nd ed.). Recursive Press.

Rule Based IT Service Management. (2007). *Rule Based IT Service Level Management*. Retrieved May 10, 2018, from http://ruleml.org/reaction/docs/ColloqiumFredericton2007.pdf

Verlaine, B., Dubois, Y., Jureta, I., & Faulkner, S. (2010). Towards automated alignment of Web Services to requirements. *2010 First International Workshop on the Web and Requirements Engineering (WeRE)*, 5-12. 10.1109/WERE.2010.5623996

Chapter 4
Power Saving Schemes for Extending the Lifetime of IoT Smart City Applications

Christopher Teh Jun Qian
Universiti Teknologi PETRONAS, Malaysia

Micheal Drieberg
Universiti Teknologi PETRONAS, Malaysia

Patrick Sebastian
https://orcid.org/0000-0001-7056-4678
Universiti Teknologi PETRONAS, Malaysia

Azrina Abd Aziz
Universiti Teknologi PETRONAS, Malaysia

Hai Hiung Lo
Universiti Teknologi PETRONAS, Malaysia

Abu Bakar Sayuti H. M. Saman
Universiti Teknologi PETRONAS, Malaysia

ABSTRACT

Currently, there is lack of implementation of practical power-saving schemes in most of the batteries powered by IoT smart city applications available in the market that can extend the battery lifetime, even though numerous researches have been carried to reduce the average power consumption. This is because electronics consume similar amounts of power during the idling state as compared to the active state, resulting in low power efficiency of the application. Thus, power consumption is affected by the modes of the electronic operations. Different electronics also have their own types of settings that can

DOI: 10.4018/978-1-7998-1253-1.ch004

be configured to reduce the power consumption, and this will be further investigated in this study. This chapter will address the issue of how to create a power-saving IoT application by applying power-saving schemes and creating an accurate model to predict the battery lifetime of the IoT application.

INTRODUCTION

Power consumption has and will always be an important factor in the IoT Smart City applications as they are required to operate continuously and for long periods of time. A non-negligible amount of power is drawn from the supply because there are usually multiple types of sensors used in these systems. Although numerous researches had been carried to reduce the sensor nodes' average power consumption, but there is still improvement that can be made in reducing the power wastage, especially during the idling state of the sensor nodes. During the idling state, similar amount of power is consumed even though there are no outputs from the sensor. As a result, power is wasted, and this will in turn affect the power efficiency of the applications.

An IoT Smart City application to monitor the ambient temperature is taken as a case study to investigate the system's power consumption. The application consists of sensor nodes and a sink node, as shown in Figure 1 (only one sensor node is shown). Each sensor node connects multiple sensors to collect different types of environmental data. In order to get an accurate ambient temperature, the sensor nodes are required to be located in multiple indoor and outdoor locations. Information collected from the sensor node will be transmitted to the sink node which act as a data collector using wireless transmission. Then, the sink node will upload the information to the Cloud for monitoring purposes. However, it is not feasible to power the sensor nodes through power points, especially in outdoor locations. Thus, using batteries is the most preferred solution because of its simplicity. There is the risk of application failure which can extend for many hours because batteries can be easily depleted from high power consumption. Worse still, not knowing when the batteries will be depleted, users will need to always monitor their application from time to time. Therefore, power saving schemes are necessary in order to extend the applications' system lifetime. With the help of power saving schemes, users can reduce the power consumption and increase the operating time of their applications. Furthermore, this will also help them to reduce the operation cost especially if the users plan for mass deployment.

To develop the power saving schemes, each component used in the application is investigated individually to find the suitable configurations for reduced power consumption. In order to achieve this, the low power modes as specified by the manufacturer's datasheet will be explored. The schemes that provide the highest power saving will be chosen and implemented. This is followed by testing to verify

Figure 1. IoT Smart City Application

the amount of power saved. And since there are multiple types of components, power consumption of each components is very much different because each consumes different amount of power based on its operation modes. It is important to know the components' power characteristics in order to be able to estimate the battery's and hence the application system's lifetime. The power consumption of each component in the system needs to be monitored so that rectification can be done immediately if the system does not meet the expected power level. Power measurement equipment are also used in this project to measure the power consumption in order to obtain accurate results.

After the power consumption of every component has been measured and recorded, a model will be developed to predict the battery's lifetime based on the given battery capacity. Then, both the model and experimental battery lifetimes will be compared to validate the accuracy of the model created. With the help of the model created from this study, users are able to estimate the battery lifetime of similar systems with different types of components before deployment.

This proposed book chapter describes the design and implementation of power saving schemes for extending the lifetime of a novel IoT Smart City Application. The book chapter outline includes the introduction, literature review, methodology, results and discussion and conclusion. From this chapter, the readers can benefit from understanding the need for power saving for smart city applications, the current state-of-the-art related development in the area of power saving, the methodology used in incorporating power saving in the system design, component selections and finally the data collection and analysis. Then, they can apply a similar power saving design methodology to their own application domain.

BACKGROUND

This chapter covers the overview of IoT Smart City Environmental Monitoring Applications and power. The related power saving works for IoT applications are also provided.

Introduction on Smart City Environmental Monitoring Applications using IoT

In the early stage, Internet was developed to allow people to access data and share resources from all over the world. Most of the interaction through the Internet is human to human interaction as the received information is interpreted and processed by human. For example, online news that is being broadcast by reporters is read by the subscribers using their electronic devices connected to the Internet. Internet is a very important technology ever invented. It has greatly influenced our daily lives and significantly transformed how today's world operates. Recently, the Internet of Things (IoT) is becoming a hot topic of interest. IoT has the capability of allowing people or electronic devices to interact and communicate with other people or devices under the same network (Hakiri, Berthou, Gokhale, & Abdellatif, 2015). Connection is offered between devices embedded with sensors and microcontroller to transfer information through wireless network to create integration between the physical and virtual world. As a result, this will help to automate any process and increase the efficiency.

The fundamental system architecture of IoT is to have sensors connected to the wireless network and users can remotely access the collected data stored in a physical or virtual server such as the Cloud (Consulting, 2019). By having reliable communication between devices, any loss of important information can be prevented during data collection stage. Then, the data will be transmitted to the Cloud for the user to process unwanted information (LaurentPierre, 2016). Data flows can be immense which may slow down the network hence, data pre-processing is required to avoid discontinuities of connection.

An environmental monitoring system should have the ability to monitor and evaluate the environment condition (Guthi, 2016). Smart City environmental monitoring can be divided into two categories which are indoor and outdoor monitoring. Examples of indoor monitoring can be seen daily in the civil structure such as controlling the air conditioner's temperature and detecting smoke. While the examples of outdoor monitoring are weather and flooding monitoring systems. Environmental monitoring is important nowadays as industries is in a rapid growth due to the high demand of goods for people. Industries without proper planning of waste management can cause environmental issues such as climate changes and pollution to the surrounding environment. With the help of integrated electronics devices, actions can be taken early to ensure the environmental parameters are kept at a healthy level.

There are also some commercial IoT smart cities applications that have been deployed. For example, CyTech Smart developed a smart home automation system that is equipped with different types of sensors (CytechSmart, 2019). The system collects data such as power consumption, temperature, lighting levels and many more. These data are transmitted to the sink node and uploaded to the online user interface for real-time monitoring. Notifications can also be sent to the users if abnormal situations are detected. Next, SmartBox has incorporated technology from Digi into their commercial product (DIGI, 2019). SmartBox offers a low cost and convenient packages storage system by using wireless transmission modules and gateways to give access to lockers based on single-use code. Moreover, SMS notifications are sent to the recipients and the system is also able to monitor the lockers from the operation centre. Since the applications are installed indoor, therefore these devices are powered by the fixed power supply. Not only that, WiseConn also utilizes the DIGI solutions to provide a platform for the agriculture sector to monitor their plantation area with low power modules and long transmission range. This platform is able to capture the environmental data such as soil moisture, weather conditions and temperature. To avoid interruption, this commercial solution uses solar power to power up their devices around the field.

Background on Power

Electric charge can produce an electric field which can be either positive or negative and the flow of electric charges is known as electric current (Britannica, 2019). However, power cannot be created or destroyed due to the law of conservation of energy where it stated that energy is a conserved quantity. Hence, human uses energy sources like potential and kinetic energy to transform the energy into power required by the system. For an example, power plants are burning fossil fuel such as coal, oil or gas to produce steam to drive large generator turbine that converts its potential and kinetic energy into electricity. But generating electricity over long period of time will cause the resources to reduce its quantities since fossil fuels are not a renewable energy (W.International, 2011). Although human had harvested renewable energy such as solar, tidal, wind and hydro to reduce the generation of electricity from fossil fuels, however these harvested energy systems are still insufficient to replace the current power system because of the high demand in electricity due to the heavy load connected to the power.

Fortunately, the awareness in conservation of energy among society had been increased due to the exploitation of resources that had caused the climate changes and in turn affected millions of people worldwide. The global energy sector is responsible for approximately two-thirds of greenhouse gases emission and this is the amount that increases the fastest compared to any other sector every year (W.International, 2011). Many people suffered from water shortage, crop failures, tropical diseases or extreme weathers (Usova & Velkin, 2018) because of poor planning and these conditions will be getting worse if the concentration of greenhouse gases created from the industries increases in the Earth's atmosphere. Hence, energy conservation is important to keep the world from depleting its natural resources because the effect can take many years before it can be seen.

Power electronics is the heart of each electronic device that handles the conversion of electrical power and signal with high efficiency switching mode (Zhang, Li, Zhang, & Halang, 2018). Back in the few decades, power electronics are mostly used in electrical machines. They can be very bulky and expensive due to the hardware and design limitations and they are not user friendly. But throughout many years of researches, more power electronics technologies have been developed to improve power electronics efficiency and reduce the wastage of energy. The development of power electronics had revolutionized industries and contributed to many fields including IoT where complex circuit found in those tiny sensing devices used in an IoT application are built up by multiples types of power electronics. This allows users to perform faster rate of data processing and obtain the result they wanted.

To fulfil the demands of customers, numerous types of power electronic systems are incorporated into the electronic systems aiming to reduce the power consumption and to increase the products' functionalities. Hence, customers have the options to choose the product that meets their requirement and suitable for their application.

IoT Smart City Environment Monitoring Applications

This section will discuss the related works in IoT Smart City environment monitoring applications. In (Jaladi, 2017), a wireless sensor network system equipped with light, moisture, humidity, temperature, pressure and pollution sensors is developed to monitor the environmental parameters around the campus area. The data collected by the sensor nodes is transferred to the sink node using a wireless communication module based on ZigBee protocol. ZigBee is chosen to perform the task because it has the capability to multi route the data to the sink node if the nodes are connected under the same network. The nearest router will be chosen to relay the data until the data is finally transmitted to the destined sink node. However, there is lack of power saving in the system and the system consumes a large amount of power because a lot of sensors are used and connected.

An IoT environmental monitoring application that detects the environmental parameters using Raspberry-Pi 3 is discussed in (Ibrahim, Elgamri, Babiker, & Mohamed, 2015). The work uses different types of sensors that are only giving digital output to the microcontroller. Next, the data will be uploaded to the digital devices through Wi-Fi network so that the users can monitor the results online. But the work is not scalable because Raspberry Pi is not capable of creating a network without an external module.

An environmental temperature monitoring application using the concept of wireless sensor network is presented in (Sastra & Wiharta, 2016). Although this work proposed two ways to construct the network, but each of the sensor node is connected to the network individually using ESP8266 WI-FI. Multi-routing and scalability are not possible in this work.

In (Cerchecci et al., 2018), an application to monitor the filling level of dustbin using ultrasound is introduced in which an external timer is used to control the activation of sensor. The timer will send a logic output to AT328 to activate the MCU so that it can control the subsystems such as ultrasound sensor and LoRa to operate when required. However, there is lack of power saving scheme in the subsystems whereby power consumption is possibly high when the system is idling.

Indoor environmental monitoring is proposed in (Kelly, Suryadevara, & Mukhopadhyay, 2013) to monitor water temperature and light intensity through the network connected using ZigBee. The ZigBee protocol is connected to the gateway by translating data format to Internet Protocol (IPV6). The proposed work also allows the users to measure electrical parameters and take control of housing electrical equipment. However, the cost of the equipment is quite high.

Table 1 provides the summary of the above-mentioned IoT Smart City environmental applications. From Table 1, most of the related works did not have the power saving schemes. In this study, power saving schemes will be introduced to improve the efficiency of the IoT Smart City environmental monitoring applications and an accurate model will be developed to estimate the battery lifetime of an IoT application.

METHODOLOGY

This section presents the methods and procedure that will be carried out throughout the developed system.

Design & Development of System

There are five subsystems in the power saving system architecture. Components such as Arduino Uno, Xbee Shield, Xbee module and DHT22 temperature and humidity sensor are used to build the sensor node of the application as shown in Figure 1. The sensor node will be used to take measurements of temperature and humidity in different locations within the campus area. Data is retrieved from a digital pin from the microcontroller for analysis. Then the processed data will be transmitted wirelessly to the gateway and finally uploaded to the online platform for end user to monitor. A comparison study was also undertaken to find out whether the microcontroller, wireless communication module and sensor specifications are suitable for the application.

Table 1. Comparison of the IoT Smart City environmental works

Related Work	Description	Power Saving Schemes in microcontroller	Power Saving Schemes in sensors	Power Saving Schemes in wireless communication module
Ganesh, 2017	Multiple environmental monitoring parameters within campus area	No	No	No
(Ibrahim et al., 2015	Air, earthquake and weather IoT monitoring using Raspberry Pi.	No	No	No
Sastra & Wiharta, 2016	Ambient temperature monitoring using Arduino Uno	No	No	No
Cerchecci et al., 2018	Dustbin monitoring application and controlled by an external timer to minimize the power consumption	No	Partial	No
Kelly, Suryadevara, & Mukhopadhyay, 2013	Indoor water and temperature monitoring using IoT concept and monitored through network.	Partial	No	No

Multiple types of microcontroller unit are considered for selection to be used in this project, and comparison between Arduino Uno, Raspberry Pi 3 Model B, and Intel Galileo was conducted. The specifications of the microcontroller boards are reviewed, and they are summarized in Table 2. Arduino Uno is chosen to be used in this study because it uses ATMega328 chip with Optiboot boot loader that helps to run the program more efficiently. As the system involves simple sensors and wireless transmission module, the clock speed of 16MHz is sufficient to perform the tasks. Although higher clock speed can process data at a faster rate, but it will also cause the system to draw more power to operate, hence not suitable for this application. Moreover, Arduino Uno is also equipped with suitable and sufficient number of digital pins for circuit connection and data processing for the application.

Wireless communication is required in this project to establish the connection between the sink node and sensor node. There are four types of wireless communication available in the market: Zigbee, Wi-Fi, Bluetooth and Bluetooth Low Energy (BLE). A study has been conducted in order to select the most suitable module. The choice of module will greatly affect the battery lifetime. The comparison results are shown in Table 3. Zigbee is the best approach for the communication between the sensor nodes and sink nodes due to its low power consumption and its adequate transmission range. It also provides a high level of security protection for data transmission.

In order to get the accurate data, a suitable temperature and humidity sensor that has good sensing capabilities must be selected for this application. DHT11, DHT22 and SHT71 are being compared in Table 4 based on their specifications. DHT22 is chosen as the most suitable sensor because it has the highest measurement accuracy compared to the other two. Moreover, it also has a low and constant sampling period which would ease the user in taking measurement at a constant rate.

Considering environment parameters do not vary rapidly over a short period of time, it is unnecessary to take frequent measurement because each measurement consumes power. In order to reduce the power consumption, the operation is split into 2 stages: 1) configuring the application to take measurement between a longer interval time and; 2) implementing power saving schemes during the interval idling time. The idling state is considered the most power wasteful stage because the application does not produce output but consumes almost as high power as the active state. Hence, the sensor node is configured to take new measurement every 3.5 minutes and the operation cycle of sensor node is illustrated in Figure 2. The duration of 3.5 minutes for one complete cycle was chosen arbitrarily and this duration can be changed according to the application's requirement.

Table 2. Comparison of Microcontroller Unit

Specifications	Arduino Uno	Raspberry Pi 3 Model B	Intel Galileo
Processor	ATmega 328	Broadcom BCM2836	Intel Quack
Clock Speed	16MHz	900MHz	400MHz
Current Consumption at 5V	50mA – 1A	2.5A	800mA
RAM	32kB	1GB	1GB
Network	Via external modules	- Wi-Fi LAN (802.11b/g/n) - Bluetooth 4.1 (802.15)	- 10/100 Ethernet Connector
Language	Arduino IDE	Python, C language	Arduino IDE, Python

Table 3. Comparison of Wireless Communication Module

Specifications	Zigbee	Wi-Fi	Bluetooth	Bluetooth Low Energy
Network Topology	Star, Tree and Mesh	Star	Point-to-Point	Star, Bus
Protocol	IEEE 802.15.4	IEEE 802.11n	IEEE 802.15.1	IEEE 802.15.1
Data rate	250kbps	54 – 600Mbps	700kbps	1Mbps
Frequency	2.4GHz	2.4 – 5GHz	2.4GHz	2.4GHz
Network size	65000	255	7	Unlimited
Transmission Range	10 – 100m	50m	<30m	50m
Power Consumption	Low	High	High	Low
Security	High	Medium	Low	Low

To minimize the network interruption in the application, the authors focus the implementation of power saving schemes only on the sensor node which is constructed with Arduino Uno, Xbee, Xbee Shield, and DHT22 temperature and humidity sensor as shown in Figure 3. This is because power saving schemes may affect the performance of the sink node of the application (the coordinator to receive data from the sensor node). In order to maintain stable network connection, the coordinator must always be available in the network created to keep the devices connected.

Table 4. Comparison of Temperature and Humidity Sensor

Specifications	DHT11	DHT22	SHT71
Operating Range (a) Temperature (b) Humidity	0 to 50°C 20 – 90%RH	-40 to 80°C 0 – 100%RH	-40 to 120°C 0 – 100%RH
Accuracy (a) Temperature (b) Humidity	± 2°C ± 5%RH	± 0.5°C ± 2%RH	± 0.9°C ± 3.5%RH
Current Consumption (a) Active Mode (b) Sleep Mode	2.5mA 150µA	1.5mA 50µA	0.5mA 0.3µA
Sampling Period	>2s	2s	<3s
Power Consumption	High	Low	Lowest

Figure 2. Sensor node operation cycle

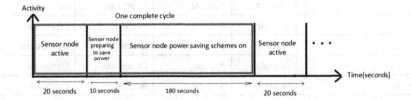

Arduino Uno Power Saving Schemes

Conserving power is crucial in order to ensure longer life span, to keep the system running for a longer period, and to avoid the need to replace the batteries frequently. In the software configuration available provided by Arduino, there are five modes available in the Arduino Uno microcontroller used in the system and each of their features (Atmel, 2015) are discussed in Table 5:

Each of the modules listed in Table 5 in different modes has its own functionality and consume different amount of power:

- Main Clock Source – Provides the frequency inputs and generates periodic signal for different devices in a system and allow them to carry out their intended function.
- Timer Oscillator - An oscillator which contain crystal and the oscillator circuit that provides signal with logic level output.
- Input/output Clock- Clock used by input or output module like Timer, Serial Peripheral Interface (SPI) and Universal Asynchronous Receiver Transmitter (USART).
- ADC Clock- Provides clock domain to ADC when halting the input/output and CPU clock to reduce the noise generated in circuit.
- Asynchronous Clock- allows the timer to drive from an external clock when the device is in sleep mode.

As shown in Table 5, the fewer modules are activated, the less power is consumed. Power down mode is the most suitable mode to be used in the Arduino Uno microcontroller because it can save the most power amongst all the available operational modes. Hence, power down mode will be implemented when the system is inactive and idling to reduce the system power consumption.

Figure 3. Sensor node setup

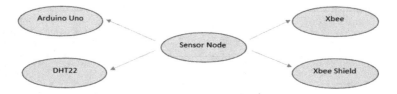

Table 5. Comparison of Power Saving Modes in Arduino

Modes	Idle	ADC	Power save	Standby	Power Down
Current saving	Lowest	Low	Medium	High	Highest
Main Clock Source	Activate	Activate	Deactivate	Activate	Deactivate
Time Oscillator	Activate	Activate	Activate	Deactivate	Deactivate
Input/output Clock	Activate	Deactivate	Deactivate	Deactivate	Deactivate
ADC Clock	Activate	Activate	Deactivate	Deactivate	Deactivate
Asynchronous Clock	Activate	Activate	Activate	Deactivate	Deactivate

In Arduino Uno, the function of Brown-Out Detector (BOD) is to sense the falling of supply voltage to the microcontroller when the microcontroller is in active mode. The purpose of BOD sensing is to prevent the microcontroller from acting abnormally during shutting down and reset due to low voltage supply. This feature will draw some power from the microcontroller even when it is in sleep mode so it will be deactivated before the mode is activated to conserve power.

Apart from the software configuration, there are some hardware configurations that can help to save power in the sensor node, for example, changing the voltage linear regulator in the microcontroller with a buck converter. Energy can be lost in the form of heat in the conversion of linear regulator and this can lead to energy inefficiency. Buck converters use a switching element to convert the power supply into a pulsed voltage which is smoothed with capacitor and inductors. When the predetermined voltage is reached at the output, the switching element will be turned off so less heat is produced during conversion and higher voltage rate conversion can be achieved.

Next, the on-board LEDs are also a power consuming device since it cannot be turned off as long there is power supply to the microcontroller. Since the LEDs are not a critical part of the operation for the purpose of this project; removing the on-board LED will help to save some power. Finally, using an individual and external microchip like AT328 will also save a lot of power since it eliminates all the power consumption from the ports, converter, clocks, SPI and USART on the microcontroller.

As discussed above, there are software and hardware configurations in power saving schemes. But due to the constrain of time, only software configuration is considered in this project.

Xbee Power Saving Schemes

The combination of IEEE 802.15.4 standard and Zigbee enables the development of wireless sensor and actuator network for short range and low power communication. IEEE 802.15.14 standard allows a basic transmission rate of 250kbps up to 10 meters range and this can be reduced to a minimum of 20kbps in Zigbee (868/915 MHz band) to further minimize the power consumption(Casilari-Pérez, Cano-García, & Manuel Campos-Garrido, 2010). Real time communication is possible with the help of this standard where it allows the scenarios of collecting burst of signals from sensor to be transmitted.

IEEE 802.15.4 also has the potential of organizing the network by itself to adapt to diverse topologies, connectivity between nodes, or even the flow of network traffic (Casilari, Cano-García, & Campos-Garrido, 2010). Past research projects usually connecting tens or hundreds of simple nodes that periodically sending data to the sinks/coordinator and this standard is conceived to regulate the power consumption of this node so they will be able to remain in a low-power state most of the time. The nodes are only required to be active when they need to sense and transmit data for a short period of time.

Xbee is one of the widely used modules based on the Zigbee technology for a wide range of services especially for low power consumption domestic application. Cyclic sleep mode is what made the Xbee Module suitable for low power application and it can be configured through Pin 9 on the Xbee Module with the help of XCTU software. Pin 13 will be the output to determine whether the Xbee should be turned on or put in sleep mode. Only Xbee module that had been flashed as End Devices are able to be configured to be in sleep mode because it does not require to route data and is able to leave the network without interrupting the connection of other Xbee Modules. Figure 4 shows the XCTU software sleep command configuration:

DHT22 Power Saving Schemes

Since the manufacturer of DHT22 does not provide any power saving mechanism for the sensor, a simple setup is implemented in the microcontroller to control the sensor's power supply. To achieve that, the sensor's positive terminal is connected to a digital port, so users are able to turn the sensor on or off by controlling the voltage supply to the sensor via programming the Arduino Uno to supply a high (5V) or a low (0V) logic gate value respectively.

RESULTS AND DISCUSSION

The power saving schemes of every component in the sensor nodes was presented in the Methodology Section. This section presents the results obtained and their discussion. Each component in the sensor node is tested to determine its power consumption and this information will be subsequently used for modelling the system.

Arduino Uno Testing

Arduino provides five power saving schemes and all of the schemes will be tested. To test these power saving schemes, 5V is supplied to the Arduino Uno through the Vin port and the current consumption is measured with the series connected multimeter, as shown in Figure 5. Arduino Uno will be programmed in advanced using the library provided to set the power saving schemes. The amount of power saved will be calculated using Equations 1 and 2 while the corresponding results are shown in Table 6.

$$Power\left(W\right) = Current\,Measured\,x\,5V\,. \tag{1}$$

Figure 4. Sleep commands configuration in XCTU software (DIGI, 2019)

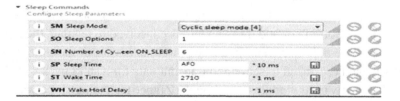

Figure 5. Arduino Uno Current Measurement

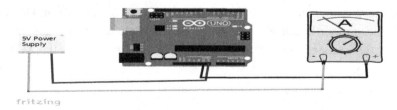

$$Power\,Saved\,(\%) = \left| \frac{\text{Normal mode}\,(\text{W}) - X\,mode\,(\text{W})}{\text{Normal mode}\,(\text{W})} \right| \text{x}100\%. \qquad (2)$$

As shown in Table 6, power down mode provides the highest power saving among the five modes as it consumes the least amount of current. This is because most of the modules inside the Arduino Uno are shut off in this mode. Therefore, power down mode is chosen to be implemented in this project.

DHT22 Testing

For the DHT22, there are four types of operation which are off, on, measure and standby in one complete measurement cycle. Each of the operation type consumes different amount of current and each of the operation lasts for 2 seconds before changing to another operation type. Due to the DHT22 operation cannot be implemented without the help of microcontroller, Figure 6 shows the set-up of DHT22 with Arduino Uno in order to allow the current measurement to be done.

Table 7 shows the current measurement of DHT22 in different operations with the help of Arduino Uno. In order to calculate the current consumed in On and Standby operations, the current measured must deduct the base current consumed by Arduino Uno which is 34.2mA. After deducting the base current, DHT22 On operation consume 1.7mA and Standby operation consume 0.6mA. While DHT22 Measure operation current is obtained by deducting the Standby operation current which is 1.5mA. The power consumption of DHT22 can be calculated using Equation 1.

The benefit of power saving schemes is that DHT22 will switch off and its current consumption will be reduced to 0mA after taking the measurement from the environment until the next cycle. While

Table 6. Current and power saved on Arduino-Uno with power saving schemes

Mode	Current measurement (mA)	Power (mW)	Power Saved (%)
Normal	34.2	171	-
Idle	26.4	132	22.8
ADC Noise Reduction	25.8	129	24.5
Power save	23.3	117	31.8
Standby	23.2	116	32.1
Power down	23.0	115	32.70

Figure 6. DHT22 sensor setup

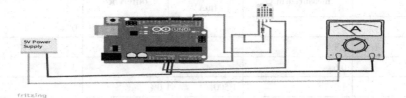

Table 7. Current measured from DHT22

DHT22 Operations	Current Measured (mA)	Description Current (mA)	Power (mW)
Off	34.2	Off Current = 0	-
On	35.9	On Current = 35.9 -34.2 =1.7	8.5
Standby	34.8	Standby Current = 34.8 -34.2 =0.6	3.0
Measure	36.3	Measure Current = 36.30 -34.8 =1.5	7.5

without power saving schemes, DHT22 will return to standby operation which consumes 0.6mA. Hence this will help to reduce the power consumption of the sensor when the system is idling.

Table 8 shows the comparison between the experiment and datasheet values. Although the power saving schemes can help to save up to 100% of the power when turned off, the amount of current saved is less than 2mA. When compared to Arduino Uno, the power saved from DHT22 is less significant. Nevertheless, any savings from the sensor node can still provide an improvement in the system's lifetime.

XBee Testing

Xbee module can be configured into three different types of devices which are Coordinator, Router or End Device. A network should contain at least one coordinator before the network can be configured. The coordinator will then create a channel with PAN ID for the other Xbee module to connect to the network. Each of the Xbee module has its own unique identifier of fixed 64-bit MAC address and the 16-bit floating network address are automatically created when it joins a network.

The Xbee module used in the network is flashed as API mode because in this mode, the 64-bit source address of a packet during transmission can be tracked and the transmission status (success or failure) can be obtained. This enables the network to be more organized and minimize the packet loss during the transmission. Not only that, API mode is preferable to AT mode because API mode allows ZigBee to transmit data to multiple locations at once while AT mode needs to establish a new connection to every destination. Hence with API mode, throughput of the system can be increased significantly.

To transmit data between Xbee modules, it is more reliable to set the end-device and coordinator to unicast transmission where the transmission path is based on the destination and the receiver address is

Table 8. DHT22 with Power saving schemes

Operations	Current measured(mA)	Current in datasheet (mA)	Percentage difference	Power measured(mW)	Power saved
Off	0	-	-	0	100%
On	1.7	-	-	8.5	-
Standby	0.6	-	-	3	-
Measure	1.5	1.500	0%	7.5	-

set to the Xbee module. If the path is found and connected, data can be transmitted, and acknowledgement can be received on both modules. Broadcast transmission will reduce the lifetime of the system and increase the throughput.

In order to create a communication path between Xbee modules, the unique identifier address of each ZigBee module is used to communicate in API frame. For an example, end device 1 has the serial address of 0x0013A200 407626D8 while coordinator 1 has the serial address of 0x0013A200 40D69FCB. Hence, both devices need to exchange their serial addresses in order to communicate. Figures 7 illustrate the communication between two ZigBee modules.

From the XCTU configuration, Xbee module maximum sleep time period in one cycle is 28 seconds, hence more cycles of sleep are needed to be set into the Xbee module so the time period can be extended. The total sleep time can be derived as the following Equation 3:

$$Sleep\,Time\,Period(s) = 28\,seconds * amount\,of\,cycles(n). \tag{3}$$

After waking up from sleep mode, the Xbee module requires at least 10 seconds for the connection to be re-established before transmitting data. This is to avoid packet losses when data is transmitted between nodes.

Current measurement from the Xbee Module is conducted with the help of Xbee Shield to determine the power drain from the batteries. Due to the multimeter and INA219 inability in sensing small spikes in the packet transmission process, an oscilloscope is used to verify the measurement by measuring the voltage drop across a low resistance power resistor (0.4 ohm). The oscilloscope set up are shown in the Figure 8

The operation of Xbee module can be categorized into three stages which are on, transceiver and sleep-state. Each of stage consumes different amount of current and it is important to know so that the user can troubleshoot and estimate the power consumed when the system is acting abnormally. Figure 9 shows that there is a current spike when the Xbee module is turned on. This is because there is a need

Figure 7. XBee Unicast Communication

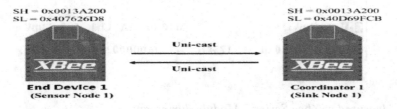

Figure 8. Oscilloscope setup for power measurement of XBee module

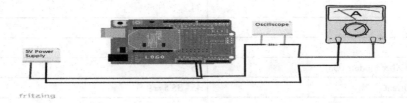

to calibrate the system clock each time when the module is switched on and clock calibration will create a spike in current while synchronizing the components.

Similar to the DHT22, the Xbee module current cannot be measured directly. The current consumption of the Xbee module is calculated by deducting the base currents of Arduino Uno and Xbee Shield from the measured total current. Therefore, each of the component is measured separately, i.e. Arduino Uno, Xbee shield and finally Xbee module. As the measurements from the oscilloscope are fluctuating, therefore an average current measurement from the multimeter is recorded. Table 9 shows the current measurement of Xbee Series 2 module during the On operation.

Figure 10 shows that the operation when Xbee module needs to transmit a packet to the coordinator. Xbee will try to search available channels within range and will go through non-beacon mode where it will ask for permission from the coordinator to allow for packet transmission. If the network is idle, the coordinator will send acknowledgement to the sensor node and allow it to start transmitting data packets. Table 10 shows the current measured of Xbee module during transmitting and receiving packet.

Figure 9. Xbee Waveform during on

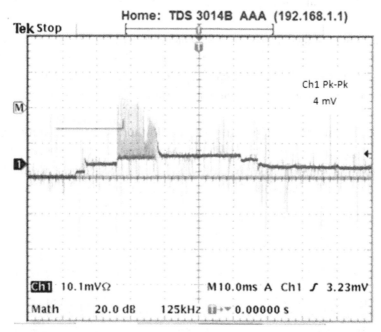

Table 9. Current Measured of Xbee Series 2 Module during on

Components	Current Measured(mA)
Uno	34.2
Uno+ Xbee Shield	35.5
Xbee Shield Current	35.5 - 34.2 = 1.3
Uno +Xbee Shield +Xbee Module (On)	45
Xbee Module On Current	45 - 35.5 = 9.5

As shown in Table 10, Xbee module consumes a higher current of up to 27mA to transmit the packet to or receive the acknowledgement from the sink node.

Figure 11 shows the waveform of Xbee module during the sleep operation and Table 11 shows the current measurement of Xbee module during sleep operation.

When Xbee module is in the Sleep mode, it only consumes a very low current of 1mA. If Sleep mode is not used, Xbee module will switch back to the Standby mode which consumes a current of 9.5mA during the iding state. By using Equation 2 to calculate the power saved in Xbee module, Table 12 shows all of the operations and the amount of power saved in Xbee with the power saving schemes.

Battery Discharge Test

The batteries used in the system are required to undergo a discharge cycle test to measure the batteries amp-hours capacity. During the test, batteries are connected to a small valued resistor which would act as a load and the values of circuit voltage and current is measured. Until the point where the voltage

Figure 10. Xbee Waveform during Packet Transmission/Receive

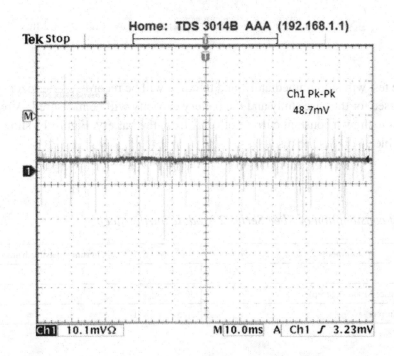

Table 10. Current consumption of Xbee Series 2 Module during transmitting and receiving packet

Components	Current Measured(mA)
Uno +Xbee Shield+ Xbee Module (On)	45
Uno +Xbee Shield+ Xbee Module (Transmitting & Receiving)	72
Xbee Module Transmitting & Receiving Current	72- 45 = 27

Figure 11. Xbee Waveform during Sleep Operation

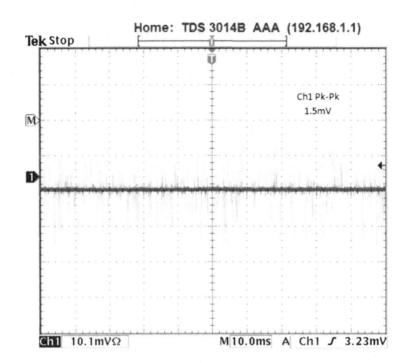

drops rapidly, the test will stop immediately, and the time will be recorded. Energizer AA LR6 alkaline batteries will be used for the case study and the battery capacity will be measured. A resistor of 62 ohm is used in this test to draw a constant current of 0.1A from the battery. Figure 12 shows the connection of the test and Table 13 shows the results:

Table 11. Current consumption of Xbee Series 2 Module during sleep

Components	Current Measured(mA)
Uno+ Xbee Shield	35.5
Uno +Xbee Shield+ Xbee Module (Sleep)	36.5
Xbee Module Sleep Current	36.5 - 35.5 = 1

Table 12. Xbee Power Saving Schemes

Operations	Current measured(mA)	Power measured(mW)	Power saved
On	9.5	48	-
Standby	9.5	48	-
Transmit & Receive	27	135	-
Sleep	1	5	89.470%

As shown in Figure 13, the Energizer AA LR6 alkaline battery has approximately 2300mAh capacity (on a 0.1A discharge rate, taken at 4V) which is similar to the capacity value stated in the datasheet. It is important to note that the Arduino Uno needs a minimum operating voltage of 4.3V to keep the oscillator and CPU functioning. And due to the drop out voltage at the Arduino Uno voltage regulator, a reduction of 1.1V is needed to be applied on the battery in order to estimate the battery lifetime accurately. Hence the battery voltage must be at least 5.4V. In this application, Arduino is powered by 4 batteries so it requires at least 5.4V for operation before the measurement stops. This value will be used for the calculation of battery lifetime of the model created. As shown in Figure 13, Energizer AA LR6 alkaline battery has approximately 920mAh capacity (on a 0.1A discharge rate, taken at 5.4V) .

System Modelling and Analysis

System modelling is required because it can help to understand the system behaviour and estimate its lifetime. Based on the result collected in previous subsection, the system will repeat one complete cycle every 3.5 minutes which consists of 3 minutes of power saving mode and 0.5 minutes of normal

Figure 12. Battery discharge test

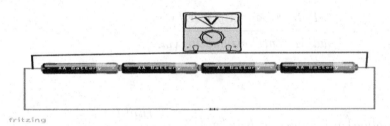

Table 13. Energizer AA LR6 Alkaline Battery Discharge Test (draws at 0.1 A)

Hours	Amp Hour	Voltage (V)
0	0.0	6.20
2	0.2	6.02
4	0.4	5.83
6	0.6	5.64
8	0.8	5.47
10	1.0	5.38
12	1.2	5.20
14	1.4	5.03
16	1.6	4.81
18	1.8	4.56
20	2.0	4.41
22	2.2	4.26
24	2.4	3.97
26	2.6	3.71

Figure 13. Graph of battery discharge rate based on 0.1A current draw

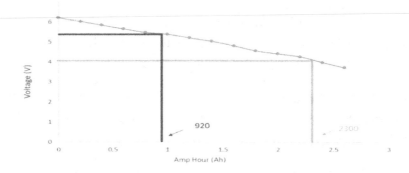

operation where all sensors are operational. Hence there will be approximately 17 cycles repeated in one hour. Power consumption analysis is carried out in two systems, one with power saving mode and the other without power saving (baseline system), to calculate the battery life. The formula to calculate the battery lifetime is shown in Equation 4. Equation 5 is used to calculate the current consumption of each component in the system.

$$
\text{Battery lifetime} \left(H \right) = \frac{Battery\,Capacity\left(mAH\right)}{Load\,Current\,Consumption\left(mA\right)}. \tag{4}
$$

$$
Current\,Consumption\left(mA\right) = current\,draw\left(mA\right) * \frac{turn\,on\,time\left(s\right)}{3600\left(s\right)}. \tag{5}
$$

where 3600 is the number of seconds in an hour

- Baseline System
  - Arduino Uno

$$
\text{Current consumption} = 34.200mA * \frac{3600}{3600}. \tag{6}
$$

$$
= 34.200mA.
$$

  - DHT22

$$
\text{Current consumption} = \left(1.700mA * \frac{2}{3600}\right) + \left(0.600mA * \frac{3564}{3600}\right) + \left(1.500mA * \frac{34}{3600}\right). \tag{7}
$$

$= 0.610mA$.

    ◦   <u>Xbee Shield</u>

$$\text{Current consumption} = 1.300mA * \frac{3600}{3600} \quad . \tag{8}$$

$= 1.300mA$.<u>Xbee Module</u>

$$\text{Current consumption} = \left(9.500mA * \frac{3192}{3600}\right) + \left(27.000mA * \frac{204}{3600}\right) + \left(27.000mA * \frac{204}{3600}\right). \tag{9}$$

$= 11.480mA$.

o Total current $= Arduino\,Uno + DHT22 + Xbee\,Shield + Xbee\,Module$.

$$= 34.200mA + 0.610mA + 1.300mA + 11.480mA. \tag{10}$$

$$= 47.590mA.$$

$$\text{Battery lifetime}\left(\text{hrs}\right) of Baseline\,System = \frac{920.000mAH}{47.590mA} . \tag{11}$$

$= 19.332\,hours$.

- Power saving system
  - ◦   <u>Arduino Uno</u>

$$\text{Current consumption} = \left(34.200mA * \frac{540}{3600}\right) + \left(23.000mA * \frac{3060}{3600}\right). \tag{12}$$

$$= 24.680mA .$$

    ◦   <u>DHT22</u>

$$\text{Current consumption} = \left(1.700mA * \frac{34}{3600}\right) + \left(0.600mA * \frac{34}{3600}\right) + \left(1.500mA * \frac{34}{3600}\right). \tag{13}$$

$$= 36.890\mu.$$

○ <u>Xbee Shield</u>

$$\text{Current consumption} = 1.300mA * \frac{3600}{3600}. \tag{14}$$

$$= 1.300mA. \text{ \underline{Xbee Module}}$$

$$\text{Current consumption} = \left(9.500mA * \frac{34}{3600}\right) + \left(27.000mA * \frac{204}{3600}\right) + \left(27.000mA * \frac{204}{3600}\right).$$

$$+ \left(1.000mA * \frac{3158}{3600}\right). \tag{15}$$

$$\mathbf{3.997mA} \quad . \text{Total current} \quad = ArduinoUno + DHT22 + XbeeShield + XbeeModule \quad .$$

$$= 24.680mA + 36.890\mu A + 1.300mA + 3.997mA. \tag{16}$$

$$= 30.020mA$$

o Battery lifetime $\left(\text{hrs}\right) of Power Saving System = \dfrac{920.000mAH}{30.020mA} \tag{17}$

$$= 30.646 hours$$

Table 14 shows the calculated power consumption and power saved by both system using Equation 1 and 2. To ease the calculation of battery lifetime from the model created, MATLAB GUI is created as shown in Figure 14 to simulate the model based on the sensors power analysis. The user is required to

Table 14. *Power Consumption of Systems Under Test*

Components	Baseline system Consumption(mW)	Power saving system Consumption (mW)	Power Saved
Arduino Uno	171	123	27.840%
DHT22	3.05	0.185	93.950%
Xbee Series 2	57.4	0.02	65.190%
Xbee Shield	6.5	6.5	0.000%
Total power consumption	238	150	36.920%

input the time for power saving and the battery capacity in order to calculate the battery lifetime of the system. Hence, approximately 37% of power had been saved with power saving schemes.

Calculation of Battery Lifetime Improvement with Power Saving Schemes

A comparison is done to investigate the effect of the power saving schemes in the application. Therefore, By using Equation 18 to calculate the efficiency improved, Table 15 summarizes the results of both baseline and power saving systems. Figure 15 and 16 show the battery lifetime during the experimental phase with and without power saving scheme.

Figure 14. *MATLAB GUI for model's simulation*

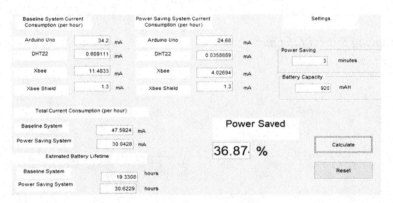

Table 15. *Power saving schemes battery lifetime improvement*

	Baseline System		Power Saving System		Battery Lifetime Improved (%)	
	Theory	Experimental	Theory	Experimental	Theory	Experimental
Battery Lifetime (hrs)	19.33 hours	18.79 hours	30.64 hours	29.13 Hours	58.53%	55.03%

$$Lifetime\,Improved\left(\%\right) = \frac{Power\ saving\ system\left(hrs\right) - Baseline\,system\left(hrs\right)}{Baseline\ system\left(hrs\right)} \text{x}100\% \qquad (18)$$

In conclusion, the power saving schemes proposed and implemented in the case study will be able to improve the battery lifetime by up to 55%.

Accuracy of Battery Lifetime between Theory and Experimental

After getting the first estimation of the battery lifetime from previous section, the results are used to compare with the model created to show the model's accuracy. The percentage difference of both systems is calculated in Table 16 using Equation 19:

$$Percentage\,Difference\left(\%\right) = \frac{Theory\left(hrs\right) - Experimental\left(hrs\right)}{Experimental\left(hrs\right)} \text{x}100\% \qquad (19)$$

Figure 15. Baseline System Lifetime

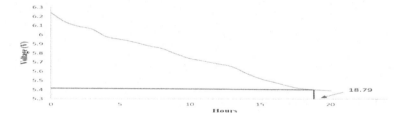

Figure 16. Power Saving System Lifetime

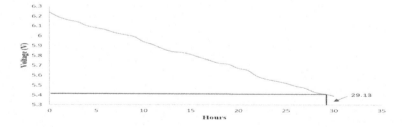

Table 16. Accuracy of battery lifetime model

	Baseline System		Power Saving System		Percentage Difference (%)	
	Theory	Experimental	Theory	Experimental	Baseline System	Power Saving System
Battery Lifetime (hrs)	19.33 hours	18.79 hours	30.64 hours	29.13 hours	2.89%	5.20%

The result shows only a small value of percentage difference between theoretical and actual values, which validates the high accuracy of the model. The difference is due to the fact that the theoretical values are calculated based on the premise that the Xbee module can successfully detect and operate each mode in every cycle. However, in practice, the Xbee module needs several attempts to switch to different modes. This stutter-like behaviour consumes more current, and in turn marginally reduces the experimental lifetime when compared to the theoretical.

FUTURE RESEARCH DIRECTIONS

The future research directions for this work include creating a user interface for the current system to monitor the battery level so that immediate replacement can be performed if the battery is depleted. Furthermore, alternative device such as the Arduino Nano that consumes lesser power can also be considered so that the system power consumption can be further reduced. Finally, energy harvesting system can also be introduced to further extend the battery lifetime. With the help of energy harvesting system, ambient energy can be harvested and stored to provide an uninterrupted source of power for the sensor node.

CONCLUSION

The implementation of power saving schemes brings many benefits to users that want to deploy low power IoT applications. It helps the user to reduce the power consumption of all the connected components, especially when the system is idling. This in turn can reduce the system operation cost and extending the lifetime of the system. Results from this study shows that implementation of power saving schemes can significantly increase the lifetime by up to 55%. With the help of the high accuracy model developed in this study, users are also able to estimate the total battery lifetime of the system without the need of testing the system in real life. Hence, users can know when the batteries need to be changed before the system goes out of order. The insights from this study is applicable to any type of IoT applications, making it an invaluable guide for applications designers.

ACKNOWLEDGMENT

This research uses software such as Arduino, Fritzing, and DIGI XCTU under Creative Common License to illustrates on how to configure the sensor node.

REFERENCES

Atmel. (2015). *ATmega48A/PA/88A/PA/168A/PA/328/P*. Author.

BritannicaE. (2019). *Energy*. Retrieved from https://www.britannica.com/science/energy

Casilari, E., Cano-García, J. M., & Campos-Garrido, G. (2010). Modeling of current consumption in 802.15.4/ZigBee sensor motes. *Sensors (Basel)*, *10*(6), 5443–5468. doi:10.3390100605443 PMID:22219671

Cerchecci, M., Luti, F., Mecocci, A., Parrino, S., Peruzzi, G., & Pozzebon, A. (2018). A Low Power IoT Sensor Node Architecture for Waste Management Within Smart Cities Context. *Sensors (Basel)*, *18*(4), 1282. doi:10.339018041282 PMID:29690552

Consulting, T. T. (2019). *Building smart (IoT) solutions with M2M-A Developer Course*. Retrieved from http://consult-timmins.com/building-smart-iot-solutions-with-m2m-a-developer-course-kl/

CytechSmart. (2019). *Smart Home Automation*. Retrieved from http://www.cytechsmart.com/product/sensor_smokeSensor.htm

DIGI. (2019). *Customer Stories*. Retrieved from https://www.digi.com/customer-stories

Guthi, A. (2016). Implementation of an Efficient Noise and Air Pollution Monitoring System Using Internet of Things (IoT). *International Journal of Advanced Research in Computer and Communication Engineering*, *5*(7).

Hakiri, A., Berthou, P., Gokhale, A., & Abdellatif, S. (2015, September 16). Publish/subscribe-enabled software defined networking for efficient and scalable IoT communications. *IEEE Communications Magazine*, *53*(9), 48–54. doi:10.1109/MCOM.2015.7263372

Ibrahim, M., Elgamri, A., Babiker, S., & Mohamed, A. (2015). Internet of things based smart environmental monitoring using the Raspberry-Pi computer. *2015 Fifth International Conference on Digital Information Processing and Communications (ICDIPC)*. 10.1109/ICDIPC.2015.7323023

Jaladi, A. R., Khithani, K., Pawar, P., Malvi, K., & Sahoo, G., (2017). Environmental Monitoring Using Wireless Sensor Networks (WSN) based on IoT. *International Research Journal of Engineering and Technology, 4*(1).

Kelly, S. D. T., Suryadevara, N. K., & Mukhopadhyay, S. C. (2013). Towards the Implementation of IoT for Environmental Condition Monitoring in Homes. *IEEE Sensors Journal*, *13*(10), 3846–3853. doi:10.1109/JSEN.2013.2263379

LaurentPierre. (2016). *IoT Past and Present: The History of IoT, and Where It's Headed Today*. Retrieved from https://www.channelfutures.com/msp-501/iot-past-and-present-the-history-of-iot-and-where-its-headed-today

Sastra, N. P., & Wiharta, D. M. (2016). Environmental monitoring as an IoT application in building smart campus of Universitas Udayana. *2016 International Conference on Smart Green Technology in Electrical and Information Systems (ICSGTEIS)* 10.1109/ICSGTEIS.2016.7885771

Usova, M. A., & Velkin, V. I. (2018). Possibility to use renewable energy sources for increasing the reliability of the responsible energy consumers on the enterprise. *2018 17th International Ural Conference on AC Electric Drives (ACED)*.

International, W. W. F. (2011). The Energy Report 100% Renewable Energy by 2050. The Energy Report 100% [Gland, Switzerland: World Wide Fund For Nature.]. *Renewable Energy*, •••, 2050.

Zhang, G., Li, Z., Zhang, B., & Halang, W. A. (2018). Power electronics converters: Past, present and future. *Renewable & Sustainable Energy Reviews*, *81*, 2028–2044. doi:10.1016/j.rser.2017.05.290

Chapter 5
AI and FPGA–Based IoT Architectures, Models, and Platforms for Smart City Application

Bishwajeet Kumar Pandey
Gyancity Research Consultancy Pvt Ltd, India

D. M. Akbar Hussain
Aalborg University, Denmark

Jason Levy
University of Hawaii, USA

ABSTRACT

Anything that has an IP address is IoT-enabled. In this chapter, the authors have surveyed nine different IoT-enabled designs from IoT-based water management cyber-physical system (IoT-WMCPS) to IoT-based random access memory (IoT-RAM). They have also surveyed a platform called Quickscript. The Quickscript platform is used to develop natural language based IoT system. The nine different IoT-enabled designs discussed in this chapter are IoT-enabled bicycle called Mo-Bike, IoT-enabled house, IoT-enabled water utility, IoT-enabled mining, IoT-enabled healthcare, IoT-enabled frame buffer, IoT-enabled RAM, IoT-enabled key generator, and IoT-enabled wi-fi encoder. In cyber physical systems for water supply, researchers are able to integrate IPv6 addresses into sensors, actuators, and controllers used in water supply systems. The IPv6 address is integrating into every object available in the city so that researchers may track any object when need occurs. We may locate freely available IoT-enabled bicycles if we need to go anywhere, and we may also trace bicycles in case of theft by criminals.

DOI: 10.4018/978-1-7998-1253-1.ch005

INTRODUCTION

In this chapter, we shall observe the enormous consequences of the internet on our lives. We are linked with so many things that are already having internet connectivity and play a vital role in our lives. As well as the Internet has gained space in our everyday work, and we are, in a way based on it. With the emergence of AI and the internet of things (IoT), the concept of incorporating smart elements/devices in our daily life is a reality now. We are more connected, secure and advanced than ever before. There are multiple possibilities of IoT enable design. Some of these are: IoT facilitates Bicycle, IoT facilitates Coffee Pot, IoT enables Bank, IoT enables Camera, IoT enables Cart, IoT enables House, IoT enables Light Bulb, IoT enables Water Utility, IoT facilitates Car, IoT enables Police Emergency, IoT enables Travel, IoT enables Frame Buffer, IoT enables RAM, IoT facilitates Key Generator, and IoT enables Wi-Fi Encoder. These possible IoT enable designs are shown in Fig. 1. Not only this there are endless possibilities by virtue of IoT can shape up our lives.

Now, the world is adopting the internet of things (IoT) and has a remarkable effect on our routine lifestyle, especially in Water Management Cyber-Physical System (Pandey et al., 2018). This chapter is motivated by the IoT concept and discusses a way through which electronic devices and other equipment will get an IPv6 address to become IoT enable electronic circuits of Frame Buffer (Musavi et al., 2015), RAM (Moudgil et al., 2015; Moudgil et al., 2015) and Encoder (Singh et al., 2015) and Key Generator (Kaur et al., 2014; Kumar, Pandey, & Das, 2013). The chapter will also discuss the hope and prospect to

Figure 1. IoT Enable Architecture of Smart City

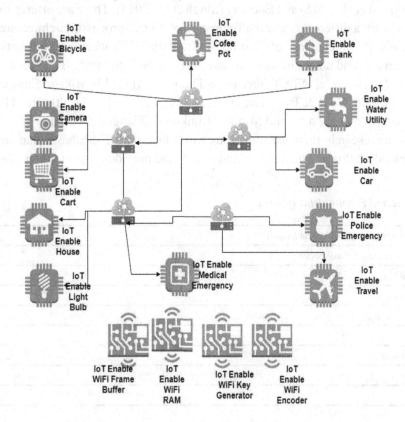

design IoT systems which is managed via natural language, with the help of Quick Script as an integrated development environment (IDE) (Khanna et al., 2016). The whole idea and motivation behind this chapter is to provide latest trends of the IoT, its background, it's possibilities in the future and the advantages and disadvantages linked with it. There is a vast scope in IoT that can lend us multiple job offers.

LITERATURE SURVEY

This WM-CPS is IoT enable because controllers used in WM-CPS always get a distinct IPv6 address for connecting with the internet (Pandey et al., 2018). As the future of the internet connectivity is IPv^ so the scientist all around the World had agreed to use IPv6 as a standard for IoT communication. Scientist analyses how few changes can be incorporated in the design of Quick Script (QS) and that result in uncomplicated and straightforward platform that leads to generation of natural language based IoT systems (Khanna et al., 2016). These few changes are simple and are easy to modify as compared to the old techniques that required to change the entire code even if any small error occurred. The researcher has inserted a 128-bit IP address in Random Access Memory (RAM) to make the IoTs enable RAM. Eventually, the researcher operated our IOTs Enable RAM with a different operating frequency of I3, I5, I7, Moto-E and Moto-X (Moudgil et al., 2015). In some other related work, researcher has designed IoT enables energy efficient and thermal-aware frame buffer to accumulate the frames and uses that frame to detect variation in object location. To make IoTs enable frame buffer design, the researcher is also embedding a 128-bit IPv6 address into the frame buffer. IoTs enable frame buffer design is controllable across the globe (Musavi et al., 2015). Researchers are making Energy Efficient Internet of Things (IoT) Enable RAM (Moudgil et al., 2015) and Encoder (Singh et al., 2015). There are efforts toward operating IOTs Enable RAM with a different operating frequency of typical processor architecture like I3, I5, I7, Moto-E, and Moto-X. Researcher also got inspiration from that IoT concept and presents a way through which electronic devices and other circuits can have a key embedded inside (Kaur et al., 2014). IoT has successfully applied in Bi-cycle("AT&T Internet of Things", 2017; "Mo-Bike in Europe", n.d.), Home Automation (Kodali, Jain, Bose & Boppana, 2016; Gubbi et al., 2013), Healthcare (Ukil et al., 2016; Kwon et al., 2016; Savola et al., n.d.) and Mining (Kunkun & Xiangong, 2014).

Whereas, in some research, there are numerous work done on IoT databases that are used for storing the data in a cloud platform, which is safe and secure and provide access to their clients at a remote

Table 1. Nine Different Application of IoTs

IoT Enable Water Management Cyber-Physical System
IoT Enable RAM Memory Design For Processor
IoT Enable Object Tracking
IoT Enable Security Hardware
IoT Enable Green Communication
IoT Enable Bi-Cycle
IoT Enable Home Automation
IoT Enable Healthcare
IoT Enable Mining

locations. Various cloud platforms such as Amazon Web Services (AWS), IBM Watson (Bluemix) and Node RED are supporting IoT based interfaces. These platforms not only provide easy access to their clients but are cheaper as well in terms of subscription that is mostly on annual basis.

Various companies are using cloud platform for the automation purposes for accessing and controlling various IoT based modules. Despite multiple security threats when it comes to the encryption methodology of the IoT connectivity, people are more and more relying on IoT modules.

The nine different IoT enable design discussed in this chapter are listed in Table 1.

Quick Script in Creation of Natural Language based IoT Systems

Researchers have discussed the likelihood and feasibility of IoT systems controllable with natural language and development platform called Quick Script (Khanna et al., 2016). Quick Script (QS) is free, easy to grasp i.e. made by a team of student developers of Chitkara University for programming virtual conversational system (Khanna et al., 2016). Their work discusses about how a few changes must be incorporated in the development of QS and that results in a deployable and straightforward architecture. They explore the platform required to create feasible policies. Their implementation reveals how the idea of turning a simple NLP tool for managing IoT systems, as shown in Fig. 2. The pros and cons of their works include sharing the power to control programming for end users (Khanna et al., 2016).

Figure 2. Conceptual Diagram for Natural Language Based IoT System (Khanna et al., 2016)

>> TURN ON THE FAN PLEASE
{ON} <fan_id>
>> TURN OFF THE FAN PLEASE
{OFF} <fan_id>
>> WILL YOU SWITCH OFF THE LED
{OFF} <led_light_id>

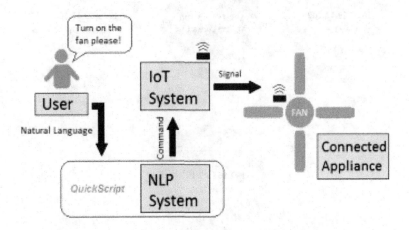

Direct Application of IoT in Smart City

Water Management Cyber-Physical System

Italian Researcher from Politecnico Di Torino and Gran Sasso Science Institutes have developed an IoT based cyber-physical system for water management (Pandey et al., 2018). As the water crisis is increasing day by day, a definite solution is required for managing the water related queries because we are running out of the clean water and if we didn't keep control of the water related issues than it might be too late. So therefore several systems are developed for the water management and one of the recent developments is Water Management Cyber- Physical System. It has four slave controllers and one master controller. They used a Wi-Fi router and gave the name of TP-LINK_807C to this router. They assign 192.168.43.100 IP to the master controller. They assign 192.168.43.102 IP address to the Slave controller at Lake water Tank. They assign 192.168.43.103 IP address to the Slave controller at Purifier water Tank. They assign 192.168.43.104 IP address to the Slave controller at Clean water tank, as shown in Fig. 3. They assign 192.168.43.102 IP address to the Slave controller at House Tank (Pandey et al., 2018).

Figure 3. Star Topology of the IoT Based Water Management Cyber-Physical System

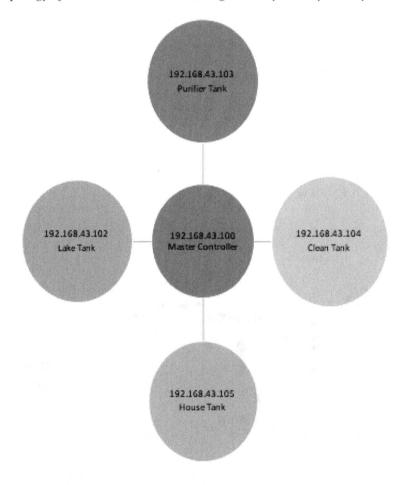

IoT Enables Bicycle

Mobike is the world's leading smart bike sharing service. Mobike is playing its bid for keeping the traffic related issues to minimum. Mobile has planning to use IoT solutions from AT&T and Qualcomm Technologies. They support its station-free smart bicycle in the U.S.A., Italy and across the globe ("AT&T Internet of Things", 2017). Mobike launched in Manchester. Manchester is the first city in Europe to get its new cycling scheme. Mobike has got enormous popularity in its native China as shown in Fig. 4 ("Mo-Bike in Europe", n.d.).

The motive of this service is to make people do exercise on the daily basis by using this services so that people can keep their health intact and by lowering the carbon footprint with the use of the smart bicycles.

IoT Based Smart Security and Home Automation System

When IoT is used for home automation, this concept can be aptly incorporated to make it smarter, safer and automated (Kodali, Jain, Bose & Boppana, 2016). The IoT project in (Kodali, Jain, Bose & Boppana, 2016) focuses on the making of security system by sending an alert to the house owner with the help of internet in case of any trespass and raises an alarm. In 2011, the number of interconnected devices on the planet overtook the actual number of people. Currently there are 9 billion interconnected devices and it is expected to reach 24 billion devices by 2020 (Gubbi et al., 2013).

Connectivity of such devices provide their clients with the sense of the security and a sigh of relief by using remote surveillance methodology that is so popularly been practiced throughout the World. Whereas, in the recent times, considering the latest development in the technology; it has become the need of the hour to make smart homes that are featured with automation for the ease of their clients so that they can lead a hassle free life.

Figure 4. The first IoT enables Bi-Cycle in the world ("Mo-Bike in Europe", n.d.)

IoT enables Healthcare

One of the critical infrastructures of IoT applications is healthcare as shown in Fig. 6 (Savola, Abie, & Sihvonen, n.d.). Long gone are the days when patients had to wait hours for getting an appointment with their doctors. Nowadays, telemedicine had changed the landscape of the traditional techniques that were previously used for the healthcare department. With the ubiquity of smartphones, cheaper storage, highly powerful edge-processors enable in-house, remote as well as preventive healthcare a near-future reality (Ukil, Bandyoapdhyay, Puri & Pal, 2016). Patients can easily access their doctors from remote locations and doctors can even operate sophisticated surgeries via surgical robots that weren't even imagined by anybody just a decade ago. In Kwon et al. (2016), IoT-based PHM for industrial applications is introduced and its opportunities and their challenges are discussed. There are many companies successfully implemented IoT-based PHM (Kwon et al., 2016). PHM consists of four dimensions: sensing, diagnosis, prognosis, and management, as shown in Fig. 5.

Figure 5. Four Dimension of PHM (Kwon et al., 2016)

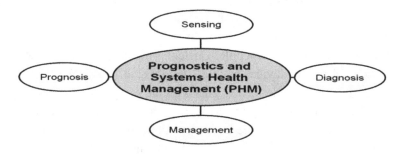

Figure 6. e-health IoT applications (Savola, Abie, & Sihvonen, n.d.)

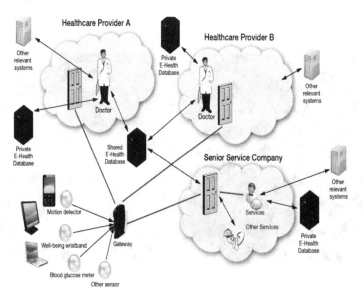

Figure 7. Internet of Things Enable RAM (Moudgil et al., 2015)

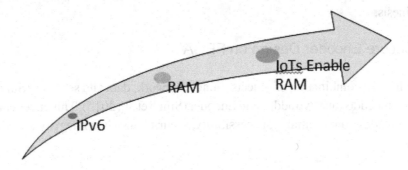

In-Direct Application of IoT in Smart City

IoT Enables Processor Specific Random Access Memory Design

Internet of Things (IoT) is a methodology in which living or nonliving thing or everything around get a unique IPv6 address. It is also the capability to send information over a network without human-to-human or human-to-computer interaction. This is revolutionizing the essence of how the Random Access Memory works. After embedding short-range mobile transceivers into devices and daily items, new forms of communication is emerging. They are using IPv6 for IoTs enable design and implementation of RAM, as shown in Fig 7. IPv6 address has a size of 128 bits. Therefore, we may allocate 100 addresses to every atom on the surface of the earth. There is plenty of IPv6 address, which we can assign for every RAM memory and make it IoT enable RAM (Moudgil et al., 2015; Moudgil et al., 2015).

IoTs Enable Object Tracking on FPGA

Researchers have developed IoTs enable energy efficient and thermal-aware frame buffer to accumulate the frames and using those frames to detect variation in object placement (Musavi et al., 2015). For IoTs enable design, a 128-bit IPv6 address is embedded into a frame buffer as shown in Fig. 8 (Musavi

Figure 8. IoTs enable frame buffer to store the image for active contour modelling (Musavi et al., 2015)

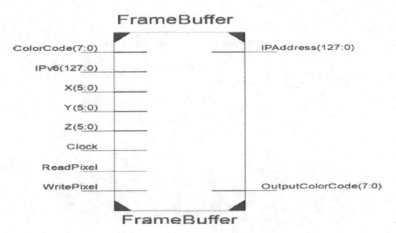

et al., 2015). Various online deep learning algorithms work similarly just like tensorflow and Amazon Web Services Kinesis.

IoT Enables Secure Encoder Design on FPGA

Fig. 9 shows that IoT is a combination of objects, things, network, data and services (Singh et al., 2015).

Researcher has embedded an IPv6 address in Encoder (Singh et al., 2015). This encoder is now network accessible. IPv6 provides confidentiality, accessibility, security and data integrity (Singh et al., 2015).

Figure 9. Short Description of IoT (Singh et al., 2015)

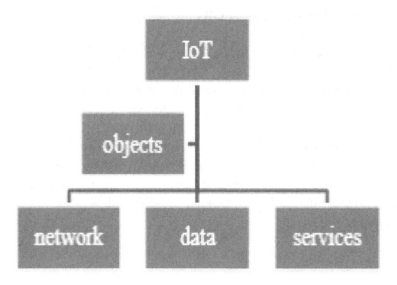

Figure 10. IoT Enable Encoder (Singh et al., 2015)

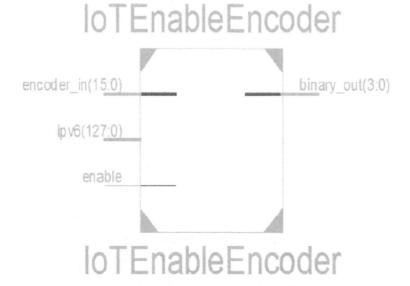

As shown in Fig. 10, encoder has 16-bit data input, 1-bit enable and 128-bit IPv6 address. This encoder encodes 16-bits information into the 4-bit encoded information. This IoT based encoder implementation was a part of real encryption project. When the researcher provides the production of this encoder into a decoder, the production of the decoder will be similar to input of encoder (Singh et al., 2015).

Internet of Things Enable Green Communication on FPGA

The key is a type of address for the communication device. To fulfill this task, researchers have developed a Fibonacci generator in Xilinx IDE. The Fibonacci Generator is power efficient. This generator generates the fibonacci number as a key for communication. The generated key will act as a code for communication equipment which will be well packed with the encryption standards (Kaur et al., 2014).

The fibonacci number 0, 1, 1, 2 generated at every clock pulse of 10ns as shown in Fig. 11-14. First number is generated at 25ns, second number is generated at 35ns, third number is generated at 45ns and fourth number is generated at 55ns. If we generalise this series then nth key will generated at $n*10+15$ ns.

Figure 11. Generation of First Fibonacci Number at 25ns (Kumar, Pandey, & Das, 2013)

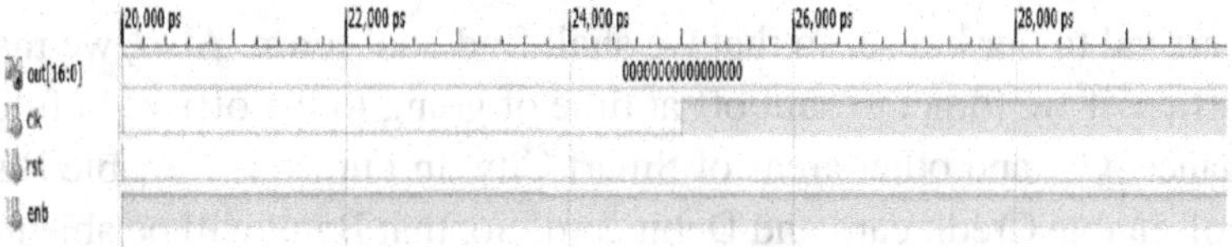

Figure 12. Generation of SecondFibonacci Number at 35ns (Kumar, Pandey, & Das, 2013)

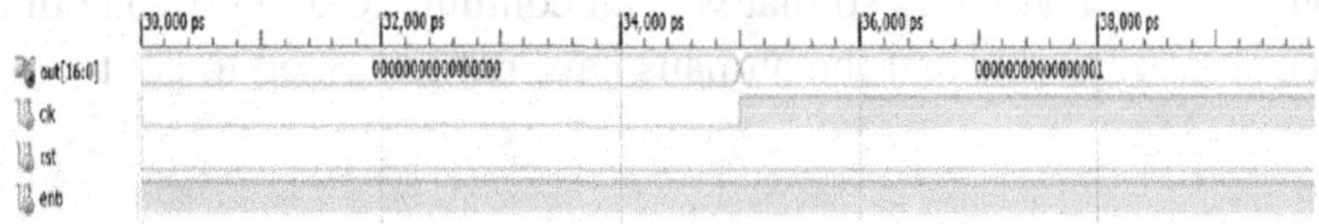

Figure 13. Generation of Third Fibonacci Number at 45ns (Kumar, Pandey, & Das, 2013)

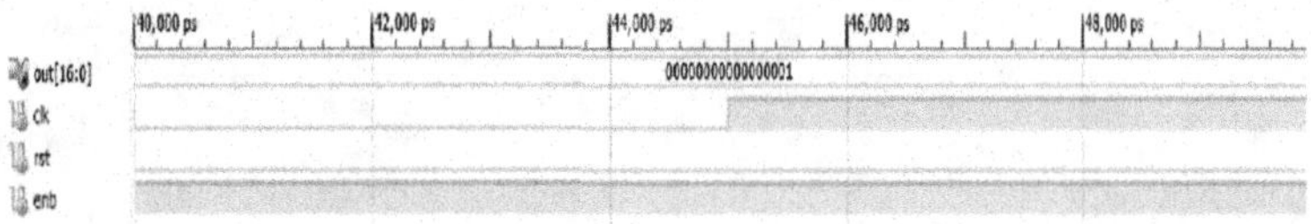

Figure 14. Generation of Fourth Fibonacci Number at 55ns (Kumar, Pandey, & Das, 2013)

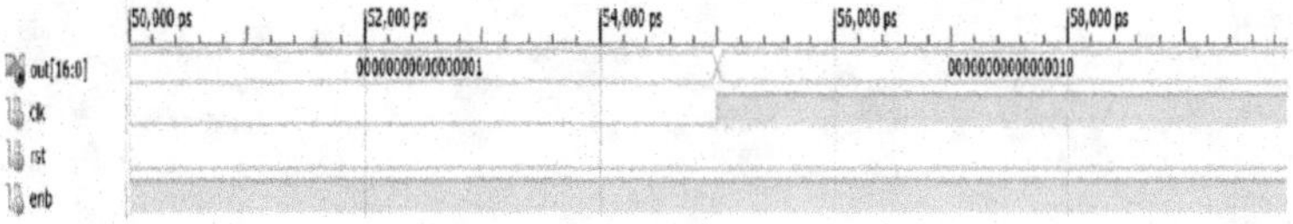

IoT in Coal Mining

In order to sense and control unavoidable circumstances of mining, the IoTs has been applied in coal mining. The safety in coal mine is dependent on the reliability of Internet of Things based coal mining (Kunkun & Xiangong, 2014).

CONCLUSION AND FUTURE SCOPE

We have discussed a new language called QuickScript, especially designed for IoT. We have also surveyed successful implementation of IoT in Water Supply System, Object Tracking, Security, Green Communication, Bicycle, Home Automation, Healthcare and mining. So, it is clear that there are vast endless opportunities of the IoT in the future that can shape up this world to be a better place to live in. Each and every field in the future will be linked with the IoT. Such as, in water supply system, researchers are able to integrate IPv6 address into sensors, actuators and controller used in water supply system. For object tracking, IPv6 address is integrating into every object available in the city. So, that researchers may track every object available in the city. After integration of IPv6 address in Bicycle, we may locate free available bicycle if we need to go anywhere, we may also locate bicycle in case of theft by anti social elements. After integrating, IPv6 address in air conditioner, we may be able to start our AC a few minutes before arrival to our house, so that we shall find cool room. Also, we may be able to close TV in house from office, if we forget to shut off at time of going to the office. In future, we may apply IoT in Banking, Finance, Car and other areas of Smart City. In Future IoT enable Banking, IoT enable ATM will support IoT enable Credit card and Debit card. So, that Bank will be able to trace where their issued card are present.

In short, IoT will simplify our lives and will save our time in such attention seeking activities that can ultimately lead us to focus on the next breakout things that can prove to beneficial not only socially and economically but also commercially so that we can continue to do good one this that we are good at and that is advance to new heights that the humans have not imagined to get to.

REFERENCES

AT&T Internet of Things Connectivity Increases Access, Lowers Environmental Impact and Enhances Transportation. (2017). Retrieved from: https://www.qualcomm.com/news/releases/2017/09/11/mobike-att-and-qualcomm-collaborate-mobile-iot-smart-bike-share-technology

Gubbi, J., Buyya, R., Marusic, S., & Palaniswami, M. (2013). Internet of Things (IoT): A vision, architectural elements, and future directions. *Future Generation Computer Systems, 29*(7), 1645–1660. doi:10.1016/j.future.2013.01.010

Kaur, K. (2014). Internet of things enabled energy efficient green communication on FPGA. *Proceedings - 2014 6th International Conference on Computational Intelligence and Communication Networks, CICN 2014*, 947-950. 10.1109/CICN.2014.200

Khanna, A., Das, B., Pandey, B., Hussain, D. M. A., & Jain, V. (2016). A discussion about upgrading the quick script platform to create natural language based IoT systems. *Indian Journal of Science and Technology, 9*(46). doi:10.17485/ijst/2016/v9i46/106917

Kodali, R. K., Jain, V., Bose, S., & Boppana, L. (2016). IoT based smart security and home automation system. In *IEEE International Conference on Computing, Communication and Automation (ICCCA)* (pp. 1286-1289). IEEE. 10.1109/CCAA.2016.7813916

Kumar, T., Pandey, B., & Das, T. (2013). Digitally controlled impedance based green design on ultra scale FPGA. In *2013 International Conference on Green Computing, Communication and Conservation of Energy (ICGCE)* (pp. 120-124). IEEE. 10.1109/ICGCE.2013.6823412

Kunkun, P., & Xiangong, L. (2014). Reliability evaluation of coal mine internet of things. In *2014 International Conference on Identification, Information and Knowledge in the Internet of Things* (pp. 301-302). IEEE. 10.1109/IIKI.2014.68

Kwon, D., Hodkiewicz, M. R., Fan, J., Shibutani, T., & Pecht, M. G. (2016). IoT-based prognostics and systems health management for industrial applications. *IEEE Access: Practical Innovations, Open Solutions, 4*, 3659–3670. doi:10.1109/ACCESS.2016.2587754

Mo-Bike in Europe. (n.d.). Retrieved from: https://news.microsoft.com/en-gb/2017/06/29/mobike-launches-smart-bike-share-service-in-uk-using-microsofts-cloud-service-azure/

Moudgil, A. (2015). GTL based Internet of Things enable processor specific RAM design on 65nm FPGA. *Proceedings Elmar - International Symposium Electronics in Marine*. 10.1109/ELMAR.2015.7334514

Moudgil, A., Garg, K., & Pandey, B. (2015). Low voltage complementary metal oxide semiconductor based internet of things enable energy efficient RAM design on 40nm and 65nm FPGA. *International Journal of Smart Home, 9*(9), 37–50. doi:10.14257/ijsh.2015.9.9.05

Musavi, S. H. A., Chowdhry, B. S., Kumar, T., Pandey, B., & Kumar, W. (2015). IoTs Enable Active Contour Modeling Based Energy Efficient and Thermal Aware Object Tracking on FPGA. *Wireless Personal Communications, 85*(2), 529–543. doi:10.100711277-015-2753-z

Pandey, B., Farulla, G.A., Indaco, M., Iovino, L., Prinetto, P., (2018). Design and Review of Water Management System Using Ethernet, Wi-Fi 802.11n, Modbus, and Other Communication Standards. *Wireless Personal Communications.*

Savola, R. M., Abie, H., & Sihvonen, M. (n.d.). Towards metrics-driven adaptive security management in e-health IoT applications. In *Proceedings of the 7th International Conference on Body Area Networks* (pp. 276-281). ICST (Institute for Computer Sciences, Social-Informatics and Telecommunications Engineering). 10.4108/icst.bodynets.2012.250241

Singh, D. (2015). Thermal aware internet of things enable energy efficient encoder design for security on FPGA. *International Journal of Security and its Applications, 9*(6), 271-278.

Ukil, A., Bandyoapdhyay, S., Puri, C., & Pal, A. (2016). IoT healthcare analytics: The importance of anomaly detection. In *2016 IEEE 30th International Conference on Advanced Information Networking and Applications (AINA)* (pp. 994-997). IEEE. 10.1109/AINA.2016.158

Chapter 6
Internet of Drones–
Enabled Smart Cities

Navuday Sharma

https://orcid.org/0000-0001-7371-0888

Tallinn University of Technology, Estonia

Maurizio Magarini

Politecnico di Milano, Italy

Muhammad Mahtab Alam

https://orcid.org/0000-0002-1055-7959

Tallinn University of Technology, Estonia

ABSTRACT

Unmanned aerial vehicles (UAVs) are expected to provide data service to users as aerial base stations, as gateways to collect the data from various sensors, and as sensor-mounted aerial platforms deployed in smart cities. The study in this chapter initially starts with the air-to-ground (A2G) channel model. Due to the unavailability of channel parameters for UAVs at low altitudes, measurements were performed using a radio propagation simulator for generalized environments developed using ITU-R parameters. Further, cell coverage analysis is shown with simulation results obtained from the ray tracing. Later, an optimal replacement to UDNs was proposed to support the flash crowds and smart cites known as ultra-dense cloud drone network. This system is advantageous as it offers reduction in total cost of ownership due to its on-demand capability. Further, work is shown on implementing parameters for 5G physical layer with generalized frequency division multiplexing modulation over A2G channel on the UAV network to provide reliable and faster connectivity for ground users and sensors.

DOI: 10.4018/978-1-7998-1253-1.ch006

INTRODUCTION

With challenges faced by today's cities in terms of sustainable growth and development, many cities tend to invest in research and innovation of Information and Communication Technology (ICT) and developing policies towards improving quality of life and sustainability. Internet-of-Things (IoT) can achieve this by creating and accessing bulks of data from the vast number of sensors and create new applications or services by post-processing of the data in the servers, thus creating an intelligent society and cleaner environment leading to smart cities (Ahlgren, 2016). IoT aims at enabling all the physical devices to be connected anytime, anywhere ideally to a centralized network and to provide any service, where the devices are equipped with a variety of sensors to offer different services. Further, interestingly from a technological perspective, Unmanned Aerial Vehicles (UAVs), commonly known as drones, can be integrated into the IoT infrastructure as Internet-of-Drones (IoD) in two possible ways as shown in Fig. 1:

1. UAVs sensor nodes: The UAVs equipped with a variety of sensors have the possibility to hover or fly over the required airspace, where data collection is needed from the environment. For example, air quality monitoring, temperature monitoring, precision agriculture, wildlife monitoring and remote sensing, etc. This data can be easily transmitted to the E-UTRAN Node B (eNodeB) or Long Term Evolution (LTE) base station.
2. UAV relays: UAVs can also be equipped with gateways, where data from various sensors or ground users can be aggregated and relayed to the nearest base station to be sent over the cloud server, where post-processing of the data can be done. This is useful mainly for scenarios such as smart hospitals, homes, industries, fleet management and health monitoring of swarm of vehicles where a large amount of data is collected from various sensors and can be easily transmitted to an LTE network via offloading to the UAV relay.

Such operations can be easily performed by UAVs due to their utmost capacity of hovering and flying close to the users and sensor mounted devices, which leads to an efficient and optimized way of data collection, aggregation and offloading, in case of heavy traffic of data from various use cases.

The contributions of this chapter mainly include the introduction to UAV based IoT platforms (Motlagh, 2017), known as IoD, equipped with different sensors and gateways depending on the use case

Figure 1. UAV architecture for IoT operations

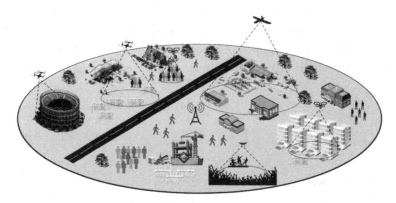

scenario. IoD provides organized connectivity in controlled airspace between the IoT sensor nodes and the cloud server, either when UAVs are deployed as relays or mounted with sensors themselves. IoD enables key performance indicators (KPIs) such as reduced latency and traffic load balancing (Fan, 2018) by exploiting computational resources of the UAVs towards edge caching (Cheng, 2018). Further, IoD also provides increased and on-demand cellular coverage (Zhao, 2018), (Sharma, 2019) encompassing a large number of users and sensor nodes. However, since UAVs are energy constrained devices, on-board processing becomes a challenging issue. Therefore, depending on the type of IoT sensor or gateway installed on the UAV, the requirement of Mobile Edge Computing (MEC) is addressed here to off-load the traffic. It also depends on various other factors such as UAV trajectory, underlying Radio Access Technology (RAT), such as LTE, WiFi, etc. Also, the selection of UAV (Motlagh, 2016) is an appropriate factor which is considered in this chapter, depending on energy, time and computational complexity for data processing and relaying. To accomplish IoD enabled smart city environment, various PHY and MAC layer issues are addressed and new system architectures and solutions are proposed. Further, future works and open challenges such as fronthauling, backhauling, energy deficiency, ABS simulator, PHY numerology, interference management, machine learning aspects etc, are provided to give insights into future research directions.

Background

Wireless Communication technology goes through a revolutionary change in every ten years. Each generation of mobile technology provides capacity enhancements to satisfy the vastly increasing data requirements of mobile users. This pertains mainly to the development of handsets or user equipment (UE) supporting high resolution video streaming, pictures, online gaming and other multimedia. Following this trend, the fifth generation of cellular technology, IMT 2020, commonly referred to as 5G, demands more data hungry devices and applications. In fact, 5G is not limited to mobile broadband but its usage patterns are also envisaged to support a wide variety of use cases in three broad categories:

- **Enhanced mobile broadband (eMBB):** eMBB is an extension of 4G broadband service to support high data rates and provide moderate data rates to cell-edge users while guaranteeing moderate reliability with packet error rate (PER) of the order of 10^{-3}.
- **Ultra-reliable and low latency communications (uRLLC):** The current 4G wireless cellular network have a latency of 50 ms which can go up to several seconds and target block error rate (BLER) of 10^{-1} before re-transmission since 4G is mainly targeted for broadband communication, unlike 5G. However, this service of 5G put strict constraints on round-trip latency of less than 1 ms along with ultra-high reliability with target BLER of 10^{-9}. This service targets applications with stringent latency and reliability requirements such as tele-surgery, intelligent transportation, industry automation, augmented/virtual reality, etc.
- **Massive machine type communications (mMTC):** This service is used to connect to a large number of IoT devices, which are sporadically active and transmit small amounts of data.

In order to accomplish these services, various 5G technologies such as denser multi-radio access technology (RAT), heterogeneous networks (HetNets), massive multi-input-multi-output (MIMO), millimeter (mm) wave signals, direct device-to-device (D2D) communication, full duplex systems, etc are being researched to enable the high-capacity mission-related data transmissions for rate-demanding applications. Integrating UAVs into 5G (and beyond) cellular systems is a promising technology to achieve such goals. Earlier UAVs were used mainly for military applications such as surveillance, reconnaissance and weapon delivery (Lyon, 2004). Later, its commercial use began with film-making, remote sensing and monitoring, goods delivery service, disaster search and rescue etc, (Hayat, 2016). Now its potential to be used as an Aerial Base Station (ABS) has been recognized by many companies such as Qualcomm, Ericsson, Nokia, China mobile etc. These companies have been performing field tests for handovers, received signal strengths, cooperative functioning in groups, autonomous control over LTE network. With interests developed to deploy ABS network, research began intensively towards assisting technologies and algorithms to support such system. Initially, the research directions were to work upon the transceiver design and channel models for ABS. Later, the research oriented more toward multi-tier ABS network to be integrated with a terrestrial network. Such enhanced interest towards the integration of UAVs into 5G cellular architecture provides the motivation to deploy ABS for IoD applications (Gharibi, 2016). However, in the development of smart cities, deployment of drones are subjected to regulations by the aviation authorities due to public and infrastructure safety (Vattapparamban, 2016). Further, there are many factors pertaining to deploy an IoD such as UAV flight, severe interference effects due to heterogeneous cellular infrastructure, UAV lifetime, energy efficiency, telecom operator support etc. Therefore, the efficient management of the multi-drone IoD framework is needed (Sharma, 2019).

ORGANIZATION AND CONTRIBUTIONS OF THE CHAPTER

Motivated with such profound interest of industry and academia, this chapter was developed to work on various aspects addressing ABS network with simulation and analytical results. The contributions of the chapter are organized as follows:

1. The contributions in this chapter initially start with the Air-to-Ground (A2G) Channel Modeling (Khawaja, 2018). Different approaches towards channel modeling will be described such as deterministic, map-based and hybrid (Nurmela, 2015). The relevance of each approach will be provided and map-based approach would be followed to accurately define A2G channel characteristics. Different large scale channel parameters, such as path loss (PL) and shadowing will be modeled. Also, the results would be mainly classified using the probabilistic Line-of-Sight (LoS) parameter, since UAVs have a higher tendency of LoS, varying with the type of environment. Many A2G channel models existing in the literature but since the work done here is to provide cellular network by UAVs, Low Altitude Aerial Platforms (LAPs) were preferred up to the altitude of 2000 m. Due to unavailability of channel parameters for LAPs, measurements would be shown using a radio propagation simulator for different environments: Suburban, Urban and Urban High Rise. These environments are generic since they are developed using ITU-R parameters for the simulator. Therefore, results from this simulator could be applied to practical environments (Sharma, 2018). The simulations would be conducted on 2.4 GHz to have an appropriate coverage area of UAV cell, which could include large amount of sensors and users.
2. Further, the work on cell coverage would be shown with simulation results obtained from the ray tracing simulator (Cileo, 2017). The results will be found with varying ABS fundamental parameters: altitude and transmission power.

3. Later, in this chapter, a new system was addressed as an optimal replacement to Ultra-Dense Networks (UDNs), to support the flash crowds events with large bulk of data arriving from the cellular users and sensors in smart city environments. This system is termed as Ultra-Dense Cloud Drone Network (UDCDN) (Sharma, 2018) and is used to offload the traffic to the nearest base stations and provide better throughput services to the users, without any delays due to large amount of data buffered on the network. Also, UDCDN is on-demand deployment system, *i.e.* it is deployed by the mobile operator only when required, based on the data traffic information obtained from the cloud. This system is advantageous due to its on-demand deployment by mobile operators, low cost and no requirement for site allocation, therefore it offers a reduction in Total Cost of Ownership (TCO) as compared to UDNs. The benefits and challenges of using such a system are provided in detail.

4. Further, in the chapter, work has been shown on implementing parameters for Low Latency Communication of 5G Physical Layer (PHY) on the ABS network to provide reliable and faster connectivity for ground users and sensors. Generalized Frequency Division Multiplexing (GFDM) will implement in the system model with Carrier Frequency Offset (CFO) for ABS downlink performance analysis, as being considered the suitable and compatible waveform, for LTE, LTE-A and LTE-Pro hybrid systems due to its backward compatibility with 4G Orthogonal Frequency Division Multiplexing (OFDM) systems. Also, parameters of low latency communication in LTE grid of 5G PHY would be used to infer tactile internet scenario. Later, various "Better than Nyquist" (BTN) pulse shaping filters will be implemented in the GFDM transceiver to obtain SER at optimal ABS altitude and show significant performance gains as compared to Nyquist pulse shaping filters (Kumar, 2016).

Issues, Controversies, Problems

Both low (LAPs) and high altitude aerial platforms (HAPs) are considered for proximity applications (Kong, 2011). However, UAVs such as quadcopters and small fixed-wing drones seems to be the only promising solution for LAPs, due to hovering capability and easy maneuverability which allows them to fly near the mobile users, the sensors placed in the environment and base stations, thus providing better services due to higher probability of LoS. On the contrary, large size airships or large drones have higher payload capacity but difficult to reach near the vicinity of ground users, sensors and servers (Sudheesh, 2018). Therefore, LAPs/UAVs were chosen for the simulations since they provide better flexibility.

However, to enable an IoD architecture as given in Fig. 1, there exist certain issues that need to be addressed:

1. **A2G Channel Model:** An appropriate channel model is needed which can provide an expected intuition of signal attenuation due to PL and multipath fading effects, due to radio propagation phenomenon such as scattering, diffusion, reflection etc. Although, the proposed ABS system is still at its infancy, there exist much literature of channel characterization. However, most of it is developed on real measurement campaigns but subject to certain constraints, explained later in this section. A survey on A2G channel modeling for UAVs is provided in (Khawaja, 2018), (Khuwaja, 2018). Much of the literature addresses the communication in two spectral bands, L-band (960-977 MHz) and C-band (5030-5091 MHz), allocated for reliable control and non-payload communication (CNPC) data links for drones, over near urban, hilly suburban, sea surface, mountains etc, with transmitter

and receiver link distance in the range of 1-19 Kms, approximately. Since realistic measurements were performed using a transportable ground transmitter and aircraft mounted receiver, the results provided are bound to be site specific and may not be feasible to be used in other environments. Further, many works in the literature address the use of new propagation models for A2G links. In (Afonso, 2016), authors perform statistical analysis over repeated measurements sets, providing received power and quality of service analysis, such as jitter and round-trip time, between a base station on building rooftop of height 11 m and receiver mounted UAV with a link distance ranging up to 3 kms, for different cellular technologies such as EDGE, HSPA+ and LTE. Also in (Simunek, 2013), statistical analysis of narrowband UAV fading channel in urban area to develop a time-series generator is shown, where an airship with on-board transmitter is flown over Prague city at an altitude of 100-170 m under low elevation angles with receiver, ranging from 1-6 deg. Reference (Yanmaz, 2011), models the downlink and uplink from field measurements in campus scenario and open fields. The KPI provided here were path loss exponent (PLE), received signal strength and throughput performance for different drone yaw angles and heights. Some studies have also been performed over A2G MIMO channel in (Willink, 2016), where authors' propose UAVs as a broadcast node and viable relay for high capacity communications. The measurements were carried out at an altitude of 200 m and 915 MHz frequency, for obtaining time varying channel characteristics with variation in velocity, elevation and roll of the UAV. Another, work on measurements is (Khawaja, 2016), for low altitudes of UAV up to 16 m in open fields at ultra-wideband to obtain stochastic PL and multipath channel model. Similar study is performed in (Amorim, 2017) for different UAV altitude of 120 m and 800 MHz transmission frequency.

All these major experimental studies have focused on developing appropriate A2G channel models to integrate UAVs into cellular networks. But there are certain limitations to these studies:

- The works are site specific (mainly suburban or near urban scenarios) and channel characteristics cannot be reciprocated for other sites easily.
- The measurement campaigns in city environments is not possible due to safety laws implemented by law enforcement agencies.
- The altitude for UAV flight are much lower, maximum up to 100 m approximately.

However, concerning the high data rate demands of flash crowds and on-demand UAV deployment, more investigation is required to come up with channel measurements. This can be applied to generalized environments, thus they can be fit in every scenario with minimal variations. Also, different altitudes of the ABS should be considered to find channel variation with respect to the height of ABS, which contributes to novelty of the system.

2. **Cellular Coverage and Capacity:** UAVs has gained substantial interest in research literature with the aim of getting an increment in cellular networks capacity and coverage area. Some previous work is available making similar analysis. In (Azari, 2016), authors provide the analytical solutions for coverage and comparison of sum rate and power gains of ABS with terrestrial base station using a generic channel model. However, they do not take into account fundamental characteristics such as, for example, PLE or shadowing. Here, verification of numerical results was not done using real measurements or by accurate channel. Similarly, reference (Al-Hourani, 2014) provides a formulation for obtaining LoS probability through ITU-R defined procedures and optimal altitude of UAV for maximum coverage area but without taking into account channel fading effects. In (Mozaffari, 2016), an optimal deployment of multiple ABSs has been proposed to cover the given geographical area using circle packing theory, with the constraints on downlink coverage prob-

ability, maximum coverage, and minimum transmit power by each ABS. In this chapter all these limitations are taken into account to provide more accurate results. Different types of generalized environments will be considered in order to get more realistic results. We also characterize A2G channel for these environments and take into account large and small scale fading effects in order to maintain high accuracy.

3. **Densification of the Network:** Due to the rapid growth in communication traffic due to eMBB and mMTC, the current macrocell network is becoming more tight and compact, eventually leading to small cell architecture or UDN. This is not just due to increase in number of users but also the data requirements, which are increasing manifold from high resolution devices, online gaming, video streaming and downloading etc. To meet these requirements, current macrocells are evolving towards multi-carrier aggregation, use of mmWave spectrum, and increased spectral efficiency, through advanced antenna solutions such as MIMO and Distributed Antenna Systems. However, the high maintenance cost and renting of a macrocell base station lead mobile operators to prefer the deployment of a UDN due to low power transmission and increase of capacity by efficient spatial reuse of the spectrum. However, major limitations of UDN are high signal to noise plus interference ratio, due to dense cell overlapping, large number of handovers occurring simultaneously, management of mobile-Xhaul, operator and vendor management, conflict resolutions between the service providers, etc (Yang, 2017). Here, such problems are addressed from a UDCDN architecture (Sharma, 2018).

4. **Waveform Design and Analysis:** Further, research on transceiver design with different modulation schemes and PHY numerology in UAV is limited. In (Wu, 2005) performance of IEEE 802.11a compatible OFDM for UAV downlink with large doppler shift and inter-carrier interference is analyzed. Reference (Blümm, 2012), address the waveform design on OFDM with customizable modulation parameters. The implementation was done on a self-designed hybrid software defined radio (SDR) platform, consisting of an FPGA (Xilinx Virtex 5) and GPP (Intel Atom), for a UAV acting as a relay between an unmanned ground vehicle and a ground control station. This area of work is complemented here in further section.

Apart from these major issues addressed in this chapter pertaining to each ABS in an IoD network, there exist a plethora of other problems pertaining to network and IoD framework management. Such issues are addressed and dealt in (Sharma, 2018).

SOLUTIONS AND RECOMMENDATIONS

In order to address the aforementioned limitations, this section explains and addresses the solutions for the transceiver design including channel propagation and information transmission. The simulation results are valid for every UAV in an IoD network to provide connectivity to the ground sensors and users.

1. **Close-In Reference Probabilistic Channel Model for Generalized Environments:** To address the issue of site-specific channels, generalized environments, Suburban, Urban and Urban High Rise, created on a design software according to ITU-R parameters, were used for ray tracing simulations as shown in Fig. 2. Here, in the simulation scenario UAV is static at the center with increasing altitude and constant transmission power of 18 dBm, while nearly 32,500 receivers are spread

on the ground covering the entire scenario, to acquire radio propagation at every point. UAV altitude with respect to the receivers are used as the fundamental design parameters for A2G channel model with KPIs as the large scale fading effects, PL and shadowing. Therefore, simulation results of PLE and standard deviation of shadow fading σ are shown. Further, LoS and Non-Line of Sight (NLoS) links were distinguished, which are other novel parameters for A2G channel. As seen from the preceding literature survey, the A2G channel for LAPs is different from the well-developed terrestrial and satellite communication channels.

Models for PL and shadow fading have been proposed in (Al-Hourani, 2014) for LAPs, as a function of the elevation angle. The elevation angle includes the PL dependence on both the transmitter-to-receiver horizontal distance and the transmitter height. Here, the Close-in (CI) propagation model, i.e., a standard approach for PL prediction that uses $d_0 = 1$ m close-in free space reference distance (Sun, 2016), is considered. The CI model depends on two parameters, PLE and σ. Both the two parameters are calculated as a function of the fundamental design parameter, transmitter height. Moreover, LoS and NLoS cases were distinguished according to the presence or absence of the free-space LoS path in the simulated link. This allows calculating the corresponding PLEs together with their associated LoS probabilities as a function of the transmitter height. Therefore, the prediction of PLE and standard deviation of shadow fading for LoS and NLoS was improved, bringing novelty to the work.

There have been several channel modeling projects such as Wireless World Initiative New Radio (WINNER I, WINNER II and WINNER+), Mobile and Wireless Communications Enablers for the Twenty-Twenty Information Society (METIS I and on-going METIS II in collaboration with 5G Infrastructure Public Private Partnership). Apart from these, there are several Millimeter-Wave channel modeling campaigns to support 5G users. METIS I addresses three different channel modeling approaches

Figure 2. Ray Tracing Simulation Setup for Urban High Rise Scenario

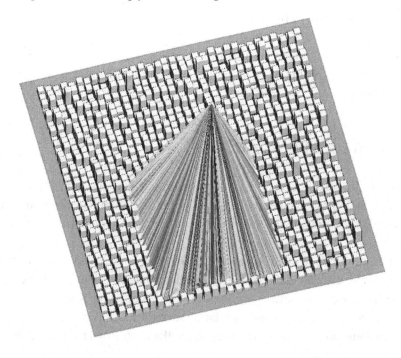

(Metis, 2015), which are currently followed by researchers and industries- Map-based, Stochastic and Hybrid. The map-based model is based on ray tracing simulation in a propagation environment, which inherently accounts for geometrical description of the environment such as building and terrain material with roughness and propagation mechanisms such as specular reflection, scattering, diffraction etc. This model provides realistic channel characteristics. The stochastic model is based on parameter distributions extracted from the measurements. The hybrid model provides scalable and flexible framework between map-based and stochastic approach. In hybrid model, large scale parameters (LSPs) such as PL and shadowing are obtained via map-based approach and small scale parameters (SSPs) via stochastic approach. Currently recognized channel models such as 3GPP/3GPP2 spatial channel model, WINNER geometry based a stochastic channel model, COST-259, 273, 2100 and ITU-R IMT-Advanced model, are based on stochastic approach and not sufficient to fulfill upcoming 5G requirements. Also, these focus on 2D channel modeling where only azimuth angular characteristics are considered, since the transmitters and receivers are at comparable altitudes. However, for an ABS, altitude becomes an important. Therefore in this chapter, a map-based channel modeling approach was emphasized instead of stochastic and hybrid, since previous experimental measurements do not cover a wide range of environments and ABS altitudes.

The large-scale shadowing PL equation is given by

$$PL(d)[\text{dB}] = 20\log_{10}\left(\frac{4\pi d_0}{\lambda}\right) + 10n\log_{10}(d) + X_\sigma,$$

where λ is the wavelength, n is the PLE, d is the link distance, $d_0 = 1$ m is the reference distance, and X_σ, in dB, is the log-normal random variable (Gaussian in dB) with standard deviation σ. Considering that for A2G communication in Suburban, Urban and Urban High Rise environments, increasing the height of the transmit antenna, the propagation characteristics result are much more sensitive to LoS and NLoS conditions. To improve path loss prediction a LoS probabilistic approach was followed, proposed in (Al-Hourani, 2014). Hence, the CI model and the probabilistic approach for LoS and NLoS PL can be combined as

$$PL_{LoS}(d)[\text{dB}] = 20\log_{10}(\frac{4\pi d_0}{\lambda}) + 10n_{LoS}\log_{10}(d) + X_{\sigma,LoS},$$

$$PL_{NLoS}(d)[\text{dB}] = 20\log_{10}(\frac{4\pi d_0}{\lambda}) + 10n_{NLoS}\log_{10}(d) + X_{\sigma,NLoS},$$

The average PL is given by

$$PL(d)[\text{dB}] = \mathbb{P}_{LoS} \cdot PL_{LoS}(d)[\text{dB}] + (1 - \mathbb{P}_{LoS}) \cdot PL_{NLoS}(d)[\text{dB}],$$

where $\mathbb{P}_{LoS}$ is the probability of having a LoS link (Al-Hourani, 2014), defined as a link where one of the paths is free space LoS, $PL_{LoS}(d)[\text{dB}]$ is the PL when the link is in LoS condition, with parameters

PLE, n_{LoS} and shadowing standard deviation, σ_{LoS}, and $PL_{NLoS}(d)[\text{dB}]$ is the PL when the link is in NLoS condition, i.e., there is no a free space LoS path, with parameters n_{NLoS} and σ_{NLoS}.

$$\mathbb{P}_{\text{LoS}} = \frac{1}{1 + p\exp(-q[\phi - p])}$$

is the probability to have a LoS link, being p and q the parameters of the LoS curve, which are related to the environment planning parameters, α, β and γ:

α = Ratio of land area covered by the buildings to the total area (dimensionless).
β = Number of buildings per unit area (building/ sq km).
γ = Variable determining the building height distribution.

The figures provided in this subsection, pertain to channel conditions for large scale fading effects for the ray tracing simulations performed on generalized environments as shown in Fig. 2. Figs. 3 and 4 show variation of PLE and σ with UAV altitude, respectively, for the three scenarios considered in the cases of LoS and NLoS links. For LoS links, PLE = 2 approximately for both figures, as expected from propagation theory, since LoS path contribution is dominant. In the NLoS case, PLE values shown in Fig. 3 range between 2.5 and 3 in Suburban and Urban environment but in Urban High Rise environment, instead, for heights less than 400m, PLE increases due to strong reflections from nearby tall buildings.

Figure 3. Path Loss Exponent vs UAV altitude

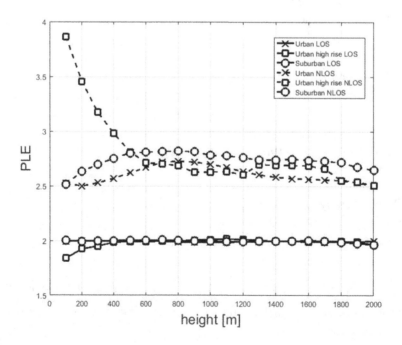

Similarly, for Fig. 4, σ is around 3 to 5 dB for LoS independently from the height. In the NLoS case, it varies between 10 to 17 dB and increase with transmitter height, showing similar values in both LoS and NLoS links. The standard deviation exhibit a clear trend for all scenarios. Standard deviation is higher for Urban High Rise scenario than Urban one because of the dense environment and tall buildings. Detailed results are highlighted in (Sharma, 2018) and (Sharma, 2019).

Further, here the receiver sensitivity was varied in ray tracing simulations (-120 dBm, -100 dBm and -80 dBm) considering the LTE standards in order to analyze the cellular coverage results in generalized city environments. Also, optimal altitude was obtained at a constant transmitting power 18 dBm of the UAV and variation of cell coverage shown with increasing power up to 46 dBm.

2. **ABS Coverage under defined A2G channel parameters from Ray Tracing**: For the coverage analysis, with respect to wireless communications, we consider it to be defined as the portion of the cell in which the received power of ground user or sensor is above the threshold, which is established by the mobile operator. Therefore, following (Richter, 2009), the cell coverage is defined by

$$C = \frac{1}{A_c} \int_{A_C} r \cdot P(P_{rx}(r) \geq P_{min}) dr d\phi \,,$$

Figure 4. Shadowing standard deviation vs UAV altitude

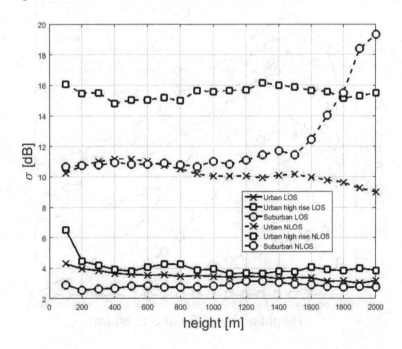

where A_C is the cell area of chosen radius 200 m, r is the distance between receiver and UAV, and P is the probability that the received power P_{rx} is greater than the threshold P_{min}. The value of the cell coverage lies in [0,1] and shown as a percentage in the simulation.

Similar to the previous simulation results, in this section results are provided for ABS cellular coverage by varying its altitude and transmission power for different receiver sensitivities or received signal strength indicator (RSSI) in various considered environments. These results indicate the number of drones that can be deployed by the operator in an IoD network to cover a specified geographic area.

From Fig. 5, it can be observed that maximum cell coverage increases with lesser received power threshold at the edge of the cell. In the simulation, the maximum coverage was obtained by setting the threshold to -120 dBm. Practical RSSI values were assumed as obtained in practical scenario to maintain the accuracy of our results. As the RSSI was increased to -80 dBm, the cell coverage decreases because less number of receivers fulfill the probability condition. Also, it was found that the optimal altitude of ABS for maximum coverage at 18 dBm was between 300-350 m for all environments. This was verified from (Mozaffari, 2016), where an analytical framework was used to find ABS coverage probability for downlink user. Lower ABS transmission power of 18 dBm was considered, in comparison to 46 dBm of terrestrial base station, because UAVs' are power constrained devices. However, with increase in transmitter power, the coverage is expected to increase as seen in Fig. 6. Finally, it was also analyze that cell coverage is higher for Suburban environment and lowest for Urban high rise for -120 dBm threshold. However, this trend was seen changing as the threshold increases, where Suburban has the least coverage than Urban and Urban high rise environments. This is because, in urban conditions, A2G channel experiences Rician fading due to the presence of LOS path. In suburban areas, a Rayleigh fading is experienced due to the presence of reflected signals that are stronger than LOS. This is opposite

Figure 5. Cell coverage variation with UAV altitude

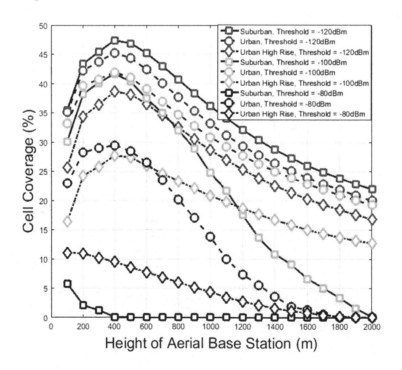

for terrestrial communication. Therefore, as received power threshold is increased, fading changes from Rayleigh to Rician in Suburban environments and vice versa in Urban. So, a generalized approach is to use a Rician distribution where both LoS and NLoS paths are considered.

As seen from Fig. 6, the cell coverage increases linearly with receiver sensitivity at -80 dBm but becomes almost constant at -120 dBm. This is because the receivers receiving -120 dBm are already receiving the least value of received power to maintain the connectivity with the UAV. Therefore, the receivers receiving lesser than -120 dBm are not present in the coverage area of the cell. Also, as expected the cell coverage is higher for Suburban environment than Urban environments, due to Rayleigh fading where multi-path and scattering effects dominate leading to constructive and destructive addition of received power with their phase and delay and therefore leading to higher received power.

3. **Ultra Dense Cloud Drone Network:** In this chapter, a novel idea of UDCDN is addressed, which can reduce the total cost of ownership (TCO) of the mobile operators. It could be argued that this is a timely and an efficient replacement for UDN in terms of on-demand deployment, energy efficiency, cost reduction and simpler network architecture with cloud-based and edge-based processing. However, some issues need to be addressed in UDCDN, starting from system design and technical aspects of administrative and legal ground for implementation. The motivation of this idea is to reduce the mobile operator's cost and radio resource continuous utilization by the real-time deployment of UDN using the drone-assisted network, while still meeting the cellular traffic requirements of 5G. Also, due to multitude of use cases of 5G, network slicing is a fundamental key aspect to be inherited with UDCDN. With powerful Network Function Virtualization (NFV)

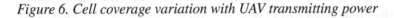

Figure 6. Cell coverage variation with UAV transmitting power

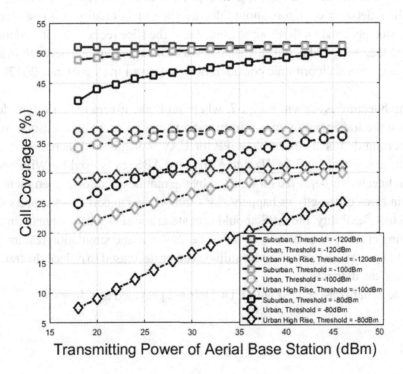

Figure 7. UDCDN architecture

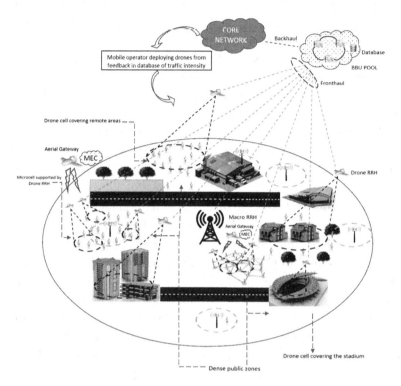

technology, quick deployment of network slices is possible with better management and utilization of resources to fulfill one-type-fits-all philosophy (Vassilaras, 2017). For employing UDCDN on a certain slice, network operators should decide slice functionality and resources, for example, processing, storage, bandwidth resources, etc. Then, the slice request is notified through a specific interface and therefore, embedding a virtual network into the physical network in an efficient way. On this aspect, several algorithmic considerations are given in (Vassilaras, 2017).

A UDCDN architecture is shown in Fig. 7, where multiple swarm of UAVs are deployed over an area depending on the traffic requirements from various mobile users and sensors. Since, there is no standardized spectrum that is allocated by 3GPP for UAV transmission, therefore, it was proposed to use LTE-Unlicensed spectrum at 2.4 GHz and 5 GHz for ABS, as is used by WiFi and Bluetooth devices. Such an architecture is deployed on-demand by the mobile operators, when there is a huge traffic demand in certain areas of the city as happens, for example, in concert zones, sports stadiums, public rally etc. Due to this flexibility, the ABS should operate at lower frequency bands in order to cover a vast cell area flying at an optimal height, as it will be shown in the simulation results. However, when there is the need to form a dense network, the altitude can be decreased to reduce the transmitter-receiver distance to increase the data rate.

Also, list of the benefits associated with UDCDNs are provided as follows:

- **Dynamic Cell Coverage Area:** Due to UAV flexibility, to hover near to the sensors and mobile users, and dynamic cellular coverage can be easily obtained depending on the UAV transmission power and sensor data rate requirements. This can enables a multi-tier IoD network also.

- **Energy efficiency:** Usually, UAVs do not require higher energy for signal transmission and can operate at lower frequency bands. However, higher transmission power and frequencies can also be enabled, if needed. However, usually, UAVs can fulfill the receiver data requirements by adjusting their flying altitude, thereby also the propagation attenuation.

- **Easy Deployment:** It is very simple to deploy UAVs currently, which are also now simple to autonomously control via LTE network.

- **Site Location:** Usually, in macrocell and microcell base stations, mobile operators need to find an appropriate site using cell planning and cost feasibility. Such cumbersome and time-consuming operation can be avoided, by deploying UDCDN when needed by the smart city environment or mobile users.

- **Cost:** The cost of UDCDN architecture is much less compared to UDN, due to much lower power requirements and on-demand deployment. Also, UAVs are solar powered and without any problem of site acquisition, TCO can be significantly decreased.

- **Data Offloading:** UAVs also can offload data to an LTE base station, if large amount of traffic is being generated by multitude of sensors or from high data requirements by mobile users. Due to the flying capacity, such an operation is much easier.

Further, there several challenges associated with UDCDN, which are provided as follows:

- **Interference Management:** Due to swarm of UAVs, trying to meet the data requirements of sensors and mobile users, there is a high probability of cell overlap and co-channel interference. To avoid such an issue, an appropriate trajectory planning and collision avoidance algorithms have to be implemented.

- **Drone Flight Standardization:** Currently, commercial drone operations for autonomous swarms are under standardization in different countries to ensure safety of the people and surrounding infrastructure in the cities.

- **Drone health monitoring and position monitoring:** To further ensure safety of people and also longer life-cycle of UAV, structural monitoring of various rotors, on-board flight management system etc. needs to be done.

- **Handover Management:** Due to dynamic cellular coverage and flight path optimization of UAVs to avoid interference and collision, frequent handovers of sensors and ground users is bound to take place. Therefore, efficient control algorithms have to be implemented to avoid such issues.

- **GFDM based ABS Transmission:** Further, in this chapter GFDM system model with low latency communication parameters in a LTE time-frequency grid with compatible transmission time interval (TTI) based frame structure (Simsek, 2016) is implemented. The transmission of multiple sub-symbols on the same sub-carrier in GFDM allows to reduce the number of sub-carriers as compared to OFDM based on the same TTI.

In this work, the GFDM system is implemented as given in (Michailow, 2014). The vector of $N = KM$ transmitted symbols is

$$d = \left[\left(\mathbf{d}_0\right)^T, \left(\mathbf{d}_1\right)^T, \ldots\ldots, \left(\mathbf{d}_{K-1}\right)^T \right]^T,$$

$$d_k = \left[d_{k,0}, d_{k,1}, \ldots\ldots, d_{k,M-1} \right]^T,$$

where $\mathbf{d}_{k,m}$ is the m-th sub-symbol transmitted on k-th sub-carrier and $(\cdot)^T$ is the transpose operator. The time-duration of each data block $\mathbf{d}_k$ is MT_s and the sub-carrier spacing is equal to $1/\mathrm{T}_s$, where T_s is sub-symbol duration associated with the data at the input.

The transmitted signal is modeled as

$$x[n] = \sum_{k=0}^{K-1} \sum_{m=0}^{M-1} d_{k,m} g_{k,m}[n], n=0,1,\ldots\ldots KM-1.$$

$$g_{k,m}[n] = g\left[(n\text{-}mK)\bmod N\right] e^{\frac{-j2\pi kn}{K}},$$

where $g[n]$ is the prototype filter, mod N is the modulo N operation, which makes $g_{k,m}[n]$ a circularly shifted version of $g_{k,0}[n]$, and the exponential function performs the frequency shifting operation.

The vector representation can be written by collecting the N samples of $g_{k,m}[n]$ in the matrix form as

$$\mathbf{x} = \mathbf{Ad},$$

where, $\mathbf{x} = [x[0], x[1], \cdots, x[N-1]]^T$, and $\mathbf{A} = \left[\mathbf{g}_{0,0} \cdots \mathbf{g}_{K-1,0}\mathbf{g}_{0,1}\mathbf{g}_{K-1,1} \ \mathbf{g}_{0,M-1}\cdots\mathbf{g}_{K-1,M-1} \right]$. Before transmission, a cyclic prefix (CP) of length N_{CP} is added to form the vector $\hat{\mathbf{x}} = \left[\mathbf{x}\left(N-N_{CP}:N-1\right)^T, \mathbf{x}^T \right]^T$. The length of CP is taken to be the same as the number of channel taps in our simulations. Transmission is done over A2G channel as described previously. However, here we also include multipath effects, which is usually modeled as Ricean for the A2G channel due to dominant LoS. The discrete time impulse response $h[n]$ can be obtained as

$$h[n] = \sum_{k=0}^{L-1} h_k \delta[n-k],$$

Where h_k is the Ricean faded k-th complex coefficient obtained from ray tracing data as $\mathrm{PG[dB]} = \mathrm{PL}(d)[\mathrm{dB}] - \mathrm{PL}_{\text{tot}}(d)[\mathrm{dB}]$ and L denotes the number of channel taps as given in Table 1. PG represents the path gain of each multipath component or channel tap and $\mathrm{PL}_{\text{tot}}(d)[\mathrm{dB}]$ is the total path loss including both large and small scale fading effects. At the receiver side of the GFDM, the length of CP must be higher than the maximum delay spread of the multipath channel, i.e, $N_{CP} \geq L$. Under these assumptions, the received signal vector after removal of the CP is

$$y = e^{\frac{j2\pi\epsilon n}{K}} Hx + w,$$

where $\epsilon = \Delta f M T_S$ is the CFO Δf normalized to the sub-carrier spacing $1/MT_S$., being T_S. the symbol interval and H a circulant matrix of size $N \times N$ based on the $N \times 1$ vector h whose first L elements coincide with the impulse response of the channel and the remaining $N - L$ elements are zero. The vector w is the noise vector of size $N \times 1$ in which each entry is an i.i.d. zero mean complex Gaussian random variable with variance σ_w^2.

Here, matched filtering (MF) receiver is considered. The equalized signal in time domain is

$$\hat{d} = B_{MF} y_{eq} = B_{MF} Ad + B_{MF} H^{-1} w,$$

where $B_{MF} = (A^H A)^{-1} A^H$ and y_{eq} is the equalized signal. The pulse shaping filter g[n] in the GFDM system affects the spectral efficiency and the performance. A standard approach for choosing the pulse shaping filter is to sample a continuous-time impulse response g(t) windowed as

$$g_w(t) = \begin{cases} g_{wdown}(t) & 1 \leq t \leq KT_s \\ g_{wup}(t) & (MK-K)Ts \leq t \leq (MK)T_s \\ 0 & otherwise \end{cases}, .$$

where g_{wup} (t)=g_{pulse} (t), g_{wdown} (t)=1-g_{pulse} (t) and T_s symbol interval, being g_{pulse} (t) one of the different types of pulse shaping filters reported below. we define the pulse shaping filters used for performance

Table 1. Power delay profile at ABS altitude of 500m

Suburban		Urban		Urban High Rise	
Delay (in ns)	Power (in dB)	Delay (in ns)	Power (in dB)	Delay (in ns)	Power (in dB)
1703	-50.5	1715	3.7	1759	113
1935	9.9	1737	-65.4	1942	99.1
2123	5.8	1752	-80.6	2293	85.2
2324	15.6	1784	-66.9	2307	78.9
2352	-12.4	2257	-26.6	2335	115.4
2504	27.8	2294	-4.1	2513	76.7
2627	-47.6	2321	-35.2	2676	47.3
2689	3.27	2524	-59.8	2723	42.4
2892	-28	2695	-13.3	2906	98.1
2911	9.3	2691	12.8	3005	130

Table 2. Parameters for GFDM simulation in LTE Grid

Parameter	Normal mode
Subframe duration	1 ms or 30.720 samples
GFDM symbol duration	66.67µs or 2048 samples
Sub-symbol duration	4.17µs or 128 samples
Sub-carrier spacing	240 KHz
Sub-carrier bandwidth	240 KHz
Sampling freq. (clock)	30.72 MHz
Sub-carrier spacing factor N	128
Sub-symbol spacing K	128
active sub-carriers	75
Sub-symbols per GFDM symbol M	15
GFDM symbols per subframe	15
CP length	4.17µs or 128 samples

evaluation with CFO in the GFDM system model. Moreover, we consider the time-domain expression that results by interchanging the independent frequency variable with the time variable for all pulse shaping filter.

Further, the performance analysis is shown in the simulation results to show the impact of CFO and specific pulse shaping filters, implemented on an ABS. The SER analysis was carried out using three BTN pulse shaping filters - Flipped-hyperbolic secant (Fsech), Flipped-inverse hyperbolic secant (Farcsech) and Reverse- Farcsech (R-Farcsech) in the GFDM system with variation in CFO and ABS altitude in different environments (Sharma, 2019). Also, low latency PHY simulation parameters are used as shown in Table 2, where the subcarrier spacing are higher and symbol duration are less, compared to LTE standards. The lower latencies would enable the drones in an IoD network to be exploited as MEC servers and provide faster services, either being data collection or relaying. The results are presented in two categories:

Group A: SER analysis with CFO variation for fixed pulse shaping filter and ABS altitude.

In GFDM, synchronization is a well-known problem, which happens due to timing offset and CFO. Here CFO is introduced in the system model to calculate the SER variation. The CFO values chosen are realistic, simply to show the SER variation in different environments. A base results without CFO is provided for comparison. In Fig. 8, SER analysis in Suburban is shown, where SER increases with the increase in the value of CFO. This happens due to the introduction of ICI between adjacent sub-carrier in all environments. A similar trend was observed for Urban and Urban High Rise scenarios in Figs. 9 and 10.

Group B: SER analysis with pulse shaping variation for fixed CFO and ABS altitude.

Further, the variation of SER with different BTN pulse shaping and RRC filters for "CFO = 0.1" and "ABS altitude = 500m" is addressed. BTN pulse shaping has been implemented, since it proves to provide a lower OOB emission and better SER performance as compared to Nyquist ones, as seen from Figs.11, 12 and 13. It can be seen that "Fsech" is an optimal BTN pulse shaping filter for the three considered scenarios with minimum SER. However, this is different from the case of Rayleigh fading,

Figure 8. SER analysis with CFO variation in Suburban Environment

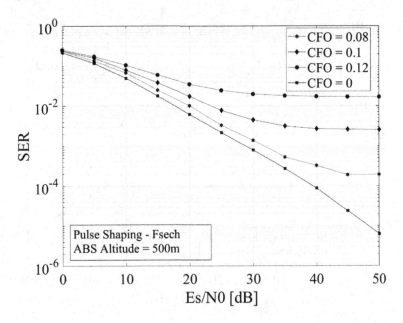

Figure 9. SER analysis with CFO variation in Urban Environment

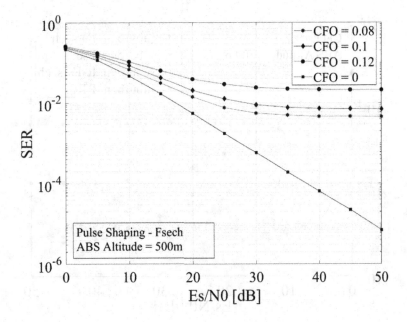

Figure 10. SER analysis with CFO variation in Urban High Rise Environment

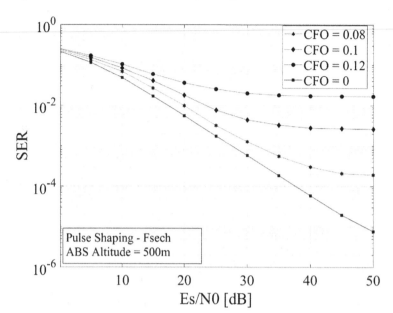

Figure 11. SER analysis with pulse shaping filters in Suburban Environment

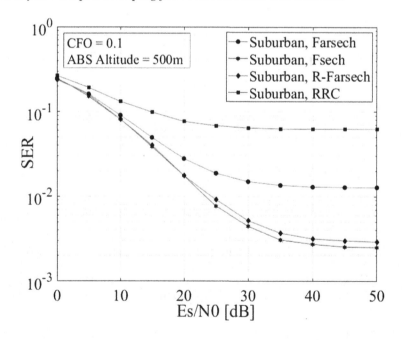

Figure 12. SER analysis with pulse shaping filters in Urban Environment

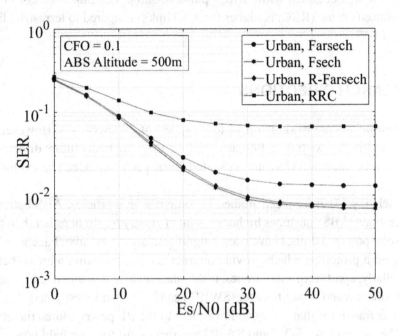

Figure 13. SER analysis with pulse shaping filters in Urban High Rise Environment

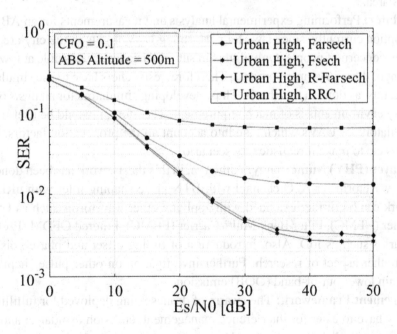

where minimum SER was obtained with "RRC" pulse shaping. The improvement in the use of BTN compared to root-raised cosine (RRC) is higher for A2G links compared to terrestrial links. This is due to predominance of LoS.

FUTURE RESEARCH DIRECTIONS

Presently, many researchers are working on various aspects of IoD networks. However, there is always room for improvement in the existing techniques. Further, there are many future directions in IoD, since it is a recently researched domain. Here are presented few aspects which can be explored further:

- **Energy Deficiency:** As it has been studied in some research articles, ABS battery is insufficient for long operations. ABS consumes higher amount of energy for flight rather than for transmission. Therefore, solar powered drones have been a significant are of research. Facebook's project *Aquila* have developed a prototype which provide internet access to suburban areas, being on-flight for months. Similarly, apart from solar drones, techniques such as stop and recharge and simultaneous wireless information and power transfer (SWIPT) can be further investigated. The benefit of using wireless power transfer is that ABS can hover near to the RF power source thereby increasing efficiency of the system since WPT and SWIPT are successful for near field power transfer.
- **Fronthauling and Backhauling**: For information transmission, from base band unit (BBU) towards ABS and from BBU to core network, techniques such as free space optics (FSO) and millimeter-wave can be investigated. However, some researchers also focused on tethered drones to address this area.
- **ABS Simulator:** Performing experimental analysis and measurements for an ABS network is not a feasible option currently, since laws for performing UAV flights in the city areas are very strict due to safety concern of people. Only flights in suburban zones are possible at lower altitudes. The development of these laws are in process. Therefore, researchers have to use simulators to get measurement results, as done in this thesis. Thus, developing simulators for analysis of such system in different city environments is of much requirement. Therefore, it would be useful to develop open source simulators for UAVs which take into account all the propagation factors, UAV maneuver, wind models etc to make it realistic city scenario.
- **Physical Layer (PHY) Numerology:** Although, in this thesis, work has been done on implementing GFDM waveform for A2G channel with BTN pulse shaping filter with uRLLC parameters, but this work can be further extended with applying other waveforms such as Universal Filtered Multi-Carrier (UFMC), Filter Bank Multi-Carrier (FBMC), Filtered OFDM (F-OFDM) etc in for other scenarios such as IoD. Also, introduction of timing offset and phase noise in this system model is another aspect of research. Further investigation on other pulse shaping filters can be done to obtain lower out-of-band (OOB) emission.
- **IoD Management Framework:** The swarm of drones being deployed for fulfilling requirements of smart city have to cater for interference management, collision avoidance and reliable control operations to accomplish the defines tasks.

Apart from these, other 5G technologies such as millimeter wave communication, HetNet interference management, Non-Orthogonal Multiple Access, Machine and Deep Learning approaches, Antenna

Beam forming and user equipment (UE) tracking can also be implemented for ABSs and better results can be expected.

CONCLUSION

To support a high density of connections by internet-of-things (IoT) devices and large bandwidth by mobile users, 5G wireless networks will be heterogeneous, being made up of both large and small cells using different technologies. Due to feasibility of Unmanned Aerial Vehicle (UAV), to hover near such devices, data collection and transmission can become a simpler task. Also, sensor mounted UAVs scan the environmental parameters and transmit the data over LTER network. This chapter is based on such motivation of internet-of-drones (IoD), which can be deployed on-demand by the mobile operators thus reducing the cost of operations as compared to a terrestrial network. Further, in this chapter, various technical aspects and research related to a UAV was studied.

Firstly, an appropriate channel model was discussed with suitable line-of-sight (LoS) and non-LoS (NLoS) probabilities, because obtaining a LoS for an ABS was much higher due to its flying and hovering potential. Later, a close-in (CI) reference path loss (PL) model was preferred as a suitable option for both LoS and NLoS channel of ABS. This was because most of the signal attenuation happens in free space for ABS. Therefore, an average PL model was defined and parameters such as path loss exponent (PLE) and standard deviation of shadow fading was obtained. This modeling was done using a deterministic approach rather than a stochastic one due to higher accuracy. The air-to-ground (A2G) modeling was done using a commercial radio propagation software, in which the environments: Suburban, Urban and Urban High Rise were imported and simulation was performed with receivers on the ground at different ABS altitudes. ABS altitude with receivers was chosen as a fundamental design parameter. Also, the environments were created on a computer-aided-design (CAD) software based on ITU-R parameters. Therefore, the environments developed were generalized, so that the results can be implied in any real city scenario with few degrees of inaccuracy.

Further, cellular coverage of an ABS with variation in altitude and transmission power was shown. The results obtained were plotted with respect to the ABS height up to 2000 m and transmission power up to 46 dBm, and an optimal altitude was obtained. The analytical expressions include all major design parameters required, such as, ABS altitude, transmission power, propagation factors and antenna gain.

Later, a novel system of Ultra-Dense Cloud Drone Networks (UDCDNs) was discussed to serve as a suitable replacement for Ultra-Dense Networks (UDNs). The major challenges and benefits associated with this system were provided against (UDNs). This system would reduce the total cost of operation (TCO) of mobile operators due to its *on-demand* deployment and lower operation cost.

Further, symbol error rate (SER) calculations for ABS with A2G channel was shown. The time frequency grid of LTE was used with low latency parameters with high signal-to-noise ratio (SNR). Also generalized frequency division multiplexing (GFDM), waveform was implemented due to its backward compatibility with orthogonal frequency division multiplexing (OFDM) system which would help the mobile operators to adapt to this new waveform. Further, "Better than Nyquist" (BTN) pulse shaping filters were used and better results than Nyquist filters were observed. Also carrier frequency offset (CFO) was introduced in the system model later to make the system more realistic and its impact was observed in the simulation results. Simulations were performed with variation in CFO value and pulse shaping in this work.

ACKNOWLEDGMENT

This research was supported by the European Union's Horizon 2020 Research and Innovation Program [grant number 668995]; European Union Regional Development Fund in the framework of the Tallinn University of Technology Development Program 2016-2022; and the NATO-SPS [grant number G5482].

REFERENCES

Afonso, L., Souto, N., Sebastiao, P., Ribeiro, M., Tavares, T., & Marinheiro, R. (2016). Cellular for the skies: Exploiting mobile network infrastructure for low altitude air-to-ground communications. *IEEE Aerospace and Electronic Systems Magazine, 31*(8), 4–11. doi:10.1109/MAES.2016.150170

Ahlgren, B., Hidell, M., & Ngai, E. C. H. (2016). Internet of things for smart cities: Interoperability and open data. *IEEE Internet Computing, 20*(6), 52–56. doi:10.1109/MIC.2016.124

Akram, A. H., Chandrasekharan, S., Kaandorp, G., Glenn, W., Jamalipour, A., & Kandeepan, S. (2016). Coverage and rate analysis of aerial base stations. *IEEE Transactions on Aerospace and Electronic Systems, 52*(6), 3077–3081. doi:10.1109/TAES.2016.160356

Al-Hourani, A., Kandeepan, S., & Jamalipour, A. (2014, December). *Modeling air-to-ground path loss for low altitude platforms in urban environments. In 2014 IEEE global communications conference* (pp. 2898–2904). IEEE.

Al-Hourani, A., Kandeepan, S., & Lardner, S. (2014). Optimal LAP altitude for maximum coverage. *IEEE Wireless Communications Letters, 3*(6), 569–572. doi:10.1109/LWC.2014.2342736

Amorim, R., Nguyen, H., Mogensen, P., Kovács, I. Z., Wigard, J., & Sørensen, T. B. (2017). Radio channel modeling for UAV communication over cellular networks. *IEEE Wireless Communications Letters, 6*(4), 514–517. doi:10.1109/LWC.2017.2710045

Azari, M. M., Rosas, F., Chen, K. C., & Pollin, S. (2016, December). Joint sum-rate and power gain analysis of an aerial base station. In 2016 IEEE Globecom Workshops (GC Wkshps) (pp. 1-6). IEEE. doi:10.1109/GLOCOMW.2016.7848947

Blümm, C., Heller, C., & Weigel, R. (2012). SDR OFDM waveform design for a UGV/UAV communication scenario. *Journal of Signal Processing Systems for Signal, Image, and Video Technology, 69*(1), 11–21. doi:10.100711265-011-0640-8

Cheng, N., Xu, W., Shi, W., Zhou, Y., Lu, N., Zhou, H., & Shen, X. (2018). Air-ground integrated mobile edge networks: Architecture, challenges, and opportunities. *IEEE Communications Magazine, 56*(8), 26–32. doi:10.1109/MCOM.2018.1701092

Cileo, D. G., Sharma, N., & Magarini, M. (2017, August). Coverage, capacity and interference analysis for an aerial base station in different environments. In *2017 International Symposium on Wireless Communication Systems (ISWCS)* (pp. 281-286). IEEE.

Fan, Q., & Ansari, N. (2018). Towards traffic load balancing in drone-assisted communications for IoT. *IEEE Internet of Things Journal, 6*(2), 3633–3640. doi:10.1109/JIOT.2018.2889503

Gharibi, M., Boutaba, R., & Waslander, S. L. (2016). Internet of drones. *IEEE Access: Practical Innovations, Open Solutions*, *4*, 1148–1162. doi:10.1109/ACCESS.2016.2537208

Hayat, S., Yanmaz, E., & Muzaffar, R. (2016). Survey on unmanned aerial vehicle networks for civil applications: A communications viewpoint. *IEEE Communications Surveys and Tutorials*, *18*(4), 2624–2661. doi:10.1109/COMST.2016.2560343

Khawaja, W., Guvenc, I., & Matolak, D. (2016, December). UWB channel sounding and modeling for UAV air-to-ground propagation channels. In *2016 IEEE Global Communications Conference (GLOBE-COM)* (pp. 1-7). IEEE. 10.1109/GLOCOM.2016.7842372

Khawaja, W., Guvenc, I., Matolak, D., Fiebig, U. C., & Schneckenberger, N. (2018). *A survey of air-to-ground propagation channel modeling for unmanned aerial vehicles.* arXiv preprint arXiv:1801.01656.

Khawaja, W., Guvenc, I., Matolak, D., Fiebig, U. C., & Schneckenberger, N. (2018). *A survey of air-to-ground propagation channel modeling for unmanned aerial vehicles.* arXiv preprint arXiv:1801.01656

Khuwaja, A. A., Chen, Y., Zhao, N., Alouini, M. S., & Dobbins, P. (2018). A survey of channel modeling for UAV communications. *IEEE Communications Surveys and Tutorials*, *20*(4), 2804–2821. doi:10.1109/COMST.2018.2856587

Kong, M., Yorkinov, O., Tran, T. H. V., & Shimamoto, S. (2011). Elevation angle-based diversity access employing high altitude platform station and unmanned aerial vehicle (uav) for urban area communications. *GITS, GITI Research Bulletin*, 3-12.

Kumar, A., & Magarini, M. (2016, November). Improved Nyquist pulse shaping filters for generalized frequency division multiplexing. In *2016 8th IEEE Latin-American Conference on Communications (LATINCOM)* (pp. 1-7). IEEE. 10.1109/LATINCOM.2016.7811588

Lyon, D. H. (2004). A military perspective on small unmanned aerial vehicles. *IEEE Instrumentation & Measurement Magazine*, *7*(3), 27–31. doi:10.1109/MIM.2004.1337910

Metis, D. (2015). *D1. 4. METIS Channel Models*. Author.

Michailow, N., Matthé, M., Gaspar, I. S., Caldevilla, A. N., Mendes, L. L., Festag, A., & Fettweis, G. (2014). Generalized frequency division multiplexing for 5th generation cellular networks. *IEEE Transactions on Communications*, *62*(9), 3045–3061. doi:10.1109/TCOMM.2014.2345566

Motlagh, N. H., Bagaa, M., & Taleb, T. (2016, December). UAV selection for a UAV-based integrative IoT platform. In *2016 IEEE Global Communications Conference (GLOBECOM)* (pp. 1-6). IEEE.

Motlagh, N. H., Bagaa, M., & Taleb, T. (2017). UAV-based IoT platform: A crowd surveillance use case. *IEEE Communications Magazine*, *55*(2), 128–134. doi:10.1109/MCOM.2017.1600587CM

Mozaffari, M., Saad, W., Bennis, M., & Debbah, M. (2016). Efficient deployment of multiple unmanned aerial vehicles for optimal wireless coverage. *IEEE Communications Letters*, *20*(8), 1647–1650. doi:10.1109/LCOMM.2016.2578312

Mozaffari, M., Saad, W., Bennis, M., & Debbah, M. (2016). Unmanned aerial vehicle with underlaid device-to-device communications: Performance and tradeoffs. *IEEE Transactions on Wireless Communications*, *15*(6), 3949–3963. doi:10.1109/TWC.2016.2531652

Nurmela, V. (2015). *METIS channel models.* FP7 METIS, Deliverable D 1.

Richter, F., Fehske, A. J., & Fettweis, G. P. (2009, September). Energy efficiency aspects of base station deployment strategies for cellular networks. In *2009 IEEE 70th Vehicular Technology Conference Fall* (pp. 1-5). IEEE. 10.1109/VETECF.2009.5379031

Sharma, N. (2018). *Increasing capacity of wireless networks through aerial base stations.* Milan, Italy: Politecnico di Milano.

Sharma, N., Kumar, A., Magarini, M., Stefano, B., & Jayakody, D. N. K. (2019, April). Impact of CFO on Low Latency-Enabled UAV using "Better than Nyquist" Pulse Shaping in GFDM. In *2019 IEEE 89th Vehicular Technology Conference (VTC)* (pp. 1-6). IEEE.

Sharma, N., Magarini, M., Dossi, L., Reggiani, L., & Nebuloni, R. (2018, January). A study of channel model parameters for aerial base stations at 2.4 GHz in different environments. In 2018 15th IEEE Annual Consumer Communications & Networking Conference (CCNC) (pp. 1-6). IEEE.

Sharma, N., Magarini, M., Jayakody, D. N. K., Sharma, V., & Li, J. (2018). On-demand ultra-dense cloud drone networks: Opportunities, challenges and benefits. *IEEE Communications Magazine*, *56*(8), 85–91. doi:10.1109/MCOM.2018.1701001

Sharma, N., Magarini, M., Reggiani, L., & Alam, M. (2019, April). Channel Characterization at 2.4 GHz for Aerial Base Station. In *2019 10th International Conference on Ambient Systems, Networks and Technologies (ANT)* (pp. 1-8). Elsevier.

Sharma, N., Sharma, V., Magarini, M., Pervaiz, H., Alam, M. M., & Moullec, Y. L. (2019). *Cell Coverage Analysis of a Low Altitude Aerial Base Station in Wind Perturbations. In 2019 IEEE GLOBECOM Workshops (GC Wkshps).* IEEE.

Sharma, V., Sharma, N., & Rehmani, M. H. (2019). *Control over Skies: Survivability, Coverage and Mobility Laws for Hierarchical Aerial Base Stations.* arXiv preprint arXiv:1903.03725.

Simsek, M., Aijaz, A., Dohler, M., Sachs, J., & Fettweis, G. (2016). 5G-enabled tactile internet. *IEEE Journal on Selected Areas in Communications*, *34*(3), 460–473. doi:10.1109/JSAC.2016.2525398

Simunek, M., Fontán, F. P., & Pechac, P. (2013). The UAV low elevation propagation channel in urban areas: Statistical analysis and time-series generator. *IEEE Transactions on Antennas and Propagation*, *61*(7), 3850–3858. doi:10.1109/TAP.2013.2256098

Sudheesh, P. G., Sharma, N., Magarini, M., & Muthuchidambaranathan, P. (2018). Effect of imperfect CSI on interference alignment in multiple-High Altitude Platforms based communication. *Physical Communication*, *29*, 336–342. doi:10.1016/j.phycom.2017.11.002

Sun, S., Rappaport, T. S., Rangan, S., Thomas, T. A., Ghosh, A., Kovacs, I. Z., . . . Jarvelainen, J. (2016, May). Propagation path loss models for 5G urban micro-and macro-cellular scenarios. In *2016 IEEE 83rd Vehicular Technology Conference (VTC Spring)* (pp. 1-6). IEEE.

Vassilaras, S., Gkatzikis, L., Liakopoulos, N., Stiakogiannakis, I. N., Qi, M., Shi, L., & Paschos, G. S. (2017). The algorithmic aspects of network slicing. *IEEE Communications Magazine, 55*(8), 112–119. doi:10.1109/MCOM.2017.1600939

Vattapparamban, E., Güvenç, İ., Yurekli, A. İ., Akkaya, K., & Uluağaç, S. (2016, September). Drones for smart cities: Issues in cybersecurity, privacy, and public safety. In *2016 International Wireless Communications and Mobile Computing Conference (IWCMC)* (pp. 216-221). IEEE. 10.1109/IWCMC.2016.7577060

Willink, T. J., Squires, C. C., Colman, G. W., & Muccio, M. T. (2016). Measurement and characterization of low-altitude air-to-ground MIMO channels. *IEEE Transactions on Vehicular Technology, 65*(4), 2637–2648. doi:10.1109/TVT.2015.2419738

Wu, Z., Kumar, H., & Davari, A. (2005, March). Performance evaluation of OFDM transmission in UAV wireless communication. In *Proceedings of the Thirty-Seventh Southeastern Symposium on System Theory, 2005. SSST'05.*(pp. 6-10). IEEE.

Yang, C., Li, J., Ni, Q., Anpalagan, A., & Guizani, M. (2017). Interference-aware energy efficiency maximization in 5G ultra-dense networks. *IEEE Transactions on Communications, 65*(2), 728–739. doi:10.1109/TCOMM.2016.2638906

Yanmaz, E., Kuschnig, R., & Bettstetter, C. (2011, December). Channel measurements over 802.11 a-based UAV-to-ground links. In *2011 IEEE GLOBECOM Workshops (GC Wkshps)* (pp. 1280-1284). IEEE.

Zhao, H., Wang, H., Wu, W., & Wei, J. (2018). Deployment algorithms for uav airborne networks toward on-demand coverage. *IEEE Journal on Selected Areas in Communications, 36*(9), 2015–2031. doi:10.1109/JSAC.2018.2864376

Chapter 7
Crop Health Monitoring Using IoT–Enabled Precision Agriculture

Uferah Shafi

National University of Sciences and Technology, Pakistan

Rafia Mumtaz

National University of Sciences and Technology, Pakistan

Syed Ali Hassan

ⓘD https://orcid.org/0000-0002-8572-7377

National University of Sciences and Technology, Pakistan

Syed Ali Raza Zaidi

University of Leeds, UK

Awais Akhtar

National University of Sciences and Technology, Pakistan

Muhammad Moeez Malik

National University of Sciences and Technology, Pakistan

ABSTRACT

Agriculture holds paramount significance in Pakistan due to its high impact on gross domestic product (GDP). However, there is huge gap between actual production and estimated production in agriculture due to manual farming system, which is time-consuming, inefficient, and labor-intensive. As of today, ultra-modern technology such as Internet of Things (IoT) can assist in acquiring timely and accurate crop information essential for the success of precision agriculture technology. Towards such ends, the

DOI: 10.4018/978-1-7998-1253-1.ch007

authors propose an IoT-based crop health monitoring system comprised of different sensors used in agricultural fields. Additionally, low altitude remote sensing platforms, such as drones, are used to capture the spectral imagery of the entire crop field of the study region. The development of such a system can be instrumental for crop status monitoring and localizing the areas under stress to maximize the agricultural output by leveraging the IoT technology.

INTRODUCTION

Food security refers to sufficient availability of safe and nutritious food to the human being. To maintain adequate food production for increasing population in the presence of climatic variation is quite challenging (McGuire, FAO, IFAD, & WFP, 2015). Although, agriculture is considered as a pillar of Pakistan's economy due to its arable land, covering several climatic and ecological zones, still Pakistan is unable to produce surplus yield (Yousaf, Zafar, Anjum & Adil, 2018). Despite of its agricultural land suitable for cultivation, there is a huge gap between the actual and estimated food production which attributed to multiple factors including lack of resources, poor farming practices, extreme climatic variations and technological constraints.

In Pakistan, multiple types of crops are harvested; most common are wheat, rice, sugar cane and maize. In (Aslam, 2016), a review of yield gap is presented between actual and potential yield. It is reported that the yield gap of rice, sugar cane and maize is 67%, 45%, 84% and 81% respectively as shown in Table-1. Multiple factors affect the health of crops including edaphic and climatic. Edaphic factors are related to soil properties such as soil organic content, soil pH, soil humidity, soil temperature and soil nutrients (phosphorous, nitrogen etc.). While climatic variations are related to the external weather conditions like change in temperature, humidity, rainfall, wind velocity, solar radiation, and atmospheric gases which have significant impact on crop health. Moreover, every crop requires different edaphic and climatic conditions suitable for its optimal growth which vary in complete life cycle of a crop. If a particular crop doesn't meet the required edaphic and climatic conditions, it will result in loss of potential food production. The technique of precision agriculture is widely used worldwide to enhance crops yield but Pakistan still relies on traditional farming practices and farmer's intuition.

Recently, several smart solutions based on technologies such as IoT are becoming common worldwide. However, Pakistani industry is slowly responding and adopting IoT technology for solving local challenges. The benefits of using IoT are automation of the system in such a way that it will produce sufficient yield with reduced human effort. IoT based systems are becoming more and more common due to smaller size,

Table 1. Gap between Actual Yield and Potential Yield

Yield tonnes / hectare	Wheat	Rice	Sugar Cane	Maize
Actual Yield tons	2.26	2.88	48.06	1.77
Potential Yield tons	6.86	5.20	300	9.20
Yield gap in %	67%	45%	84%	81%

low cost & low power consumption which make them suitable for different agriculture system (Mekala, & Viswanathan, 2017). Currently, agricultural activities like crop irrigation, crops health monitoring, pesticide spraying in case of pest attack, are all performed manually. These manual practices result not only in loss of food production but also in loss of crop organic content since farmer cannot localize the area under stress. For instance, in case of pest attack, farmers apply the pesticides on the entire field including the healthy areas as well as the affected crops. Same is the case with irrigation systems where excessive water than actually required is applied to the crop which may suppress the crop health.

Towards such end, we propose an IoT based crop health monitoring system in order to address the problems of traditional farming practices. The proposed system comprise of different sensors such as imaging sensor (multi-spectral camera) mounted on a drone for low altitude remote sensing, soil moisture sensor, soil temperature sensor, air temperature and air humidity sensors. All the sensors transmit data to the web portal, for processing data analysis, visualization and decision making. The relevant details are explained in Section-IV.

LITERATURE REVIEW

As of now, Pakistan agriculture system is still based on manual & traditional farming methods. Farmers today need to be well-informed about the crop health and must use technology based time efficient solutions to increase their crop yield. The precision agriculture technology offers real time and thorough crop status monitoring leading to the optimization of crop yield. For this reason, it is widely used and has become ubiquitous among the farmers from developed countries as well as developing countries (Zhang & Taylor, 2001).

Literature highlights various techniques that are used in agriculture worldwide for pest control and crop monitoring using ultra-modern technology such as IoT (Swain & Zaman, 2012). In Pakistan the technique used to control pests is the spray of pesticides and that too at times is over-sprayed or even the crop area not under pest attack is also sprayed which damages the crops. Worldwide, there is an increasing concern over the environmental effects of these pesticides. Due to several drawbacks regarding environment and human health, world health organization and pesticides action network banned it in several European countries. The majority of the vegetables and fruits available in markets are either deeply infected with several pesticides or are artificially grown using artificial ripeners such as calcium carbide and oxytocin respectively . An IoT based crop monitoring system is presented in (Suma, Samson, Saranya, Shanmugapriya, & Subhashri, 2017). The sensors used to monitor the environmental conditions are moisture sensor, temperature sensor and PIR sensors which is to detect the motion of people in the fields. Another solution for smart agriculture using IoT technologies is presented in (SAI, RAO, KRISHNA, & LAKSHMI, 2018) in which the main focus is the conservation of resources like water. pH sensor is used along with moisture sensor, temperature & humidity sensor. These sensors have been deployed in different locations across the field, the centralized module (Arduino Node MCU) controls the flow of water depending on the moisture level of plants, temperature, and humidity.

The optimization of resources is crucial in IoT based system including battery life time, delay in communication and etc. In (Sodhro, Pirbhulal, Luo, & de Albuquerque, 2019), a framework to provide high data transmission with longer battery life time is presented for smart city applications. In the proposed work, two cost effective algorithms were proposed for resource optimization named as 'HABPA' and 'DSA' which minimized the energy requirements. Moreover, with the rapid increase in IoT devices, there are numerous challenges in IoT based systems such as stable communication with minimum delay and power requirements. To overcome these problems, FoG Computing and Edge Computing are used which distribute the computation burden on edge devices (Baccarelli, Naranjo, Scarpiniti, Shojafar & Abawajy, 2017). In (Naranjo, Shojafar, Mostafaei, Pooranian, & Baccarelli, 2017), an energy efficient protocol is proposed. The proposed protocol divides the energy evenly among all connected fog devices in a wireless sensor network. Consequently, the life time of the system network is increased.

Water management is very important to grow healthy crops since shortage can destroy the crops health as well as excessive irrigation can damage the crop. A smart irrigation system using IoT and embedded technologies is presented in (Monica, Yeshika, Abhishek, Sanjay, & Dasiga, 2017). The hardware components of the systems are Arduino Uno, relay and pump, GSM module and WIFI module. The proposed system is able to control the water motor depending on the moisture level of soil and to control the quantity of water. Similarly, another IoT based system is proposed for crop monitoring and automated irrigation in (Rao, & Sridhar, 2018, January). Sensors are used to monitor the temperature, humidity and duration of sunshine in a day, depending on the values generated by these sensors, the moisture level of soil is calculated by the system which is later used to estimate the amount of water required of fields. In (Durga, Nalini, & M. Ramakrishna, June 2018; Surai, Kundu, Ghosh, & Bid, 2018), smart agriculture systems are presented using IoT. Soil moisture level is monitored using a soil moisture sensor. Systems intelligently decide when to water the plants.

The traditional method of monitoring of pest relies on the farmers experience, visual observation, intuition and periodical surveys that he has to perform over a widespread plantation (Azfar, Nadeem, & Basit, 2015). The fundamental limitations of these approaches are that they are labor intensive and time consuming, and the disease symptoms are only visible at an advance stage and could not be detected at an early phase. It would be of great advantage for the farmers to have a cost effective system for automating this task. The efficient and precise use of pesticides can be made by deploying sensors and image capturing devices in the crop field which are inter-connected via internet for appropriate decision making (Srivastavai, Chopra, Jain, Khatter, 2013). In literature several pest monitoring and control systems have been developed such as systems based on acoustic detection technology and wireless sensor network (Singh, Singh, 2016; Srinivas, Harsha, Sujatha, Kumar, 2013; Al-Manie, & Alkanhal, 2004). These systems incorporate the acoustic sensors which record the noise level of the pests and whenever the noise breaches a predefined threshold, they alert the farmer where the infestation is occurring. The energy consumption of such systems is very low and they offer wide area coverage. In addition to this, the farmer doesn't need to explore the entire crop region for pest and thus reducing the crop survey effort significantly.

There also exist systems which find the relationship between pests, inter related diseases and weather data using wireless sensor network. Several data mining techniques have been applied to develop a predictive model for pest detection at an early stage (Azfar, Nadeem, & Basit, 2015). Some developed systems only employ weather data to detect specific diseases at an early stage such as (downy mildew) in Grapes (Datir, & Wagh, 2014). There are solutions which are based on wireless imaging sensors for monitoring pest traps. These image sensors capture the images and send them to remote web portal with high temporal resolution thus enabling accurate monitoring of pest population (López et.al, 2012). There are prototypes which are developed based on wireless sensor network to detect pest at an early stage and additionally incorporates the air temperature observations to measure the spread of disease vector as the pest disease proliferate in warmer temperature. Once the temperature goes beyond a predefined threshold an alert was sent to the farmer to act accordingly. Alongside this approach, pesticides will only be used when it is absolutely necessary. The crop growers were able to reduce their pest control cost by 25% each season with this new system. A disadvantage of this method is the cost and time required to deploy the wireless sensor network across the crop region (Mauro, 2011).

In Pakistan, the monitoring of crop health is a key issue as significant amount of crop is destroyed every year owing to ineffective methods of pest control, irrigation, and application of fertilizers. The pest control is typically operated through recurring surveys by farmers coupled with commonly used techniques such as field burning, destruction of infected plants, air guns, hunting, poisoned bait, and poison spray etc. to protect their fields. Additionally, in order to maintain the crop moisture, the excessive water is applied to the entire crop without properly identifying the target areas, which may suppress its growth. All these methods are labor intensive and it would be of great advantage for farmers to have an affordable system of doing this task automatically. Based on the above review, we propose a crop monitoring based on latest technology such as IoT for reporting real-time status of the crop in order to response promptly in an event of crop stress.

The rest of the paper is organized as follows: Section-II of the paper discusses the related work, Section-III presents the factors affecting the health of crop; Section-IV indicates the proposed system while results of data Analysis have been discussed in Section V. The challenges are discussed in Section-VI and Section-VII concludes the paper.

Study Area: The study area is selected from field of National Agriculture Research Center (NARC) in Islamabad, Pakistan with particular location of 33°, 40' N and Long: 73°, 07' E as shown in Figure 1. The area of the particular field selected is 1.4375 hectare where wheat crop was grown. The climate of particular region is humid subtropical with an average rainfall of 790.8 mm with average temperature of 21.74 °C.

FACTOR EFFECTING THE HEALTH OF CROP

Wheat is a rabi crop which is sown in September-October and harvested in April-May. Several factors may influence the health of wheat crop including temperature, *intensity & frequency of rainfall, soil*

Figure 1.

properties which have direct impact on the yield. The growth cycle of wheat includes seeding, tillering, stem elongation, flowering, grain filling and grain ripening as shown in Figure 2.

Multiple factors are involved that effect the growth of wheat are following:

- **Temperature:** Temperature is considered to be the most important factor for the growth of wheat crop. Each growth stage has its own climatic requirements. In early growing stage, a cool and moist weather is required while heading and flowering stages require dry weather; ripening stages require warm weather. However, very high or very low temperature can damage the growth cycle of the wheat crop. The excessive cloudy weather with high humidity and low temperature may result in rust attack which ultimately affects the yield productivity. The germination stage starts from 95 to 110 days after sowing the seeds, during this time period, average temperature required is 20°C to 25°C. At the stage of grain filling, an optimal average temperature required is 25°C, high or low temperature can cause to depress grain weight. Similarly, ripening stage of wheat crop require an optimal average temperature of 25°C to 30°C. Table-2 shows the temperature requirements for optimal growth of wheat in different stages.

- **Soil Properties:** Soil types play an important role in holding the water content which define the requirement of water for a particular crop. The soil is classified into different categories based on the composition of the minerals, water content, organic matter, and multiple gasses which are present in the soil. The four main classes of soil are sandy soil, clay Soil, loamy soil and slit soil. The sandy soil is composed of rock particles having large spaces which cannot hold water.

Figure 2.

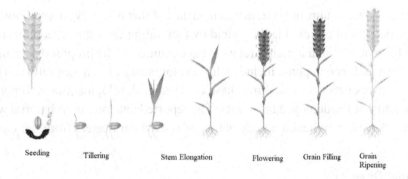

| Seeding | Tillering | Stem Elongation | Flowering | Grain Filling | Grain Ripening |

Table 2. Ideal Temperature Requirements for Wheat Crop

Sr #	Wheat Growth Stage	Temperature Requirements °C
1	Germination Stage	20 to 25
2	Accelerated Growth Stage	20 to 25
3	Grain Filling Stage	23 to 25
4	Grain Ripening Stage	25 to 30

Additionally, sandy soil has deficiency of nutrients which make it unsuitable for plant growth. The slit soil is composed of minerals and rock particles but these particles are much smaller as compared to the sand. This type of soil is considered more fertile which is mostly used to enhance the fertility of soil in agriculture domain. The clay soil is composed of very small particles which are packed very closely with each other so that there is minimal air space between these particles. It has good capability to store water which makes it suitable for plants growth. While loam soil is considered as the most suitable soil for plants growth because it poses all properties of sand soil, clay soil and slit soil. This particular type of soil has ability to retain the soil moisture and soil nutrients. It can tolerate the severe variation of temperature because it dry out and warms up slowly. So clay loams and drained loams are considered to be most suitable for optimal growth of wheat crop.

- **Rainfall:** Rainfall is another important factor that has direct influence on the soil temperature, soil moisture which may affect the health and growth cycle of wheat crop. The frequency and intensity of the rain are two important aspects while assessing the effects of rainfall on the crops. In Pakistan, rainfall is the primary resource of irrigation where the shortage of rainfall results in water scarcity which can affect the food production. The extreme shortage of rainfall may result in drought. Whereas excessive rainfall may cause to damage the crop as it results in soil erosion which remove the upper fertile layer of the soil. Thus, for optimal growth of wheat crop, rainfall with moderate intensity & frequency is required.

The variation in above factors may cause different diseases in the crops which is loss of production. The Table-3 shows most common crops harvested in Pakistan along with their common diseases:

PROPOSED SYSTEM

We proposed a crop health monitoring system based on the IoT that is widely adopted worldwide by farmers. IoT has the capability of optimizing crop yield by facilitating crop status monitoring via collecting data in real time to create optimal agricultural growing conditions. The proposed system is divided into four phases. The first and second phase includes the development of IoT nodes followed by the development of wireless sensors network. The third phase consists of development of web portal to visualize the real time telemetry of the deployed IoT nodes. The reported data on the web portal will be analyzed temporally to monitor the crop health and deviation of sensed parameters from the ideal crop profile.

Table 3. Crops and Diseases

Sr #	Crop	Common Diseases
1	Wheat (Bockus et.al, 2010)	Loose smut, powdery mildew, rust, flag smut, leaf blight, seeding blight
2	Rice (Khush, 1977)	Bacterial blight, brown spots, false smut, rice ragged stunt, sheath rot, rice stripe
3	Maize (Long & Hensley, 1972)	Corn fungal, corn rust, downy mildew, giberrella stalk & ear rot, leaf blight
4	Sugar Cane (Payak, & Sharma, 1985)	Sugar cane eyespot, leaf scald, ring spot, ratoon stunting

The fourth phase includes the capturing of spectral data using drone. The spectral images are used for NDVI mapping to monitor the crop health. The NDVI mapped images and the corresponding spectra & optical imagery are then uploaded on the web portal for further analysis. The system architectural diagram is shown in Figure 3.

1. Phase -1 Development of IoT Nodes:

    Every IoT node consists of the following components as described below and shown in Figure 4.

- **Arduino UNO & Arduino Mega Board:** These are micro-controllers based on ATmega328. All sensors are connected with this board which further collect the data and transmit it to the web portal. Additionally, it is responsible for all communication among the nodes i.e. 1)- Communication among slave nodes and master nodes, 2)-Communication between master node and web portal.

Figure 3.

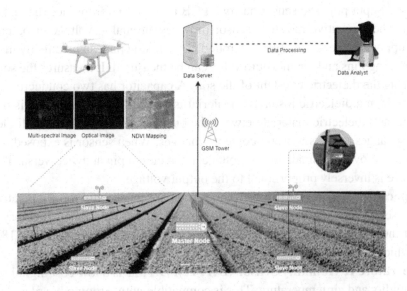

Figure 4.

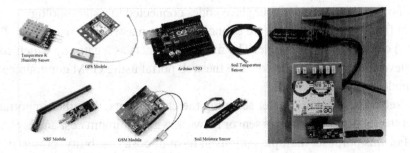

- **GSM Module (AI thinker A7):** The master node collect the data from the salve nodes and transmit it to the web portal using GSM communication module. In proposed system, AI thinker A7 GSM module is used due to its low cost and reliable communication.

- **NRF Module:** For communication, NRF24L01+PA+LNA is used. The selection of the module is based on the pre-analysis of different wireless module. NRF are preferred due to its low cost and high performance in short range communication. It works on the Industrial, Scientific and Medical (ISM) band which is 2.4GHz. This band is used internationally for unlicensed low power devices. The modulation technique of this module is Gaussian frequency-shift keying (GFSK). The NRF24Lo1+ use Enhanced ShockBurst protocol for communication. It enables the improvement of power efficiency for the uni-directional and bi-directional system. This protocol is controlled by the NRF24 without adding the complexity on the host controller side. Using this protocol, it is feasible to configure the maximum number of the delay in packet transmission without intervention of host micro controller.

- **GPS Module (NEO-6M):** The GPS module is used to fetch the location of the wireless nodes. It can track up to 22 satellites on 50 channels. It has the sensitivity level of -161 dB tracking while consuming 45mA.

- **Capacitive Soil Moisture Sensor:** The capacitive moisture is a single sided Surface Mount Device (SMD) consisting of only one module. The sensor has three pins i.e. power (3.3v – 5v), Ground and Analog Output pin. The sensor has two PCB traces on its front face that act as two plates of capacitors. The capacitive moisture sensor provides an analog voltage at output pin anywhere between supply voltage (e.g. 3.3v) and ground. This analog pin can be directly interfaced with the Arduino Analog Pins and the moisture value can be measured. It measures the soil water contents by measuring the dielectric constant of the soil. A capacitor has two conductive metal plates and in between them a dielectric insulating material is placed. When the sensor is inserted into soil, the soil acts as a dielectric material between the plates of the capacitor. The di-electric properties of the soil changes as the soil water contents changes. When sensor is exposed to a large amount of moisture, it provides a small analog voltage at the output pin and vice-versa. The amount of the soil moisture is inversely proportional to the output voltage.

- **Soil Temperature Sensor (DS18B20):** The particular sensor sense the temperature and using the one wire it send back the value in fraction in Celsius. It contains its own memory and mechanism to convert the reading to the Celsius. The operating Temperature range of DS18B20 is -55°C to +125°C which has the accuracy of ±0.5°C over the range of -10°C to +85°C.

- **Air Temperature & Humidity Sensor (DHT11):** DHT11 is a low cost digital sensor to capture the air humidity and air temperature. This is compatible with Arduino board and provides humidity and temperature status of air with reasonable accuracy.

    2. **Phase-II Development of Wireless Sensor Network:** A cluster of wireless nodes comprising of one master node and four slave nodes connected in a star topology is deployed into the wheat fields. The slave nodes are connected to the master node using Near Radio Frequency (NRF) communication module. The master node acts as a gateway which collects data from the slaves node and send this data to the web portal using GSM communication technology. All nodes are solar powered.

- **Wireless Network Topology:** After selecting the components, the other important consideration is to select the topology of wireless sensor network with minimum cost and high reliable communication. For this purpose, multiple options in term of cost, reliability, power and scalability and tradeoff between the parameters that fits in our particular scenario were considered. One possible option is to make every single node independent and collect the data and send it to the web portal but it is not cost effective solution since we need to provide internet connectivity to each node.

After performing multiple experiments, we found that star topology for wireless communication of nodes would be a cost effective solution. Although star topology is considered to be unreliable because of single point of failure, but it provides stable communication with reduced cost. Every node collects the data and sends it to the single master node. The slave nodes are 75 meters apart from each other and 35 meters far from master node. The master node collects the data from other slave nodes and transmits the data to the web portal as shown in Figure 5.

- **Wireless Communication Setup and Evaluation:** For wireless communication, two communication modules are used (i) GSM, and (ii)NRF. The GSM module provides a standard communication link that is acknowledged worldwide by using a SIM Card. GSM is used by master node to transmit data to the web portal. Our main communication module is NRF.

For testing the performance of NRF communication modules, a pair of wireless transceiver system are designed so that both can communicate and acknowledge each other as shown in Figure6 where '*h*' denotes the height of the particular wireless node from ground level where '*d*' is the distance between two wireless nodes. The height has the direct relation with the communication distance i.e. higher alti-

Figure 5.

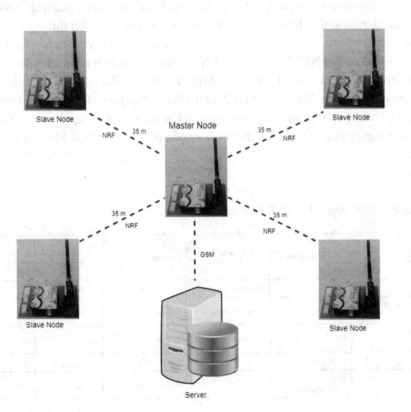

Figure 6.

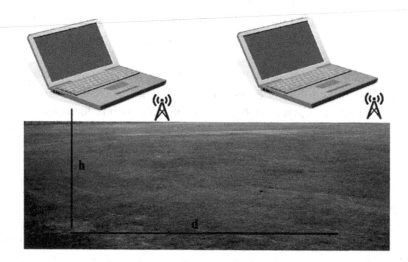

tude achieves longer distance. The range tests were conducted in open air and in the closed environment such as "inside building".

Multiple experiments were performed to test different communication modules against communication range, throughput, underground communication and power consumption as shown in Table-4. It is observed that RF433MHZ has very high packet drop at a mere distance of 20m. Moreover, it is unidirectional so it cannot be used in our particular application. The module HC-12 can be easily integrated with the system and consumes less power. While the NRF24L01 perform relatively good in comparison to other communication modules. It provides multi-channel supports, higher throughput and Long-Range communication with low cost. NRF24L01 exists mainly in two variants i.e. one is NRF24L01 and other is NRF24L01+PA+LNA. The NRF24L01+PA+LNA comes with the special RFX2401C with integrated PA (Power Amplification) and LNA (Low Noise Amplification). NRF24L01 with printed antenna gives the 100meter range in open air. Whereas, NRF24L01+PA+LNA provides increased range and stability. Finally, NRF24L01 was found promising communication module among all other. The final design is based on NRF as an inter-communication device between nodes and GSM Module is used to send data to Web portal.

Table 4. Communication Setup for NRF Module

Sr #	Module	Interface Protocol	Communication Protocol	Communication Type	Channels Support	Distance ('d') Measurements (m)	
						Open Air	Underground
1	NRF24L01	SPI	Enhanced ShockBurst	Bi-Directional	100+	25	2 – 4
2	NRF24L01+PA+LNA (Without Base)	SPI	Enhanced ShockBurst	Bi-Directional	100+	350	5 – 7
3	NRF24L01+PA+LNA (Base Module)	SPI	Enhanced ShockBurst	Bi-Directional	100+	600+	5 – 8
4	RF 433MHz	No Protocol	-	Uni-Directional	16	20	4 - 6
5	HC – 12	Serial Communication	-	Bi-Directional	100+	120	5 - 10

After selecting the components and network topology, IoT nodes were developed and deployed across NARC fields as shown in Figure 7.

3. **Phase -III Development of web portal for data visualization**: A web portal is developed for visualization of the recorded IoT sensors data and NDVI mapping. The system development started during November 2018 but the deployment of the system completed during March 2019. Hence, the entire crop cycle was not covered and data was collected from March 2019 to May 2019 (grain filling stage to grain ripening stage). Since, IoT nodes are connected in a star topology, the slave nodes send the data to the master node which transmit the data after every five minutes to the web portal using HTTP get request. At the web portal end, these values are processed to remove any invalid values. The values are then stored in a MySQL database on the web portal. After data acquisition, data is visualized into a tabular form and in the form of graphs using 'chart-js' and 'flot-charts' libraries. The four vital parameters are being analyzed which include soil temperature, soil moisture, air temperature and air humidity level. The snapshot of web portal is shown in Figure 8.

4. **Phase-IV NDVI Mapping for Crop Health Monitoring:** The multi-spectral images are collected by drone with multi-spectral camera mounted on it. For this purpose, DJI Phantom-4 Advanced drone is used which has only optical camera. To obtain multi-spectral imagery, a separate multi-spectral camera "Sentera Single sensor" is mounted on to the DJI platform to take imagery in Red, and NIR spectral bands. Figure 9-A shows the drone with multi-spectral camera, while Figure 9-B shows the drone taking fight in NARC fields to capture multi-spectral images.

Due to security concerns in the territory of the capital of Pakistan, the drone cannot be flown very frequently to obtain spectral images. Hence the spectral images were captured twice in a month starting from April 2019 to May 2019. These images were further analyzed for NDVI mapping to monitor the crop health. NDVI value ranges from -1 to 1 where 1 represents high chlorophyll content in the crop and a value below 0 indicates very small chlorophyll content (Mahajan, & Bundel, 2017). For NDVI mapping, we extracted the NDVI and Red-light bands from the image taken by the NIR single sensor. The image taken by this sensor consists of red-light and NIR light in the first channel where the third channel contains only NIR light. For NDVI computation, we subtracted the third channel from the first channel to get the red-light as illustrated in Eq-1 (Oliver, 2010).

Figure 7.

Figure 8.

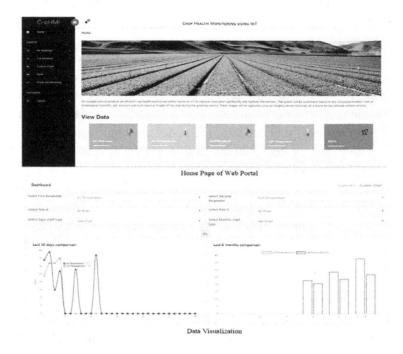

Home Page of Web Portal

Data Visualization

Figure 9.

Where, Ch1 and Ch3 are the pixel values of the first and third channel of the image taken by the single sensor respectively. The NDVI values are color-coded for better visualization. The smaller NDVI values ranging from 0 to -1 are coded as red; NDVI values ranging from 0 to 0.5 are coded as gradient from red to yellow whereas NDVI values ranging from 0.5 to 1 are coded as gradient from yellow to green.

DATA ANALYSIS

We performed an analysis of climate variability on wheat phenology by considering meteorological behavior. Two types of analysis are performed i.e. analysis on the data acquired from IoT nodes and analysis of NDVI mapping on multi-spectral imagery acquired from low altitude platform.

1. *Analysis of IoT Nodes Data:* We collected the data from IoT nodes starting from March 2019 to May 2019. Since data is generated after every five minutes, so data is averaged over 24 hours. The

deviation of temperature profile from ideal temperature profile during grain filling stage to grain ripening stage is shown in Figure 10.

By analyzing the recorded air temperature, we can find behavior of air temperature with air humidity, soil temperature and soil humidity. The air temperature and air humidity are negatively correlated as shown in Figure 11.

Similarly, we collected temperature normal data which indicate the behavior of normal temperature of past thirty years. Figure 12 shows the deviation of actual temperature from temperature normal and ideal temperature.

The air temperature has a direct influence on the soil temperature and soil moisture level. The relationship between air temperature and soil temperature is shown in Figure 13 which shows that increase in air temperature causes to increase the soil temperature i.e. soil temperature and air temperature are positively correlated.

Air temperature and soil moisture are negatively correlated i.e. increase in air temperature will cause to decrease the soil moisture level as shown in Figure 14.

Analysis of Multi-spectral Images by NDVI Mapping: For the purpose of crop health monitoring using multi-spectral imagery, the NDVI Sentera camera is mounted on the drone. The imagery with the help of drone has been taken at altitude of 50 ft, with speed of the DJI set to 8 mph. The field boundary was marked in the FieldAgent mobile app which is shown in Figure 15. The Sentera camera takes images in three bands Red band at the wavelength of 625 nm, Near-Infrared band at wavelength of 850 nm and Red-Edge band at wavelength of 720 nm. The Field of View of Sentera lens is 60 degree horizontal and 47 degree vertical.

The multi-spectral images of month April & May 2019 are captured when wheat crop is in grain ripening stage then NDVI against each image is computed by using Eq-1. In the grain ripening stage of wheat, the NDVI value should be small because of low chlorophyll content at the particular stage i.e. the crop starts to get yellow color from green color. The Figure16 shows the multi-spectral image captured in April 23, 2019 along with NDVI mapping. The green color in NDVI mapping indicates naturally grown unwanted plants on the crops while red color indicates the visibility of soil. The NDVI mapping

Figure 10.

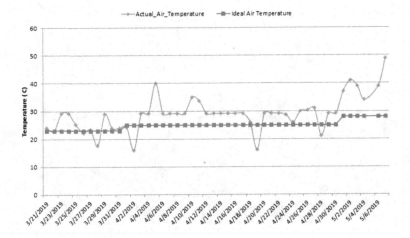

Figure 11.

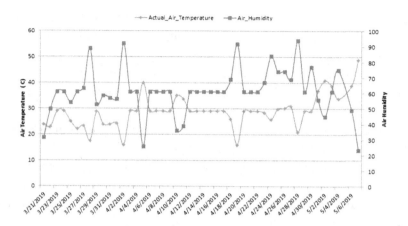

Figure 12.

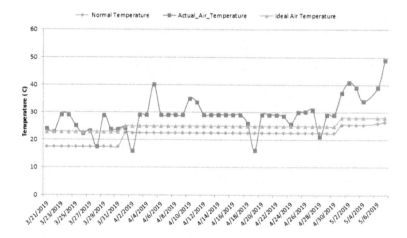

Figure 13.

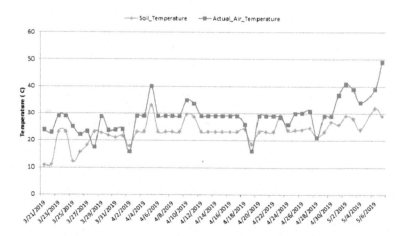

Figure 14.

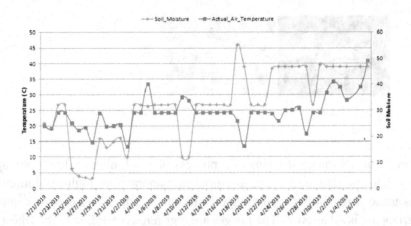

show that crop is not healthy because of large area is red which indicates the visibility of soil i.e. crop is not grown properly. Moreover, crop is in grain ripening stage, so smaller NDVI value indicates the normal growth of wheat crop and vice versa.

The multi-spectral image captured on May 8, 2019 when wheat crop is in mature stage i.e. grain ripening stage is shown in Figure17. The altitude for drone flight was set at 70 ft. After acquiring the images, NDVI is computed using Eq-1. The NDVI mapping of this particular multi-spectral image indicates that the particular area is healthy as compared to Figure16, since there is less green color i.e. less naturally grown unwanted plants are observed. Moreover, the histogram shown in Figure 16 and Figure 17 indicate that NDVI values are decreased with passage of time from April to May because grains are in ripening phase.

The captured multi-spectral images cover a specific region in the field. To visualize the whole field, we performed image stitching to get detail view of complete field by merging whole multicultural im-

Figure 15.

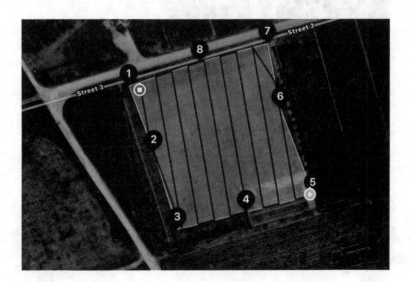

Figure 16.

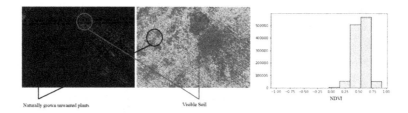

ages as shown in Figure18 Image stitching is a process of combining multiple photographic images with overlapping fields of view to produce a segmented panorama or high-resolution image. For this purpose, images are acquired for harvesting stage of the wheat crop. 75 Images are captured on May 16, 2019 where overlapping is set as 50 %. The images are registered according to the wheat field boundary and the area exceeding the field boundary was cut off according to the shape file of the field using the FieldAgent application as shown in Figure 18-A. All images are stitched to give a single high-resolution image of the wheat field from the acquired 75 images. With the help of the generated stitched image, NDVI analysis is performed which gave a whole picture to the farmer regarding the state of wheat crop. The image acquired was for the harvesting stage where wheat crop had golden ears. The analysis on the overall stitched image showed the region of wheat field having greenery at some regions, which is due to the naturally grown grass as shown in Figure 18-C.

The results of NDVI mapping indicates that the computed NDVI values lie in smaller range because of: 1) Crop is in grain ripening stage, 2) Naturally grown grass. If we identify green content in NDVI mapping in the grain ripening stage, then we need to perform ground survey. After performing ground survey, rust attack is also observed. Consequently, the yield obtained from the particular field is 1.6

Figure 17.

Figure 18.

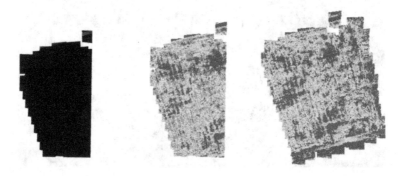

tonne per hectare while expected optimal wheat yield is 2.26 tonne per hectare. The deviation of actual food production from optimal food production leads toward food security concerns which also cause to decline the GDP of Pakistan. This decline in yield is attributed to the rust attack, naturally grown grass and fluctuation of temperature during these stages.

CHALLENGES

Several challenges were faced while designing and deploying the system which are mentioned below:

- **Deployment Issues**: Agricultural land is typically located away from urban setup which makes the deployment of the system expensive and hard to maintain. The IoT nodes need to be fixed properly in the field in order to be resilient to the extreme weather conditions. The identification of physical points where the IoT nodes are to be installed require rigorous testing for reliable wireless communication. The distance from master to slave node should be decided after appropriate measurement and sufficient testing. The main reason for this is that once the node is deployed at a certain point as once deployed it is difficult to relocate.
- **Maintenance Issues:** The IoT based system deployed in agricultural fields is expensive to maintain. The testing and debugging of the remote system are major challenges as the identification of faulty node / sensor at run time is quite challenging. The issues faced in our system were reliable data transmission, impedance matching with antenna, power issues and weariness of sensors. For this reason, a dedicated engineer needs to be assigned to look after the fields regularly. The engineer should have necessary equipment during field visit to repair / replace the faulty equipment.
- **Drone Interfacing Issues With Multi-Spectral Camera:** The drone and multi-spectral camera were from different vendors which has its own challenges. The first challenge was how to integrate Sentera multi-spectral camera with DJI Phatom-4 advance Drone, as there were no official Senetera customer support point in Pakistan. For this reason the Sentera customer in US were contacted for customer support but due to time zone difference the immediate support could not be provided which incur the time delay in resolving the issues. The other major hurdle was that the drone and the multi-spectral camera were operated through two different softwares which do not function in parallel. For this reason, the optical and multi-spectral imagery has to be captured separately.
- **Equipment Security:** As the IoT nodes are deployed in open field without secure casing, therefore, the probability of equipment theft is high in such systems.

CONCLUSION AND FUTURE WORK

Food security has become a rising concern for developing countries like Pakistan. To enhance the food production, the state of the art technologies need to be implemented. Toward this end, a system to monitor the health of crops is presented which utilizes state of the art technologies such as IoT for collecting the key parameters of the crop and capturing multispectral imagery using low altitude platforms. The developed system is deployed into wheat fields and data is acquired for further analysis. In the particular phenological cycle of wheat (November 2018 - May 2019), an extreme fluctuations in the temperature of Islamabad has been observed which resulted in deviation of normal wheat growth cycle and attack of some deceases i.e. wheat rust attack. Consequently, reduction in the wheat yield from 2.6 tonne per hectare to 1.6 tonne per hectare in the particular field is observed.

Currently, we are only monitoring the health of crop, in future we will incorporate the control part where in parallel to automated monitoring, the curative actions will also be automated. The predictive model will also be developed in future that will help the IoT-based agricultural system to perform correlation and sensitivity analysis of various crop growth parameters to analyze existing state and forecast potential harvest. Consequently, the quality of agricultural output can be enhanced because farmers monitor the entire crop growth cycle by leveraging this IoT-based decision support system in real time.

ACKNOWLEDGMENT

This research has been conducted in IoT Research Lab at NUST-SEECS in collaboration with NARC, Pakistan.

REFERENCES

Al-Manie, M. A., & Alkanhal, M. I. (2004). Acoustic detection of the red date palm weevil. *Int. J. Signal Process*, *1*, 1–12.

Aslam, M. (2016). Agricultural productivity current scenario, constraints and future prospects in Pakistan. *Sarhad Journal of Agriculture*, *32*(4), 289–303. doi:10.17582/journal.sja/2016.32.4.289.303

Azfar, S., Nadeem, A., & Basit, A. (2015). Pest detection and control techniques using wireless sensor network: A review. *Journal of Entomology and Zoology Studies*, *3*(2), 92–99.

Baccarelli, E., Naranjo, P. G. V., Scarpiniti, M., Shojafar, M., & Abawajy, J. H. (2017). Fog of everything: Energy-efficient networked computing architectures, research challenges, and a case study. *IEEE Access: Practical Innovations, Open Solutions*, *5*, 9882–9910. doi:10.1109/ACCESS.2017.2702013

Bockus, W. W., Bowden, R. L., Hunger, R. M., Murray, T. D., & Smiley, R. W. (2010). Compendium of wheat diseases and pests (No. Ed. 3). American Phytopathological Society (APS Press).

Datir, S., & Wagh, S. (2014). Monitoring and detection of agricultural disease using wireless sensor network. *International Journal of Computers and Applications*, *87*(4).

Khush, G. S. (1977). Disease and insect resistance in rice. []. Academic Press.]. *Advances in Agronomy*, *29*, 265–341.

Long & Hensley. (1972). Insect pests of sugar cane. *Annual Review of Entomology*, *17*(1), 149–176. doi:10.1016/S0065-2113(08)60221-7

López, O., Rach, M., Migallon, H., Malumbres, M., Bonastre, A., & Serrano, J. (2012). Monitoring pest insect traps by means of low-power image sensor technologies. *Sensors (Basel)*, *12*(11), 15801–15819. doi:10.3390121115801 PMID:23202232

Mahajan, U., & Bundel, B. R. (2017). Drones for Normalized Difference Vegetation Index (NDVI), to Estimate Crop Health for Precision Agriculture: A Cheaper Alternative for Spatial Satellite Sensors. In *International Conference on Innovative Research in Agriculture, Food Science, Forestry, Horticulture, Aquaculture, Animal Sciences, Biodiversity, Ecological Sciences and Climate Change (AFHABEC-2016)*. Jawaharlal Nehru University.

Mauro Prevostini. (2011). *Wireless Sensor Network for Pest Control, Commission for Technology and innovation CTI*. Retrieved from https://1pdf.net/wireless-sensor-network-for-pest-control-dolphin-engineering_59159fd8f6065d4311b1fb6d

McGuire, S. (2015). *FAO, IFAD, and WFP. The state of food insecurity in the world 2015: meeting the 2015 international hunger targets: taking stock of uneven progress*. Rome: FAO.

Mekala, M. S., & Viswanathan, P. (2017, August). A Survey: Smart agriculture IoT with cloud computing. In *2017 international conference on microelectronic devices, circuits and systems (ICMDCS)* (pp. 1-7). IEEE.

Monica, M., Yeshika, B., Abhishek, G. S., Sanjay, H. A., & Dasiga, S. (2017, October). IoT based control and automation of smart irrigation system: an automated irrigation system using sensors, GSM, bluetooth and cloud technology. In *2017 International Conference on Recent Innovations in Signal processing and Embedded Systems (RISE)* (pp. 601-607). IEEE. 10.1109/RISE.2017.8378224

Nalini & Ramakrishna. (2018). Smart irrigation system based on soil moisture using iot. *International Research Journal of Engineering and Technology, 5*(6).

Naranjo, P. G. V., Shojafar, M., Mostafaei, H., Pooranian, Z., & Baccarelli, E. (2017). P-SEP: A prolong stable election routing algorithm for energy-limited heterogeneous fog-supported wireless sensor networks. *The Journal of Supercomputing, 73*(2), 733–755. doi:10.100711227-016-1785-9

Oliver, M. A. (Ed.). (2010). *Geostatistical applications for precision agriculture*. Springer Science & Business Media. doi:10.1007/978-90-481-9133-8

Payak, M. M., & Sharma, R. C. (1985). Maize diseases and approaches to their management in India. *International Journal of Pest Management, 31*(4), 302–310.

Rao, R. N., & Sridhar, B. (2018, January). IoT based smart crop-field monitoring and automation irrigation system. In *2018 2nd International Conference on Inventive Systems and Control (ICISC)* (pp. 478-483). IEEE. 10.1109/ICISC.2018.8399118

Singh, T., & Singh, T. (2016). Hand Held Device for Detection of Pesticides using NDVI. *International Journal of Computer Applications, 154*(9).

Sodhro, A. H., Pirbhulal, S., Luo, Z., & de Albuquerque, V. H. C. (2019). Towards an optimal resource management for IoT based Green and sustainable smart cities. *Journal of Cleaner Production, 220*, 1167–1179. doi:10.1016/j.jclepro.2019.01.188

Srinivas, S., Harsha, K. S., Sujatha, A., & Kumar, N. (2013). Efficient protection of palms from RPW Larvae using WSN. *IJCSI, 10*(3), 2.

Srivastavai, N., Chopra, G., Jain, P., & Khatter, B. (2013). Pest Monitor and Control System Using Wireless Sensor Network (with special reference to acoustic device sensor). *International Conference on Electrical and Electronics Engineering.*

Suma, N., Samson, S. R., Saranya, S., Shanmugapriya, G., & Subhashri, R. (2017). IOT based smart agriculture monitoring system. *International Journal on Recent and Innovation Trends in Computing and Communication, 5*(2), 177-181.

Surai, S., Kundu, R., Ghosh, R., & Bid, G. (2018). An IoT Based Smart Agriculture System with Soil Moisture Sensor. *Journal of Innovation and Research, 1*(1).

Swain, K. C., & Zaman, Q. U. (2012). Rice crop monitoring with unmanned helicopter remote sensing images. *Remote Snsing of Biomass-Principles and Applications*, 254-272.

Yousaf, H., Zafar, M. I., Anjum, F., & Adil, S. A. (2018). Food security status and its determinants: A case of farmer and non-farmer rural households of the Punjab, Pakistan. *Pakistan Journal of Agricultural Sciences, 55*(1), 217–225. doi:10.21162/PAKJAS/18.6766

Zhang, N., & Taylor, R. K. (2001). Applications of a field–level geographic information system (fis) in precision agriculture. *Applied Engineering in Agriculture, 17*(6), 885. doi:10.13031/2013.6829

Chapter 8
Streamlining IPv6 Functionality for Low Power Nodes

Bhawana Rudra
National Institute of Technology, Karnataka, India

Thanmayee S.
iD https://orcid.org/0000-0002-8815-7891
National Institute of Technology, Karnataka, India

ABSTRACT

The internet of things is a new paradigm where smart embedded devices are connected to the internet. In this context, wireless sensor networks (WSN) are becoming an important alternative for sensing and actuating critical applications like industrial automation, healthcare, etc. 6LoWPAN provides a means of carrying packet in the form of IPv6 over IEEE 802.15.4 and other networks. It provides end-to-end IPv6, and as such, it is able to provide direct connectivity to a huge variety of networks and to the internet. It uses an adaptation layer for fragmenting and reassembling of the IPv6 packets. Due to its low-cost communication network, it allows IoT connectivity with limited power and throughput. It can be used to overcome the challenges that are faced during the integration of WSN and IP protocols. This chapter briefly discusses IoT followed by an introduction to IPv6 and 6LoWPAN in detail along with architecture that suits IoT, 6LoWPAN mote design features and functions. It also focus on the advantages of LoWPAN with respect to IoT and its security along with smart city case studies.

INTRODUCTION

The Internet has paved a way for every "thing" on every corner of the world to be connected to each other. Day by day the number of things that operates on a single network is increasing. This gave rise to the concept of the "Internet of Things (IoT)" (Mainetti, Patrono and Vilei, 2011)(Gomez, Paradells, Bormann and Crowcroft, 2017). The connectivity allows collecting information from all over the world with higher granularity. It offers a wide range of sophisticated services to its users. This has increased as it is inexpensive, easy to deploy and use in various environments like agriculture, healthcare, smart

DOI: 10.4018/978-1-7998-1253-1.ch008

cities and so on. The wireless sensor networks complaint with proprietary and non-proprietary solutions with high heterogeneity. The solutions in various areas are delayed due to the challenges such as i) extensive deployment of the technologies to obtain a sensor network ii) ability to add the new sensor networks to the existing ones iii) interoperability in the heterogeneous sensing systems iv) the abstraction between lower layers to higher layers (Gomez, Paradells, Bormann and Crowcroft, 2017)(Lamkimel, Naja, Jamali and Yahyaoui, 2018).

The proprietary systems (Vasseur and Dunkels, 2010) have limited connectivity communication with the external world. For this purpose of communication, we must use gateways that are embedded with specific application knowledge in order to transfer data to other devices over the Internet. The system follows different standards for various applications and no direct communication among them. To facilitate smooth communication in a heterogeneous environment there is a need for embedding application-specific standards on the gateways or proxies as shown in Figure 1.

The Internet Protocol (IP) is used to achieve the communication over the Internet. It allows the connectivity of multiple wireless sensor networks to the Internet. It provides an open standard in which every thing has an IP address of its own. With the IP address every thing or smart objects can be interconnected to communicate with each other. These things or smart objects that will allow us to collect useful information about the smart environments present around. It provides this information for developing more accurate and increase the lifetime of the objects or things. The web-based smart object can deliver more flexible and customized information and will be adjusted to the future Internet. The use of IP in IoT is for the following reasons (Vasseur and Dunkels, 2010), (Shelby, Bormann, 2009), (Kushalnagar, Montenegro, Hui, Culler,2007), (Kushalnagar, Montenegro, and Schumacher, 2007), (Deering, Hinden, 1988):

Figure 1. Interworking among Heterogeneous Networks

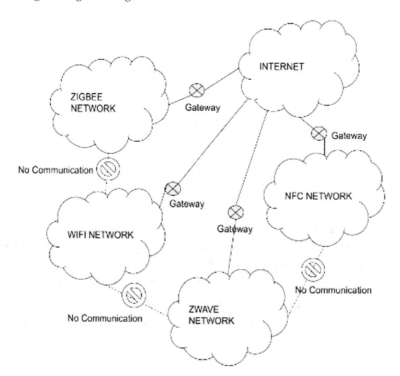

- It is easy to connect the IP devices to available networks using no extra gateways or proxies.
- It is easy to reuse the existing infrastructure for connecting IP networks.
- These networks are in use for decades and well known to work. The wide use of socket API proves to be a promising technology in networks.
- This technology has standard documents that is freely available for research. As a result, it encourages innovations in the area and is easy to understand by a wider range of audiences.
- The tools for deployment and maintenance are readily available in the network and makes it easy to adopt by many researchers.

IoT devices cannot support a powerful processor, IP based communication as it proves to be an overhead on the tiny devices. The IoT consists of low power devices for network communication over wired or wireless network technologies. Wireless devices and network communication with low power and transmission of data in the channel are the various challenges of IP to support IoT.

- **Security:** IPv6 supports IP Security, authentication and encryption. It makes use of SSL and TLS protocols too. The low power devices in IoT may be burdened with this complex service.
- **Web Services:** The services provided by the Internet rely on web services like HTTP, SOAP, XML and TCP along with some sophisticated transaction patterns.
- **Frame Size:** The IP protocol has MTU of 1280 bytes which is not suitable for embedded devices that support low bandwidth..
- **Power and Duty-Cycle:** The wireless devices require to keep low duty cycles in order to deliver the information and increase their lifetime. This is in contrast to IP's assumption that the devices are always connected to the network.
- **Management:** A Simple Network Management Protocol (SNMP) and web services are inefficient and result in complex for embedded devices.
- **Multicast:** The wireless technologies do not support multicast such as IEEE 802.15.4 and flooding is a waste of power and bandwidth.
- **Mesh Topologies:** The wireless applications can use the multihop mesh to reach the destination with cost-efficiency. The available IP solution may not be suitable for such device networks.
- **Bandwidth and Frame Size:** Usage of mesh topology will decrease the bandwidth as the channel is shared and can reduce the multihop forwarding. IEEE 802.15.4 standard specifies an MTU of 127-byte. IPv6 specifies MTU to be 1280 bytes. Thus there is a requirement for fragmentation.
- **Reliability:** The protocols of IP were not designed to support the low power networks. TCP is not capable of differentiating packet drops because of congestion or packet loss on wireless channels. The reliability is lost due to the failure of nodes, loss of energy or sleep duty cycle.

The IETF has come up with a solution called 6LoWPAN to solve the above-mentioned problems and enable IPv6 for the wireless embedded networks. 6LoWPAN incorporates all the features of IPv6 with a simple header structure and uses its hierarchical addressing model which can be adopted by the IoT devices for communication.

6LoWPAN

Low power Wireless Personal Area Network (LoWPAN) is a network with the devices that conform to the IEEE 802.15.4-2003 standard. The main features of these devices are short-range communication, low throughput, low bandwidth and low cost. They have limited processing power, low memory and low energy consumption (Mc Gee and Collier, 2019), (Lin, Fan, Zhong, Zi and Xiao, 2017),(Honggang, Chen and Leyu, 2018). The nodes with limited capacity must be able to communicate with the remote nodes on the Internet. *"But the high capacity Internet Protocol proves to be heavy for low capacity embedded devices in LoWPAN. To streamline the functionalities of IPv6 over IEEE 802.15.4, 6LoWPAN is placed as an adaptation layer in between IPv6 and IEEE802.15.4(PHY/MAC). So the goal is to use IPv6 to enable the LoWPAN usage over the low power wireless networks. It allows communication with the help of 6LoWPAN adaptation layer. It also requires optimization of upper layer protocols"* (Shelby, Bormann, 2009),(Kushalnagar, Montenegro, Hui, Culler, 2007), (Kushalnagar, Montenegro, and Schumacher, 2007).

Characteristics of 6LoWPAN

6LoWPAN has the following characteristics: i) Small packet size ii) Allows two representations of MAC address: 16 bit short address or IEEE 64 bit extended address iii) Support low bandwidth, low power devices v) Providing a way to deploy large number of devices during the lifetime improvement of technology (Chere, Ngqondi and Bembe, 2019).

Architecture of 6LoWPAN

There exist three kinds of LoWPANs: a) Ad-Hoc LoWPANs - they have no connectivity to the Internet and they are infrastructure less, b) Simple LoWPANs - they have connectivity to the Internet via edge routers, and c) Extended LoWPANs - formed by interconnecting multiple edge routers using a backbone link (Shelby, Bormann, 2009), (Kushalnagar, Montenegro, and Schumacher, 2007) and (Vinay Kumar, Sudarshan Tiwari, 2012). The edge routers help in communication between the LoWPANs. Figure 2 represents 6LoWPAN Architecture. There are various nodes that may be routers or hosts and the edge routers. Neighbor discovery (ND), is an important process in 6LoWPAN as it allows the devices to register with the edge routers to perform efficient operations in the network. With the help of ND, routers will know how to communicate with hosts on the same link. The devices move freely in the area of LoWPAN, they can move among the edge routers and even among the LoWPANs.

It uses IEEE802.15.4 as a link-layer protocol. It supports three kinds of nodes: the Personal Area Network coordinator (PAN coordinator), Full-Function Device (FFD) and Reduced-Function Device (RFD) (Chere, Ngqondi and Bembe, 2019). RFDs are simple nodes with restricted resources. For example RFDs may sense and forward data. FFDs are the nodes that may sense and make decisions on routing it to the destination. They can act as PAN coordinators with responsibilities like the creation, control, and maintenance of the network. The fixed nodes are the PAN coordinators. FFDs are categorized into fixed nodes and mobile nodes. The 6LoWPAN as a whole is divided into multiple sub-PANs. Each sub-PAN has a gateway node, cluster node, and cluster member node. The Gateway node is a PAN coordinator, the cluster node acts as an FFD coordinator and supports forwarding and routing functions and Cluster member node acts as an RFD without routing and forwarding functions. One sub-PAN can be divided into multiple clusters and each cluster has one cluster head and a set of cluster members. Two types of

Figure 2. 6LoWPAN Architecture

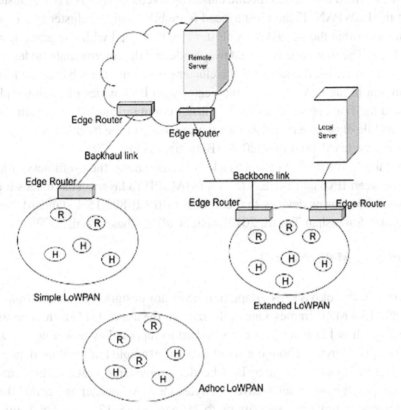

Figure 3. 6LoWPAN Protocol Stack

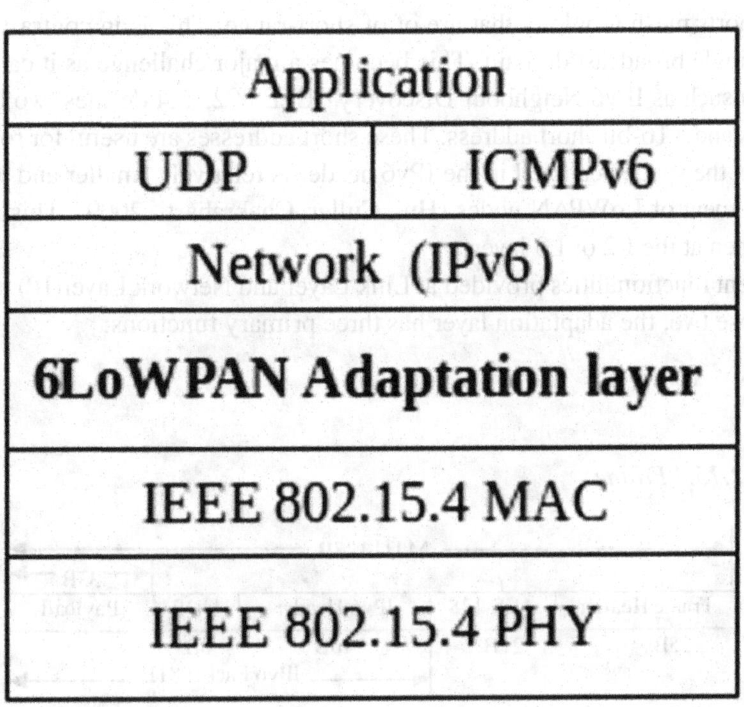

Application	
UDP	ICMPv6
Network (IPv6)	
6LoWPAN Adaptation layer	
IEEE 802.15.4 MAC	
IEEE 802.15.4 PHY	

cluster can be formed: fixed cluster and mobile cluster. A fixed cluster has a fixed cluster head that does not move within the LoWPAN. If the cluster head is mobile then the cluster is a mobile cluster. The mobile cluster moves within the sub-PAN. A cluster tree is formed with one gateway and fixed cluster head in one sub-PAN. The root node is the gateway node and the intermediate nodes are the leaf nodes along with the fixed cluster head nodes. All the cluster trees construct a backbone routing network. A mobile cluster present in the LoWPAN communicates with IPv6 nodes through the cluster tree of the same sub-PAN and the fixed head nodes in the cluster communicate directly with the mobile cluster head node of the mobile cluster i.e called as the associate node of the mobile cluster. The mobile cluster has only an associate node (Ma and Luo, 2008) (Bouaziz, Rachedi, 2014)

Figure 3 shows the 6LoWPAN Protocol Stack. It clearly shows the usefulness of 6LoWPAN as an adaptation layer between IPv6 and IEEE 802.15.4 (MAC/PHY) layers. That means it enables IP communication between low power devices that conform to IEEE 802.15.4 standard (Shelby, Bormann, 2009), (Vinay Kumar, Sudarshan Tiwari, 2012), (Hui, Culler, Chakrabarti, 2009)

Primary Functions of 6LoWPAN

The basic functions of the 6LoWPAN adaptation layer are designed to enable transmission of IPv6 packets in IEEE 802.15.4 MAC frames. One of the reasons the use of MTU is the size specified by IEEE 802.15.4 standard which is 127 bytes as it is a standard to support low power nodes, whereas the IPv6 MTU requirement is 1028 bytes. Though a small data for example temperature data can fit in a single MAC frame although the space occupied by IPv6 header is quite large, that is 40 bytes as shown in Figure 4. UDP header occupies 8 bytes, which leaves 79 bytes for MAC header and actual data. MAC header can be 25 bytes large with link-layer security up to 21 bytes (AES-128). This ends up with 31 bytes of space left for actual data (Shelby, Bormann, 2009),(Hui, Culler, 2007), (Huiqin and Yongqiang, 2010), (Degermark, Nordgren, Pink, 1999), (Hui, and Thubert, 2011)

LoWPAN supports mesh topology that are of of short-range. This is in contrast to the assumption that the link is a single broadcast domain. This becomes a major challenge as it can affect the core of IP based functions such as IPv6 Neighbour Discovery. IEEE 802.15.4 defines two types of addresses: EUI-64 bit address and a 16-bit short address. These short addresses are useful for routing and forwarding in LoWPAN as the space occupied in the IPv6 header is relatively smaller and thus supporting the low energy requirement of LoWPAN nodes (Hui, Culler, Chakrabarti, 2009). This allows routing and forwarding to happen at the L2 or L3 layer.

With the efficient functionalities provided at Link Layer and Network Layer(IP), to provide compatibility between those two, the adaptation layer has three primary functions:

Figure 4. IEEE 802.15.4 Frame

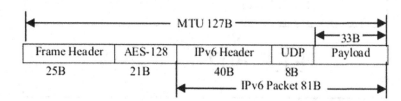

Figure 5. 6LoWPAN Encapsulation

6LoWPAN Dispatch (1 byte)	IPv6 Header (40 byte + 8 byte UDP)	Payload

1. **Header Compression:** 6LoWPAN allows compression of IPv6, UDP, TCP header by identifying the redundant data in the header and removing them, thereby reducing the size of the IP header from 40 bytes to at least 3 bytes in MAC frame.
2. **Fragmentation:** Along with IP layer fragmentation and reassembly that happens only at source and destination according to IPv6, 6LoWPAN also provides fragmentation at the adaptation layer to allow IP packets that conform to MTU of 1280 bytes to be encapsulated in IEEE 802.15.4 defined MAC frames. Fragmentation and reassembly which is at the adaptation layer happen for every hop in LoWPAN.
3. **Mesh Routing:** 6LoWPAN supports Layer 2 forwarding and routing which is called Mesh under routing. This basically uses layer 2 addresses that can be EUI-64 bit address or 16-bit short address of next hop.

6LoWPAN provides these functionalities and makes it explicit in IP packets in the form of an encapsulation header that is called a dispatch byte. An IPv6 packet encapsulated in LoWPAN is shown in Figure 5.

Dispatch byte will indicate what functionalities have been applied to an IP packet to be transmitted in LoWPAN (Hui, and Thubert, 2011) (Bormann, 2001). The list of values for Dispatch byte is shown in Table 1.

Table 1. 6LoWPAN Dispatch Values

Dispatch value	Header Type	Description
00 xxxxxx	NALP	Not a LoWPAN frame
01 000001	IPv6	Uncompressed IPv6 Addresses
01 000010	LOWPAN_HC1	IPv6 Header Compression - stateless
01 010000	LOWPAN_BC0	Broadcast
01 1xxxxx	LOWPAN_IPHC	IPv6 Header Compression - context based
01 111111	ESC	Additional Dispatch byte follows
10 xxxxxx	Mesh Header	Mesh header
11 000xxx	FRAG1	Initial fragment
11 1100xx	FRAGN	Subsequent fragments

Header Compression

The adaptation layer can compress 40 byte IPv6 header and 8 byte UDP header. It assumes that most of the information in the IP and UDP headers are redundant which means they can be derived from lower-level layers. Thus it elides those information and thereby reducing the overall size of IPv6 and UDP headers. 6LoWPAN defines two types of header compression (Hui, and Thubert, 2011) (Bormann, 2001) (Casner and Jacobson, 1999) (Jacobson, Braden, Borman, 1990) (Nuno, da Silva, 2010) and (Rawat, Priyanka, and Jean-Marie Bonnin, 2010)

1. **Stateless Header Compression:** This is also called HC1 Header compression. It is an encoding scheme for compressing the IPv6 header. It can be extended to next headers currently specified for UDP as defined in RFC 4944. It is optimized for link-local addresses.
2. **Context-Based Header Compression:** A node in LoWPAN may wish to send packets to a remote server on the Internet which involves routable addresses. In this case, the HC1 header compression scheme cannot compress a 128-bit IPv6 address and it has to be sent inline. This is a primary limitation of the Stateless Header compression scheme. Context-based header compression overcomes this limitation by providing a scheme for compressing routable addresses.

Stateless Header Compression

Stateless header compression does not depend on any flow state. There is no need for context information to be stored in the routers along the destination path. Traditionally, IP header compression is status based provided the flow between two endpoints is stable which is in case of point-to-point connections. Communication over multiple hops requires hop-by-hop compression and decompression. For a network like LoWPAN which is a dynamically changing multiple hops network, stateless and shared-context compression is used, which does not require any state and allows routing protocols e.g., RPL to dynamically choose routes without affecting compression efficiency. Without the state, there is no synchronization problem and algorithm will become simple.

Stateless Header compression is specified using HC1 encoding in 6LoWPAN header. The 6LoWPAN format specification [RFC4944] defines two types of header compression: HC1 and HC2 compression. HCI is used to compress IPv6 headers and HC2 is for UDP header compression. HC1 and HC2 can be used together to compress 48 bytes (40 bytes IPv6 and 8 bytes UDP) of IP and UDP headers.

Assumptions made in Stateless Header compression for **IPv6 Header Compression:**

1. The version number (4 bits) is always 6 and thus it need not be sent.
2. Traffic class (1 byte) and the flow label (20 bits) are often zero in IPv6 header. Thus it can be elided.
3. The 2 bytes payload length field can be inferred from the link-layer frame or from the fragmentation mechanism and hence can be ignored.
4. Next header field (1 byte) consumes 1 byte but it has few values that are much more likely than others e.g., TCP, UDP, ICMP. Thus it can be represented using only a few bits in the HC1 header.
5. Hop limit is not compressed and hence this 1-byte hop limit is always sent inline.
6. 128-bit IPv6 address (source and destination makes it up to 256 bits) has two parts: Network prefix(64 bits) and Interface Identifier(64 bits). If the IPv6 address is link-local (HC1 is optimized for

Figure 6. 6LoWPAN HC1 Encoding

0	1	0	0	0	0	1	0	SA 2 bits	DA 2 bits	TF	NH	0	Non compressed fields

<----------Dispatch Byte------><--------- HC1 Header --------->

Table 2. SA and DA encoding

SA Bits	Description
0 0	Prefix and IID are sent in-line (no compression, 128-bit source address is sent in-line).
0 1	Prefix is sent in-line. IID is elided. (Address is reduced to 64 bits)
1 0	Prefix is elided (It is link-local). IID is sent in-line. (Address is reduced to 64 bits)
1 1	Prefix and IID are elided. (Complete compression. The address field is 0 bits)

link-local), the network prefix is by default FE80::/64 and hence it need not be sent and thus save 64 bits space in IPv6 header. IID can be derived from the MAC frame header which contains IID in the form of EUI-64 bit address or 16-bit short address and thus it can be elided.

Putting all the assumptions together, HC1 encoding done using a dispatch byte of LOWPAN_HC1 (01000010) as shown in Figure 6.

Description of HC1 Header

1. The first byte is a dispatch value that indicates HC1 header compression has been applied on IPv6 Header. What follows dispatch byte is the HC1 header.
2. First two bits in HC1 header indicates the state of the Source address (1 bit for Prefix and 1 bit for IID)
3. The next two bits indicate the status of the destination address. Encoding is same as that of source address.
4. One bit TF field indicates the status of Traffic class (1 byte) and Flow label (20 bits) field in IPv6 Header.

    TF=1 Traffic class and Flow label are not sent (compressed)

    TF=0 Traffic class and Flow label are sent (not compressed)
5. Two bits NH field indicates the Next header field (1 byte). HC1 encoding specifies compression of three next headers but compression is defined only for UDP header (HC2 encoding)
6. If the NH bit is set to 01 that means IPv6 header is followed by UDP header. The last bit in HC1 header if set to 1, then HC2 header will follow HC1 header indicating UDP header compression.

Table 3. NH encoding

Bits	Description
00	Next header is sent in-line
01	Next header = 17 i.e., UDP
10	Next header = 1 i.e., ICMP
11	Next header = 6 i.e., TCP

Figure 7. HC1 and HC2 encoding

0	1	0	0	0	0	1	0	SA	D A	TF	NH	1	S	D	L	-	-	-	-	-	Non compressed fields

`<-----Dispatch Byte------><-----HC1 Header-------><------HC2 Header----->`

UDP header has four fields. Each of 2 bytes. It has Source Port, Destination Port, Length and Checksum field. HC2 encoding compresses source port and destination ports by assuming that some port number ranges are more likely than others. So the well-known range is 61616-61631 (16 different values) which can be represented using 4 bits (e.g., 0000 - 61616 and 1111 - 61631). HC2 encoding can reduce 4 bytes of Source and Destination port numbers into 1 byte (4 bits Source port and 4 bits Destination port).

As per the encoding is shown in Figure 7 HC2 Header start with Source port number compression status. If S is set to 1 then Source port is compressed to 4 bits else it will be 2 bytes. Next bit D, if set to 1 then Destination port is compressed to 4 bits else it will be 2 bytes. L bit indicates if the length field is compressed. If L is set to 1 then a length field is elided and it can be derived from lower layers. If L is 0 then 2 bytes length field is sent in-line.

Example: Consider a header compression encoding as follows:

01000010 11111011 11100000 Followed by uncompressed data

Here the first byte is LoWPAN dispatch byte indicating HC1 compression.

This is followed by HC1 header with bits SA=11, DA=11, TCF=1, NH=01 (UDP), the last bit set to 1 means HC2 header follows. In HC2 header, field S=1, D=1, L=1 and remaining 5 bits are reserved. Now the total IPv6 header is reduced to 1-byte dispatch +1 byte HC1 header + 1 byte HC2 header + 1 byte Hop limit + 1-byte source and destination port + 2 bytes checksum, which is just 7 bytes!

Thus 48 bytes IPv6 and UDP header are now reduced to 7 bytes overcoming the header size overhead.

Context-Based Header Compression

Though HC1 and HC2 are good at compressing IPv6 and UDP headers:

1. They are not sufficient for most real use cases in 6LoWPAN.
2. HC1 is optimized for link-local addresses that are used for tasks such as Neighbour discovery, DHCPv6 or Routing protocols.
3. For communication with devices that are outside 6LoWPAN, routable addresses must be used. In such a case, a 64-bit prefix must be carried in-line in the header.
4. For multicast address, HC1 requires the full 128-bit address to be carried in-line.
5. Hop Limit is carried sent without compression.
6. The Checksum field in the UDP header was carried in-line.
7. No scheme for compressing extension headers (hop-by-hop, source routing, etc).

To tackle the above limitations of the HC1 header compression scheme, the context based header compression scheme is defined in RFC 6282. LoWPAN_IPHC is an encoding format for effective compression of Local, Global and multicast IPv6 addresses. It also allows compression of most commonly used Hop Limit values. LoWPAN_NHC is an encoding format for arbitrary next headers. It specifies a scheme for extension headers too.

Assumptions made by LoWPAN_IPHC:

i) Version 6, Traffic class and flow label are set to zero
ii) Payload length can be inferred from lower layers from either the fragmentation header or the IEEE 802.15.4 header.
iii) Hop Limit will be set to a well-known value by the source.
iv) Addresses assigned to 6LoWPAN interfaces will be informed using the link-local prefix or a small set of routable prefixes assigned to the entire 6LoWPAN. A small set of routable prefixes can be stored in-context information.
v) Addresses assigned to 6LoWPAN interfaces are formed with an IID derived directly from either 64-bit extended or 16-bit short addresses.

LOWPAN_IPHC base format:
The base LoWPAN_IPHC encoding can be 2 bytes long. When context (CID=1) is used it becomes 3 bytes long as it appends context information to the base encoding. 4 bits context for Source Prefix and 4 bits context for Destination Prefix is added. A total of 16 contexts are defined. If CID is set to 0 but SAC/DAC is set to 1 then default context (Context = 0) is considered. Non-compressed IPv6 fields are placed immediately after the 6LoWPAN_IPHC header.

TF: Indicates compression of Traffic class (8 bit) and Flow label (20 bit) fields in IPv6 header. The traffic class field is divided into two fields. 2-bit Explicit Congestion Notification (ECN) and 6-bit Differentiated Services Code Point (DSCP).

Traffic class and Flow label are encoded as follows:

Figure 8. LoWPAN_IPHC base encoding

0	1	1	TF	NH	HLIM	CID	SAC	SAM	M	DAC	DAM

Table 4. LoWPAN_IPHC fields

Fields	Bits	Description
TF	2 bits	Traffic Class and Flow Label
NH	1 bit	Next Header
HLIM	2 bits	Hop Limit
CID	1 bit	Context Identifier Extension
SAC	1 bit	Source Address Context
SAM	1 bit	Source Address Mode
M	1 bit	Multicast Address Compression
DAC	1 bit	Destination Address Context
DAM	2 bits	Destination Address Mode

TF=00 ECN + DSCP + 4 bit Padding + Flow label

TF=01 ECN + 2 bit padding + Flow label

TF=10 ECN + DSCP

TF=11 Traffic class and Flow label are elided

HLIM: LoWPAN_IPHC allows compression of Hop limit field. According to the assumption made, commonly used Hop limit values are 1,64,255 and thus field is compressed to 2 bits.

HLIM=00 Hop limit is carried in-line

HLIM=01 Hop limit =1

HLIM=10 Hop limit = 64

HLIM=11 Hop limit = 255

CID: Context Identifier Extension is used to include source and destination context information which is a 1-byte field (4 bit each)

CID=0 No Context information

CID= 1 1 byte context information is appended

SAC: Source Address Compression is used to indicate if the header compression is stateless of context-based compression.

Figure 9. LoWPAN_IPHC with Context Information

0	1	1	TF	NH	HLIM	1	S A C	SAM	M	D A C	DAM	Source context	Dest Context t

Table 5. SAC/SAM and DAC/DAM (when M=0)encoding

SAC/ DAC	SAM /DA M	Address Compression	Description
0	00	128 bits	No compression. The 128-bit address is carried in-line
	01	64 bits	The first 64-bits of the address are elided. The prefix is link-local. Remaining 64-bits are carried in-line
	10	16 bits	The first 112-bits are elided. The prefix is link-local. Next 64 bits are 0000:00FF:FE00:XXXX. XXXX are carried in-line.
	11	0 bits	The address is fully elided. The prefix is link-local. IID is computed from the lower layer headers.
1	00	Reserved	The UNSPECIFIED address,::
	01	64 bits	64 bit IID is carried in-line. The prefix is derived from the Source context field/Destination context field.
	10	16 bits	The 16-bit short address is carried in-line. 112 bits are derived from the Source context field/Destination context field.
	11	0 bits	The address is derived from context and the lower layer headers.

SAC=0 Stateless header compression is used
SAC=1 Context-based compression is used

SAM: Source Address Mode field is dependent on the value of SAC for compression of IPv6 address.
Similarly DAC: Destination Address Compression can be Stateless or context-based compression and the value of DAM: Destination Address Mode is dependent on DAC.

The following table shows the encoding scheme and description for SAC/SAM, DAC/DAM fields (when Multicast field M=0, i.e, the destination address is not a multicast address but a Unicast address)

The remaining fields in the LOWPAN_IPHC encoding are related to the destination address. The destination address can be a multicast address or a global unicast address. LOWPAN_IPHC has encoding schemes for these addresses.

M: Multicast compression (B.Haberman and D.Thaler, 2002). IPv6 multicast address prefix is FF00::/8. General format is

M=0 Destination address is not a multicast address

M=1 Destination address is a multicast address

Figure 10. IPv6 Multicast address

F(4 bits)	F(4 bits)	Flags(4 bits)	Scope(4 bits)	0	Interface ID

Table 6. DAC/DAM encoding when M=1

DAC	DAM	Address bits	Description
0	00	128	Full Address sent in-line
	01	48	Address is FFXX::00XX:XXXX:XXXX (X indicates bits that are carried in-line)
	10	32	Address is FFXX::00XX:XXXX (X indicates bits that are carried in-line)
	11	8	Address is FF02::00XX
1	00	48	Multicast Address takes the form FFXX:XXLL:PPPP:PPPP:PPPP:PPPP:XXXX: XXXX. X is the nibbles carried in-line, P represents bits to encode prefix. L is used to encode the prefix length. Prefix information P and L is taken from context.
	01	Reserved	-
	10	Reserved	-
	11	Reserved	-

According to RFC 6282 how the contexts are shared and maintained and what information is contained within a piece of context information is out of scope.

LOWPAN_NHC

It is a compression scheme to compress the UDP header. In stateless header compression, UDP header compression was defined to compress source and destination ports which fall under a well-known range, 61616-61631, and elide payload length. But the checksum field remained untouched. LOWPAN_NHC provides a scheme for compressing checksum field too provided there exist higher-layer end-to-end integrity checks.

If the NH field in LOWPAN_IPHC is set then LOWPAN_NHC is appended after non-compressed IP fields.

Figure 11. LOWPAN_IPHC and LOWPAN_NHC encoding

LOWPAN_IPHC	Non-compressed IPv6 fields	LOWAN_NHC	Non-compressed Next header fields	Payload

Figure 12. LOWPAN_NHC encoding for UDP header

1	1	1	1	0	C (1 bit)	P (2 bits)

LOWPAN_NHC can be encoding for UDP or Extension Header.

Note that in stateless header compression encoding all the non-compressed fields appear after the compression encodings (Dispatch+HC1+HC2+Non compressed field). But in Context-based compression non-compressed fields appear immediately after the compression encodings. Hence it is possible to compress Extension headers that appear between IPv6 Fixed header and UDP/TCP headers.

LOWPAN_NHC encoding for UDP header is as follows:

C: 1-bit checksum compression field. The 2-byte checksum field is compressed to 0 bits.

C=0 Checksum is carried in-line

C=1 Checksum is elided

P: 1 bit Port Compression. Source port(2 bytes) and Destination port(2 bytes) is reduced to 1 byte (4 bits for source port and 4 bits for destination port)

P=00 Source port and destination port is sent in-line

P=01 Source port is sent in-line, the Destination port is compressed to 4 bits. Dest=F0XX

P=10 Destination port is sent in-line, Source port is compressed to 4 bits. Src=F0XX

P=11 Source and Destination ports are compressed to 4 bits each. Src= F0BX,Dest=F0BY

LOWPAN_NHC provides a compression scheme for Extension headers too which is shown in Figure 13.
EID: Extension Header ID denotes which Extension header follows IPv6 header.
NH: Next Header field indicates if the next header is carried in-line or elided

NH=0 Full 8 bits for Next Header are carried in-line

NH=1 The Next Header field is elided and encoded using LOWPAN_NHC

Figure 13. LOWPAN_NHC encoding for Extension Headers

1	1	1	0	EID (3 bits)	NH(1 bit)

Table 7. EID for Extension Headers

EID value	Extension Header
0	Hop-by-Hop Options header
1	Routing Header
2	Fragment Header
3	Destination Options Header
4	Mobility Header
5	Reserved
6	Reserved
7	IPv6 Header (in case of nested IPv6 header)

Among different fields in IPv6 Extension Header, most of the part is sent in-line immediately after LOWPAN_NHC byte. Length and Next Header field are elided. The Next Header field is elided when the NH field in LOWPAN_NHC is set. The Length field in the compressed Extension Header specifies the number of bytes pertaining to the compressed extension header that follows the Length field. Pad1 or PadN options used in Hop-by-Hop and Destination Headers for meeting alignment requirements. It can be elided when there is a single trailing Pad1 or PadN option of 7 octets or less and the header in which it is contained is a multiple of 8 bytes. It can be elided only if they are present at the end. Otherwise, they must be carried in-line as they are used to align subsequent options.

Example: Consider the following encoding:

In the example shown in Figure 14, LOWPAN_IPHC encoding compresses all fields in the IPv6 header. Hop limit is now represented using 2 bits (Hop limit is now a well-known value 64). The source address and Destination address are completely elided and constructed using context information and encapsulating headers(For example MAC). In this case, no extra byte of context information is appended to LOWPAN_IPHC so default context information contained in ID = 0000 (SCI and DCI = 0000) is considered. Thus IPv6 header is compressed to 2 bytes. UDP is compressed to 2 bytes. So the best case context-based compression achieved is 4 bytes. The checksum is compressed by assuming that end-to-end integrity is ensured by upper layers.

Figure 14. LOWPAN_IPHC and LOWPAN_NHC encoding for Hoplimit, Global unicast address compression, and UDP checksum compression

IPHC Dispatch	T F	N H	H L I M	CID	S A C	S A M	M	D A C	D A M	NHC Dispatch	C	P	Non-Compressed Fields(UDP)	Payload
011	11	1	10	0	1	11	0	1	11	11110	1	11	Source and Destination Ports (1 byte)	Payload

Figure 15. Initial 6LoWPAN fragment

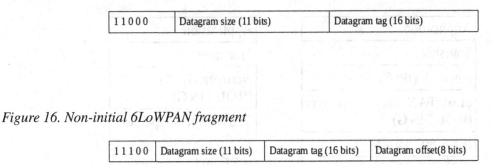

1 1 0 0 0	Datagram size (11 bits)	Datagram tag (16 bits)

Figure 16. Non-initial 6LoWPAN fragment

1 1 1 0 0	Datagram size (11 bits)	Datagram tag (16 bits)	Datagram offset(8 bits)

Fragmentation

A network is formed with links that are capable of carrying varying size packets. An IPv6 packet may be as small as 40 bytes (Just a header with no payload) or it may be as big as 4,2,94,967,295 bytes(Jumbo payload) or 65,575 bytes. Most Subnetworks like Ethernet define a Maximum Transmission Unit (MTU) below that large packet size. For example, Ethernet defines an MTU of 1500 bytes. When IPv6 defines MTU of 1280 bytes, LoWPAN has low power nodes for which the IEEE 802.15.4 standard defines an MTU of 127 bytes. Thus fragmentation and reassembly mechanism needs to at the 6LoWPAN adaptation layer (Shelby, Bormann, 2009), (Kushalnagar, Montenegro, Hui, Culler, 2007), (Kushalnagar, Montenegro, and Schumacher, 2007) (Hui, Culler, Chakrabarti, (2009) and (Tanaka, Minet and Watteyne, 2019).

During fragmentation, an initial fragment will contain compressed headers. Other fragments will contain the remaining part of the fragmented payload. Datagram size is included in all the fragment headers because the fragments may arrive out of order at the destination and there is a need to allocate reassembly buffer for reordering of fragments. The datagram tag is the identity for fragments belonging to the same packet. The datagram offset field is for reordering purpose and it is present in non-initial fragments only. Fragmentation header for initial and non-initial fragments are shown in Figures 15 and 16.

Mesh Routing

A key area of LoWPAN is the mesh networking of nodes. It plays an important role because nodes in LoWPAN are of low energy, low power radio. A mesh can extend the device's reach by providing multiple paths between nodes. Mesh provides reliability through path diversity Mulligan (2007). Routing in 6LoWPAN can be based on layering decisions or application-based. Based on layering decision there exists two types of routing: Mesh Under and Route over. Application-based routing types are data-aware routing, probabilistic routing, geographic routing, event-driven, probabilistic routing and hierarchical routing (Shelby, Bormann, 2009) and (Vinay Kumar, Sudarshan Tiwari, 2012) .

Routing decisions can happen at the IP layer or at the Adaptation layer. Based on which layer the routing decision takes place a LoWPAN has two types of routing and forwarding: Mesh-under and Route-over. If the routing decision happens at the IP layer, it is called Route-over routing. If the routing decision happens at the adaptation layer, it is called Mesh-under routing.

Figure 17. (a) Mesh-under routing (b) Route-over routing

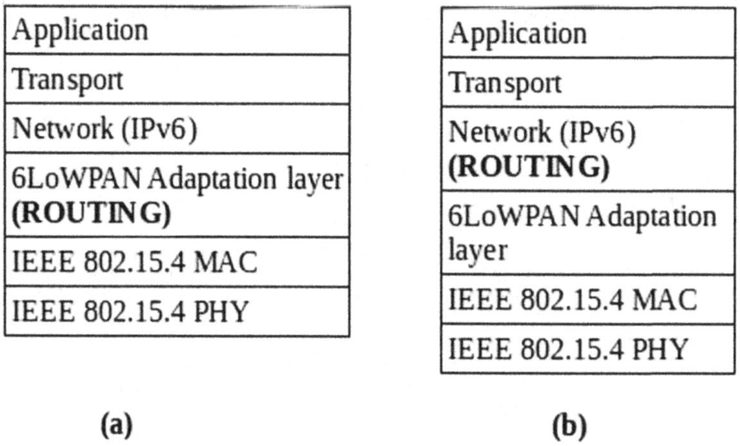

| Application |
| Transport |
| Network (IPv6) |
| 6LoWPAN Adaptation layer **(ROUTING)** |
| IEEE 802.15.4 MAC |
| IEEE 802.15.4 PHY |

(a)

| Application |
| Transport |
| Network (IPv6) **(ROUTING)** |
| 6LoWPAN Adaptation layer |
| IEEE 802.15.4 MAC |
| IEEE 802.15.4 PHY |

(b)

The route-over scheme as shown in Figure 17(b) has all routing decisions taken in the network layer. In this, each node acts as an IP router and each link layer hop is an IP hop. It makes use of IP routing tables. Here the adaptation layer receives all the fragments and reassembles the fragments and forwards the IP packet to the network layer. If the packet is intended to be for itself then the network layer forwards it to the transport layer, otherwise forwards to next-hop based on the routing table information. If any fragment is missing then all fragments are retransmitted to one-hop distance.

In the Mesh-under scheme as shown in Figure 17(a), routing decisions happen at the 6LoWPAN adaptation layer. Routing and forwarding are performed at the link layer based on the IEEE 802.15.4 frame or 6LoWPAN mesh header. It makes use of EUI-64 bit address or the 16-bit short address to send packets to a neighbor node in order to move the packet close to the destination. Multiple link-layer hops make one IP hop. Different fragments can go through different paths as they reach the destination. If all fragments reach the destination successfully, then the destination node's adaptation layer reassembles all the fragments and forwards it to the IP layer. If any fragment goes missing then all fragments pertaining to this IP packet is retransmitted to the destination.

During mesh forwarding, when the packet is being forwarded, at each hop, the link-layer source and the destination address is overwritten. This information is useful for functions like Reassembly. Thus it becomes important to store original source and destination address somewhere and this is done using 6LoWPAN Mesh Header. It has the hop limit field to limit the hops in the network. Mesh header shown in Figure 18, is the first header in the header stack of 6LoWPAN which is followed by Fragmentation header and Header compression header.

Figure 18. 6LoWPAN Mesh addressing

| 1 0 | V | F | Hops left (4 bits) | Originator address(16 or 64 bits), Final destination address(16 or 64 bits) |

Figure 19. 6LoWPAN Mesh addressing with Additional Hops left field

10	V	F	1 1 1 1	Hops left (8 bits)	Originator address(16 or 64 bits), Final destination address(16 or 64 bits)

Figure 20. 6LoWPAN Header Stack

Mesh Header	Fragment Header	Header compression	Uncompressed fields	Payload

V: very first address or originator address.

V=0 Originator is EUI-64 bits address

V=1 Originator is 16-bit short address

F: Final address or destination address

F=0 Destination is EUI-64 bits address

F=1 Destination is 16-bit short address

Hops left the field: It is a 4-bit field that can define the number of hops up to 16. If the number of hops is more than 16 then an extra byte of Hops left field is added soon after the Hops left the field in Mesh header as shown in Figure 19.

Stack of 6LoWPAN headers:

When all three functionalities of 6LoWPAN are applied on the IPv6 packet, headers must be stacked as per the order is shown in Figure 20. Each header begins with corresponding dispatch values.

6LoWPAN APPLICATIONS

1. **Healthcare:** 6LoWPAN devices can be used in the medical field for patient monitoring that can save lives by remotely monitoring the patient's health and take actions by triggering medical devices. Advances in healthcare monitoring with the development of technologies for the Internet of Things have led to the design of a system for global healthcare monitoring applications such as ECG, SpO$_2$, etc. A 6LoWPAN node with biomedical sensors are placed on the patient's body can monitor the patient for biomedical data. Each and every node has IP-addresses. Thus, it helps in transferring the data of the patient to the service provider or doctor in real-time. The patient can freely move inside the PAN or hospital area and service providers will be able to receive biomedical

data efficiently (Singh, Tiwary, Lee and Chung, 2009) (Wireless Medium Access Control (MAC) and Physical Layer (PHY), 2007) (Antonio J. Jara, Miguel A. Zamora, Antonio F.G. Skarmeta, 2010)

2. **Intelligent Home:** A home is made of many things that can be connected to the Internet to make it IoT enabled. 6LoWPAN sensor nodes can be embedded in furniture (e.g., a chair that can monitor body temperature, sitting posture), electronic appliances (e.g., Refrigerator, washing machine, oven) and they can be connected to the Internet via gateway (Ma and Luo, 2008) (Gomez and Paradells, 2010)

3. This system will collect data from water meter, gas meter, ammeter, along with detecting and alerting the owners about fire or robbery, communicate to the management of the residential area. For example, information about water usage of every house in the city can be sent to the corporate office for analysis and make major decisions about saving water resources (Arndt, Krause, Wunderlich and Heinen, 2017) (Huang, Xiao, Liu and Lin, 2016) .

4. **Environmental Monitoring:** 6LoWPAN nodes can be placed in areas where it is difficult for a human to visit and monitor (Rghioui, Bouhorma and Benslimane, 2013). For example, forest monitoring, in which monitoring of rare species of trees is really important. 6LoWPAN nodes can sense and collect data about the environment and help prevent natural disasters (Liang and Yao, 2018)

5. **Industrial Monitoring:** LoWPAN can be used in industrial monitoring. It can help in remotely monitoring the machines, production quality (Rghioui, Bouhorma and Benslimane, 2013). 6LoWPAN devices are easy to implement and inexpensive too. They can be manipulated easily via the Internet. It can be used in stock and storage operations monitoring to make quick decisions on the collected data.

6. **Structure Monitoring:** Monitoring the construction of large projects such as bridges or monitoring the constructed projects for their lifespan becomes important to prevent any disasters they may occur due to poor maintenance or monitoring. 6LoWPAN nodes can play an important role in monitoring large structures by sensing and providing data for analysis. (Rghioui, Bouhorma and Benslimane, 2013) and (Guo-Bin Li, Sheng-Hui Wang and Ting Xu, 2015).

7. **Transport/Traffic Management:** LoWPAN nodes can be embedded in vehicles, roads, traffic lights, toll gates for easy management of traffic and thereby reducing traffic congestion during peak time. For instance, it is observed that during peak time there will be a huge queue of vehicles at toll gates. Sensors (e.g., camera sensors) can be used to capture the vehicle information and generate toll fee and send it to the owner of the vehicle via app or SMS for which the owner can make an online payment on the go.

6LoWPAN CHALLENGES

Some of the research challenges that could improve the capabilities and effectiveness of 6loWPAN are summarized (Shelby, Bormann, 2009) (Vinay Kumar, Sudarshan Tiwari, 2012) (Ma and Luo, 2008) (Bouaziz, Rachedi, 2014) (Nuno, da Silva, 2010) (Mulligan 2007) (Wireless Medium Access Control (MAC) and Physical Layer (PHY)*2007)*(Mainetti, Patrono and Vilei, 2011)(Vohra and Srivastava, 2015) (Qiu and Ma, 2018) (Seliem and Elgazzar, 2018)(Shirbhate and Solapure, 2018)(Shah and Sharma, 2018)

1. **Mobility Support:** There is a need for low-cost mobility support for 6LoWPAN. It is important in 6LoWPAN due to the increased demand for mobile services. 6LoWPAN has to support mobility in order to be applicable in various smart applications. Currently, tunnel-based mobility protocols and routing-based mobility schemes are available for mobility support in 6LoWPAN. But they cannot be used directly without some optimization. Tunnel-based mobility protocols require mobile nodes to communicate by sending and receiving a lot of control information which consumes a lot of energy. Similarly, in the case of routing-based mobility schemes, nodes have to send control messages periodically to maintain mobility management and this consumes a lot of network resources. Existing schemes are performed at the network layer which adds overhead in the form of IPv6 header which affects the energy consumption.

2. **Quality of Service:** This is one of the greatest challenges in Wireless Sensor Networks with 6LoWPAN as it has to work with the constrained network. For example, a) *Scalability:* It needs to be achieved in mobility management i.e., performance must not degrade with the increased density of nodes. b) *Low data loss rate*: It is another QoS requirement in 6loWPAN nodes. A home automation application requires the routing protocol to support 250 devices of a network. A metropolitan-scale sensor network requires the routing protocol to support the clustering of a large number of sensing nodes in regions containing 100 to 10,000 sensing nodes.

3. **Resource Management:** Resource management in constrained networks is a challenging task due to the unavailability of the resources in LoWPAN in terms of power, processing capacity, memory, and bandwidth. Thus there is a need for reducing communication overhead and processing of signaling messages.

4. **Security:** 6LoWPAN may be threatened with external attacks from the Internet or internal attacks due to malicious nodes. Cryptography mechanisms can be used to prevent external attacks but the difficulty raises with the internal attacks. Fragmentation attacks like Tiny fragmentation, Ping of Death may occur while performing fragmentation at 6LoWPAN which is one of the primary tasks of 6LoWPAN. RPL is threatened with Rank attack, Local Repair attack, and Resource depletion attack. Also, false information can be introduced due to attacks that can disturb the communication in LoWPAN. It can be tackled by introducing optimized integrity, authorization, authentication, confidentiality services. For example, public-key cryptography primitives are typically avoided as they are relatively heavyweight when compared to conventional encryption methods.

CONCLUSION

The major objective of IoT is to improve the quality of human mankind. This technology has already become an integral part of many major projects around the world. The technology is meant for making every tiny thing around the world to communicate with each other. The tiny things mean that they are limited in their processing capacity. The communication between these tiny devices must focus on low energy consumption. Thus the IEEE802.15.4 standard for the Data link layer and Physical layer specifies low data rate, low throughput, and low power consumption standard for tiny things. However, it becomes undeniable to send and receive data to and from and IP network. Thus there is a requirement for carrying IPv6 packets over LoWPAN. Considering the incompatibility between the services that are provided by IPv6 and IEEE 802.15.4, an intermediary layer called 6LoWPAN was introduced. 6LoW-PAN can operate on IPv6 packets and make them well suited for transport over LoWPAN. It provides three major functions: Header Compression, Fragmentation, and Mesh Routing. These dominant features have made 6LoWPAN a supreme technology in IoT. Various technical challenges are to be tackled for the enhancement of the applicability of 6LoWPAN in projects like smart cities. This chapter reveals various technical challenges to be addressed in the view of streamlining IPv6 capabilities into low power nodes. It also describes the relevance of 6LoWPAN in various applications. The chapter reflects the importance of 6LoWPAN in IoT.

REFERENCES

Approved IEEE Draft Amendment to IEEE Standard for Information Technology-Telecommunications and Information Exchange Between Systems-Part 15.4: Wireless Medium Access Control (MAC) and Physical Layer (PHY) 2007 Specifications for Low-Rate Wireless Personal Area Networks (LR-WPANS): Amendment to Add Alternate Phy (Amendment of IEEE Std 802.15.4). (2007). *IEEE Approved Std P802.15.4a/D7*. Retrieved from http://ieeexplore.ieee.org/stamp/stamp.jsp?tp=&arnumber=4152704 &isnumber=4152703

Arndt, J., Krause, F., Wunderlich, R., & Heinen, S. (2017). Development of a 6LoWPAN sensor node for IoT based home automation networks. *2017 International Conference on Research and Education in Mechatronics (REM)*, 1-4. 10.1109/REM.2017.8075226

Bormann. (2001). *Robust Header Compression*. RFC 3095 IETF.

Bouaziz & Rachedi. (2014). A survey on mobility management protocols in wireless sensor networks based on 6LoWPAN technology. *Computer Communications*.

Casner & Jacobson. (1999). *Compressing IP/UDP/RTP Headers for Low-Speed Serial Links*. IETF RFC 2508.

Chere, N., & Bembe. (2019). Wireless Low Power Area Networks in the Internet of Things: A Glimpse on 6LoWPAN. *International Conference on Electronics, Information, and Communication (ICEIC)*, 1-10. doi: 10.23919/ELINFOCOM.2019.8706392

Deering, S., & Hinden, B. (1988). *Internet Protocol, Version 6 (IPv6) Specification*. IETF RFC 2460.

Degermark, M., Nordgren, B., & Pink, S. (1999). *IP Header Compression, RFC 2507*. IETF.

Gomez, C., & Paradells, J. (2010). Wireless home automation networks: A survey of architectures and technologies. *IEEE Communications Magazine*, *48*(6), 92–101. doi:10.1109/MCOM.2010.5473869

Gomez, C., Paradells, J., Bormann, C., & Crowcroft, J. (2017). From 6LoWPAN to 6Lo: Expanding the Universe of IPv6-Supported Technologies for the Internet of Things. *IEEE Communications Magazine*, *55*(12), 148–155. doi:10.1109/MCOM.2017.1600534

Haberman & Thaler. (2002). *Unicast-Prefix-based IPv6 Multicast Address*. RFC 3306.

Honggang, Z., Chen, S., & Leyu, Z. (2018). Design and Implementation of Lightweight 6LoWPAN Gateway Based on Contiki. *2018 IEEE International Conference on Signal Processing, Communications and Computing (ICSPCC)*, 1-5. 10.1109/ICSPCC.2018.8567741

Huang, L., Xiao, Y., Liu, J., & Lin, H. (2016). LED intelligent lighting system based on 6LoWPAN. *2016 11th International Conference on Computer Science & Education (ICCSE)*, 529-532. 10.1109/ICCSE.2016.7581636

Hui & Thubert. (2011). *Compression Format for IPv6 Datagrams over IEEE 802.15.4-Based Networks.* RFC 6282.

Hui, C. & Chakrabarti. (2009). *6LoWPAN: Incorporating IEEE 802.15.4 into the IP architecture.* Internet Protocol for Smart Object (IPSO) Alliance White Paper.

Hui & Culler. (2007). *Stateless IPv6 Header Compression for Globally Routable Packets in 6LoWPAN Subnetworks.* draft-hui-6lowpan-hc1g-00.

Huiqin, W., & Yongqiang, D. (2010). An Improved Header Compression Scheme for 6LoWPAN Networks. *2010 Ninth International Conference on Grid and Cloud Computing*, 350-355. 10.1109/GCC.2010.74

Jacobson, Braden, & Borman. (1990). *Compressing TCP/IP headers for low-speed serial links IETF.* Network working group, RFC 1144.

Jara, Zamora, & Skarmeta. (2010). Intra-mobility for Hospital Wireless Sensor Networks based on 6LoWPAN. 6th IEEE (ICWMC), 389–394.

Kumar, V., & Tiwari, S. (2012). Routing in IPv6 over Low-Power Wireless Personal Area Networks (6LoWPAN): A Survey. *Journal of Computer Networks and Communications, Hindawi Publishing Corporation, 2012*, 1–10. doi:10.1155/2012/316839

Kushalnagar, Montenegro, Hui, & Culler. (2007). *Transmission of IPv6 Packets over IEEE 802.15.4 Networks.* IETF RFC 4944.

Kushalnagar, Montenegro, & Schumacher. (2007). *IPv6 over Low-Power Wireless Personal Area Networks (6LoWPANs): overview, assumptions, problem statement, and goals.* IETF RFC 4919.

Lamkimel, M., Naja, N., Jamali, A., & Yahyaoui, A. (2018). The Internet of Things: Overview of the essential elements and the new enabling technology 6LoWPAN. *2018 IEEE International Conference on Technology Management, Operations and Decisions (ICTMOD)*, 142-147. 10.1109/ITMC.2018.8691271

Li, G.-B., Wang, S.-H., & Xu, T. (2015). Application of 6LoWPAN in monitoring system for transmission line. *2015 12th International Computer Conference on Wavelet Active Media Technology and Information Processing (ICCWAMTIP)*, 412-415. doi: 10.1109/ICCWAMTIP.2015.7494021

Liang, D., & Yao, J. (2018). Application of IPv6 in Coal Mine Safety Production Monitoring. *2018 International Conference on Sensor Networks and Signal Processing (SNSP)*, 45-48. 10.1109/SNSP.2018.00018

Lin, W., Fan, Z., Zhong, Y., Zi, S., & Xiao, J. (2017). The Research of Long-Chain Wireless Sensor Network Based on 6LoWPAN. *2017 5th International Conference on Enterprise Systems (ES)*, 143-147. 10.1109/ES.2017.30

Ma, X., & Luo, W. (2008). The analysis of 6LowPAN technology. *Proceedings of the Pacific-Asia Workshop on Computational Intelligence and Industrial Application (PACIIA '08)*, 963–966.

Mainetti, L., Patrono, L., & Vilei, A. (2011). Evolution of wireless sensor networks towards the Internet of Things: A survey. *SoftCOM 2011, 19th International Conference on Software, Telecommunications and Computer Networks*, 1-6.

Mainetti, L., Patrono, L., & Vilei, A. (2011). Evolution of wireless sensor networks towards the Internet of Things: A survey. *SoftCOM, 19th International Conference on Software, Telecommunications and Computer Networks*, 1-6.

Mc Gee, K., & Collier, M. (2019). 6LoWPAN Forwarding Techniques for IoT. *2019 IEEE 5th World Forum on Internet of Things (WF-IoT)*, 888-893. 10.1109/WF-IoT.2019.8767174

Mulligan, G. (2007). The 6LoWPAN architecture. *Proceedings of the 4th Workshop on Embedded Networked Sensors (EmNets '07)*, 78–82. 10.1145/1278972.1278992

Nuno, R., & da Silva, M. (2010). *Mobility support in Low Power Wireless Personal Area Networks (MLoWPAN)*. Coimbra University.

Qiu, Y., & Ma, M. (2018). Secure Group Mobility Support for 6LoWPAN Networks. IEEE Internet of Things Journal, 5(2), 1131-1141. doi:10.1109/JIOT.2018.2805696

Rawat, P., & Bonnin, J.-M. (2010). Designing a header compression mechanism for efficient use of IP tunneling in wireless networks. *Consumer Communications and Networking Conference (CCN C), 7th IEEE*. 10.1109/CCNC.2010.5421788

Rghioui, A., Bouhorma, M., & Benslimane, A. (2013). Analytical study of security aspects in 6LoWPAN networks. *2013 5th International Conference on Information and Communication Technology for the Muslim World (ICT4M)*, 1-5. 10.1109/ICT4M.2013.6518912

Seliem, M., & Elgazzar, K. (2018). IoTeWay: A Secure Framework Architecture for 6LoWPAN Based IoT Applications. *2018 IEEE Global Conference on Internet of Things (GCIoT)*, 1-5. 10.1109/GCIoT.2018.8620137

Shah, M. K., & Sharma, L. K. (2018). Study on 6LoWPAN Routing Protocols with SD aspects in IoT. *2018 2nd International Conference on I-SMAC (IoT in Social, Mobile, Analytics and Cloud) (I-SMAC) I-SMAC (IoT in Social, Mobile, Analytics and Cloud) (I-SMAC), 2018 2nd International Conference on*, 60-65. 10.1109/I-SMAC.2018.8653660

Shelby & Bormann. (2009). *6LoWPAN: The Wireless Embedded Internet*. New York: Wiley.

Shirbhate, M. D., & Solapure, S. S. (2018). Improving existing 6LoWPAN RPL for content based routing. *2018 Second International Conference on Computing Methodologies and Communication (ICCMC)*, 632-635. 10.1109/ICCMC.2018.8487866

Singh, D., Tiwary, U. S., Lee, H., & Chung, W. (2009). Global healthcare monitoring system using 6lowpan networks. *11th International Conference on Advanced Communication Technology*, 113-117.

Tanaka, Y., Minet, P., & Watteyne, T. (2019). 6LoWPAN Fragment Forwarding. IEEE Communications Standards Magazine, 3(1), 35-39. doi:10.1109/MCOMSTD.2019.1800029

Vasseur, J., & Dunkels, A. (2010). *Interconnecting Smart Objects with IP - The Next Internet*. Morgan Kaufmann.

Vohra, S., & Srivastava, R. (2015). A Survey on Techniques for Securing 6LoWPAN. *2015 Fifth International Conference on Communication Systems and Network Technologies*, 643-647. 10.1109/CSNT.2015.163

Chapter 9
Antennas for IoT Application:
An RF and Microwave Aspect of IoT

Badar Muneer
Mehran University of Engineering and Technology, Pakistan

Faisal Karim Shaikh
Mehran University of Engineering and Technology, Pakistan

Qi Zhu
University of Science and Technology of China, China

ABSTRACT

Under the umbrella of 5G there are many technology projects (e.g., internet of things, in-vehicle communication, smart cities, e-health systems, etc.). To understand the concept of IoT, the authors first understand the revolution of technological networks and later discuss what IoT is, the importance of antennas, and future vision.

INTRODUCTION

The diverse ecosystem of Internet of Things (IoT) brings along uncountable end-devices utilizing all sorts of radio modules, sensors/actuators, batteries/cells, MEMS devices, energy harvest techniques, and on top of all, antennas. The choice and design of the antenna is application dependent and varies depending on the frequency range, transmission strength and availability of space. Unlike the high-throughput wireless networks such as 5G, IEEE 802.11ax and WiGig etc. that utilize vast continuous spectrum space, IoT network smartly transmits/receivers small chunks of data in an IoT network in various network topologies like star, mesh and/or point-to-point. Most of the times, the job of establishing such types of links is accomplished by some common and relatively less complex types of omni-directional antennas such as wire antennas, rubber duck, patch, whip, PCB and on-chip antenna structures. Several IoT development kits and platforms such as Arduino GSM and Qualcomm IoE make use of similar antennas structures for GPS, Bluetooth and Wifi communication. Some applications such as Medical Body Area Networks

DOI: 10.4018/978-1-7998-1253-1.ch009

(MBAN) and wearable electronics also require antennas to be low-profile and conformal to the surface of the device. This persuades the need of developing antennas specific to end-device and tailored to meet specialized applications requirements. Antennas for IoT can either be categorized according to their bands of operation or the application; Unlicensed ISM bands e.g. frequencies around 2.4 GHz are more common in IoT development platforms. Whereas, some applications also include antennas for licensed bands such as Avionics applications. The table below highlights few antennas frequently used in IoT applications with their frequency bands.

Antenna technology has hit its limits providing sustainable communication medium to lot of commercial markets such as IoT, Radar, aerospace market. Many companies are developing antenna devices by using different approaches that were previously not envisioned. There are several antenna types to choose depending on different radio bands and each band requires different types of antennas. When choosing an antenna size, cost, and performances are the most important factor.

Let us look at the sampling of different antenna technologies that have gained our attention over the recent years.

Printed Antennas

The printed antennas have chosen to become favorite option in modern wireless communication systems. The required architecture for manufacturing these printed antennas differ from already available hardware being utilized in wireless routers, smart phones, laptops etc. The main advantage of printed antennas is their low manufacturing cost, weight and the capability of miniaturization, and ease of integration with on-board circuitry. Some common designs of printed antennas used are discussed below:

Micro Strip Patch Antenna

The integration of novel sensing systems with printed antennas have opened doors for smart sensors and wireless sensor network, which was unconceivable just few years ago. The most popular among printed

Table 1 Frequency bands and IoT applications

Application	Technology	Frequency band
Smart homes/Smart buildings	Wifi	2.4 GHz,
	GPS	1575.42 MHz, 1227.6 MHz, 1176.45 MHz
	Zigbee	915 MHz, 2.4 GHz
	Z-wave	2.4 GHz
	Bluetooth	2.4 GHz
	HART	2.4 GHz
	ISA 100.11a	2.4 GHz
Smart Agriculture, Smart cities	LoRa	433 MHz, 868 MHz, 915 MHz
	Sigfox	868 MHz, 902 MHz
Medical	MBAN/WBAN IEEE 802.15.6	400 MHz, 800 MHz, 900 MHz, 2.36 GHz, 2.4 GHz
Avionics (intra-com)	WAIC	4.2 GHz, 4.4 GHz

antennas is micro strip antennas. The topology is shown in Figure 1 with scheme of sensing device shown in Figure 2. A microstrip antenna comprises of a radiating patch separated by a dielectric material with an electrically big ground plane. Radiation pattern of these antennas differ according to patch shape, commonly which are: rectangular (Werfelli, Tayari, Chaoui, Lahiani, & Ghariani, 2016) and circular etc.

Rectangular antennas (Sivia & Bhatia, 2015) are linearly polarized showing good results of return loss VSWR and Gain, obtaining better suppression for side lobe level especially in 4x1 array (Melad M. Olaimat, 2016). While circularly polarized antennas (Kumar, Ghivela, & Sengupta, 2019) have dual feeding lines show better results on bandwidth, radiation pattern, side lobes and impedance matching (Shailza Gotra Gaurav Varshney Rajveer Singh Yaduvanshi Vinay Shankar Pandey, 2019).Other shapes in micro strip patch antenna can also be used (Tripathy, Ranjan, Kumar, & Kumar, 2015) by keeping typical patch size of λg/2, where λg is the wavelength in dielectric material over which patch is sketched. A high quality factor is achieved by microstrip antennas, however with the resonant frequency limited to 5-10% of bandwidth. The possibility of miniaturization by means of high permittivity substrate or even with ground slotted planes is yet another advantage of micro strip antenna. Dual wireless system (Wi-Fi or WiMax) can be developed using dual micro strip antenna example: on-body communication

Figure 1: Topology of microstrip patch antenna

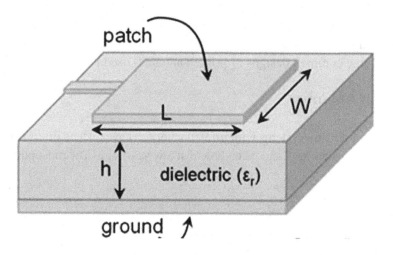

Figure 2: Scheme of sensing device, with tentative implementation of microstrip patch antenna

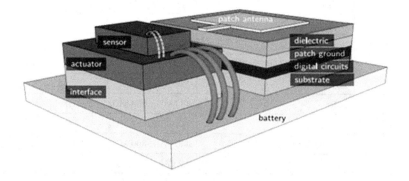

system, medical sensor network, radio links and short-range personal communication can be included in microstrip patch antenna applications for IoT (Lizzi, Ferrero, Monin, Danchesi, & Boudaud, 2016). In recent times, wearable (Lee & Choi, 2017) and body WBAN applications, spiral printed antennas (S. Zhang et al., 2015) using textile substrate have been proposed with dual band operation for GSM 900, DCS1800 (Goncalves, Carvalho, Pinho, Loss, & Salvado, 2013; Loss, Gonçalves, Lopes, Pinho, & Salvado, 2016; Mustaqim et al., 2019) including GPS and LoRa band (Lizzi et al., 2016)frequency. This patch intended to obtain geo location information through GPS and send it by using LoRa transceiver.

Slot Antenna

Different kinds of physical layer technologies are used in IoT nodes; one of them is slot antennas. A typical slot antenna is shown in Figure 3. Slot antennas have a pattern of bidirectional radiation with a broader bandwidth than antennas using microstrip technology. Their fundamental issue is the difficulty of incorporating them into the electronics. CPW feed systems are usually used to enhance integration possibilities and achieving even wider bandwidths. Traditional slot antenna technology is now being integrated in substrate integrated waveguide structure (SIW) due to their compactness and ease of integration with existing circuity on a microstrip substrate. These types of antennas are used in Radio Frequency Identification (RFID) with different shapes providing automated wireless identification and tracking capabilities operating in UHF band (860-950 MHz) being complimented with ISO 15693 (13.6MHz) for performance analysis of food logistics (Eom, Kim, Lee, & Lee, 2012).

Some other novel applications including battery less solar powered RF tags (Amendola, Lodato, Manzari, Occhiuzzi, & Marrocco, 2014; Lakafosis et al., 2010; Shoykhetbrod, Niibler, & Hommes, n.d.), T.Mishra et al(Eltresy, Elsheakh, Abdallah, & Elhennawy, 2019) made power management system for wireless energy harvesting application using SIW based slotted array antenna.

Other type of printed antennas like folded-F, monopole, quasi-Yagi antennas that are being used in commercial applications are summarized in Table 2.

Future Antennas

In many commercial and aerospace markets, traditional antenna technology has hit its limit such as 5G, IoT and Radar Telecommunication companies are developing new ways to innovate, improve the antennas performance for next generation enabling new applications that were not previously envisioned. The

Figure 3: Slot antenna with ground plane

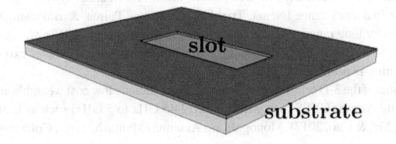

Table 2: Types of Antennas used in commercial wireless system

System	Frequency Band (s)	Antenna(s)
RFID tags	30MHz to 2.4 GHz	Loop, folded-F, patch or monopole
GSM Handsets	T: 880-915 MHz R:925-960 T:1710-1785 R:1805-1880 MHz T:1850-1910 MHz R:1930-1990 MHz	Monopole, sleeve dipole, folded-F or patch
GPS receivers	1227 and 1575 MHz	Microstrip patch, bifilar helix
Bluetooth, WLAN	2.4-2.5 GHz 5.15-5.35GHz 5,725-5.820 GHz	Monopole, sleeve dipole, folded-F or patch
DBS subscribers	11.7-12.5 GHz	Offset fed reflector, strip line slot array

requirement to achieve high reliability and low latency for internet of things (IoT) applications, product engineers are using 3D printing techniques to make antennas with smaller size, lighter and more powerful than ever before. In next few years many new exciting technologies are going to revolutionized antenna technology, few of the unique approaches currently introduced are 3D printing, metamaterial and fractal antennas that is going to address many challenges that are being faced today in 5G, IoT, SATCOM and Radar applications. Some major technologies in future antennas that have come to our attention are as discussed under.

3-D printed Antenna

The technology of 3-D printing is rapidly growing due to ease of use and variety of its applications in field. Additive manufacturing has enabled recent advances in 3-D printing by realizing complex RF structures. 3-D printing material used in the characterization of these structures have shown accurate results in predicting the performance but they are found to be critical in designing. In the realm of 3-D printing manufacturers have led to the development of traditional antennas shapes with novel RF structures with less weight at lower cost.

The production of microwave antennas and devices via 3-D printing method such as focused ion beam chemical vapor deposition (FIB-CVD), micro stereo lithography (MSL), Ultra Visible assisted 3-D printing, Conformal printing are suitable, common techniques. Few of such products include micro strip band pass filters (Araujo et al., 2017; Choi, Stubbs, & Park, 2003), horn antennas (Miralles, Schoenlinner, Belenguer, Esteban, & Ziegler, 2019) for Ka Band, bowtie antenna (Mirzaee, Noghanian, Wiest, & Chang, 2015), U-Helix antenna using micro-electro mechanical systems(MEMS) novel technology for 1 THz frequency range (Nenzi, Tripaldi, Varlamava, Palma, & Balucani, 2012), harmonic planar transponder for long range covering up to 4 meters (Palazzi et al., 2017), waveguides, resonator, antennas pad, etc. So far, these devices are using 2-step procedure, which includes extrusion and curing methods along with 3-D printers.

Meanwhile some of the 3-D printed antenna applications include low cost wearable antenna for global Navigation satellite system (GNSS) using ISM band (2.45 GHz to 5 GHz) such as Button Antenna (X. Y. Zhang, Wong, Mo, & Cao, 2017), Monopole zip Antenna (Mantash, Tarot, Collardey, & Mahdjoubi,

2011) Conformal Antenna on 3-D printed wearable bracelet (Jun et al., 2018), etc, depending on the specific nature of IoT application. Few 3-D printed Antennas are shown below in Figure 4.

Metamaterial Based Antennas

Metamaterials are not found naturally instead they are arranged in a way so that they can produce electromagnetic response that is not found in nature (Dong & Itoh, 2012). The periodic structures have created similar wavelengths, negative indexes as influenced from the naturally occurred materials; in short, these materials are controlled structures in a way that cannot be done with natural materials. The traditional active electronically scanned arrays (AESA), phase shifters are embedded in control circuitry. While metamaterial based AESA reduces the complexities involved in phased array antennas by steering the beam without phase shifters eliminating the power loss and heat dissipation.

A couple of antenna structures made up of unique metamaterials such as (Ali & Biradar, 2017) describes compact multi band antenna by utilizing a novel meta material based split ring resonator (SRR) working on IEEE 802.11n (WLAN) and IEEE 802.16e (WiMAX) for the frequency band 2.4-5.8 GHz. Similarly (Stevenson, Sazegar, Bily, Johnson, & Kundtz, 2016) Kymeta company has developed a metamaterial surface antenna technology based on a diffractive metamaterial concept using thin film resistor acting as tunable dielectric as depicted in Figure 5. They use liquid crystal (LC) also known as High-birefringence liquid crystal in-between glass structure to form holographic beams that can receive and transmit satellite signal and maintain the link while antenna is in motion which looks like LCD flat television. It has replaced traditional satellite dish antenna by creating thousands of phase arrays generating separate signal. Kymeta's antenna technology provides internet connectivity and uses software

Figure 4: 3D printed antennas for various IoT applications (a) Hemisphere meandering antenna (b) Optisys Ka-Band 16-element tracking array (d) Harmonic Transponder (d) Wrist band antenna

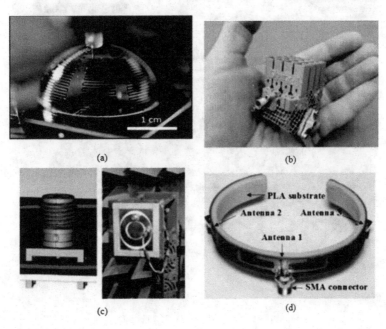

to steer antenna towards satellite replacing mechanical parts (gimbals) shown in Figure 5. Key features of this technology are:

1. Via single aperture, it can transmit and receive data.
2. Excellent beam performance and wide-angle scanning
3. Electronically controllable polarization and beam pointing.

Previously it was inaccessible for industries like satellite, maritime and aviation industry to implement satellite technology in across smaller vessels and aircraft.

Another company named **Echodyne**,(Bob Yirka, n.d.) has developed first metamaterial-based electronically scanning array(MESA) Radar antenna making it a high performance radar antenna by reducing the cost, size (up to 10 times smaller) and easier to deploy. Echodyne Radar combines high resolutions

Figure 5: Kymeta's 70cm Ku-band Meta surface on the assembly line

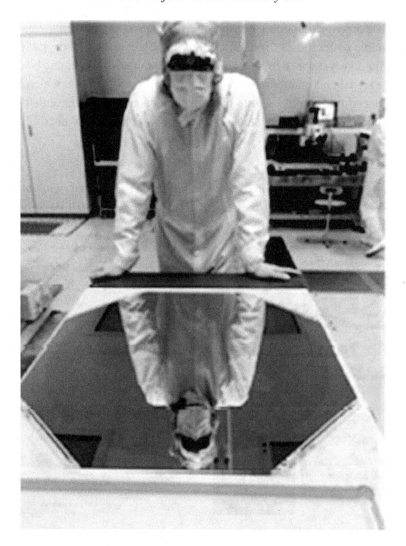

imaging capabilities with the all-weather, long range and ground truth measurement working in X-Band. In practice, such technology works similarly as bats do to avoid obstacles such as unmanned craft i.e. drones. The technology Echodyne Radar is utilizing is able to switch to multi beams steering in less than 1 micro seconds, operating at 24 GHz with range of 3.4 Km. Figure 6 depicts the Echodyne Radar vision that can replace next iPhone.

Fractal Antennas

The repetition of simple shapes out of complex patterns is known as "fractal". It is the proposed method by using some iterative mathematical rule to design fun shapes that if you zoom in zoom out the structure remains the same. Such technique is used to increase the bandwidth of traditional antenna. Using fractal geometry, fractal antenna can be created enabling the better radiation properties and compact size; making it excellent choice for wideband and multi band applications. This type of antenna was produced by the company named as Fractal Antenna that visions to reproduce all the existing antennas as shown in Figure 7, through fractal technology that is attained through geometry of the conductor rather than the accumulation of separate components that increases the complexity and cost.

This company was the first to demonstrate unique RF and microwave invisible cloaking and deflection technology via fractal structures. In their demonstration a test signal from 750 to 1250MHz was attenuated by only 0.5 dB over 50% bandwidth while normal signal takes 6 to 15 dB.

Fractal technology meets the different design requirements aiming to incorporate in mobile devices and IoT end-devices. Mousa et al. (Mousa, Abdullah, & El Din Abo El-Soud, 2018) presented a novel RFID tag employing multi resonators stub with two fractal microstrip antennas having 12 dB signal strength, can encode 12 bit data operating in UWB band ranging from 3 to 6.2 GHz with the gain twice the tag antennas. Similarly Marco et al (Salucci, Anselmi, Goudos, & Massa, 2019) proposed fractal

Figure 6. Echodyne's radar vision unit next to an iPhone.

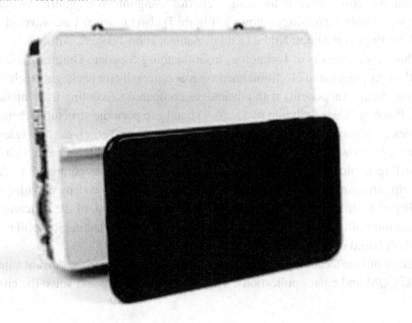

Figure 7. Fractal bow-tie antenna

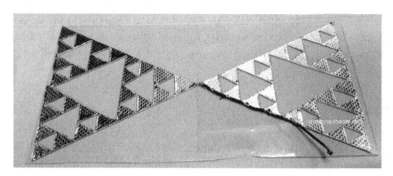

antenna for Narrow band IoT application by means of system by design (SbD) paradigm operating over multi bands using different software modules.

Other Promising Technologies

Plasma Antenna is yet another upcoming future antenna technology started with an idea of coaxial plasma closing switch (Ted Anderson, Alexeff, & 10.1., 2011; Theodore Anderson, 2014) which demonstrated stealth, reconfigurability and protection from electronics warfare. This remarkable discovery of plasma antenna (PSiAN) have range of innovative plasma silicon devices (PSiD) that can replace RF switches, phase shifters and attenuators with one loss less device. The PSiD offers wideband switching, multi-port accessibility, high power handling device with high precision for the mass market at low cost. Small cell backhaul at V band (60GHz)(V-Band 60GHz Millimeter Wave MMW Technology, n.d.), gigabit wireless LAN, intelligent transport system at 63 GHz and vehicle radar (77GHz) are some of the possible applications of PSiAN plasma antenna. This technology (Alexeff, Anderson, Farshi, Karnam, & Pulasani, 2008) has already been tested up to 40W showing that it does not need any calibration and has the potential to solve different handling scenarios using intrinsic qualities of plasma silicon.

Gap waveguide Technology (shown in Figure 7) also known as Gap wave AB was first experimented in 2011 by Professor Simon Kildal (Kildal, Zaman, Rajo-Iglesias, Alfonso, & Valero-Nogueira, 2011) from Chalmers University of Technology in Gothenburg, Sweden. The aim of this technology is to provide contactless propagation of electromagnetic waves especially for packaging technology for mm-Wave and Terahertz circuit components with advantages compared to existing transmission line and waveguide. The GAP waveguide is built into two parts 1) band gap periodic structured metal surface with ridges on both sides (Alfonso et al., 2010), (Ebrahimpouri, Quevedo-Teruel, & Rajo-Iglesias, 2017) and 2) a flat metal surface allowing air to flow between the two parts for high gain and high efficiency applications. This GAP technology has made antennas to achieve lesser loss compared to that of an antenna using microstrip structure, Substrate Integrated Waveguide (SIW) and rectangular waveguide. The design flexibility of multilayer waveguide has enabled to achieve 80% of the efficiency; effective cooling for active circuits with gain of 38 dBi for E-Band antenna system making it useful for high-power amplifiers and CMOS based control circuits.

The new unique technologies which promises to revolutionize the current antenna technology for 5G, IoT, SATCOM and radar applications. They aim to overcome and solve the challenges that traditional

Figure 8: Waveguide internal structure

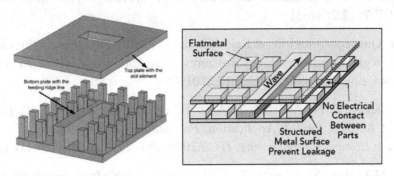

antennas technologies such as 3-D printing, metamaterial and fractal antennas was not able to solve in the next few years.

REFERENCES

Alexeff, I., Anderson, T., Farshi, E., Karnam, N., & Pulasani, N. R. (2008). Recent results for plasma antennas. *Physics of Plasmas*, *15*(5), 057104. doi:10.1063/1.2919157

Alfonso, E., Baquero, M., Kildal, P. S., & Valero-Nogueira, A. RajoIglesias, E., & Herranz, J. I. (2010). Design of microwave circuits in ridge-gap waveguide technology. IEEE MTT-S International Microwave Symposium Digest, (l), 1544–1547. 10.1109/MWSYM.2010.5514731

Ali, T., & Biradar, R. C. (2017). A compact multiband antenna using λ /4 rectangular stub loaded with metamaterial for IEEE 802.11N and IEEE 802.16E. *Microwave and Optical Technology Letters*, *59*(5), 1000–1006. doi:10.1002/mop.30454

Amendola, S., Lodato, R., Manzari, S., Occhiuzzi, C., & Marrocco, G. (2014). RFID technology for IoT-based personal healthcare in smart spaces. *IEEE Internet of Things Journal*, *1*(2), 144–152. doi:10.1109/JIOT.2014.2313981

Anderson, T. (2014). Plasma frequency selective surfaces. IEEE Antennas and Propagation Society, AP-S International Symposium (Digest), 35(2), 2096–2097. 10.1109/APS.2014.6905375

Anderson, T., & Alexeff, I. (2011). Plasma antennas. Frontiers in Antennas Next Generation Design & Engineering. *Plasma Antennas*, *34*(2), 226.

Araujo, L. S., Shang, X., Lancaster, M. J., de Oliveira, A. J. B., Llamas-Garro, I., Kim, J. M., ... de Rijk, E. (2017). 3-D printed band-pass combline filter. *Microwave and Optical Technology Letters*, *59*(6), 1388–1390. doi:10.1002/mop.30547

Bob Yirka, T. X. (n.d.). Echodyne uses metamaterials to make drone sized radar system. Academic Press.

Choi, B. G., Stubbs, M. G., & Park, C. S. (2003). A Ka-band narrow bandpass filter using LTCC technology. *IEEE Microwave and Wireless Components Letters*, *13*(9), 388–389. doi:10.1109/LMWC.2003.817139

Dong, Y., & Itoh, T. (2012). Metamaterial-based antennas. *Proceedings of the IEEE, 100*(7), 2271–2285. doi:10.1109/JPROC.2012.2187631

Ebrahimpouri, M., Quevedo-Teruel, O., & Rajo-Iglesias, E. (2017). Design guidelines for gap waveguide technology based on glide-symmetric holey structures. *IEEE Microwave and Wireless Components Letters, 27*(6), 542–544. doi:10.1109/LMWC.2017.2701308

Eltresy, N. A., Elsheakh, D. N., Abdallah, E. A., & Elhennawy, H. M. (2019). RF Energy Harvesting Using Transparent Antenna for IoT Application. *Proceedings of 2019 International Conference on Innovative Trends in Computer Engineering, ITCE 2019*, 287–291. doi:10.1109/ITCE.2019.8646423

Eom, K. H., Kim, M. C., Lee, S., & Lee, C. W. (2012). The vegetable freshness monitoring system using RFID with oxygen and carbon dioxide sensor. *International Journal of Distributed Sensor Networks, 2012*, 1–6. doi:10.1155/2012/472986

Goncalves, R., Carvalho, N. B., Pinho, P., Loss, C., & Salvado, R. (2013). Textile antenna for electromagnetic energy harvesting for GSM900 and DCS1800 bands. IEEE Antennas and Propagation Society, AP-S International Symposium (Digest), 1, 1206–1207. 10.1109/APS.2013.6711263

Gotra, Varshney, & Singh, Vinay, & Pandey. (2019). Dual-band circular polarisation generation technique with the miniaturisation of a rectangular dielectric resonator antenna. *IET Microwaves, Antennas & Propagation*.

Jun, S. Y., Elibiary, A., Sanz-Izquierdo, B., Winchester, L., Bird, D., & McCleland, A. (2018). 3-D printing of conformal antennas for diversity wrist worn applications. *IEEE Transactions on Components, Packaging, and Manufacturing Technology, 8*(12), 2227–2235. doi:10.1109/TCPMT.2018.2874424

Kildal, P.-S., Zaman, A. U., Rajo-Iglesias, E., Alfonso, E., & Valero-Nogueira, A. (2011). Design and experimental verification of ridge gap waveguide in bed of nails for parallel-plate mode suppression. *IET Microwaves, Antennas & Propagation, 5*(3), 262. doi:10.1049/iet-map.2010.0089

Kumar, P., Ghivela, G. C., & Sengupta, J. (2019). Design and Analysis of Multiple bands Spider Web Shaped Circular Patch Antenna for IoT Application. India International Conference on Power Electronics, IICPE, 2018–Decem, 1–5. 10.1109/IICPE.2018.8709444

Lakafosis, V., Rida, A., Vyas, R., Yang, L., Nikolaou, S., & Tentzeris, M. M. (2010). Progress towards the first wireless sensor networks consisting of inkjet-printed, paper-based RFID-enabled sensor tags. *Proceedings of the IEEE, 98*(9), 1601–1609. doi:10.1109/JPROC.2010.2049622

Lee, H., & Choi, J. (2017). A polarization reconfigurable textile patch antenna for wearable IoT applications. *2017 International Symposium on Antennas and Propagation, ISAP 2017*, 1–2. doi:10.1109/ISANP.2017.8228882

Lizzi, L., Ferrero, F., Monin, P., Danchesi, C., & Boudaud, S. (2016). Design of miniature antennas for IoT applications. 2016 IEEE 6th International Conference on Communications and Electronics, IEEE ICCE 2016, 234–237. 10.1109/CCE.2016.7562642

Loss, C., Gonçalves, R., Lopes, C., Pinho, P., & Salvado, R. (2016). Smart coat with a fully-embedded textile antenna for IoT applications. [PubMed]. *Sensors (Switzerland), 16*(6), 938. doi:10.339016060938

Mantash, M., Tarot, A. C., Collardey, S., & Mahdjoubi, K. (2011). Wearable monopole zip antenna. *Electronics Letters*, *47*(23), 1266. doi:10.1049/el.2011.2784

Miralles, E., Schoenlinner, B., Belenguer, Á., Esteban, H., & Ziegler, V. (2019). A 3-D Printed PCB Integrated TEM Horn Antenna. *Radio Science*, *54*(1), 158–165. doi:10.1029/2018RS006594

Mirzaee, M., Noghanian, S., Wiest, L., & Chang, I. (2015). Developing flexible 3D printed antenna using conductive ABS materials. IEEE Antennas and Propagation Society, *AP-S International Symposium (Digest)*, 1308–1309. 10.1109/APS.2015.7305043

Mousa, M. E., Abdullah, H. H., & El Din Abo El-Soud, M. (2018). Compact Chipless RFID Tag Based on Fractal Antennas and Multiple Microstrip Open Stub Resonators. Progress in Electromagnetics Research Symposium, 1332–1338. 10.23919/PIERS.2018.8598207

Mustaqim, M., Khawaja, B. A., Chattha, H. T., Shafique, K., Zafar, M. J., & Jamil, M. (2019). Ultra-wideband antenna for wearable Internet of Things devices and wireless body area network applications. International Journal of Numerical Modelling: Electronic Networks, Devices and Fields, 1–12. doi:10.1002/jnm.2590

Nenzi, P., Tripaldi, F., Varlamava, V., Palma, F., & Balucani, M. (2012). On-chip THz 3D antennas. Proceedings - Electronic Components and Technology Conference, 102–108. 10.1109/ECTC.2012.6248813

Olaimat, M. M. (2016). Comparison between Rectangular and Circular Patch AntennasArray. *International Journal of Computational Engineering Research*, *6*(9).

Palazzi, V., Alimenti, F., Kalialakis, C., Mezzanotte, P., Georgiadis, A., & Roselli, L. (2017). Highly Integrable Paper-Based Harmonic Transponder for Low-Power and Long-Range IoT Applications. *IEEE Antennas and Wireless Propagation Letters*, *16*, 3196–3199. doi:10.1109/LAWP.2017.2768383

Salucci, M., Anselmi, N., Goudos, S., & Massa, A. (2019). Fast design of multiband fractal antennas through a system-by-design approach for NB-IoT applications. Eurasip Journal on Wireless Communications and Networking, 2019(1). doi:10.118613638-019-1386-4

Sivia, J. S., & Bhatia, S. S. (2015). Design of fractal based microstrip rectangular patch antenna for multiband applications. Souvenir of the 2015 IEEE International Advance Computing Conference, IACC 2015, 1(151302), 712–715. 10.1109/IADCC.2015.7154799

Stevenson, R., Sazegar, M., Bily, A., Johnson, M., & Kundtz, N. (2016). Metamaterial surface antenna technology: Commercialization through diffractive metamaterials and liquid crystal display manufacturing. 2016 10th International Congress on Advanced Electromagnetic Materials in Microwaves and Optics, METAMATERIALS 2016, 349–351. 10.1109/MetaMaterials.2016.7746395

Tripathy, M. R., Ranjan, P., Kumar, A., & Kumar, S. (2015). A compact dual band antenna for IOV applications. *Lecture Notes in Computer Science*, *9502*, 315–323. doi:10.1007/978-3-319-27293-1_28

Werfelli, H., Tayari, K., Chaoui, M., Lahiani, M., & Ghariani, H. (2016). Design of rectangular microstrip patch antenna. *2nd International Conference on Advanced Technologies for Signal and Image Processing, ATSIP 2016*, 798–803. doi:10.1109/ATSIP.2016.7523197

Zhang, S., Speight, D., Paraskevopoulos, A., Fonseca, D., Luxey, C., Whittow, W., & Pinto, J. (2015). On-body measurements of embroidered spiral antenna. *2015 Loughborough Antennas and Propagation Conference*, 1–5. doi:10.1109/LAPC.2015.7366131

Zhang, X. Y., Wong, H., Mo, T., & Cao, Y. F. (2017). Dual-Band Dual-Mode Button Antenna for On-Body and Off-Body Communications. [PubMed]. *IEEE Transactions on Biomedical Circuits and Systems*, *11*(4), 933–941. doi:10.1109/TBCAS.2017.2679048

Chapter 10
Industry 4.0 Privacy and Security Protocol Issues in Internet of Things

Jayapandian N.
(iD) https://orcid.org/0000-0002-7054-0163
Faculty of Engineering, Christ University, Bangalore, India

ABSTRACT

The main objectives of this chapter are to discuss the basics of IoT and its applications and to solve data security and privacy issues in Industry 4.0. Industry 4.0 is mainly focus on IoT technology. The IIoT is generating digital data, and that data is stored in cloud server. There are two major issues in this IIoT. The first one is data storage, and the second one is data security. Industry 4.0 is not only involved in the manufacturing industry. It is also in the transportation and automobile industries. Electrical, electronic, mechanical, and computer technology fields are involved in Industry 4.0. This chapter enhances the hybrid security protocol in Industrial IoT. This hybrid mechanism combines lightweight protocol and the probabilistic encryption (LPP) algorithm.

INTRODUCTION

Internet of Things (IoT) is a heart of modern technology. IoT is bridging between the hardware device and software component by using internet communication. There are two types of machine: traditional machine and digital machine. The major difference between these two machines is the activities performed by the machine, which can be mechanical, electrical or computational. Digital machine solely relies on direct current and thus its activities are computational, for instance, computers. The traditional machine comprised of analog inputs and also works mechanically such as motors and automobiles. The digital machine is controlled and monitored from remote location that is named as IoT based digital machine. This IoT based digital machine is an application, which is combination of mechanical, electrical and computer machine. The modern industry revolution focuses on automation. Automation emphasizes on manpower reduction with the help of machine. Almost 70% of jobs currently are automated in mechani-

DOI: 10.4018/978-1-7998-1253-1.ch010

cal industry; there are two major reasons behind this automation. The primary reason is to reduce the manufacturing cost and manpower. The secondary reason, this automation is providing higher quality in product (Kolberg & Zühlke, 2015). Industry 4.0 majorly focuses on computing and Internet technology. The computing technology is widely spread and involves several domains such as cloud computing, distributed computing and fog computing (Dizdarević, Carpio, Jukan & Masip-Bruin, 2019). The aim of industry 4.0 is to use modern technology in industry and increase the quality of service (Gilchrist, 2016). The word smart is used in effective usage of existing technology in different applications. Smart industry is a final destination of industry 4.0 with inclusion of IoT. Smart industry means usage of existing machine and incorporate that machine in latest IoT technology (Wang et al., 2016). IoT devices control and monitor the entire machine activities. IoT has been modernized in Industrial Internet of Things (IIoT). The recent survey shows that more than 45% of industry has already implemented IoT technology in their industry. In coming years, it will reach approximately 70% (Wollschlaeger, Sauter & Jasperneite, 2017). The financial growth of IIoT is excepted to reach nearly 123 Billion US dollar by the year 2021 (Manavalan & Jayakrishna, 2019). Transportation and logistics companies have also inclined to implement IIoT technology for the purpose of better service provision (Liu et al., 2019). The IoT security is one of the emerging topics in modern industry, since huge number of industry machines is inter-connected with IoT devices. Lightweight protocol has been used previously to reduce the memory space; and probabilistic algorithm provides higher security in machine data encryption. The IoT security protocols face several issues that are: cross layer connection establishment and device data security. The major advantage of IoT is reduction in computational cost and it provides a new business model. The objective of this chapter is to enhance additional IoT security system by using Lightweight Protocol with Probabilistic (LPP) algorithm.

APPLICATION OF SMART IoT

Internet of Things (IoT) is analogous to operating system; the basic working principle of operating system is to establish the connection between machine components and human. The same mechanism is involved in IoT technology. IoT is establishing the network connection and transferring the machine data from physical device to other physical device or cloud server (Guo et al., 2013). Machine to Machine communication is a next advanced communication protocol system in industry (Theoleyre & Pang, 2013). This device to device communication system is established with the help of internet communication. Internet is a global network communication for connecting multiple computers in single domain. IoT is widely spread in multiple domains. In the recent days, government has also taken some initiative to use this technology in governance projects (Mueller, Mathiason & Klein, 2007). For example, smart city is one of the government projects using IoT; the purpose of smart city is to use technological solutions and reshape life style for civilians (Jayapandian, 2019).

The smart city concept has been introduced in the year 2004 (Midgley, 2009), which uses modern IoT devices such as sensors, biometric detectors and automatic data collecting from devices (Su, Li & Fu, 2011). These devices generate digital data, manage and control that information in centralized server by using Internet communication. The objective of smart city concept is minimizing manpower and optimizing entire city operation by using information technology and network communication system. The combination of communication and information technology provides better performance. Communication technology is a primary and information technology is a secondary pillar of smart city (Kramers,

Höjer, Lövehagen & Wangel, 2014). These two technologies are providing better quality, at the same time increase the smart city performance. The introduction of IoT technology has resulted in smart home, which has been replaced by smart city concept (Zanella et al., 2014). The IoT is major component of smart city for the past ten years. Technology based society is unavoidable in future; increasing demand of modern life style is promoting this kind of smart technology (Ahmad, Paul, Rathore & Change, 2016). There are many IoT projects running under smart city concept; one of the major applications is traffic management and monitoring system (Al-Shammari, Al-Aboody & Al-Raweshidy, 2018). The recent research focuses on controlling traffic system by using network routing algorithm (Yang et al., 2014). The concept of IoT based traffic management system helps in monitoring traffic scenario in centralized system, some private service providers provide alternate route, thus reducing traffic on a certain road (Foschini, Taleb, Corradi & Bottazzi, 2011). Smart city establishes surveillance in public places; this system helps to identify thefts and illegal activities (Abas, Taleb, Porto & Obraczka, 2014). The smart city dealing with different level of problem, it also provides solution in major divisions of smart city such as smart homes or smart buildings. Nowadays, more than 70% of home appliances are interconnected with IoT technology (Noury, Barralon, Vuillerme & Fleury, 2012). Development of modern society smart home is a structured home; at the time of building construction, IoT devices are installed. Examples of smart home interconnection are smart TV, smart washing machine, and smart surveillance camera (Miller, 2015). These are some of the products apart from this, many applications are mutually interconnect and establish the centralized communication (Petrolo, Loscri & Mitton, 2017).

The figure 1 elaborates smart city applications. Smart energy management system is integrated unit of smart city. Under this energy division, IoT technology related to energy is utilized (Zhou et al., 2016). The objective of smart energy is providing computational energy service with lower cost. Smart grid is one of the sub-division of energy division; smart grid establishes power connection from one city to another city (Stojkoska & Trivodaliev, 2017). The aim of smart grid technology is establishing connection in the shortest distance in order to reduce cost and at the same time, power loss is also avoided. The expected market growth of smart grid technology is considered 61 billion US dollars (Strong, 2019). This technology helps to improve the grid reliability and provide efficient reduction in power outage. Power generation is one of the major problems in developing country. The investment of power generation unit is very high, thus, it is very unlikely to establish power unit in different locations (Järventausta, Repo, Rautiainen & Partanen, 2010). The solution to this very problem is transmitting power from one power unit to nearest cities/locations; during the power transmission power loss is unavoidable. IoT technology is used in this smart grid in reducing the power loss during transmission (Jaradat et al., 2015).

Smart meter is also major part in smart city development. Manpower is used for measuring the traditional method for consumer power usage; sometime power theft is one of the major issues in this field. Government and private sector have faced heavy loss due to power theft (Morello, De Capua, Fulco & Mukhopadhyay, 2017). Almost 15% electricity of overall power production is illegally stolen (Smith, 2004) in developing countries. Manual detection of power theft is next to impossible, that is the reason IoT based power monitoring system has been adopted, which helps to trace electricity theft. Smart meter measures electricity usage of consumers and sends its data to centralized unit on the day-by-day basis. This technology helps in reducing electricity theft and also reduces manpower (Depuru, Wang & Devabhaktuni, 2011). Using smart energy concept, electricity wastage is also solved; for instance, public lighting system is connected with centralized IoT device. Cloud based smart solar management system is also used in modern homes (Jayapandian, Rahman, Poornima & Padmavathy, 2015).

Figure 1. Smart City Applications.

Smart mobility is an unavoidable aspect in smart city, under this technology e-transportation; intelligent vehicle monitoring and traffic management system are some of the examples (Benevolo, Dameri & D'Auria, 2016). In the next 20 years, vehicle fuel would be an important problem in transportation sector. That is the reason many governments should encourage alternate fuel vehicle system, for instance, electric vehicle (Yang, Ding, Zhu & Bia, 2010). Developed countries have taken initiatives for these technological solutions in public transportation, people also like these kind of transportation due to less cost, pollution and safety. Public transportation safety is most important factor; several countries started installing IoT based safety system in vehicles (Melis, Prandini, Sartori & Callegati, 2016). The purpose of such devices is helping to monitor vehicle moments and also provide surveillance.

Smart water management system monitors entire water flow and its usage. Water management is essential task in efficient resource management and productivity. Because of modernization, ground water level is decreasing every year. Population is one of the additional factors in broadening water problem; this water management challenges requires attention of government officials and authorities to remedial solutions (Koo, Piratla & Matthews, 2015). The smart water management system particularly monitors two different systems first one is water distribution, and second one is storm water management system. These are some important IoT based smart city applications.

INTERNET OF THINGS LAYERS

Internet of Things (IoT) is a combination of multiple technologies. All these technology comes under the category of Service Oriented Architecture (SOA). The aim of SOA is providing quality service to consumer at reasonable cost. Under SOA umbrella, many services and technologies are working such as cloud computing and physical cyber system (Zhiliang, Yi, Lu & Wei, 2011). Internet of Things also comes under this category. Several technologies have remained unsuccessful due to lack of investments; however, IoT has taken great attention and has remained success story within short duration. Reason behind its success is the reliability, security, vulnerabilities and interoperability (Sulyman, Oteafy & Hassanein, 2017). IoT allows to establish heterogeneous network connection to transfer the machine data.

There are four different layers are available in IoT technology (Da Xu, He & Li, 2014). The figure 2 demonstrates different layer involved in IoT. Sensing layer is an important layer to establish the connection of existing hardware device. Example of this layer is sensors, RFID device and actuators. These devices help in sensing or reading the data and sending to hardware terminal. Internet is network of networks; similarly, IoT is an interconnected network system (Perera, Zaslavsky, Christen & Georgakopoulos, 2012). The sensor allows sensing data automatically, that data is exchanged or transfered from one particular device to other device. The RFID is working with the help of sensing layer using Universal Unique Identifier (UUID). This layer transmits data from one remote location device to other remote location device.

Figure 2. Internet of Things Layers.

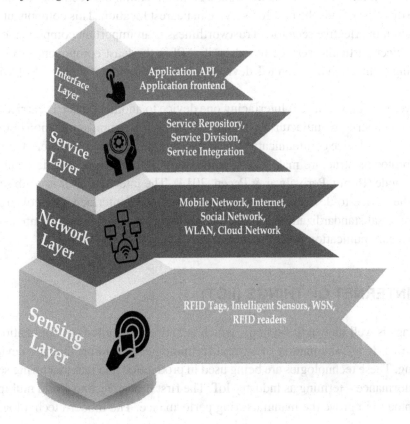

Second layer of IoT technology is network layer; basic working principle of network layer is establishing connection from one IoT device to other (Bello, Zeadally & Badra, 2017). This network layer helps to accumulating the data from remote server machine. Real time example of network layer is gathering the health care data (Bitra, Jayapandian & Balachandran, 2018). This network layer is directly adopts SOA; quality measurement is fixed based on the service. The major difference between traditional network layers into IoT network layer is dynamically mapped device in remote location. The basic mechanism of network layer is allocating the schedule for certain tasks (Centenaro, Vangelista, Zanella & Zorzi, 2016). This layer decides the certain device role, whether it is scheduler or dispatcher. Network layer has two different sub divisions; primary division is routing layer and secondary division is encapsulation layer. The routing helps to transmitting the data packets from source node to destination node (Han, Jornet, Fadel & Akyildiz, 2013). The example of routing protocols is RPL protocol, which stands for Routing Protocol in Low power. The basic working mechanism of RPL is distance vector structure; it is modular part of data link layer. The cognitive RPL is another extended protocol structure; this is mainly used in cognitive network structure. This protocol maintains forward information in parent node.

Service layer is third layer of IoT, which helps to establish and integrate the service from application. This layer is working with middleware technology; it confirms the cost effectiveness in IoT service. The middleware technology is also providing reusability concept, to reuse the IoT software and hardware platform. The role of service layer is to maintain the service specification in middleware technology. It also handles multiple problems such as storage management, network communication and information exchange. There are four major components involved in this service layer namely, service composition, service API, Service trust worthiness and service discovery (Swetina et al., 2014). The service composition creates interaction and establishes the communication between one IoT devices to another device. Service discovery finds the best IoT service in nearest location. This component helps in finding service information in effective scenario. Trustworthiness is an important component of network layer; customer may select particular service based on it. API is the least component of network layer that helps establishing connection between IoT devices to service provider. (Yashiro, Kobayashi, Koshizuka & Sakamura, 2013).

Interface layer is last layer of IoT. Interfacing one device to another device is carried out at this layer. There are several industries manufacturing IoT based devices for certain application domains. The major challenge is device-to-device communication; where each industry may use different protocol structure. This different protocols structure makes very unlikely to establish the dynamic connection from one node to another node (Bontu, Periyalwar & Pecen, 2014). The interface layer is a sub set of service layers to manage the device-to-device interconnection. This kind of interface protocol structure is used to maintain the universal standardization. Device interfacing is one of the main components in IoT, since device-to-device communication is the essence of IoT.

INDUSTRY INTERNET OF THINGS (IIOT)

Internet of Things is well known technology, which is in use of hundreds of application domains from home to industries. It is combination of several technologies including Internet device, sensors and cloud computing. These technologies are being used in production and manufacturing sector to improve quality and performance – terming as Industry IoT. The first time in techno world multiple technologies have been adopted to improve the manufacturing performance. The modern technologies are big data, device to device communication, sensor monitoring and decision making algorithms are convoluted in this modern Industry IoT platform (Trappey et al., 2017). Before unfolding these kind of technologies, industry should use automated technology in production department. Automated technology means to control the machine activity based on user input, for example, robots usage in automobile industry. The problem with this kind of automation is lack of 100% accuracy; further, decision-making concept is also missing in such automation. In manufacturing sector, manual monitoring and controlling is next to impossible, which lead towards use of Industry based IoT products in manufacturing and production units. The combination of operational and information technology system create enterprise Internet based industry. The Internet based machines help in increasing operational performance and production; it also reduces the machine complexity in manufacturing sector. The primary aim of industry is quality and cost, at the same time secondary aim of the industry is safety parameter (Peralta et al., 2017). Industry IoT technology is fulfilling both the primary and the secondary objective of industry.

Industry 1.0 Vs Industry 4.0

The growth of industry 4.0 has been introduced in the year of 2010. The growth of industry 1.0 to industry 2.0 is almost crossed 85 years. Similarly, industry 2.0 to industry 3.0 took nearly 98 years; however, industry 3.0 to Internet based industry 4.0 just took 40 years. The modern technology grows with a very fast pace as compared to existing industry growth. The figure 3 shows industry evaluation and its growth (Wahlster, 2012). The industry 1.0 is manpower oriented growth and partial machine involvement, for instance, steam engine that was introduced in year 1784. The industry 2.0 is an assembly line manufacturing process, which was introduced in automobile manufacturing plant. This technique was invented in Henry Ford. First time, mass manufacturing has been tested in industry. This method tests in manufacturing assembly unit and nearly half of the manpower has been saved. This could be considered partial involvement of automated devices in industry. In 1969, one of the major revolutions came into existence – known as robotics. It was named as industry 3.0, the combination of electronic and robotics technology have been used in the process. The basic working mechanism of industry 3.0 is to use predefined microprocessor programs to control the robot machine, which has been used in production and assembly plant to minimize manpower and increase production - aiming at automation and quality. This automation helped in computational cost reduction.

The vision of enterprise industry machine connectivity is implemented in Industry 4.0. The enterprise system means connecting the device in common domain. This enterprise system concept is successfully implemented in computer by using internet technology. The developer should decide to implement similar method in manufacturing sector. The concept of IoT is very simple but interconnecting the device is more complex. IoT technology is collection of many computer and electronic components. The smart device connection is possible with the help of Internet; same technology incorporates with industry machine. The concept of Industry IoT establishes enterprise machine connection by using Internet technology. Industry 4.0 has been introduced in 2010; there are multiple advantages to implement this technology. The major advantage is smart control and smart monitoring system (Lasi et al., 2014). The term smart is most important parameter in Internet based technology. Previous growth only focused on production and quality, but Industry 4.0 is multi-focused system to optimize and improve industry manufacturing. The modern machine learning algorithms are also used in Industry 4.0 leading towards decision making, which eventually help in increasing level of decision-making in machine and reduce 90% manpower (Tsukada, Washio & Motoda, 2001). The resource optimization and real time machine monitoring is

Figure 3. Of Industry 1.0 – Industry 4.0

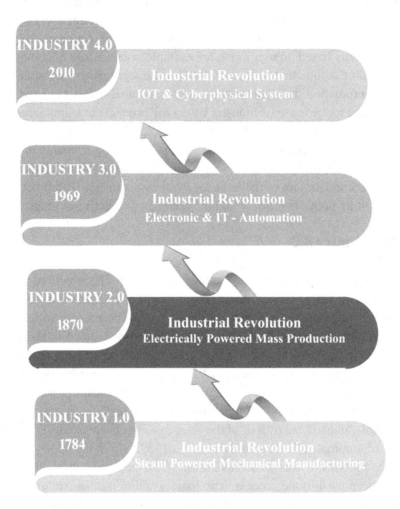

an additional features of Industry 4.0 technologies. The modern technology remote desktop and server access is possible by using Internet technology; similarly, remote machine diagnosis is also possible by using Industry IoT technology.

Drivers in Industry 4.0

The driver's help to maintain the machine to human interaction, there are three major drivers involved in Industry IoT concept. Frist driver is technology; without technology nothing is possible. Sensor is an old but smart sensor is newly established concept that is implemented in Industry IoT. The machine performance is monitored using these sensors, which sense machine activity and transfer details in centralized server with the help of Internet communication (Drath & Horch, 2014). Cloud computing is another key technology in IoT. The recent Internet growth has reached at doorsteps of common people, thus, introducing cloud computing platform. Cloud computing is a server oriented platform that works in the presence of Internet connectivity. The cloud computing and data storage technology are usually used to store industry machine information (Jayapandian & Zubair Rahman, 2018). Later, this information is used in predicting future growth and industrial performance applying data analytics concept. The manufacturing industry produce immense data, therefore, normal analytics tools may not be feasible in data processing. Big data analytics concept is adopted to predict future industry growth. The unique identification number is most important in computer system; the same internet protocol number is assigned in industry machine for the purpose of machine monitoring and controlling process. The second driver is customer, the purpose of this driver is providing quality service and maintaining customer satisfaction level. The service-based system always depends upon customer feedback. The last driver of this technology is economic driver. The private and government both should provide means for industry development. Industry IoT also comes under smart city development. India has taken an initiative of technology based industry development know as "Make in India". Similarly, other nations also take initiatives and frame technology based policies (Liao, Deschamps, Loures & Ramos, 2017). Beijing government has implemented IoT in agriculture sector (Xiaojun, Weirui & Jianping, 2012).

Economy Growth in Industry 4.0

The growth of Industry 4.0 is fully technology based industry development. It directly helps to increase the country GDP level. This technology allows providing the novel products and eliminates the risk factors in industry products. The intimate objective of industry is financial growth with sustainable development. The name digital industry now interconnects all the service and manufacturing sectors in digitalization (Rüßmann et al., 2015). The modern population more than three billion people slowly moved into smart mobile technology that helps in 10% yearly growth. This mobile usage has opened means of online business. The online shopping mechanisms have started using machine-learning algorithms and IoT based voice assistant mechanisms. The growth of online business has nearly 30% increased compared to last financial year; it has reached 4.5 billion US dollars. In future, it is expected to reach more than 20%. IoT technology also monitors the consumer products and easy way to trace the shipping. Product shipping is having unique computer bar code; it is recognized and traced by IoT scanner.

APPLICATIONS OF INDUSTRY IOT

The Industry IoT is one of the modern applications. The Industry IoT has two major pillars: one is to increase the production and Quality. Second one is optimizing resource management in manufacturing plant (Bandyopadhyay & Sen, 2011). In general, Industry IoT is categorized into three major applications, that is Healthcare Industry using IoT, Production & Manufacturing Industry Safety Using IoT, and Transportation & logistics Industry using IoT.

Healthcare Industry Using IoT

Healthcare is one of the booming and more technology surrounded in modern world. IoT technology is perfectly utilized in monitoring entire patient information. The most of the medical equipment are interlinked with IoT technology. The purpose of maintaining health record is to foresee disease prediction. In recent days, number of hospitals has maintained patient's health information in centralized system. This e-health record is very useful to analyze the patient health issues and easy to compare the existing or

Figure 4. Industry IoT Applications

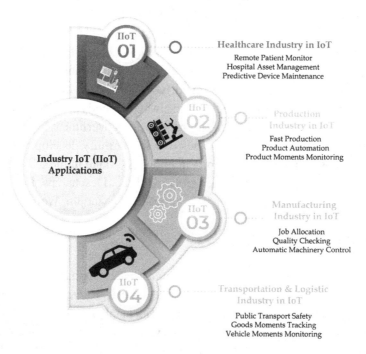

others health records (Jabbar et al., 2017). IoT devices enable communication between medical devices to patient and are also used for service provider and customer. The customer here is patient and service provider is hospital and doctors. The user wears IoT enabled product for their health and continuously monitoring of health condition. The service provider monitors user information by remote machine. Anytime user may face health issue, it automatically notifies doctor and hospital system (Hassanalieragh et al., 2015). Later, doctor may provide some first aid treatment. This system helps significant reduction in time and provides immediate treatment. Apart from this, from business point of view, health insurance companies need patient health information for providing financial support. This kind of IoT based health record provides original patient condition, thus, duplicate health reports are avoided by using modern Industry based IoT devices. The major advantage in healthcare IoT sector is reduction of treatment cost, easy and fast disease diagnosis and improvement in treatment quality.

Production and Manufacturing Industry Safety Using IoT

Industry IoT technology is one of the fastest growing sectors in technological field. More than 60% of manufacture companies use IoT based analytics tool and they optimize product-line production. The manufacturing industry directly affects GDP growth of a country. IoT technology allows increasing the production quality and production line in short duration. The safety parameter is one of the major problems in automobile, mining and mechanical industry. That is the reason most of the mechanical industry gives higher weightage in safety (Riel, Kreiner, Macher & Messnarz, 2017). After emergence of IoT based machine monitoring and controlling system, 90% of industry accidents are prevented. For example, mining production industry is at high risk factor, employees work underground. If an accident occurs, several human lives may be harmed. That is the reason, modern industry uses IoT based accident prediction. IoT enabled device helps to predict the mining accident and give alarming signals. These devices also may help for disaster furcating and improve the safety parameter in underground mining works. IoT based wireless communication establishes the connection between the underground and land surface. IoT device is fixed with employee that traces the employee underground moments with help of IoT remote monitoring unit. Recently, GPS watch and other equipment has been used to trance the location. The sensors fixed in underground send data to remote sever; the data is analyzed and used for safety measures. The decision making algorithms are used to predict and provide the higher safety. The sensors help in sensing temperature and give the warning alarm. In industry fire alarm is also working in similar principle; all fire detecting IoT devices are connected with centralized server in wireless communication. The fire accident, in case, happens; the information is passed from these devices to main server.

Transportation & Logistics Industry Using IoT

Transportation and logistics are two hands of manufacturing industry. The manufacturing industry sends their goods from one location to another location by using some logistics service. IoT technology plays a vital role in this particular service. The product having a unique bar code; RFID scanner can be used to scan the particular product details moments (Anand et al., 2015). This bar code scanner sends the information from one device to other device without human intervention. This should help customer to easily trace their goods details online. The trend of online shopping is increasing day-by-day, based on such growth; logistics service companies foresee a better future. That is the reason logistic companies invest much in establishing IoT based solutions. The advantage of IoT based technology is reduction in computational time and increase quality service and performance. The modern vehicles have inbuilt IoT based GPS device, which is used for tracking vehicle moments and activities. Example for this system is BMW, which is equipped with iDrive system that intelligent based vehicle moment's system. This kind of IoT products helps in avoiding vehicle theft and provides safety. Public transportation service such as taxi services may use these tracking systems to avoid undesired activities. Also this system can be installed in school and college buses to monitor bus speed and location, and notify automatically to parents about moments of buses for the better monitoring of kids (Jisha, Jyothindranath & Kumary, 2017).

INTERNET OF THINGS SECURITY PROTOCOL

The previous section discussed about basics of IoT and Industry 4.0 applications. Network of things is the basic structure of IoT, where wireless sensor network allows connectivity of several smart applications such as smart city, smart grid, smart appliances (Zhao & Ge, 2013). IoT is an emerging domain and this field is still evolving, privacy and security is the major concerned in IoT applications. The reason behind it is the IoT devices are interconnected with the public wireless network. IoT technology allows multiple devices connectivity and creates intelligent communication; at the same time different device use a different security protocol; this is the main drawback of IoT technology. Different protocols using different security mechanism is very difficult to establish and maintain the device interconnection. Wireless communication is only possible way to exchange the data from one device to other device. During communication, security is one of the major elements of concern. Suppose third party service providers provide communication service; it means data privacy is another major problem in this domain. Institute

Figure 5. Security Protocols in IoT

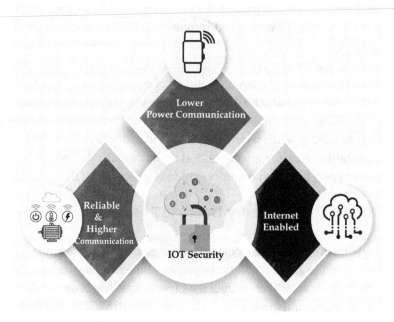

of Electrical and Electronics Engineers (IEEE) communities have developed these kinds of network protocols. Internet Engineering Task Force (IETF) is also focuses on wireless communication protocol development. The focus of IoT security protocol is mainly on three elements that is higher and reliable communication. It is a portable device that is required for low power communication. All devices needed for wireless communication connection become interconnected with Internet. Low power allows devices to establish battery connection, because portable device cannot be connected with high power. That is the reason IoT devices are developed with light weight both object and security protocol. The purpose of reliable communication is uninterrupted wireless network connection, since IoT device do not work without Internet connection. The primary aim of IoT device is device-to-device and device-to-customer communication, which communication is only possible through Internet connection.

Constrained Application Protocol (CoAP)

Constrained Application Protocol is an IoT application layer protocol designed by IETF. The main focus of CoAP is constrained recourse IoT device. Also it is a subset of HTTP protocol working with interoperable network structure. The working structure of CoAP is UDP with lightweight protocol system (Bormann, Castellani & Shelby, 2012). The common HTTP commands are used in establishing user to server connection, which has GET, PUT and POST commands. This is a client server architecture system that establishes wireless device communication. This protocol is working with system response and request structure in combination of synchronous and asynchronous communication. The lightweight protocol requires lesser bandwidth, which is the reason CoAP uses UDP connection. It naturally reduces the bandwidth and improves the performance compared to TCP. This works for both unicast and multicast protocol systems; it also helps to increase communication reliability. The UDP system automatically increases reliability of IoT communication. There are two major elements that are available in header file; one is message type and other one is QoS level. The message type contains four different types: 1) confirmable - it means the message is sent from one node to another node and acknowledgement message is received from the receiver. The total duration of message sending and acknowledgement is called as computational time. The message type works in both structures - synchronous and asynchronous. 2) non-confirmable - this type of message does not expect acknowledgement message. 3) acknowledgement - once a message is reached at destination, an automatic ACK message is received at source side. 4) Reset - this message type makes sure that certain type of data is not processed. The CoAP is created for IoT security protocol for the purpose of machine-to-machine communication. It does not have inbuilt security mechanism, DTLS protocol is created. DTLS stands for Datagram Transport Layer Security protocol. This protocol provides data authentication, confidentiality and data integrity. DTLS does not work in multicast structure, which is a major advantage of IoT application layer. The disadvantage of DTLS system is that it requires higher network traffic during handshake process (Alghamdi, Lasebae & Aiash, 2013). CoAP is suitable structure of HTTP connection, but at the same time DTLS system has an additional problem in HTTP because of their packet structure.

IEEE 802.15.4 Protocol

The IEEE 802.15.4 protocol is a low rate wireless personal area network structure. It is standard format for the physical layer in low rate wireless communication. Similarly, it specifies media access control protocol system (Sastry & Wagner, 2004). This protocol is to be maintained by IEEE group, it is updated in regular interval. This protocol is low power as well as low cost to establish connection with nearby devices. The higher transmission power technology requires high bandwidth and higher battery power. This is short-range communication with 10-meter device-to-deice communication. The maximum transfer rate of this communication is 250 kbit/s. This protocol has been established in the year of 2003; initially it has higher security risk. Later in 2006, other group of IEEE solved its security issues and provided better version. The packet length frequency transmission ratio is 128 bytes. This protocol controls source and destination by using MAC layer. In 2008, the concept of Time Synchronized Channel Hopping has been introduced; it directly helps improving IoT device security. This security protocol is used to avoid network security attacks and threats. This also provides various security services (Jayapandian, Rahman, Radhikadevi & Koushikaa, 2016). Advanced Encryption Standard algorithm used different key size for the process of encryption with 32, 64 and 128 bits. This data encryption provides data confidentiality and authentication. The access control mechanism is used to maintain the security information.

Message Queue Telemetry Transport (MQTT)

Message Queue Telemetry Transport (MQTT) is a commonly used protocol in IoT. IBM developed this for the purpose of machine-to-machine communication. This is kind of lightweight security protocol; it works on top of the TCP layer. The request and response time is minimized; network bandwidth consumption is very less. MQTT maintains message information, and it acts as broker (Hwang, Park & Shon, 2016). As a broker, it creates topic based on user data, when user sends message from client machine to MQTT broker; the component automatically replies based on the topic. MQTT works based on Internet bandwidth and battery level; example of this protocol is WhatsAPP and Facebook Massager. MQTT maintains three quality levels. First quality level is fire and forget; it is not required in acknowledgment for sending message. Second quality level is delivery at least once; acknowledgment is required and message is send at least once from device to device. Third level is delivery exactly once; it needs acknowledgement for both sender and receiver that is named as four way handshake communication. The protocol using these quality levels takes less message delivery time and less network bandwidth usage. MQTT broker architecture system needs username and password for authentication. The packet loss and message delay depends on message quality.

Extensible Messaging and Presence Protocol (XMPP)

Extensible Messaging and Presence Protocol is a message chatting communication protocol. This protocol was developed by Internet Engineering Task Force (IETF) for the purpose of secure internet chatting application. This protocol structure is most suitable for IoT application. XMPP is working in TCP with the concept of request and response structure, which means synchronous message passing system (Bendel et al., 2013). This was specially designed for short message communication using Internet. The main advantage of this protocol is real time message passing; also acknowledgement is received within the short duration. The additional functionality is increased in extension protocol termed as XEP. The main core value of this protocol is to inbuilt security mechanism known as TLS or SSL. Main advantage of XMPP is that it is open source protocol; anyone can use and implement this protocol in their application. The working structure of XMPP is decentralized, it means any client machine cannot send request directly. Within network connection, anyone can execute server. Example of this decentralized server is AOL instant massager.

Advanced Message Queuing Protocol (AMQP)

Advanced Message Queuing Protocol is a message oriented structure and open standard protocol. There are many unique features available in AMQP. It's main feature is message oriented system. This works in queuing procedure with an additional component of point-to-point communication (Vinoski, 2006). AMQP has a higher security with reliable communication protocol. It has methodology of interoperable structure similar to SMTP and HTTP protocol. AMQP is middleware technology and interoperable between the multiple device. It is wired communication protocol that sends data stream from one device to another device over network. This protocol is mainly used in financial industry with a transport layer protocol. Compared to other protocols, main feature of AMQP is its working in store and forward method. That means after network disruption, message is stored and later, it tries to send it to destination terminal. The message reliability works in three methods - "At most once", "At least once", "Exactly once". More than 2000 users per day have used AMQP protocol and it processes more than 300 million messages per day.

INDUSTRY IOT SECURITY ISSUES

The manufacturing and transportation industry are getting more benefits in Industry IoT technology. There are many industrial IoT projects implemented for consumer products. The water purifier and water heater companies are implementing IOT sensors inside their products. These sensors are used to monitor the performance of the equipment and send reports to the concern industry. For example, water purifier needs change of filter and needs service in regular interval. This sensor helps to indicate the current situation of the product; if the service is required, it intimates to the concerned service center.

The manufacturing industry nowadays has more than 80% implementation of these IoT sensors for monitoring and controlling industry machines. The key problem of this technology is its data security, since almost all industry activity is connected with remote server and controlled by remote location. The hackers may get access to these services; thus, entire system is at higher security threat. All devices are connected with public Internet connection that is another major security issue in IoT. The entire industry machine is controlled by IoT device. Therefore, safety in industry is very dangerous to implement using Industry IoT control (Kimani, Oduol & Langet, 2019). Chemical industry or power industry safety are at the highest risk factor; since any one hack it and control it. Some critical case study of security issues are reported form 2011 to 2016; multiple number of water plants are hacked and have been stopped resulting in stoppage of water supply. US power grid industry faces similar problems. In just two years, more than 17 times hacker hacked the power station. Unfortunately, a few countries face nuclear power plant hacking; between 2009 to 2015, Iraq and North Korea faced this issue. This section discussed about various security issues faced in industry. Data security has been considered as major issue in industry. In particularly some service industry applications have been hacked from third party server.

HYBRID SECURITY FOR INDUSTRY 4.0

The previous sections discuss about security and privacy issues in Industry Internet of Things. Based on the literature survey, more than 80% of industry machineries are interconnected with IoT technology. The aim of Industry 4.0 is technology based industry development. The technology purely depends upon Internet communication. This Internet based industry development creates positive environment at the same time reduces manpower. Major problem of Internet based connectivity is its security. Currently, Industry based IoT machines use lightweight protocols. The purpose of using lightweight protocol is that these IoT devices are portable device and have less power. The figure 6 outlines the concept of proposed LPP algorithm, which is lightweight protocol. It consumes less power and provides reasonable security, however, industry based IoT technology requires more security compared to the existing security mechanism. The reason of acquiring more security is industry based IoT devices, which handle higher sensitive data. For example, healthcare industry deals patients' personal data; it is highly sensitive compared to normal Internet based data. This is the main reason behind proposed system. The proposed algorithm introduces additional security mechanism. It combines Lightweight Protocol with Probabilistic (LPP) encryption algorithm; thus, it is named as hybrid encryption. The basic working mechanism of probabilistic algorithm is encrypting data in randomized manner (Jayapandian & Rahman, 2017). The concept of the proposed probabilistic algorithm is encrypting the original message at more than one time. Proposed system also uses lightweight protocol for security. The encrypted data, which is stored in local devices, this algorithm encrypts the data again. Using this probabilistic algorithm, the encryption process is carried out. The process works in temporary memory and flash memory concept.

The temporary memory concept is used to reduce the storage space required in additional encryption process. The figure 6 elaborates hybrid encryption process, which is Lightweight Protocol with Probabilistic (LPP) encryption security system. Advantage of the proposed LPP algorithm is improved security system in Industry IoT devices. The entire process is implemented in Internet protocol, since the purpose of proposed algorithm is providing security for IoT devices at network.

Figure 6. Hybrid Lightweight Protocol with Probabilistic (LPP) Algorithm

RESULT AND DISCUSSION

The hybrid encryption concept is already implemented in various computing platforms, but this concept is unique and noval for IoT platform. The purpose of LPP algorithm is providing higher security and maintaining Qulaity of Service (QoS). LPP algorithm is simulated and tested using NetSim. NetSim is a network protocol simulation tool that helps to create entire virtual IoT environment. The simulation is tested with two conditions: i) only using lightweight protocol for connecting industry device to server, at the same time, machine-to-machine communication is also simulated. ii) Use of LPP algorithm meaning that after successful lightweight protocol, additional encryption using probabilistic algorithm for secure transaction. The simulation measures four major parameters namely - encryption time, security attack ratio, throughput, and data delivery percentage.

The figure 7 and table 1 report data encryption time for different devices. The encryption time is measured with inside device. In encryption, average lightweight protocol (LP) encryption time is 0.539ms. On the other hand, LPP algorithm takes 0.5654ms. There is difference of 0.02634ms; it means 2.634% different is observed between LP algorithms to LPP algorithm. LPP algorithm took 2.63% additional time for data encryption as compared to LP algorithm.

The table 2 and figure 8 discuss about IoT device attack ratio. The device is identified based on device id; for the purpose of simulation, virtual attack environment has been created. The virtual attacker tried to attack IoT devices. The LP algorithm average attack ratio is 13.2%, where as LPP algorithm's

Figure 7. Data Encryption Analysis

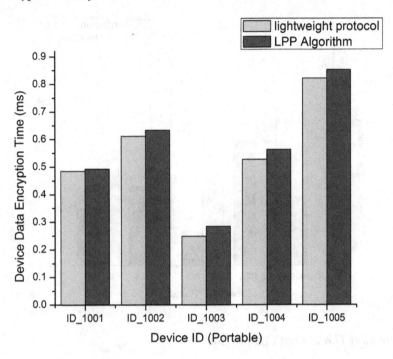

Table 1. Device Data Encryption Time Comparison

Device ID	lightweight protocol (ms)	LPP Algorithm (ms)
ID_1001	0.4856	0.4931
ID_1002	0.6123	0.6341
ID_1003	0.2491	0.2843
ID_1004	0.5273	0.5629
ID_1005	0.8213	0.8529

Table 2. Device Attack Ratio Comparison

Device ID	Lightweight Protocol (LP) (%)	LPP Algorithm (%)
ID_1001	12	6
ID_1002	14	11
ID_1003	8	3
ID_1004	18	7
ID_1005	14	5

Figure 8. Attack Ratio Analysis

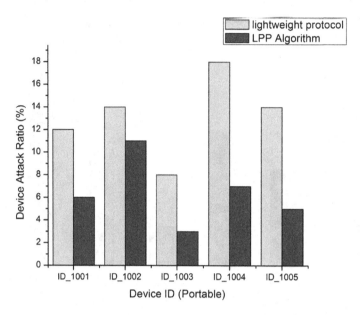

Table 3. Communication Throughput Comparison

Number of Device	lightweight protocol (Kbps)	LPP Algorithm (Kbps)
10 - 20 Device	5.2	5.3
20 - 40 Device	6.2	6.289
40 - 60 Device	6.7	7
60 - 100 Device	8.4	8.93

Figure 9. Throughput Analysis

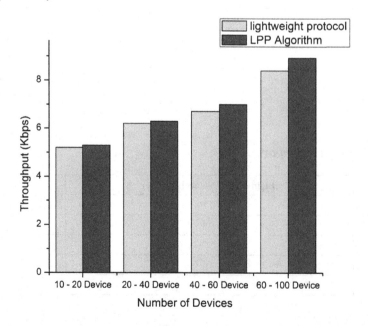

Table 4. Data Delivery Percentage Comparison

Device ID	Lightweight protocol (LP) (%)	LPP Algorithm (%)
ID_1001	80	89
ID_1002	87	94
ID_1003	84	93
ID_1004	86	95
ID_1005	87	96

Figure 10. Data Packet Delivery Analysis

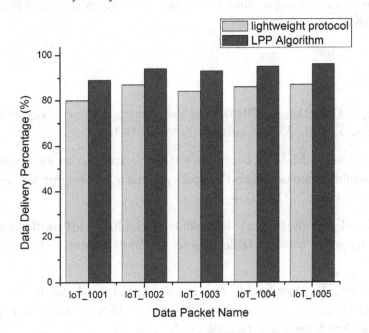

attack ratio is only 6.4%. The difference between two methods is 6.8%; it means proposed LPP algorithm provides 6% additional security in comparison with existing method.

The table 3 and figure 9 show throughput - IoT device communication bandwidth analysis. The average bandwidth utilization of LP algorithm is 5.3 Kbps, whilst LPP algorithm takes 5.5038 Kbps. The difference between the two algorithms is 0.2038 Kbps. This is quite reasonable variation; which does not affect device performance.

The table 4 and figure 10 demonstrate IoT data delivery percentage. The average data delivery percentage of LP method is 84.8%, and LPP algorithm has 93.4% in average delivery time. Compared to LP method, LPP algorithm delivery percentage is increased 8.6%. This shows 8.6% security level increased compared to existing method.

CONCLUSION

This chapter discussed several IoT applications. Industry 4.0 has been the main focus of the chapter and motivation for implementing IoT based industry development. The major challenge of IoT environment is its security. The main contribution of the chapter is proposed security protocols in Industry IoT devices. The proposed security algorithm additionally encrypts data to ensure its security for the IoT enabled devices. The proposed algorithm is Lightweight Protocol with Probabilistic Algorithm. It provides better security environment compared to existing Lightweight protocol (LP). The experimental results, which have been simulated, show that the proposed LPP algorithm performs better in comparison to LP algorithm. Particularly, data attack ratio is 6% and data packet delivery ratio is 8.6%. The proposed hybrid LPP algorithm took little bit additional execution time, which is negligible and it doesn't affect IoT device performance.

REFERENCES

Abas, K., Porto, C., & Obraczka, K. (2014). Wireless smart camera networks for the surveillance of public spaces. *Computer*, *47*(5), 37–44. doi:10.1109/MC.2014.140

Ahmad, A., Paul, A., Rathore, M. M., & Chang, H. (2016). Smart cyber society: Integration of capillary devices with high usability based on Cyber–Physical System. *Future Generation Computer Systems*, *56*, 493–503. doi:10.1016/j.future.2015.08.004

Al-Shammari, B. K., Al-Aboody, N., & Al-Raweshidy, H. S. (2018). IoT traffic management and integration in the QoS supported network. *IEEE Internet of Things Journal*, *5*(1), 352–370. doi:10.1109/JIOT.2017.2785219

Anand, T. M., Banupriya, K., Deebika, M., Anusiya, A., Anand, T. M., Banupriya, K., & Anusiya, A. (2015). Intelligent transportation systems using iot service for vehicular data cloud. *International Journal for Innovative Research in Science and Technology*, *2*(2), 80–86.

Bandyopadhyay, D., & Sen, J. (2011). Internet of things: Applications and challenges in technology and standardization. *Wireless Personal Communications*, *58*(1), 49–69. doi:10.100711277-011-0288-5

Bello, O., Zeadally, S., & Badra, M. (2017). Network layer inter-operation of Device-to-Device communication technologies in Internet of Things (IoT). *Ad Hoc Networks*, *57*, 52–62. doi:10.1016/j.adhoc.2016.06.010

Benevolo, C., Dameri, R. P., & D'Auria, B. (2016). Smart mobility in smart city. In *Empowering Organizations* (pp. 13–28). Cham: Springer. doi:10.1007/978-3-319-23784-8_2

Bitra, V. S., Jayapandian, N., & Balachandran, K. (2018, August). Internet of Things Security and Privacy Issues in Healthcare Industry. In *International Conference on Intelligent Data Communication Technologies and Internet of Things* (pp. 967-973). Springer.

Bontu, C. S., Periyalwar, S., & Pecen, M. (2014). Wireless wide-area networks for internet of things: An air interface protocol for IoT and a simultaneous access channel for uplink IoT communication. *IEEE Vehicular Technology Magazine*, *9*(1), 54–63. doi:10.1109/MVT.2013.2295068

Bormann, C., Castellani, A. P., & Shelby, Z. (2012). Coap: An application protocol for billions of tiny internet nodes. *IEEE Internet Computing, 16*(2), 62–67. doi:10.1109/MIC.2012.29

Centenaro, M., Vangelista, L., Zanella, A., & Zorzi, M. (2016). Long-range communications in unlicensed bands: The rising stars in the IoT and smart city scenarios. *IEEE Wireless Communications, 23*(5), 60–67. doi:10.1109/MWC.2016.7721743

Da Xu, L., He, W., & Li, S. (2014). Internet of things in industries: A survey. *IEEE Transactions on Industrial Informatics, 10*(4), 2233–2243. doi:10.1109/TII.2014.2300753

Depuru, S. S. S. R., Wang, L., & Devabhaktuni, V. (2011). Electricity theft: Overview, issues, prevention and a smart meter based approach to control theft. *Energy Policy, 39*(2), 1007–1015. doi:10.1016/j.enpol.2010.11.037

Dizdarević, J., Carpio, F., Jukan, A., & Masip-Bruin, X. (2019). A survey of communication protocols for internet of things and related challenges of fog and cloud computing integration. *ACM Computing Surveys, 51*(6), 116. doi:10.1145/3292674

Drath, R., & Horch, A. (2014). Industrie 4.0: Hit or hype? *IEEE Industrial Electronics Magazine, 8*(2), 56–58. doi:10.1109/MIE.2014.2312079

Foschini, L., Taleb, T., Corradi, A., & Bottazzi, D. (2011). M2M-based metropolitan platform for IMS-enabled road traffic management in IoT. *IEEE Communications Magazine, 49*(11), 50–57. doi:10.1109/MCOM.2011.6069709

Gilchrist, A. (2016). *Industry 4.0: the industrial internet of things*. Apress. doi:10.1007/978-1-4842-2047-4

Guo, B., Zhang, D., Wang, Z., Yu, Z., & Zhou, X. (2013). Opportunistic IoT: Exploring the harmonious interaction between human and the internet of things. *Journal of Network and Computer Applications, 36*(6), 1531–1539. doi:10.1016/j.jnca.2012.12.028

Han, C., Jornet, J. M., Fadel, E., & Akyildiz, I. F. (2013). A cross-layer communication module for the Internet of Things. *Computer Networks, 57*(3), 622–633. doi:10.1016/j.comnet.2012.10.003

Hassanalieragh, M., Page, A., Soyata, T., Sharma, G., Aktas, M., Mateos, G., & Andreescu, S. (2015, June). Health monitoring and management using Internet-of-Things (IoT) sensing with cloud-based processing: Opportunities and challenges. In *2015 IEEE International Conference on Services Computing* (pp. 285-292). IEEE. 10.1109/SCC.2015.47

Hwang, H. C., Park, J., & Shon, J. G. (2016). Design and implementation of a reliable message transmission system based on MQTT protocol in IoT. *Wireless Personal Communications, 91*(4), 1765–1777. doi:10.100711277-016-3398-2

Jabbar, S., Ullah, F., Khalid, S., Khan, M., & Han, K. (2017). Semantic interoperability in heterogeneous IoT infrastructure for healthcare. *Wireless Communications and Mobile Computing, 2017*.

Jaradat, M., Jarrah, M., Bousselham, A., Jararweh, Y., & Al-Ayyoub, M. (2015). The internet of energy: Smart sensor networks and big data management for smart grid. *Procedia Computer Science, 56*, 592–597. doi:10.1016/j.procs.2015.07.250

Järventausta, P., Repo, S., Rautiainen, A., & Partanen, J. (2010). Smart grid power system control in distributed generation environment. *Annual Reviews in Control*, *34*(2), 277–286. doi:10.1016/j.arcontrol.2010.08.005

Jayapandian, N. (2019). Business Transaction Privacy and Security Issues in Near Field Communication. In *Network Security and Its Impact on Business Strategy*. IGI Global. doi:10.4018/978-1-5225-8455-1.ch005

Jayapandian, N. (2019). Threats and Security Issues in Smart City Devices. In *Secure Cyber-Physical Systems for Smart Cities*. IGI Global. doi:10.4018/978-1-5225-7189-6.ch009

Jayapandian, N., & Md Zubair Rahman, A. M. J. (2018). Secure Deduplication for Cloud Storage Using Interactive Message-Locked Encryption with Convergent Encryption, To Reduce Storage Space. *Brazilian Archives of Biology and Technology*, 61.

Jayapandian, N., & Rahman, A. M. Z. (2017). Secure and efficient online data storage and sharing over cloud environment using probabilistic with homomorphic encryption. *Cluster Computing*, *20*(2), 1561–1573. doi:10.100710586-017-0809-4

Jayapandian, N., Rahman, A. M. Z., Koushikaa, M., & Radhikadevi, S. (2016, February). A novel approach to enhance multi level security system using encryption with fingerprint in cloud. In *2016 World Conference on Futuristic Trends in Research and Innovation for Social Welfare (Startup Conclave)* (pp. 1-5). IEEE. 10.1109/STARTUP.2016.7583903

Jayapandian, N., Rahman, A. M. Z., Poornima, U., & Padmavathy, P. (2015, November). Efficient online solar energy monitoring and electricity sharing in home using cloud system. In *2015 Online International Conference on Green Engineering and Technologies (IC-GET)* (pp. 1-4). IEEE. 10.1109/GET.2015.7453775

Jayapandian, N., Rahman, A. M. Z., Radhikadevi, S., & Koushikaa, M. (2016, February). Enhanced cloud security framework to confirm data security on asymmetric and symmetric key encryption. In *2016 World Conference on Futuristic Trends in Research and Innovation for Social Welfare (Startup Conclave)* (pp. 1-4). IEEE. 10.1109/STARTUP.2016.7583904

Jisha, R. C., Jyothindranath, A., & Kumary, L. S. (2017, September). Iot based school bus tracking and arrival time prediction. In *2017 International Conference on Advances in Computing, Communications and Informatics (ICACCI)* (pp. 509-514). IEEE. 10.1109/ICACCI.2017.8125890

Kimani, K., Oduol, V., & Langat, K. (2019). Cyber security challenges for IoT-based smart grid networks. *International Journal of Critical Infrastructure Protection*, *25*, 36–49. doi:10.1016/j.ijcip.2019.01.001

Kolberg, D., & Zühlke, D. (2015). Lean automation enabled by industry 4.0 technologies. *IFAC-PapersOnLine*, *48*(3), 1870–1875. doi:10.1016/j.ifacol.2015.06.359

Koo, D., Piratla, K., & Matthews, C. J. (2015). Towards sustainable water supply: Schematic development of big data collection using internet of things (IoT). *Procedia Engineering*, *118*, 489–497. doi:10.1016/j.proeng.2015.08.465

Kramers, A., Höjer, M., Lövehagen, N., & Wangel, J. (2014). Smart sustainable cities–Exploring ICT solutions for reduced energy use in cities. *Environmental Modelling & Software*, *56*, 52–62. doi:10.1016/j. envsoft.2013.12.019

Lasi, H., Fettke, P., Kemper, H. G., Feld, T., & Hoffmann, M. (2014). Industry 4.0. *Business & Information Systems Engineering*, *6*(4), 239–242. doi:10.100712599-014-0334-4

Liao, Y., Deschamps, F., Loures, E. D. F. R., & Ramos, L. F. P. (2017). Past, present and future of Industry 4.0-a systematic literature review and research agenda proposal. *International Journal of Production Research*, *55*(12), 3609–3629. doi:10.1080/00207543.2017.1308576

Manavalan, E., & Jayakrishna, K. (2019). A review of Internet of Things (IoT) embedded sustainable supply chain for industry 4.0 requirements. *Computers & Industrial Engineering*, *127*, 925–953. doi:10.1016/j.cie.2018.11.030

Midgley, P. (2009). The role of smart bike-sharing systems in urban mobility. *Journeys*, *2*(1), 23–31.

Miller, M. (2015). *The internet of things: How smart TVs, smart cars, smart homes, and smart cities are changing the world*. Pearson Education.

Morello, R., De Capua, C., Fulco, G., & Mukhopadhyay, S. C. (2017). A smart power meter to monitor energy flow in smart grids: The role of advanced sensing and IoT in the electric grid of the future. *IEEE Sensors Journal*, *17*(23), 7828–7837. doi:10.1109/JSEN.2017.2760014

Mueller, M., Mathiason, J., & Klein, H. (2007). The Internet and global governance: Principles and norms for a new regime. *Global Governance*, *13*(2), 237–254. doi:10.1163/19426720-01302007

Noury, N., Barralon, P., Vuillerme, N., & Fleury, A. (2012). Fusion of multiple sensors sources in a smart home to detect scenarios of activities in ambient assisted living. *International Journal of E-Health and Medical Communications*, *3*(3), 29–44. doi:10.4018/jehmc.2012070103

Peralta, G., Iglesias-Urkia, M., Barcelo, M., Gomez, R., Moran, A., & Bilbao, J. (2017, May). Fog computing based efficient IoT scheme for the Industry 4.0. In *2017 IEEE International Workshop of Electronics, Control, Measurement, Signals and their Application to Mechatronics (ECMSM)* (pp. 1-6). IEEE. 10.1109/ECMSM.2017.7945879

Perera, C., Zaslavsky, A., Christen, P., & Georgakopoulos, D. (2012, November). Ca4iot: Context awareness for internet of things. In *2012 IEEE International Conference on Green Computing and Communications* (pp. 775-782). IEEE. 10.1109/GreenCom.2012.128

Petrolo, R., Loscri, V., & Mitton, N. (2017). Towards a smart city based on cloud of things, a survey on the smart city vision and paradigms. *Transactions on Emerging Telecommunications Technologies*, *28*(1), e2931. doi:10.1002/ett.2931

Riel, A., Kreiner, C., Macher, G., & Messnarz, R. (2017). Integrated design for tackling safety and security challenges of smart products and digital manufacturing. *CIRP Annals*, *66*(1), 177–180. doi:10.1016/j. cirp.2017.04.037

Smith, T. B. (2004). Electricity theft: A comparative analysis. *Energy Policy, 32*(18), 2067–2076. doi:10.1016/S0301-4215(03)00182-4

Stojkoska, B. L. R., & Trivodaliev, K. V. (2017). A review of Internet of Things for smart home: Challenges and solutions. *Journal of Cleaner Production, 140,* 1454–1464. doi:10.1016/j.jclepro.2016.10.006

Strong, D. R. (2019). Impacts of diffusion policy: Determinants of early smart meter diffusion in the US electric power industry. *Industrial and Corporate Change.* doi:10.1093/icc/dtz011

Sulyman, A. I., Oteafy, S. M., & Hassanein, H. S. (2017). Expanding the cellular-IoT umbrella: An architectural approach. *IEEE Wireless Communications, 24*(3), 66–71. doi:10.1109/MWC.2017.1600433

Swetina, J., Lu, G., Jacobs, P., Ennesser, F., & Song, J. (2014). Toward a standardized common M2M service layer platform: Introduction to oneM2M. *IEEE Wireless Communications, 21*(3), 20–26. doi:10.1109/MWC.2014.6845045

Theoleyre, F., & Pang, A. C. (Eds.). (2013). *Internet of Things and M2M Communications.* River Publishers.

Trappey, A. J., Trappey, C. V., Govindarajan, U. H., Chuang, A. C., & Sun, J. J. (2017). A review of essential standards and patent landscapes for the Internet of Things: A key enabler for Industry 4.0. *Advanced Engineering Informatics, 33,* 208–229. doi:10.1016/j.aei.2016.11.007

Tsukada, M., Washio, T., & Motoda, H. (2001). Automatic web-page classification by using machine learning methods. *Asia-Pacific Conference on Web Intelligence Springer,* 303-313. 10.1007/3-540-45490-X_36

Vinoski, S. (2006). Advanced message queuing protocol. *IEEE Internet Computing, 10*(6), 87–89. doi:10.1109/MIC.2006.116

Wahlster, W. (2012). From industry 1.0 to industry 4.0: Towards the 4th industrial revolution. *Forum Business Meets Research.*

Wang, S., Wan, J., Zhang, D., Li, D., & Zhang, C. (2016). Towards smart factory for industry 4.0: A self-organized multi-agent system with big data based feedback and coordination. *Computer Networks, 101,* 158–168. doi:10.1016/j.comnet.2015.12.017

Wollschlaeger, M., Sauter, T., & Jasperneite, J. (2017). The future of industrial communication: Automation networks in the era of the internet of things and industry 4.0. *IEEE Industrial Electronics Magazine, 11*(1), 17–27. doi:10.1109/MIE.2017.2649104

Xiaojun, Y., Weirui, W., & Jianping, L. (2012). Application mode construction of internet of things (IOT) for facility agriculture in Beijing. *Nongye Gongcheng Xuebao (Beijing), 4,* 1–14.

Yang, F., Wang, S., Li, J., Liu, Z., & Sun, Q. (2014). An overview of internet of vehicles. *China Communications, 11*(10), 1–15. doi:10.1109/CC.2014.6969789

Yang, Y., Ding, X., Zhu, J., & Bai, Y. (2010). Assumption of internet of things applied in electric vehicle charging facilities. *Dianli Xitong Zidonghua, 34*(21), 95–98.

Zanella, A., Bui, N., Castellani, A., Vangelista, L., & Zorzi, M. (2014). Internet of things for smart cities. *IEEE Internet of Things Journal, 1*(1), 22-32.

Zhou, B., Li, W., Chan, K. W., Cao, Y., Kuang, Y., Liu, X., & Wang, X. (2016). Smart home energy management systems: Concept, configurations, and scheduling strategies. *Renewable & Sustainable Energy Reviews, 61*, 30–40. doi:10.1016/j.rser.2016.03.047

Chapter 11
Reliability and Security Challenges in Electrical/ Optical On–Chip Interconnects for IoT Applications

Muhammad Rehan Yahya

iD https://orcid.org/0000-0002-6777-4022

Nanjing University of Aeronautics and Astronautics, China

Ning Wu

Nanjing University of Aeronautics and Astronautics, China

Zain Anwar Ali

iD https://orcid.org/0000-0002-2143-2879

Sir Syed University of Engineering and Technology (SSUET), Pakistan

ABSTRACT

The evolution of internet of things (IoT) applications, cloud computing, smart cities, and 4G/5G wireless communication systems have significantly increased the demands for on chip processing. Network on chip (NoC) is a viable alternative that can provide higher processing and bandwidth for increasing demands. NoC offers better performance and more flexibility with lower communication latency and higher throughput. However, use of NoC-based IoT devices have raised concerns on security and reliability of integrated chips (IC), which is used in almost every application. IoT devices share data that becomes vulnerable to attack and can be compromised during the data transfer. Keeping in view these security challenges, a detailed survey is presented that covers the security issues and challenges focusing on NoCs along with proposed countermeasures to secure on-chip communication. This study includes on-chip security issues for electrical as well as optical on-chip interconnects.

DOI: 10.4018/978-1-7998-1253-1.ch011

INTRODUCTION

The evolution of internet of things (IoT) inspires smart devices that are permeating in our lives, where smart services and applications are performing critical tasks that raise security concerns. Data proliferation is one of the critical issues, which designers and researchers are facing with the advent of IoT based smart cities projects (Samaila, Neto, Fernandes, Freire, & Inácio, 2018). With the increase in processing demand for IoT applications in every day of life, security and dependability have become key concerns while designing a network on chip based CMPs. Intellectual property (IP) hardware from third-parties are frequently used in order to reduce design time. The use of these IPs could cause leakage of data/information due to presence of some malicious Hardware Trojan (HT) (Basak, Bhunia, Tkacik, & Ray, 2017), (Tehranipoor & Koushanfar, 2010). The reason for information leakage may be unverified IPs, malicious foundry or untrusted design procedure. This problem of security lead researchers and designers to focus on security and reliability issues of on-chip interconnects (Bhunia et al., 2013). Network on Chip (NoC) has evolved as a practical solution that can provide future interconnection and processing requirements for IoT applications in chip multiprocessors (CMPs) (Bertozzi, Dimitrakopoulos, Flich, & Sonntag, 2015). In past, few works have been proposed to discuss security challenges in NoC based systems (Ben Achballah, Ben Othman, & Ben Saoud, 2017). However, more research needs to be accomplished for both electrical and optical NoC domains for secure on-chip communication. Figure 1 shows the IoT system setup with smart applications and services (Samaila et al., 2018).

As technology has exponentially evolved over the last few years, the number of cores on a single die has increased at a rapid pace, especially during the last decade. In this regard, the trend of technological developments in terms of increase in per chip core count, the increase in number of transistors, escalation in frequency and power consumption has been presented in form of trending plot titled "35 Years of Microprocessor Trend Data", which has been initially presented by M. Horowitz et. al till 2010 (M. Horowitz, F. Labonte, O. Shacham, K. Olukotun, L. Hammond, and C. Batten, 2018). Later, the plots have been updated by K. Rupp from 2010-2017. It can be observed from the Figure 2 that the number of per chip cores is increasing with a power law. Since the number of transistors is increasing as per Moore's Law, therefore chip count is increasing in form on-chip additional cores.

NoC based design has access to all the communication among different cores (Benini & De Micheli, 2002). Most of the work and research being done has recognized that NoC based architectures are suitable for secure on-chip communication. Since, components used in NoC architecture are homogeneous, taking that advantage designers have proposed several security mechanisms / schemes in an NoC based designs that provide better security than software approaches (Frey & Yu, 2017). Using hardware circuit among routers to secure data communication between different IPs is proposed in (Boraten & Kodi, 2018). Several threat models and countermeasures are proposed in literature to secure on-chip communication. Encryption and cryptographic algorithms are proposed in NoC links with additional area overhead and

Figure 1. Smart City Concept based on IoT System including smart applications of mobility, health and daily life

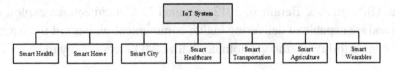

Figure 2. Original data up to the year 2010 collected and plotted by M. Horowitz, F. Labonte, O. Shacham, K. Olukotun, L. Hammond, and C. Batten. New plot and data collected for 2010-2017 by K.Rupp

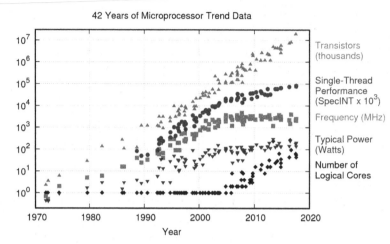

communication latency. Another way to secure on-chip communication is to define a particular set of rules that can act as a firewall to secure communication links. However, in case of third-party IP usage, NoC itself can be a source of threat. During the process of fabrication, malicious hardware can be injected into the chip that can cause serious security issues. In that case different design schemes e.g. denial of service / special hardware modules may be used that can prohibit the HT to access the information. Due to variety of different HTs, it is still an open challenge to tackle all threat scenarios and provide appropriate protection countermeasures.

Photonic NoCs have emerged as an alternative to electrical NoCs that can provide higher bandwidth, lower power consumption and minimal latency (Biberman & Bergman, 2012), (Yahya, 2018). Photonic NoC comprised of waveguides that are used for transmission of data using dense wavelength division multiplexed (DWDM) wavelengths. Microrings (MRs) are an essential component in optical communication and can be used as modulators, detector or filters (Bahadori, Rumley, Nikolova, & Bergman, 2016). These MRs are vulnerable to security threats from HTs (Pasricha, Chittamuru, Thakkar, & Bhat, 2018). MR tuning circuits that are used to provide control for MRs during data transmission among different cores can be easily accessible during the process of tuning that may lead to HT attach which can snoop the data from the optical bus. An HT can influence the tuning process the MR by partially tune MR to different wavelength which can be used to snoop the data from the optical bus. Such kind of malicious functionality in MRs can cause serious concerns in photonic NoC architectures. Architectural level security schemes can be utilized to secure optical on-chip communications. Securing optical on-chip communication is also a big challenge in future manycore processor systems that are widely used in several IoT applications.

Silicon photonics provides a natural solution for many issues that are related to high-performance computing, cloud computing, and IoT systems. The components used in photonics don't require high consumption of power per bit, as well as provide higher bandwidth of data that uses WDM instead of signal frequencies (Biberman & Bergman, 2012). Optical NoC architectures exploit these features of silicon photonics and are capable of delivering higher communication rates of up to terabits per second. Furthermore, the compatibility of silicon photonics with CMOS technology makes it highly suitable in integrating with electrical on-chip interconnects, where electrical and optical layers are integrated via 3D TSV technology. The optical NoCs give an advantage of using the same bandwidth for complete on-chip communication by closing the gap between processor and memory interface, which also provides benefits in terms of scalability of networks. Using the non-blocking optical switches with higher radix and scale with low power consumption and insertion loss, the higher bandwidth options can be utilized where simultaneous transmission of data is accomplished (Biberman & Bergman, 2012), (Duro, Pascual, Petit, Sahuquillo, & Gómez, 2018), (Yahya, Wu, Gaizhen, et al., 2019). To achieve higher bandwidth of data with low power consumption and minimized communication latency, these optical switches with higher radix are highly suitable in optical NoC topologies which enable optical interconnects to achieve a higher level of performance up to petascale and exascale and maybe beyond (Biberman & Bergman, 2012).

Keeping in view the above-mentioned upcoming challenges in IoT applications, in this work, a comprehensive review of security and reliability issues in the NoC paradigm is presented. State of the art proposed design schemes and architectures are discussed in this work which emphasizes mainly on secure on-chip communication using NoCs in the electrical domain as well as optical on-chip communication. Different possible solutions and efforts of designers are presented, that would provide an exhaustive insight in security and reliability issues of NoC based on-chip communication. In this chapter, the main focus is on security threats and different threat models for NoC are discussed. Furthermore, countermeasure methodologies and schemes for threat avoidance for electrical and optical NoCs are also provided. Finally, key challenges and future research directions are furnished at the end of this chapter.

Background

Security and confidentiality of information disseminated via IoT based applications and devices is a major concern, which requires special efforts and measures to be taken for secure communication in IoT (Granjal, Monteiro, & Sa Silva, 2015). Its a necessity of time to address the security challenges caused due to advancements in technology. An extensive review of existing solutions for the security of IoT applications, featuring confidentiality, privacy, reliability, integrity, and trust with critical challenges of IoT based applications is presented in (Sicari, Rizzardi, Grieco, & Coen-Porisini, 2015). System-on-chip has gained much attention to meet the requirements of IoT systems, which requires multiple processors on a single chip to fulfill higher processing demands (Candel, Petit, Sahuquillo, & Duato, 2018). With the progression of technology and evolution of multi/manycore era during the past few years, the replacement of conventional wiring and bus-based on-chip communication has been replaced with Network on-chip. The NoC based communications allow on-chip multi-processors, memories and other peripherals to share information by packet-based communication via an on-chip network (Dally & Towles, 2001). NoC provides designers, the flexibility to utilize higher bandwidth, low power consumption and flexibility for the stability of the system on chip (SoC). A lot of literature in the form of textbooks is available for NoC basic and advanced concepts such as 2D-NoC, 3D-NoC and photonic network on chip design (Dally & Towles, 2003),(Peh & Jerger, 2017), (Elfadel, 2016), (Bergman, Carloni, Chan, & Hendry, 2014). Before proceeding further in this chapter, a brief discussion on the basics of electrical and optical NoC design flow is provided for the ease of readers in this Section.

Basic NoC architecture consists of a particular topology, nodes consisting of routers, processor core, and communication links/channels. Nodes of NoC are arranged in different structures/arrangements called topologies, e.g. Mesh, Torus, Butterfly, and Fat-tree. Each router is connected with a processing core as well as interconnected to other routers via electrical/optical link. Basic NoC architecture consisting of routers and processing cores is shown in Figure 3, where each router consists of 5-ports, i.e. local, east, west, north, and south. The local port connects the processing core to the router, while the other four ports provide communication links between different routers. Once the NoC topology is finalized, it is important to define some scheme for routing of data, which is responsible to select a communication path between source and destination node. The design of the routing scheme/algorithm determines the performance of overall NoC architecture. Resourceful utilization of network resources decides the flow control of NoC design, where bandwidth allocation, the capacity of buffers plays an important role. An effective scheme for flow control can achieve higher bandwidth and low latency in NoC architecture. There are different flow control schemes that are available, e.g. packet switching, circuit switching, and bufferless flow control. The integration of all the aforementioned components leads to build an NoC architecture (Dally & Towles, 2003).

The design of an electrical NoC includes topology, routing and flow control, the internal architecture of router and link architecture (Dally & Towles, 2003). The routers are mainly responsible for intra-core communication and transmission of data. Therefore, the most crucial component from the security point of view is a router in electrical NoCs. However, in 3D-NoC the TSVs have significant role in reliable communication among different stacks of die layers. The thermal variation and peak temperature of routers affect the transmission of data through TSVs and can cause physical damages, timing errors and increased cost of cooling (Keramati, Modarressi, & Rezaei, 2017), (Z. Li et al., 2012), (Abellan et al., 2017). However, several techniques and management schemes to address these issues in electrical NoCs have been proposed to achieve reliable communication in on-chip networks (Killian, Tanougast, Monteiro, & Dandache, 2014), (Yan & Gao, 2017), (Yan & Gao, 2017), (Werner, Navaridas, & Luján, 2016).

Optical on-chip interconnects are realized using the integration of photonic components such as lasers, microring resonators based modulators and photo-detectors, the optical waveguides, and the couplers. The continuous wave stream of light with different wavelengths, generated by a laser source is injected into the chips via optical waveguides. The laser sources are considered as possibly the most challenging devices to integrate into on-chip silicon die. The efficient hybrid silicon/III-V lasers capable of lesser power consumption are proposed which significantly reduces the cost of packaging (Duro et al., 2018). Microring resonators are the fundamental component in optical communication to exploit

Figure 3. 4x4 Mesh NoC Architecture, with internal architecture of NoC node (IP Core, L1 Cache, Router Microarchitecture)

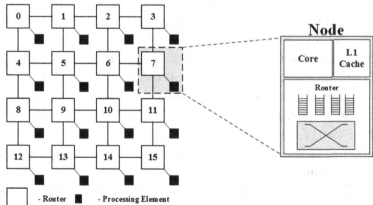

the wavelength division multiplexing (WDM), which permits the optical signal to split into several independent wavelengths. Microring resonators are used as modulators and photo-detectors in on-chip communication. Once the wavelength enters into the optical waveguide, the electrical to optical conversion is accomplished at the particular modulator and on reception, at respective photo-detector, the optical to electrical is achieved. The modulators also determine the switching capacity of the on-chip communication system which leads to decide the operational bandwidth of the photonic on-chip system (Duro et al., 2018). Lastly, the photo-detectors which are used as optical receivers, control and convert the amplitude and phase of an incoming optical signal back to the electrical paradigm and complete the data transmission from source to destination (Duro et al., 2018). Different layers of optical NoC are shown in Figure 4 connecting electrical and optical layers via 3D-TSV technology.

Since electrical interconnects limit the performance of on-chip communication for high-performance applications, optical NoCs is proposed which provides a promising solution to upcoming demands. On-chip optical communication contains four main components: a laser source, microring resonator (MR), waveguide and coupler. To generate a continuous light having a certain wavelength λ_i, a laser source is required either on-chip or off-chip. The light wave with particular wavelength λ_i is encoded and optical to electrical conversion is completed at the sender side, which is then transmitted to the specific receiver using the photo-detector. Photo-detector is responsible for optical to electrical conversion on the receiver's end. Optical on-chip communication is illustrated in Figure 5. In general, a laser source generates different wavelengths i.e. $(\lambda_1, \lambda_2 \ldots \lambda_n)$ using external laser source, which is coupled to waveguide via couplers and transmitted through the waveguide. Silicon waveguides act as a carrier and hence responsible for the optical signal transmission, exploiting wavelength division multiplexing (WDM) carrying multiple wavelengths. MR is a basic component of optical on-chip communication and acts as modulator or demodulator at source and destination respectively. Finally, the coupler is used for physical interface between the chip and a laser source (Bahadori et al., 2016), (Rumley et al., 2017), (Yahya, 2018).

The lasers are the main source of injecting light to optical waveguides, which can be used either as on-chip or off-chip. Normally the material is stimulated known as "gain material" to generate a light beam that is amplified and transmitted (Bashir, Peter, & Sarangi, 2019). The gain medium is placed between a pair of optical mirrors, where light gets bounce among those mirrors and the gain medium is used to generate light beam by injection of charge or transmission of optical signal. Once, the light

Figure 4. Layers of optical on-chip interconnects connecting electrical and optical layers via 3D-TSV technology

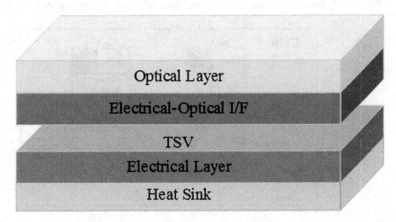

gets out of area between the mirrors called a cavity, the output of laser is generated (Bashir et al., 2019). Different types of lasers have been proposed such as DFB (Distributed Feedback) lasers, which provide an advantage of broad-spectrum and are widely used, the DBR (Distributed Bragg Reflector) laser are the most common type of lasers and preferred over other lasers, MQW (Multiple QuantumWell) lasers are difficult from manufacturing point of view due to small size, while VCSEL (Vertical Cavity Surface Emitting) lasers are highly suitable for on-chip communication due to small size with higher yield rates and can be easily integrated on the chip and used as an on-chip lasers (Bashir et al., 2019). The off-chip lasers should persist in on state, in order to avoid latency issue, which can occur if the laser source is turned off to save the consumption of power, therefore not an automatic choice for on-chip communication. The detailed discussion of each laser type is reviewed and discussed in (Bashir et al., 2019).

The light signal is propagated via optical waveguides, which provides the feature of WDM in on-chip communication. The waveguides are the propagation medium and can be utilized as tapers which are employed as off-chip waveguides, bends which are used to provide a turn in a waveguides. The transfer of optical power from one waveguide to another is main responsibility of couplers/beam-splitters. The directional couplers provide an interface to switch optical signals between different waveguides. Lastly, the Y-junction which is used to split an optical waveguide into two structures and used a splitter (Bashir et al., 2019), (Tu, Song, Huang, Chen, & Fu, 2019). Moreover, optical NoCs are constructed by using combination of electrical and optical layers having electrical to optical interfaces and vice versa connected via 3D-TSV technology as shown in Figure 6.

In literature, a number of research publications have been proposed over the period of time evaluating the performance of electrical and optical NoCs. Recently, a comprehensive comparative study between optical and electrical interconnects exploring the advantages and shortcomings of optical NoC as compared to electrical NoCs has been presented in (Yahya, Wu, Ali, & Khizar, 2019). The comparisons of 64 and 144 nodes NoC architectures in both domains have been explored and studied, comparing the effect of different data sizes on throughput and latency in NoC architectures under different traffic patterns. In addition, the impact of insertion loss and crosstalk noise under real-time video applications have also been analyzed and investigated in (Yahya, Wu, Ali, et al., 2019). Another study explored the comparison of different electrical NoC topologies evaluating the cost-efficiency in chip multiprocessors is presented in (Ortín-Obón, Suárez-Gracia, Villarroya-Gaudó, Izu, & Viñals-Yúfera, 2016). A circuit-switched optical network, which uses an electrical domain for path setup and transmission of smaller

Figure 5. On-Chip Optical Communication with laser, modulators, photo-detectors, and waveguide

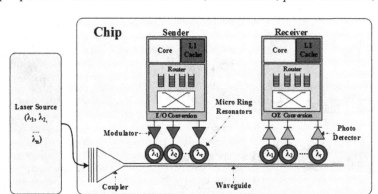

data packets while utilized optical layer for transmission of large data packets is presented and proposed in (Shacham, Bergman, & Carloni, 2008). As an example, a mesh-based NoC topology for both electrical and optical domains is shown in Figure 6 (Yahya, Wu, Ali, et al., 2019). It can be seen from Figure 6(a), that the electrical mesh NoC topology consists of a number of processing elements attached to the corresponding router connected via electrical links. However, optical NoC consists of two layers upper (optical) and lower (electrical) layer, connected via 3D-TSV technology as shown in Figure 6(b). The cores in the optical layer are connected through optical waveguide links, however, the electrical layer utilized conventional on-chip interconnects used for path setup and data transmission of smaller packets.

A brief introduction to HT is provided for ease of understanding. Hardware Trojans can cause a critical threat to manycore systems, as a result, the chip may lead to malfunctioning or complete failure (Sengupta, 2017). Recently, manycore processors are extensively employed in SoC designs providing high-performance computing. These systems utilize NoC to exchange data among cores (M. J. Sepúlveda, Diguet, Strum, & Gogniat, 2015). The foremost SoC threats which cause is due to the sharing of resources when malicious processes breaches and ultimately extraction of data incurs. On-chip communications may be checked by attackers to steal critical data. As resource sharing among malicious and safe processes happens often, performance degradation becomes more prominent (Bazzazi, Manzuri Shalmani, & Hemmatyar, 2017).

Figure 6a. Electrical Mesh NoC architecture with 16 tiles,

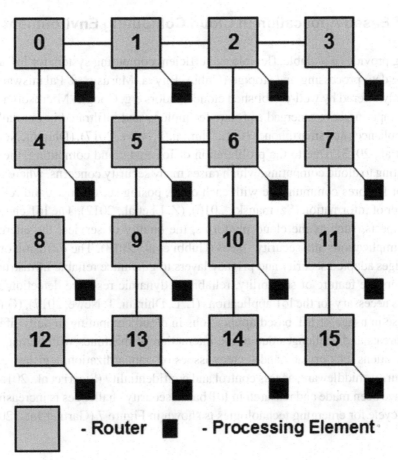

Figure 6b. Optical Mesh NoC with optical (upper) and electrical (bottom) layers

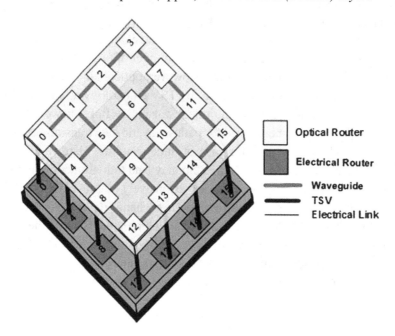

Impact of IoT Based Application in Cloud Computing Environment

Cloud computing provides a scalable, flexible and efficient computing system for IoT applications having cost-effective data processing and storage (Gubbi, Buyya, Marusic, & Palaniswami, 2013). These services are mainly offered by well-established cloud vendors e.g. Google, Microsoft and Amazon. The IoT and cloud computing have emerged as future technology and infiltrated in our daily life e.g. smart devices, home appliances and smartphones (L. L. Dhirani, T. Newe, 2017), (Dhirani, Newe, & Nizamani, 2019), (Gubbi et al., 2013). Due to the proliferation of IoT and cloud computing, the multiprocessors thrive on connecting to cloud computing, which raises many security concerns, where multiple applications on different IP cores communicate with each other, posing serious trust and reliability concerns during the transfer of information (Szymanski, 2016), (Z. Li et al., 2012). The IoT enabled applications opens various aspects, such as the cloud platforms, the quality of service, the energy consumption, the data mining implications and security issues (Gubbi et al., 2013). The diffusion of IoT application and services obliges adapted security and privacy layers to guarantee reliable infrastructure. The cloud computing delivers the feature of scalability, reliability, dynamic resource detection and independent ubiquitous access necessary for the IoT applications (L. L. Dhirani, T. Newe, 2017), (Gubbi et al., 2013). Moreover, the rise in usage of IoT based applications in cloud computing in daily life at a wide-scale raises security threats and challenges due to the interaction of machines with humans. The IoT based end-to-end applications lack privacy and secrecy issues of standardization, legislative, authentication, trust, mobile security, middleware, access control and confidentiality (Sicari et al., 2015). In this regard, several efforts have been made and research in IoT based security challenges is increasing during recent years. The hype cycle for emerging technologies is shown in Figure 7 (Gartner Inc., 2012).

The IoT based sensor analytics applications are promising paradigm with lower energy requirements, however, poses security challenges in real-life examples such as secure autonomous aerial surveillance, local face detection, and seizure detection. The Unmanned Aerial Vehicle (UAV) are used to secure autonomous aerial surveillance with the deployment of convolutional neural networks (CNN). However, the usage of CNN requires more external storage for storing information, which is vulnerable to security issues and data can be leaked, accessed and modified by the hijacking agents (Schroff, Kalenichenko, & Philbin, 2015). Therefore, to avoid these issues, strong encryption on crucial information can be utilized at the cost of an extra overhead required as an overlay on original data. Another example of end-to-end IoT application is local face detection with secured remote recognition, where billions of operations are required for the face recognition and detection (Schroff et al., 2015). Therefore, the complete computation on a single device is not advantageous and can be divided into two-stage computation. The first stage can take an input image and scan the face for further processing and another stage can achieve the recognition of scanned faces. Hence, continuous face detection and scanning can be done on low-power smartwatch and the recognition can be completed on smartphone or the cloud to accomplish the two-stage computation. Moreover, the seizure detection for healthcare applications such as electrocardiogram (ECG), electroencephalogram (EEG) and electromyogram (EMG) has become a huge market that can be used in IoT devices (Analytics et al., 2017). However, the security remains one of the main concern due the sensitive information, acquired and transmitted to network for analysis, hence requires encryption scheme to accomplish secure communication. The aforementioned cases for IoT applications are detailed discussed and presented in IoT endpoint SoC secure communication system (Analytics et al., 2017).

SECURITY CHALLENGES IN NOC PARADIGM

In literature, several surveys and reviews are available on the security challenges of SoC, however, for the NoC domain, more work is required. Since NoC is considered as future on-chip interconnection scheme in manycore processors, therefore, more efforts and work are vital to make NoC architecture secure for communication. A survey on emerging and forthcoming challenges on NoC is provided in (Ben Achballah et al., 2017), (Papastefanakis, Maitre, & Ragot, 2015). However, a detailed and up-to-date survey on NoC security issues in both optical and electrical is yet to be discussed and this chapter is an attempt to furnish a comprehensive survey. This survey is divided into two parts; first, the security issues in the electrical NoC domain and second, covers the security challenges in optical NoCs.

SECURITY CHALLENGES AND COUNTERMEASURES IN ELECTRICAL NoCs

The security challenges for both electrical and optical NoCs are presented in this article. In addition, we have presented a few schemes and methodologies proposed by researchers in the recent past to overcome these security and reliability issues in NoCs. In order to avoid and circumvent the attacks caused due to memory in NoC, a data protection unit is utilized, which delivers features as a conventional "firewall" in on-chip interconnection networks (Gbali Fayez, Elmiligi Haytham, 2009). This data protection module/system is capable of enforcing an access control mechanism to the memory system by defining a specific transaction initiated by an IP to access the shared memory system in NoC. These specifications separate the non-sensitive and sensitive data by partitioning the memory blocks for different processors in NoC.

Figure 7. Gartner 2019 Hype Cycle of emerging technologies, Source: Gartner Inc. [10]

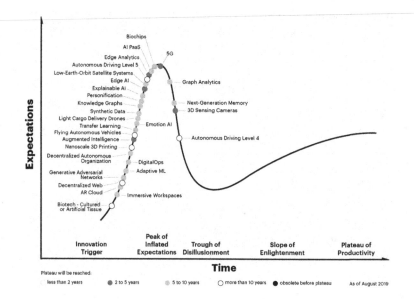

Another method of avoiding security issues in NoC is the use of for secure network interface by using a security configuration manager, which is a dedicated core taking care of hardware configurations as well as their communication and keeping track of their behavior. By monitoring the behavior of subsystems that are closely connected in NoC architecture, the security manager controls by warning the different monitors to secure communication of data among different processors. Lastly, the protection from the side-channel attacks by using cryptographic algorithms in NoC via key exchange at the start of communication. The aim of the cryptographic schemes in NoCs is to introduce an enhanced security level in a network to protect from attackers capable of leakage of information (Gbali Fayez, Elmiligi Haytham, 2009). This section deliberates the aforementioned security challenges and proposed countermeasures in electrical NoCs. Security attacks can be classified into three categories; software attacks, side-channel attacks and physical attacks (Samyde, 2002).

1. Software attacks include a malicious piece of code e.g. viruses, trojans that intrude and affect the NoC performance.
2. Physical attacks are based on hardware intrusion at the time of chip fabrication.
3. Side-channel attacks are HT using side-channel parameters such as power consumption, time delay, thermal radiation, and electromagnetism to deteriorate the performance of NoC.

A detection method for HT, based on a neural network by analyzing its power consumption of the suspicious circuit is proposed in (J. Li, Ni, Chen, & Zhou, 2017). From NoC point of view, three different kinds of attacks can be defined.

1. First, Denial of Service (DoS) attacks, which degrades overall system performance in terms of bandwidth minimization that causes higher on-chip communication latency to saturate the network. Another way to employ DoS is that attacker injects certain packets having false path address, such

that either theses packets don't reach to the desired destination or trapped into some closed loop. DoS make the system power-hungry that leads to a high rate of battery power drainage in embedded systems.

2. Second, extracting secret data/information, since, NoC provides access to all information across the chip, the extraction of critical data is possible which is kept in different memory areas. Exploiting buffer overflow, the data can be extracted using this method (Chien & Szor, 2002).

3. Last, the Hijacking attacks, which are triggered by attackers to perform additional functions in special configurations (Fiorin, Silvano, & Sami, 2007).

A comprehensive survey of NoC security issues and countermeasures which are proposed by researchers to secure on-chip communication is presented in this chapter. A data protection unit (DPU) based secure NoC architecture is proposed in (Fiorin, Palermo, Lukovic, Catalano, & Silvano, 2008). DPU is employed into network interface which is controlled by a network security manager. A reconfigurable environment is provided that gives flexibility to assist the dynamic system properties. DPU is responsible for secure communication between sender and receiver by securing the memory accesses. DPU protects critical information from malicious cores to access the load and store functions. This design methodology doesn't involve time-consuming encryption schemes and delivers a secure communication system to secure shared memory accesses in NoC.

A security framework that divides the network into two zones i.e. secure zone and un-secure zone using Authentication Encryption (AE) scheme is proposed in (Kapoor, Rao, Arshi, & Trivedi, 2013). AE scheme provides secure communication, which is employed in the network interface of each node in NoC architecture. AE denies the memory accesses to illegal transactions caused by malicious sources. AE exploits a scheme to first authenticate the memory access using session keys among the cores of NoC. These keys are only used between secure and un-secure zones, however, secure zones can communicate, using their permanent keys. Since this scheme requires an extra AE module to be employed, thus an increase in area overhead is noticed, which affects the latency of overall network.

The NoCs are often designed utilizing the IP cores taken from third-party, to minimize the time of the design cycle. However, these third-party cores may contain some HT or extra logic, which can pose severe damage to NoC architecture where it is employed. Such compromised NoC along with software assistance can pose serious security threats that are discussed in (Ancajas, Chakraborty, & Roy, 2014). In addition, countermeasures to above threats and protection schemes for compromised NoC are proposed called Fort-NoCs. This methodology restricts hidden side-channel attacks to deny accesses that secures the on-chip communication.

Countermeasure schemes to protect NoC architectures cause's different implications on hardware and software design, which can affect the physical characteristics e.g. power, latency, and area required to implement extra logic for protection of compromised NoC. To ensure the secure transmission of data, even the safe data has to pass through secure mechanism, which can cause extra overheads and thus deteriorate the performance of overall network. An efficient scheme to check the memory accesses using firewall, based on hardware approach between system-level memory requests, is presented in (Grammatikakis et al., 2014).

An efficient scheme to inject a firewall into NoC routers for securing the network information is proposed in (Hu, Müller-Gritschneder, Sepulveda, Gogniat, & Schlichtmann, 2015). The proposed scheme reduces the extra overhead caused due to the extra logic required for security purposes. An automatic approach, based on Integer Linear Programming (ILP) to find the optimal configuration of the firewall is used such that the extra overhead is minimized and security necessities are full filed. Compared to other solutions, this scheme effectively reduces overhead by almost 63% as a result of the ILP solver.

A new router attack scenario, which is targeted towards network-on-chip with possibility inside the router along with a survey on different potential attack scenarios in MPSoCs is presented in (Biswas, Nandy, & Narayan, 2015). Since Multi-Processor System on Chip (MPSoCs) consists of many Trusted Execution Environments (TEEs). All NoC architectures are considered to be vulnerable to such kind of attacks. Initiation of such a router attack can allow the attacker to take control of the whole chip and thus poses a severe threat to the SoC. Routing tables are susceptible to such kind of attacks, which are addressed in this article. Countermeasures based on monitoring against routing table attacks with many TEE are proposed.

Smart security zones are efficiently implemented by taking advantage of protocols based on robust group key agreement along with routing of NoC architecture is proposed in (J. Sepúlveda, Flórez, & Gogniat, 2016). Creation, modification, and removal of malicious security zones are efficiently managed using this design approach. The architecture of the proposed scheme consists of data routers for transmission of data, service routers that control the security feature. Secure units are responsible for group key agreement and a security manager is used to control the parameters for security protocol. For key agreement, Diffie-Hellman is implemented in this design scheme, which assigns a group key for the security protocol (Systems & Kocher, 1996). Validation of the scheme is accomplished through software-based simulations.

Another architecture employing NoC firewall at the network interface layer using certain rules to check the physical address, where illegal processor requests to access on-chip memory are rejected, which protects the legal processes to safely run on the SoC is proposed in (Grammatikakis et al., 2015). Adversary to other approaches, this scheme is realized at the hardware level to implement the firewall. Using the gem5 simulation environment and integrating the ARM processor with STMicroelectronics (STNoC), a comprehensive framework is designed to evaluate the performance of this design scheme. The implementation of this firewall scheme has the advantage of reducing power consumption and communication delays in NoC.

A runtime scheme for HT mitigation to strengthen the NoC, against trojan attack caused due to insertion of malicious logic in NoC by untrusted third-party vendor or in-house disloyal employee is proposed and discussed (Frey & Yu, 2017). This scheme features countermeasures contrary to software or hardware design approach to secure the NoC architecture. Router level Trojan detection and mitigation are performed which control the multi-hop communications and prevent the malicious packet to not reach its desired destination. The check on flit integrity allows the termination of HT once detected and mitigates the effect of HT which can modify the flit data.

Another work based on security zones, where the routing algorithm is utilized for implementation of such zones to employ secure on-chip commutation by establishing secure communication links is proposed in (Fernandes et al., 2016). This scheme exploits the Region-based Routing algorithm to implement security zones along with a deadlock avoidance scheme called Segment-based Routing (Flich, Mejia, Lopez, & Duato, 2007), (Mejia et al., 2006).

Implications of HT on FPGA devices along with the classification of specific HT types in FPGAs, which can be inserted by an attacker in FPGAs is presented in (Mal-Sarkar et al., 2016). Taxonomy of FPGA trojans is shown in Figure 8 (Mal-Sarkar et al., 2016). Based on combined logic-testing and side-channel attacks analysis, a combined scheme is proposed for efficient HT detection in FPGAs. Authors also proposed a scheme called Adapted Triple Modular Redundancy (ATMR), for the protection of

FPGA devices against different HT types. This approach can detect arbitrary HT which is inserted into FPGA device by attackers. Compared to traditional TMR, this design scheme provides protection with a lesser overhead of power.

NoC allows all nodes to share and access data in the network. Compromised IP core becomes a serious point of concern when malicious logic or a piece of software is executed. Using snooping, information can be accessed and secret data can be acquired. Since NoC is prone to side-channel attacks, the affected cores can implement a special type of attack i.e. distributed timing attack (DTA). To counter the DTA attack, a secure NoC solution called Gossip NoC is proposed which exploits traffic management to avoid the side-channel attacks (Reinbrecht, Susin, Bossuet, & Sepúlveda, 2016). A traffic monitor is installed in each router, which transmits the gossip alert whenever a threat is detected. In response, whenever that gossip alert is received, the neighboring node ignores the message and router deviates the path, using the different routing algorithm.

FPGA based reconfigurable NoC with fault tolerance and security via signature exchange and adaptive routing, exploiting FPGA property of partial reconfiguration is proposed in (Chip & Ram, 2016). The network used for NoC is X-network, which requires a lesser number of routers as compared to traditional Mesh topology. Rivest-Shamir-Adleman (RSA) encryption/decryption algorithm is used for signature exchange. Speed of RSA has increased through Montgomery modular multiplication. This architecture offers all characteristics of a secure SoC i.e. CIA (confidentiality, integrity, authentication). Implementation of security features with a minimal overhead of resource consumption is carried out on Xilinx FPGA.

Another FPGA based reconfigurable secure on-chip communication system, utilizing a security module called identity and address verification (IAV) is proposed in (Saeed, Ahmadinia, & Just, 2016). The IAV module is integrated at each router which is responsible for verification of identity and address used for data communication in multicore systems, built using NoC architecture. IAV is validated using FPGA using the run-time reconfiguration feature of the FPGA device. This work shows efficient power and area consumption in comparison to similar architectures.

Since, NoCs are vulnerable to security attacks, if not properly configured in MPSoCs. To prevent these attacks, source authentication at the router level while the configuration of packets can secure on-chip communication. Source authentication scheme ensures that only trusted source is allowed to send configuration packets to the router. Hashing is one of the schemes that is widely used for source authentication. Similar to Secure Hash Algorithm-3 (SHA-3), this work proposed a hashing scheme for source authentication with minimal area and power consumption for router configuration packets in NoCs (Biswas, 2016).

Figure 8. Taxonomy of FPGA based Trojans

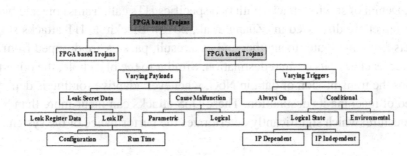

An efficient implementation to create security zones for hierarchical group key based NoC in MPSoCs system is proposed in (Sepulveda, Flórez, Immler, Gogniat, & Sigl, 2017). This hierarchical configuration provides security features with improved scalability and performance of MPSoCs. The proposed architecture consists of a global manager assisted by multiple local managers to implement a layered protocol. IP cores are used as local managers to handle the critical applications which belong to the security zone. Three types of hierarchical group-wise protocols are implemented including hierarchical Diffie-Hellman. This architecture efficiently implements security zones to secure on-chip communication.

To reduce the design cycle time and meet the stringent constraints of time to market, the use of third-party intellectual property (3PIP) has increased. Though time to market is reduced while using 3PIP components, but the reliability and verification of these components still raise questions. Any 3PIP may have some hidden malicious logic that can trigger a critical instance and deteriorate the performance of NoC. To explore the hidden threat in 3PIP used in NoC, a model, based on security measures against compromised NoC is proposed in (JayashankaraShridevi, Ancajas, Chakraborty, & Roy, 2017). The compromised NoC is called rouge NoC (rNoC), which causes the bottleneck in performance of MPSoCs. An on-chip runtime latency auditor (RLAN) is integrated for screening, to ensure the trust and dependability of NoC.

To counter, side-channel attacks, a method for real-time randomization in NoC route to increase the efficacy and resilience of NoC is proposed in (Indrusiak, Harbin, & Sepulveda, 2017). To achieve the route randomization, optimization approach is employed which effectively controls the task in real-time. Test setup for guaranteed performance under side-channel attacks, to provide security measures is also introduced in this architecture.

The capability of MPSoCs to detect the threat of DoS caused due to hardware trojans and its mitigation is a challenging task. A new lightweight HT model named target activated sequential payload (TASP) to inject the faults in data packets for deployment of new DoS attack is proposed in (Boraten & Kodi, 2018). This threat model incurs the network resource starvation, which leads to malfunctioning of chip. To prevent this attack, link obfuscation method is used as countermeasure to avert the HT triggering, which reroutes the packets within NoC. Optimized algebraic manipulation detection (AMD) code implementation is also proposed for detection of fault injections in this work.

To detect the HT in runtime requires certain methodologies and techniques to covert the effect of HTs in integrated chips. A methodology to detect the runtime invasions caused by HT is proposed, which is based on burst mode communication protocol (Khalid, Hasan, Hasan, & Awwad, 2018). A three-phase design methodology includes; linear temporal logic (LTC) used for behavioral modeling and its verification. Runtime monitors are inserted based on LTC based behavioral model at susceptible links. Finally, integrating runtime monitors in the system. Without knowing the netlist details, this scheme gives an advantage of reuse in design for runtime monitoring.

NoCs are widely used in manycore systems and susceptible to the intrusion of HTs during manufacturing or design phases. Denial of service attacks with two specifics HTs called sinkhole and blackhole having NoC as the main target are discussed in (Zhang et al., 2018). Blackhole HT attacks stop the forwarding of data packets from one router to another and as a result, packets are dropped from NoC network, hence, packet never reaches to its desired destination. Similar to the blackhole, the other type of HT i.e. sinkhole also stops the transmission of data in NoC, whenever adaptive routing is deployed, hence the packet is deprived of reaching its destination. These DoS attacks can incur more than 30% packet loss rate in NoC architecture, which significantly deteriorates the performance of the system. Modeling and quantification on the effects of the above-mentioned HT attacks, along with countermeasures against attacks are also proposed. Process of blackhole and sinkhole are presented in Figure 9 (Zhang et al., 2018).

Hybrid NoC routers are widely presented, combining the features of both packet and circuit switching which can meet varying demands of application in an efficient manner (Lotfi-Kamran, Modarressi, & Sarbazi-Azad, 2016). However, the different application can pose diverse security threats and one application can extract information from other using time side channel or secretly using covert time channel attacks. To secure the hybrid routers, three different schemes i.e. separate hybrid (SH), combined and separate hybrid (CSH) and combined hybrid (CH) are proposed in (Biswas, 2018). Proposed methodologies effectively secure the hybrid NoC routers from time channel attacks.

Data sharing among different IoT devices are very common, using a cache memory shared model, which is highly exposed to side-channel attacks. Using the side channel, encryption keys are more prone to attacks, which can be acquired during data sharing. A comprehensive review of side-channel attacks, where the main target of attacks is cache memory and their countermeasures are presented in (Lyu & Mishra, 2018). Common encryption/decryption algorithms, which are the main target by side channels in cache memory systems are Advanced Encryption Standard (AES), Rivest-Shamir-Adleman (RSA) and Elliptic Curve Digital Signature Algorithm (ECDSA). Different side-channel attacks in the cache memory system are categorized into two classes i.e. time-driven and access driven attacks. In time-driven attacks, the attacker calculates the total execution time taken by the encryption algorithm and later used it for stealing of critical data. Access driven attacks, lead attackers to check the particular module which uses encryption scheme. Based on time and access driven attacks, different methods are proposed for cache memory side-channel attacks, which are as follows:

1. **Prime + Probe:** The contents of cache memory are filled by the attacker's data and monitor, which one evicts as a result of encryption scheme (Osvik, Shamir, & Tromer, 2006).
2. **Evict + Time:** This scheme belongs to time-driven attacks, where the execution time of the compromised process is measured, which evicts the data of a particular process from a buffer (Osvik et al., 2006).

Figure 9. Illustration of Blackhole and Sinkhole (a). Blackhole (b). Sinkhole

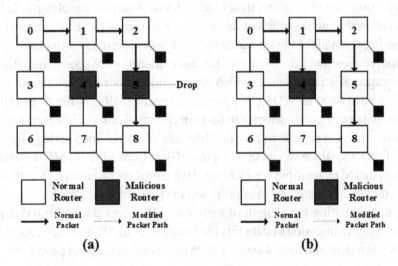

3. **Flush + Reload:** This attack flushes the content of the cache memory line and monitor, when particular victim process is executed, as soon as the process runs, the attacker calculates the time and reload the memory with its contents (Yarom & Falkner, 2014).

Different variants of Prime + Probe scheme to attack cache memory of NoC architectures, named P+P Firecracker and P+P Arrow are proposed in (Reinbrecht, Susin, Bossuet, Sigl, & Sepúlveda, 2017). The P+P Firecracker identifies all non-accessed sets of cache memory during the encryption/decryption process, while P+P Arrow identifies all accessed sets of cache memory, which allows the attacker to extract the information from the cache memory in NoC architectures. Year-wise secure NoC architectures and quantification of threat models are listed in Table 1.

SECURITY CHALLENGES AND COUNTERMEASURES IN OPTICAL NoCs

In recent years, different optical NoC topologies have been proposed and demonstrated which include mesh, torus, butterfly, fat-tree and clos architectures (Werner, Navaridas, & An, 2017). In addition to conventional NoC topologies, several customized topologies for on-chip interconnects have been presented and proposed to optimize the power consumption, reduce communication latency and increase the overall network throughput (Yahya, 2018). In this regard, recently, a comprehensive review is presented, which studied different optical and hybrid NoC topologies providing a comprehensive overview about proposed design scheme, optimization parameters which include latency, power, throughput, bandwidth, insertion loss, scalability, SNR and fault tolerance. The summarized form of performance parameters are listed in Table 2 (Yahya, 2018). The optical layer of ONoC can cause unreliable communication due to temperature variation and thermal sensitivity caused due to non-ideal behavior of optical switching elements. The control of mirroring's wavelength on which it resonates its signal is critical during communication and can lead to erroneous data transmission if the demodulator's wavelength at destination gets misaligned with the wavelength of incoming data signal. Therefore, fault-tolerant approaches are required for reliable communication of data in ONoCs (Bakhtiar, Hosseinzadeh, & Reshadi, 2017). Another method is the use of hardware redundancy where redundant MRs are used with same wavelengths having different temperatures. The MRs in redundant schemes are tuned in such a manner that original wavelength shift is achieved by increasing the temperature, thus spare MRs with narrow wavelengths help to accomplish reliable communication despite the effect of thermal variations in MRs (Bakhtiar et al., 2017).

With the increasing demands of higher bandwidth and lower communication latency with minimized power consumption, conventional electrical on-chip interconnects have shown limitations. Optical NoC technology has emerged as an alternative, which can provide higher bandwidth and minimized power consumption taking advantage of WDM. Microring resonator (MRs) is the most critical component which is used as modulator or photo-detector in on-chip communication. However, it has been observed that process variation plays a critical role in functionality of MRs. The driving signal of MR can be manipulated by HT attacks, which can incur snooping of data from adjacent MR's wavelength in optical waveguide, which is shared by multiple wavelengths. Using process variations, an authentication scheme to secure optical on-chip communications is proposed in (Pasricha et al., 2018).

Partial tuning to modulating wavelength of malicious MR draws power from that particular wavelength, which results in modification of data bits i.e. from bit '1' to '0'. Similarly, during reception, data duplication incurs when demodulating wavelength drops a small amount of power onto photo-detector.

Table 1. Summary of year wise NoC security proposals

Reference	Type	Proposal	Other Features
(Fiorin et al., 2008)	SW	Data protection Unit	Secure Communication
(Fiorin et al., 2008)	HW	Illegal Access Probe	Denial-of-Service Probe
(Sepulveda et al., 2012)	SW	Quality of Security Service	Firewall
(Kapoor et al., 2013)	SW	Authentication Encryption	Secure Zone
(Ancajas et al., 2014)	SW	Fort-NoCs	Side Channel Attacks
(Grammatikakis et al., 2014)	HW	Firewall	Memory Access
(Hu et al., 2015)	SW	Firewall	Integer Linear Programming
(Grammatikakis et al., 2015)	HW	Firewall	Reduce power and area
(Sepulveda et al., 2016)	SW	Rekeying Process	Hierarchical Group Key
(J. Sepúlveda et al., 2016)	SW	Group Key	Smart Secure Zone
(Fernandes et al., 2016)	SW	Region based Routing	Secure Zone
(Mal-Sarkar et al., 2016)	HW	HT Detection in FPGA	Side Channel Attacks
(Reinbrecht et al., 2016)	SW	Distributed Timing Attack	Side Channel Attacks
(Chip & Ram, 2016)	HW	Rivest-Shamir-Adleman	Signature Exchange
(Saeed et al., 2016)	HW	Identity and Address Verification	FPGA Reconfiguration
(Biswas, 2016)	SW	Secure Hash Algorithm-3	Source authentication
(Frey & Yu, 2017)	SW	HT Mitigation	Router Level Detection
(Sepulveda et al., 2017)	SW	Diffie-Hellman	Hierarchical Group Key
(JayashankaraShridevi et al., 2017)	SW	Runtime Latency Auditor	Rouge NoC, 3PIP
(Indrusiak et al., 2017)	SW	Route Randomization	Side Channel Attacks
(Reinbrecht et al., 2017)	SW	Prime + Probe	Side Channel Attacks
(Boraten & Kodi, 2018)	SW	TASP*	Denial of Service, AMD
(Khalid et al., 2018)	SW	Burst Mode Communication	linear temporal logic
(Zhang et al., 2018)	SW	Blackhole and Sinkhole	Denial of Service
(Biswas, 2018)	SW	SH, CSH and CH*	Time Side Channel

* Terms are abbreviated at the end of chapter

The process of alteration in optical data bits is shown in Figure 10 (Pasricha et al., 2018). This altered data eventually reaches to destination and can pose serious threat in optical NoC. To address this problem a framework named SOTERIA, which provides secure communication taking advantage of process variations in optical NoCs is proposed in (Vineel, Chittamuru, Thakkar, Bhat, & Pasricha, 2018). The generation of encryption keys is completed using the process variation of destination's detector MR's gateway interface. Due to process variation cloning of MRs is not possible, which inhibits the duplication of encryption keys.

Table 2. Optical and Hybrid NoC Topologies with Optimization Parameters

Reference	Routing Strategy	Achieved Optimized Parameters
(Gu, Chen, Yang, Chen, & Zhang, 2017)	WDM	LAT, PWR, TP, SC
(Gu, Wang, Zhang, Yang, & Wang, 2017)	TDM-WDM	LAT, PWR, SNR
(X. Li, Gu, Chen, Song, & Hao, 2016)	WDM	LAT, TP, PL, WC
(Wang, Gu, Yang, Wang, & Hao, 2016)	WDM-SDM	LAT, PWR, TP, C, DIA, SC
(Werner et. al, 2015)	WDM + CN	PWR, MR, WC, A
(Koohi & Hessabi, 2014)	WDM	LAT, PWR, DIA
(Koohi, Yin, Hessabi, & Yoo, 2014)	WDM	LAT, PWR, SC, A
(Hamedani, Jerger, & Hessabi, 2015)	WDM + CN	LAT, PWR, BW, WL, IL
(Wu et al., 2014)	WDM + CN	LAT, PWR, TP, PL
(Power-efficient et al., 2014)	WDM	LAT, PWR, TP, SC, MR
(Zheng Chen, Gu, Yang, & Fan, 2014)	WDM	LAT, PWR, C
(Sebastien Le Beux et al., 2014)	WDM	LAT, PWR, SC
(K. Chen, Gu, Yang, & Fan, 2014)	WDM+SDM	A, WL, IL
(Ye et al., 2013)	WDM	LAT, PWR, NS
(Koohi & Hessabi, 2012)	WDM	LAT, PWR
(Z. Chen, Gu, Yang, & Chen, 2012)	WDM	LAT, PWR, OL
(S Le Beux et al., 2011)	WDM	SC, WG
(Joshi et al., 2009)	WDM	LAT, PWR, TP, BW
(Pan, Kim, & Memik, 2010)	WDM	PWR, FL
(Vantrease et al., 2008)	WDM	LAT, PWR, BW, NS
(W. Tan, Gu, Yang, Wang, & Wang, 2017)	SDM + WDM	LAT, TP, OL, NS
(Werner, Navaridas, & Lujan, 2017)	DWDM + SWMR	LAT, PWR, TP, A, PDP
(Ben Ahmed & Ben Abdallah, 2015)	CW + CN	PWR, SC, FL
(Ahmed, Meyer, Okuyama, & Abdallah, 2016)	CW + CN	PWR, TP, BL
(X. Tan, Yang, Zhang, Wang, & Jiang, 2014)	WDM	LAT, PWR, TP, SC, FL
(H. Li & Gu, 2010)	CW	LAT, TP
(Fu, Chen, & Liu, 2014)	DWDM + Token	LAT, PWR, TP
(Bahirat & Pasricha, 2014)	WDM + CN	LAT, PWR, TP, A, EDP
(Ye et al., 2012)	CW + CN	LAT, PWR, TP, C
(Koohi & Hessabi, 2011)	WDM	LAT, PWR, SC
(Z. Li et al., 2011)	CW	LAT, PWR, TP,
(Kurian et al., 2010)	WDM	LAT, PWR, NS
(Pan et al., 2009)	WDM+R-SWMR	LAT, PWR, EDP, SC, NS
(Pasricha & Bahirat, 2011)	WDM + CN	LAT, PWR, TP
(Cianchetti et al., 2009)	WDM	LAT, PWR
(Mo et al., 2010)	CW + CN	LAT, PWR, TP
(Shacham et al., 2008)	CW + CN	LAT, PWR

Abbreviations of Optimization Parameters:
Latency/ETE Delay (LAT), Power/ Energy Efficiency (PWR), Throughput (TP), Cost (C), Fault Tolerance (FT), Bandwidth (BW), Wavelength Division Multiplexing (WDM), Control Network (CN), Circuit-Switched (CW), Waveguide Count (WL), Waveguide Crossings (WC), Time Division Multiplexing (TDM), Area (A), Insertion Loss (IL), Power Loss (PL), Normalized Speedup (NS), Optical Loss (OL), Space Division Multiplexing (SDM), Diameter (DIA), Energy Delay Product (EDP), Scalibilty (SC), Signal to Noise Ratio (SNR), Wavelengths Count (WL), Flexibility (FL), Reservation SWMR (R-SWMR)

Figure 10. Alteration in Optical Data (a). MR Modulator (b). MR Photo-Detector

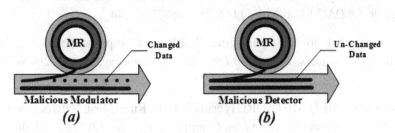

CONCLUSION AND FUTURE RESEARCH DIRECTIONS

The evolution of IoT systems and its usage in daily life applications and computing demands has increased during the past few years. These high-performance computing demands can be realized using multiple cores on a single chip, which are connected through network-on-chip infrastructure. However, the shared memory system of NoC poses several security issues for upcoming processing demands. This chapter provides a comprehensive survey on reliability and security challenges in both electrical and optical on-chip interconnects for IoT applications used in smart cities. We present, recently proposed potential security threats that can incur in NoC architectures and their countermeasures, to address the security features of on-chip communication. However, with the advancements of technology, types of HTs and threats are increasing and to counter each and every Trojan type is still an issue that needs to be addressed. The evolution of 4G/5G wireless communication would require substantial attention to address issues of security for wireless channels. From NoC perspective, wireless NoCs are also employed for different signal processing applications, where radio frequencies (RF) channels are used for transmission of data. Hence, requires considerable framework and methodologies to control the data extraction in wireless NoCs.

ACKNOWLEDGMENT

This work was supported by the National Natural Science Foundation of China [grant number 61774086]; the Natural Science Foundation of Jiangsu Province [grant number BK20160806]; and the Fundamental Research Funds for the Central Universities [grant numbers NP2019102, NS2017023].

REFERENCES

Abellan, J. L., Coskun, A. K., Gu, A., Jin, W., Joshi, A., Kahng, A. B., ... Zhang, T. (2017). Adaptive Tuning of Photonic Devices in a Photonic NoC Through Dynamic Workload Allocation. *IEEE Transactions on Computer-Aided Design of Integrated Circuits and Systems*, 36(5), 801–814. doi:10.1109/TCAD.2016.2600238

Analytics, E. N., Conti, F., Schilling, R., Schiavone, P. D., Pullini, A., Rossi, D., ... Benini, L. (2017).. . *An IoT Endpoint System-on-Chip for Secure and.*, 64(9), 2481–2494.

Ancajas, D. M., Chakraborty, K., & Roy, S. (2014). Fort-NoCs: Mitigating the Threat of a Compromised NoC. *Proceedings of the DAC-51*, 1–6. 10.1145/2593069.2593144

Bahadori, M., Rumley, S., Nikolova, D., & Bergman, K. (2016). Comprehensive Design Space Exploration of Silicon Photonic Interconnects. *Journal of Lightwave Technology*, *34*(12), 2975–2987. doi:10.1109/JLT.2015.2503120

Bahirat, S., & Pasricha, S. (2014). METEOR: Hybrid Photonic Ring-Mesh Network-on-Chip for Multicore Architectures. *ACM Transactions on Embedded Computing Systems*, *13*(3s), 1–33. doi:10.1145/2567940

Bakhtiar, L. A., Hosseinzadeh, M., & Reshadi, M. (2017). Reliable communications in optical network-on-chip by use of fault tolerance approaches. *Optik (Stuttgart)*, *137*, 186–194. doi:10.1016/j.ijleo.2017.03.015

Basak, A., Bhunia, S., Tkacik, T., & Ray, S. (2017). Security Assurance for System-on-Chip Designs with Untrusted IPs. *IEEE Transactions on Information Forensics and Security*, *12*(7), 1515–1528. doi:10.1109/TIFS.2017.2658544

Bashir, J., Peter, E., & Sarangi, S. R. (2019). A Survey of On-Chip Optical Interconnects. *ACM Computing Surveys*, *51*(6), 1–34. doi:10.1145/3267934

Bazzazi, A., Manzuri Shalmani, M. T., & Hemmatyar, A. M. A. (2017). Hardware Trojan Detection Based on Logical Testing. *Journal of Electronic Testing: Theory and Applications*, *33*(4), 381–395. doi:10.100710836-017-5670-0

Ben Achballah, A., Ben Othman, S., & Ben Saoud, S. (2017). Problems and challenges of emerging technology networks−on−chip: A review. *Microprocessors and Microsystems*, *53*, 1–20. doi:10.1016/j.micpro.2017.07.004

Ben Ahmed, A., & Ben Abdallah, A. (2015). Hybrid silicon-photonic network-on-chip for future generations of high-performance many-core systems. *The Journal of Supercomputing*, *71*(12), 4446–4475. doi:10.100711227-015-1539-0

Ben Ahmed, A., Meyer, M., Okuyama, Y., & Ben Abdallah, A. (2016). Hybrid Photonic NoC Based on Non-Blocking Photonic Switch and Light-Weight Electronic Router. *Proceedings - 2015 IEEE International Conference on Systems, Man, and Cybernetics, SMC 2015*, 56–61. 10.1109/SMC.2015.23

Benini, L., & De Micheli, G. (2002). Networks on chips: A new SoC paradigm. *Computer*, *35*(1), 70–78. doi:10.1109/2.976921

Bergman, K., Carloni, L. P., Chan, J., & Hendry, G. (2014). *Photonic Network- on-Chip Design*. Academic Press.

Bertozzi, D., Dimitrakopoulos, G., Flich, J., & Sonntag, S. (2015). The fast evolving landscape of on-chip communication selected future challenges and research avenues. *Design Automation for Embedded Systems*, *19*(1), 59–76. doi:10.100710617-014-9137-6

Beux, S. L., Li, H., O'Connor, I., Cheshmi, K., Liu, X., Trajkovic, J., & Nicolescu, G. (2014). Chameleon: Channel efficient Optical Network-on-Chip. *Design, Automation & Test in Europe Conference & Exhibition*, *2014*, 1–6. doi:10.7873/DATE.2014.317

Bhunia, S., Abramovici, M., Agrawal, D., Hsiao, M. S., Plusquellic, J., Tehranipoor, M., & Bradley, P. (2013). Protection against hardware trojan attacks: Towards a comprehensive solution. *IEEE Design and Test*, *30*(3), 6–17. doi:10.1109/MDT.2012.2196252

Biberman, A., & Bergman, K. (2012). Optical interconnection networks for high-performance computing systems. *Reports on Progress in Physics*, *75*(4), 046402. doi:10.1088/0034-4885/75/4/046402 PMID:22790508

Biswas, A. K. (2016). Source Authentication Techniques for Network-on-Chip Router Configuration Packets. *ACM Journal on Emerging Technologies in Computing Systems*, *13*(2), 1–31. doi:10.1145/2996194

Biswas, A. K. (2018). Efficient Timing Channel Protection for Hybrid (Packet/Circuit-Switched) Network-on-Chip. *IEEE Transactions on Parallel and Distributed Systems*, *29*(5), 1044–1057. doi:10.1109/TPDS.2017.2783337

Biswas, A. K., Nandy, S. K., & Narayan, R. (2015). Router Attack toward NoC-enabled MPSoC and Monitoring Countermeasures against such Threat. *Circuits, Systems, and Signal Processing*, *34*(10), 3241–3290. doi:10.100700034-015-9980-0

Boraten, T., & Kodi, A. (2018). Mitigation of Hardware Trojan based Denial-of-Service attack for secure NoCs. *Journal of Parallel and Distributed Computing*, *111*, 24–38. doi:10.1016/j.jpdc.2017.06.014

Candel, F., Petit, S., Sahuquillo, J., & Duato, J. (2018). Accurately modeling the on-chip and off-chip GPU memory subsystem. *Future Generation Computer Systems*, *82*, 510–519. doi:10.1016/j.future.2017.02.012

Chen, K., Gu, H., Yang, Y., & Fan, D. (2014). A novel two-layer passive optical interconnection network for on-chip communication. *Journal of Lightwave Technology*, *32*(9), 1770–1776. doi:10.1109/JLT.2014.2311119

Chen, Z., Gu, H., Yang, Y., & Chen, K. (2012). Low Latency and Energy Efficient Optical Network-on-chip Using Wavelength Assignment. *IEEE Photonics Technology Letters*, *24*(24), 1–1. doi:10.1109/LPT.2012.2226939

Chen, Z., Gu, H., Yang, Y., & Fan, D. (2014). A hierarchical optical network-on-chip using central-controlled subnet and wavelength assignment. *Journal of Lightwave Technology*, *32*(5), 930–938. doi:10.1109/JLT.2013.2294863

Chien, E., & Szor, P. (2002). Blended attacks exploits, vulnerabilities and buffer-overflow techniques in computer viruses. *Virus Bulletin Conference*, 1–36.

Chip, F., & Ram, B. (2016). Secure and Dependable NoC-Connected Systems. *IEEE Transactions on Reliability*, *65*(4), 1852–1863. doi:10.1109/TR.2016.2606883

Cianchetti, M. J., Cianchetti, M. J., Kerekes, J. C., Kerekes, J. C., Albonesi, D. H., & Albonesi, D. H. (2009). Phastlane: a rapid transit optical routing network. *International Symposium on Computer Architecture*, *37*(3), 9. 10.1145/1555754.1555809

Dally, W. J., & Towles, B. (2001). *Route packets, not wires: on-chip interconnection networks*. doi:10.1109/dac.2001.935594

Dally, W. J., & Towles, B. (2003). *Principles and Practices of Interconnection Networks*. San Francisco, CA: Morgan Kaufmann Publishers Inc.

Dhirani, L. L., & Newe, T. (2017). Cloud Computing and Internet of Things Fusion. Academic Press.

Dhirani, L. L., Newe, T., & Nizamani, S. (2019). Can IoT escape cloud QoS and cost pitfalls. *Proceedings of the International Conference on Sensing Technology, ICST,* 65–70. 10.1109/ICSensT.2018.8603570

Duro, J., Pascual, J. A., Petit, S., Sahuquillo, J., & Gómez, M. E. (2018, June). Modeling and analysis of the performance of exascale photonic networks. *Concurrency and Computation,* 1–12. doi:10.1002/cpe.4773

Elfadel, I. A. M. (2016). *3D Stacked Chips.* doi:10.1007/978-3-319-20481-9

Fayez & Haytham. (2009). *Network-on chip theory and practice*. Academic Press.

Fernandes, R., Marcon, C., Cataldo, R., Silveira, J., Sigl, G., & Sepulveda, J. (2016). A security aware routing approach for NoC-based MPSoCs. *Proceedings - SBCCI 2016: 29th Symposium on Integrated Circuits and Systems Design: Chip on the Mountains.* 10.1109/SBCCI.2016.7724054

Fiorin, L., Palermo, G., Lukovic, S., Catalano, V., & Silvano, C. (2008). Secure memory accesses on networks-on-chip. *IEEE Transactions on Computers, 57*(9), 1216–1229. doi:10.1109/TC.2008.69

Fiorin, L., Palermo, G., & Silvano, C. (2008). *A security monitoring service for NoCs.* doi:10.1145/1450135.1450180

Fiorin, L., Silvano, C., & Sami, M. (2007). Security aspects in networks-on-chips: Overview and proposals for secure implementations. *Proceedings - 10th Euromicro Conference on Digital System Design Architectures, Methods and Tools, DSD 2007,* (7945), 539–542. 10.1109/DSD.2007.4341520

Flich, J., Mejia, A., Lopez, P., & Duato, J. (2007). Region-based routing: An efficient routing mechanism to tackle unreliable hardware in network on chips. *Proceedings - NOCS 2007: First International Symposium on Networks-on-Chip,* 183–194. 10.1109/NOCS.2007.39

Frey, J., & Yu, Q. (2017). A hardened network-on-chip design using runtime hardware Trojan mitigation methods. *Integration, the VLSI Journal, 56,* 15–31. doi:10.1016/j.vlsi.2016.06.008

Fu, W., Chen, T., & Liu, L. (2014). Energy-efficient hybrid optical-electronic network-on-chip for future many-core processors. *Elektronika ir Elektrotechnika, 20*(3), 83–86. doi:10.5755/j01.eee.20.3.6682

Gartner's hype cycle special report for 2011. (2012). Retrieved from http://www.gartner.com/technology/research/hype-cycles/

Grammatikakis, M. D., Papadimitriou, K., Petrakis, P., Papagrigoriou, A., Kornaros, G., Christoforakis, I., & Coppola, M. (2014). Security effectiveness and a hardware firewall for MPSoCs. *Proceedings - 16th IEEE International Conference on High Performance Computing and Communications, HPCC 2014, 11th IEEE International Conference on Embedded Software and Systems, ICESS 2014 and 6th International Symposium on Cyberspace Safety and Security,* 1032–1039. 10.1109/HPCC.2014.173

Grammatikakis, M. D., Papadimitriou, K., Petrakis, P., Papagrigoriou, A., Kornaros, G., Christoforakis, I., ... Coppola, M. (2015). Security in MPSoCs: A NoC Firewall and an Evaluation Framework. *IEEE Transactions on Computer-Aided Design of Integrated Circuits and Systems*, *34*(8), 1344–1357. doi:10.1109/TCAD.2015.2448684

Granjal, J., Monteiro, E., & Sa Silva, J. (2015). Security for the internet of things: A survey of existing protocols and open research issues. *IEEE Communications Surveys and Tutorials*, *17*(3), 1294–1312. doi:10.1109/COMST.2015.2388550

Gu, H., Chen, K., Yang, Y., Chen, Z., & Zhang, B. (2017). MRONoC: A low latency and energy efficient on chip optical interconnect architecture. *IEEE Photonics Journal*, *9*(1), 1–12. doi:10.1109/JPHOT.2017.2651586

Gu, H., Wang, Z., Zhang, B., Yang, Y., & Wang, K. (2017). *Time-Division-Multiplexing – Wavelength-Architecture for ONoC*. Academic Press.

Gubbi, J., Buyya, R., Marusic, S., & Palaniswami, M. (2013). Internet of Things (IoT): A vision, architectural elements, and future directions. *Future Generation Computer Systems*, *29*(7), 1645–1660. doi:10.1016/j.future.2013.01.010

Hamedani, P. K., Jerger, N. E., & Hessabi, S. (2015). QuT: A low-power optical network-on-chip. *Proceedings - 2014 8th IEEE/ACM International Symposium on Networks-on-Chip, NoCS 2014*, 80–87. 10.1109/NOCS.2014.7008765

Horowitz, M., Labonte, F., Shacham, O., Olukotun, K., Hammond, L., & Batten, C. (2018). *35 Years of Microprocessor Trend Data*. Retrieved from https://www.karlrupp.net/2015/06/40-years-of-microprocessor-trend-data

Hu, Y., Müller-Gritschneder, D., Sepulveda, M. J., Gogniat, G., & Schlichtmann, U. (2015). Automatic ILP-based firewall insertion for secure application-specific networks-on-chip. *Proceedings - 2015 9th International Workshop on Interconnection Network Architectures: On-Chip, Multi-Chip, INA-OCMC 2015*, 9–12. 10.1109/INA-OCMC.2015.9

Indrusiak, L. S., Harbin, J., & Sepulveda, M. J. (2017). Side-channel attack resilience through route randomisation in secure real-time Networks-on-Chip. *12th International Symposium on Reconfigurable Communication-Centric Systems-on-Chip, ReCoSoC 2017 - Proceedings*. 10.1109/ReCoSoC.2017.8016142

JayashankaraShridevi, R., Ancajas, D. M., Chakraborty, K., & Roy, S. (2017). Security Measures Against a Rogue Network-on-Chip. *Journal of Hardware and Systems Security*, 173–187. doi:10.100741635-017-0008-z

Joshi, A., Batten, C., Kwon, Y. J., Beamer, S., Shamim, I., Asanović, K., & Stojanović, V. (2009). Silicon-photonic clos networks for global on-chip communication. *Proceedings - 2009 3rd ACM/IEEE International Symposium on Networks-on-Chip, NoCS 2009*, 124–133. 10.1109/NOCS.2009.5071460

Kapoor, H. K., Rao, G. B., Arshi, S., & Trivedi, G. (2013). A security framework for NoC using authenticated encryption and session keys. *Circuits, Systems, and Signal Processing*, *32*(6), 2605–2622. doi:10.100700034-013-9568-5

Keramati, M., Modarressi, M., & Rezaei, S. H. S. (2017). Thermal management in 3d networks-on-chip using dynamic link sharing. *Microprocessors and Microsystems, 52*, 1339–1351. doi:10.1016/j.micpro.2017.05.011

Khalid, F., Hasan, S. R., Hasan, O., & Awwad, F. (2018). Runtime hardware Trojan monitors through modeling burst mode communication using formal verification. *Integration, the VLSI Journal, 61*, 1–15. doi:10.1016/j.vlsi.2017.11.003

Killian, C., Tanougast, C., Monteiro, F., & Dandache, A. (2014). Smart reliable network-on-chip. *IEEE Transactions on Very Large Scale Integration (VLSI) Systems, 22*(2), 242–255. doi:10.1109/TVLSI.2013.2240324

Koohi, S., & Hessabi, S. (2011). Hierarchical opto-electrical on-chip network for future multiprocessor architectures. *Journal of Systems Architecture, 57*(1), 4–23. doi:10.1016/j.sysarc.2010.07.003

Koohi, S., & Hessabi, S. (2012). Scalable architecture for a contention-free optical network on-chip. *Journal of Parallel and Distributed Computing, 72*(11), 1493–1506. doi:10.1016/j.jpdc.2012.02.003

Koohi, S., & Hessabi, S. (2014). All-optical wavelength-routed architecture for a power-efficient network on chip. *IEEE Transactions on Computers, 63*(3), 777–792. doi:10.1109/TC.2012.171

Koohi, S., Yin, Y., Hessabi, S., & Ben Yoo, S. J. (2014). Towards a scalable, low-power all-optical architecture for networks-on-chip. *ACM Transactions on Embedded Computing Systems, 13*(3s), 1–30. doi:10.1145/2567930

Kurian, G., Miller, J. E., Psota, J., Eastep, J., Liu, J., Michel, J., … Agarwal, A. (2010). ATAC: a 1000-core cache-coherent processor with on-chip optical network. *Proceedings of the 19th International Conference on Parallel Architectures and Compilation Techniques - PACT '10*, 477. 10.1145/1854273.1854332

Le Beux, S, Trajkovic, J., O'Connor, I., Nicolescu, G., Bois, G., & Paulin, P. (2011). Optical Ring Network-on-Chip (ORNoC): Architecture and design methodology. *2011 Design, Automation & Test in Europe*, 1–6. doi:10.1109/DATE.2011.5763134

Li, H., & Gu, H. (2010). *A Hierarchical Cluster-based Optical Network-on-Chip*. Academic Press.

Li, J., Ni, L., Chen, J., & Zhou, E. (2017). A novel hardware Trojan detection based on BP neural network. *2016 2nd IEEE International Conference on Computer and Communications, ICCC 2016 - Proceedings*, 2790–2794. 10.1109/CompComm.2016.7925206

Li, X., Gu, H., Chen, K., Song, L., & Hao, Q. (2016). STorus: A new topology for optical network-on-chip. *Optical Switching and Networking, 22*, 77–85. doi:10.1016/j.osn.2016.04.004

Li, Z., Mohamed, M., Chen, X., Dudley, E., Meng, K. K., Shang, L., … Sun, Y. (2012). Reliability Modeling and Management of Nanophotonic On-Chip Networks. *IEEE Transactions on Very Large Scale Integration (VLSI). Systems, 20*(1), 98–111. doi:10.1109/TVLSI.2010.2089072

Li, Z., Mohamed, M., Chen, X., Zhou, H., Mickelson, A., Shang, L., & Vachharajani, M. (2011). Iris: A Hybrid Nanophotonic Network Design for High-Performance and Low-Power on-Chip Communication. *ACM Journal on Emerging Technologies in Computing Systems, 7*(2), 1–22. doi:10.1145/1970406.1970410

Lotfi-Kamran, P., Modarressi, M., & Sarbazi-Azad, H. (2016). An Efficient Hybrid-Switched Network-on-Chip for Chip Multiprocessors. *IEEE Transactions on Computers*, *65*(5), 1656–1662. doi:10.1109/TC.2015.2449846

Lyu, Y., & Mishra, P. (2018). *A Survey of Side-Channel Attacks on Caches and Countermeasures*. doi:10.100741635-017-0025-y

Mal-Sarkar, S., Karam, R., Narasimhan, S., Ghosh, A., Krishna, A., & Bhunia, S. (2016). Design and Validation for FPGA Trust under Hardware Trojan Attacks. *IEEE Transactions on Multi-Scale Computing Systems*, *2*(3), 186–198. doi:10.1109/TMSCS.2016.2584052

Mejia. (2006). An Efficient Fault-Tolerant Routing Methodology for Meshes and Tori. *20th International Parallel and Distributed Processing Symposium*, 10. 10.1109/IPDPS.2006.1639341

Mo, K. H., Ye, Y., Wu, X., Zhang, W., Liu, W., & Xu, J. (2010). A hierarchical hybrid optical-electronic network-on-chip. *Proceedings - IEEE Annual Symposium on VLSI, ISVLSI 2010*, 327–332. 10.1109/ISVLSI.2010.17

Ortín-Obón, M., Suárez-Gracia, D., Villarroya-Gaudó, M., Izu, C., & Viñals-Yúfera, V. (2016). Analysis of network-on-chip topologies for cost-efficient chip multiprocessors. *Microprocessors and Microsystems*, *42*, 24–36. doi:10.1016/j.micpro.2016.01.005

Osvik, D., Shamir, A., & Tromer, E. (2006). *Cache Attacks and Countermeasures: The Case of AES\nTopics in Cryptology – CT-RSA 2006*. doi:10.1007/11605805_1

Pan, Y., Kim, J., & Memik, G. (2010). FlexiShare: Channel sharing for an energy-efficient nanophotonic crossbar. *HPCA - 16 2010 The Sixteenth International Symposium on High-Performance Computer Architecture*, 1–12. 10.1109/HPCA.2010.5416626

Pan, Y., Kumar, P., Kim, J., Memik, G., Zhang, Y., & Choudhary, A. (2009). *Firefly : Illuminating Future Network-on-Chip with Nanophotonics Categories and Subject Descriptors*. Academic Press.

Papastefanakis, E., Maitre, B., & Ragot, D. (2015). Security Challenges in ManyCore Embedded Systems based on Networks-on-Chip (NoCs). *Proceedings of the WESS'15: Workshop on Embedded Systems Security - WESS'15*, 1–6. 10.1145/2818362.2818372

Pasricha, S., & Bahirat, S. (2011). OPAL: A multi-layer hybrid photonic NoC for 3D ICs. *Proceedings of the Asia and South Pacific Design Automation Conference, ASP-DAC*, 345–350. 10.1109/ASP-DAC.2011.5722211

Pasricha, S., Chittamuru, S. V. R., Thakkar, I. G., & Bhat, V. (2018). Securing Photonic NoC Architectures from Hardware Trojans. *2018 Twelfth IEEE/ACM International Symposium on Networks-on-Chip (NOCS)*, 1–8. 10.1109/NOCS.2018.8512167

Peh, L.-S., & Jerger, N. E. (2017). On-chip networks (2nd ed.). Morgan and Claypool.

Reinbrecht, C., Susin, A., Bossuet, L., & Sepúlveda, J. (2016). Gossip NoC - Avoiding timing side-channel attacks through traffic management. *Proceedings of IEEE Computer Society Annual Symposium on VLSI, ISVLSI*, 601–606. 10.1109/ISVLSI.2016.25

Reinbrecht, C., Susin, A., Bossuet, L., Sigl, G., & Sepúlveda, J. (2017). Timing attack on NoC-based systems: Prime+Probe attack and NoC-based protection. *Microprocessors and Microsystems*, *52*, 556–565. doi:10.1016/j.micpro.2016.12.010

Rumley, S., Bahadori, M., Polster, R., Hammond, S. D., Calhoun, D. M., Wen, K., ... Bergman, K. (2017). Optical interconnects for extreme scale computing systems. *Parallel Computing*, *64*, 65–80. doi:10.1016/j.parco.2017.02.001

Saeed, A., Ahmadinia, A., & Just, M. (2016). Secure On-Chip Communication Architecture for Reconfigurable Multi-Core Systems. *Journal of Circuits, Systems, and Computers*, *25*(08), 1650089. doi:10.1142/S0218126616500894

Samaila, M. G., Neto, M., Fernandes, D. A. B., Freire, M. M., & Inácio, P. R. M. (2018). Challenges of securing Internet of Things devices: A survey. *Security and Privacy*, *1*(2), e20. doi:10.1002py2.20

Samyde, D. (2002). Side channel cryptanalysis. *Computer*, 179–184.

Schroff, F., Kalenichenko, D., & Philbin, J. (2015). FaceNet: A unified embedding for face recognition and clustering. *Proceedings of the IEEE Computer Society Conference on Computer Vision and Pattern Recognition*, 815–823. 10.1109/CVPR.2015.7298682

Sengupta, A. (2017). Hardware Vulnerabilities and Their Effects on CE Devices: Design for Security Against Trojans. *IEEE Consumer Electronics Magazine*, *6*(3), 126–133. doi:10.1109/MCE.2017.2684940

Sepúlveda, J., Flórez, D., & Gogniat, G. (2016). Efficient and flexible NoC-based group communication for secure MPSoCs. *2015 International Conference on ReConFigurable Computing and FPGAs, ReConFig 2015*. 10.1109/ReConFig.2015.7393301

Sepulveda, J., Flórez, D., Immler, V., Gogniat, G., & Sigl, G. (2016). Hierarchical group-key management for NoC-based MPSoCs protection. *Journal of Integrated Circuits and Systems*, *11*(1), 38–48.

Sepulveda, J., Flórez, D., Immler, V., Gogniat, G., & Sigl, G. (2017). Efficient security zones implementation through hierarchical group key management at NoC-based MPSoCs. *Microprocessors and Microsystems*, *50*, 164–174. doi:10.1016/j.micpro.2017.03.002

Sepulveda, J., Pires, R., Gogniat, G., Chau, W. J., & Strum, M. (2012). QoSS Hierarchical NoC-Based Architecture for MPSoC Dynamic Protection. *International Journal of Reconfigurable Computing*, *2012*, 1–10. doi:10.1155/2012/578363

Sepúlveda, M. J., Diguet, J. P., Strum, M., & Gogniat, G. (2015). NoC-Based Protection for SoC Time-Driven Attacks. *IEEE Embedded Systems Letters*, *7*(1), 7–10. doi:10.1109/LES.2014.2384744

Shacham, A., Bergman, K., & Carloni, L. P. (2008). Photonic networks-on-chip for future generations of chip multiprocessors. *IEEE Transactions on Computers*, *57*(9), 1246–1260. doi:10.1109/TC.2008.78

Sicari, S., Rizzardi, A., Grieco, L. A., & Coen-Porisini, A. (2015). Security, privacy and trust in Internet of things: The road ahead. *Computer Networks*, *76*, 146–164. doi:10.1016/j.comnet.2014.11.008

Systems, O., & Kocher, P. C. (1996). Timing Attacks on Implement at ions of. *Advances*, 104–113.

Szymanski, T. H. (2016). Securing the Industrial-Tactile Internet of Things with Deterministic Silicon Photonics Switches. *IEEE Access: Practical Innovations, Open Solutions*, 4, 8236–8249. doi:10.1109/ACCESS.2016.2613512

Tan, W., Gu, H., Yang, Y., Wang, K., & Wang, X. (2017). Venus: A Low-Latency, Low-Loss 3-D Hybrid Network-on-Chip for Kilocore Systems. *Journal of Lightwave Technology*, 35(24), 5448–5455. doi:10.1109/JLT.2017.2764956

Tan, X., Yang, M., Zhang, L., Wang, X., & Jiang, Y. (2014). A hybrid optoelectronic networks-on-chip architecture. *Journal of Lightwave Technology*, 32(5), 991–998. doi:10.1109/JLT.2013.2296145

Tehranipoor, M., & Koushanfar, F. (2010). A survey of hardware trojan taxonomy and detection. *IEEE Design & Test of Computers*, 27(1), 10–25. doi:10.1109/MDT.2010.7

Tu, X., Song, C., Huang, T., Chen, Z., & Fu, H. (2019). State of the art and perspectives on silicon photonic switches. *Micromachines*, 10(1), 51. doi:10.3390/mi10010051 PMID:30642100

Vantrease, D., Schreiber, R., Monchiero, M., Mclaren, M., Jouppi, N. P., Fiorentino, M., … Ahn, J. H. (2008). Corona: System implications of emerging nanophotonic technology. *Proceedings - International Symposium on Computer Architecture*, 153–164. 10.1109/ISCA.2008.35

Vineel, S., Chittamuru, R., Thakkar, I. G., Bhat, V., & Pasricha, S. (2018). SOTERIA: Exploiting Process Variations to Enhance Hardware Security with Photonic NoC Architectures. *2018 55th ACM/ESDA/IEEE Design Automation Conference (DAC)*, 1–6. 10.1145/3195970.3196118

Wang, X., Gu, H., Yang, Y., Wang, K., & Hao, Q. (2016). A Highly Scalable Optical Network-on-Chip with Small Network Diameter and Deadlock Freedom. *IEEE Transactions on Very Large Scale Integration (VLSI) Systems*, 24(12), 3424–3436. doi:10.1109/TVLSI.2016.2561299

Werner, S., Navaridas, J., & Lujn, M. (2015). Amon: An Advanced Mesh-like Optical NoC. *Proceedings - 2015 IEEE 23rd Annual Symposium on High-Performance Interconnects, HOTI 2015*, 52–59. doi:10.1109/HOTI.2015.18

Werner, S., Navaridas, J., & An, M. L. (2017). A Survey on Optical Network-on-Chip Architectures. *ACM Computing Surveys*, 50(6), 1–37. doi:10.1145/3131346

Werner, S., Navaridas, J., & Luján, M. (2016). A Survey on Design Approaches to Circumvent Permanent Faults in Networks-on-Chip. *ACM Computing Surveys*, 48(4), 1–36. doi:10.1145/2886781

Werner, S., Navaridas, J., & Lujan, M. (2017). Designing Low-Power, Low-Latency Networks-on-Chip by Optimally Combining Electrical and Optical Links. *Proceedings - International Symposium on High-Performance Computer Architecture*, 265–276. 10.1109/HPCA.2017.23

Wu, X., Xu, J., Ye, Y., Wang, Z., Nikdast, M., & Wang, X. (2014). SUOR: Sectioned Undirectional Optical Ring for Chip Multiprocessor. *J. Emerg. Technol. Comput. Syst.*, 10(4), 29:1–29:25. doi:10.1145/2600072

Yahya, M. R. (2018). Review of Photonic and Hybrid On Chip Interconnects for MPSoCs in IoT Paradigm. *2018 21st Saudi Computer Society National Computer Conference (NCC)*, 1–6. 10.1109/NCG.2018.8593055

Yahya, M. R., Wu, N., Ali, Z. A., & Khizar, Y. (2019). Optical Versus Electrical: Performance Evaluation of Network On-Chip Topologies for UWASN Manycore Processors. *Wireless Personal Communications*. doi:10.100711277-019-06630-5

Yahya, M. R., Wu, N., Gaizhen, Y., & Ahmed, T., Yasir, & Zhang, J. (2019). An Algorithmic Framework to Construct Optical Switch via Scaling from N-to-2N Ports for Optical Network on Chip. *IEEE Access: Practical Innovations, Open Solutions*, 1–1. doi:10.1109/ACCESS.2019.2930754

Yan, F., & Gao, J. (2017). Reliable NoC design with low latency and power consumption. *Electronics Letters*, *53*(6), 382–383. doi:10.1049/el.2016.4665

Yarom, Y., & Falkner, K. (2014). FLUSH+RELOAD: A High Resolution, Low Noise, L3 Cache Side-Channel Attack. *Proceedings of the 23rd USENIX Security Symposium*, 719–732. Retrieved from https://www.usenix.org/conference/usenixsecurity14/technical-sessions/presentation/yarom

Ye, Y., Xu, J., Huang, B., Wu, X., Zhang, W., Wang, X., ... Wang, Z. (2013). 3-D mesh-based optical network-on-chip for multiprocessor system-on-chip. *IEEE Transactions on Computer-Aided Design of Integrated Circuits and Systems*, *32*(4), 584–596. doi:10.1109/TCAD.2012.2228739

Ye, Y., Xu, J., Wu, X., Zhang, W., Liu, W., & Nikdast, M. (2012). A Torus-Based Hierarchical Optical-Electronic Network-on-Chip for Multiprocessor System-on-Chip. *ACM Journal on Emerging Technologies in Computing Systems*, *8*(1), 1–26. doi:10.1145/2093145.2093150

Zhang, L., Wang, X., Jiang, Y., Yang, M., Mak, T., & Singh, A. K. (2018). Effectiveness of HT-assisted sinkhole and blackhole denial of service attacks targeting mesh networks-on-chip. *Journal of Systems Architecture*, *89*(July), 84–94. doi:10.1016/j.sysarc.2018.07.005

Compilation of References

Abas, K., Porto, C., & Obraczka, K. (2014). Wireless smart camera networks for the surveillance of public spaces. *Computer, 47*(5), 37–44. doi:10.1109/MC.2014.140

Abdelwahab, S., Hamdaoui, B., Guizani, M., & Rayes, A. (2014). Enabling Smart Cloud Services Through Remote Sensing: An Internet of Everything Enabler. IEEE Internet of Things Journal, 1(3).

Abellan, J. L., Coskun, A. K., Gu, A., Jin, W., Joshi, A., Kahng, A. B., ... Zhang, T. (2017). Adaptive Tuning of Photonic Devices in a Photonic NoC Through Dynamic Workload Allocation. *IEEE Transactions on Computer-Aided Design of Integrated Circuits and Systems, 36*(5), 801–814. doi:10.1109/TCAD.2016.2600238

Afonso, L., Souto, N., Sebastiao, P., Ribeiro, M., Tavares, T., & Marinheiro, R. (2016). Cellular for the skies: Exploiting mobile network infrastructure for low altitude air-to-ground communications. *IEEE Aerospace and Electronic Systems Magazine, 31*(8), 4–11. doi:10.1109/MAES.2016.150170

Ahlgren, B., Hidell, M., & Ngai, E. C. H. (2016). Internet of things for smart cities: Interoperability and open data. *IEEE Internet Computing, 20*(6), 52–56. doi:10.1109/MIC.2016.124

Ahmad, A., Paul, A., Rathore, M. M., & Chang, H. (2016). Smart cyber society: Integration of capillary devices with high usability based on Cyber–Physical System. *Future Generation Computer Systems, 56*, 493–503. doi:10.1016/j.future.2015.08.004

Akram, A. H., Chandrasekharan, S., Kaandorp, G., Glenn, W., Jamalipour, A., & Kandeepan, S. (2016). Coverage and rate analysis of aerial base stations. *IEEE Transactions on Aerospace and Electronic Systems, 52*(6), 3077–3081. doi:10.1109/TAES.2016.160356

Alexeff, I., Anderson, T., Farshi, E., Karnam, N., & Pulasani, N. R. (2008). Recent results for plasma antennas. *Physics of Plasmas, 15*(5), 057104. doi:10.1063/1.2919157

Alfonso, E., Baquero, M., Kildal, P. S., & Valero-Nogueira, A. RajoIglesias, E., & Herranz, J. I. (2010). Design of microwave circuits in ridge-gap waveguide technology. IEEE MTT-S International Microwave Symposium Digest, (l), 1544–1547. 10.1109/MWSYM.2010.5514731

Al-Hourani, A., Kandeepan, S., & Jamalipour, A. (2014, December). *Modeling air-to-ground path loss for low altitude platforms in urban environments. In 2014 IEEE global communications conference* (pp. 2898–2904). IEEE.

Al-Hourani, A., Kandeepan, S., & Lardner, S. (2014). Optimal LAP altitude for maximum coverage. *IEEE Wireless Communications Letters, 3*(6), 569–572. doi:10.1109/LWC.2014.2342736

Ali, M., Khan, S. A., Rahimoon, A. Q., Hussain, F., Abro, S. A., & Hussain, I. (2019). *Triboelectric Nanogenerator Scavenging Sliding Motion Energy.* Paper presented at the 2019 2nd International Conference on Computing, Mathematics and Engineering Technologies (iCoMET).

Ali, A., Hwang, E. Y., Choo, J., & Lim, D. W. (2018a). Nanoscale graphene oxide-induced metallic nanoparticle clustering for surface-enhanced Raman scattering-based IgG detection. *Sensors and Actuators. B, Chemical*, *255*, 183–192. doi:10.1016/j.snb.2017.07.140

Ali, A., Hwang, E. Y., Choo, J., & Lim, D. W. (2018b). PEGylated nanographene-mediated metallic nanoparticle clusters for surface enhanced Raman scattering-based biosensing. *Analyst (London)*, *143*(11), 2604–2615. doi:10.1039/C8AN00329G PMID:29741172

Ali, T., & Biradar, R. C. (2017). A compact multiband antenna using λ/4 rectangular stub loaded with metamaterial for IEEE 802.11N and IEEE 802.16E. *Microwave and Optical Technology Letters*, *59*(5), 1000–1006. doi:10.1002/mop.30454

Al-Manie, M. A., & Alkanhal, M. I. (2004). Acoustic detection of the red date palm weevil. *Int. J. Signal Process*, *1*, 1–12.

Al-Shammari, B. K., Al-Aboody, N., & Al-Raweshidy, H. S. (2018). IoT traffic management and integration in the QoS supported network. *IEEE Internet of Things Journal*, *5*(1), 352–370. doi:10.1109/JIOT.2017.2785219

Amendola, S., Lodato, R., Manzari, S., Occhiuzzi, C., & Marrocco, G. (2014). RFID technology for IoT-based personal healthcare in smart spaces. *IEEE Internet of Things Journal*, *1*(2), 144–152. doi:10.1109/JIOT.2014.2313981

Amorim, R., Nguyen, H., Mogensen, P., Kovács, I. Z., Wigard, J., & Sørensen, T. B. (2017). Radio channel modeling for UAV communication over cellular networks. *IEEE Wireless Communications Letters*, *6*(4), 514–517. doi:10.1109/LWC.2017.2710045

Analytics, E. N., Conti, F., Schilling, R., Schiavone, P. D., Pullini, A., Rossi, D., ... Benini, L. (2017).. . *An IoT Endpoint System-on-Chip for Secure and.*, *64*(9), 2481–2494.

Anand, T. M., Banupriya, K., Deebika, M., Anusiya, A., Anand, T. M., Banupriya, K., & Anusiya, A. (2015). Intelligent transportation systems using iot service for vehicular data cloud. *International Journal for Innovative Research in Science and Technology*, *2*(2), 80–86.

Ancajas, D. M., Chakraborty, K., & Roy, S. (2014). Fort-NoCs: Mitigating the Threat of a Compromised NoC. *Proceedings of the DAC-51*, 1–6. 10.1145/2593069.2593144

Anderson, T. (2014). Plasma frequency selective surfaces. IEEE Antennas and Propagation Society, AP-S International Symposium (Digest), 35(2), 2096–2097. 10.1109/APS.2014.6905375

Anderson, T., & Alexeff, I. (2011). Plasma antennas. Frontiers in Antennas Next Generation Design & Engineering. *Plasma Antennas*, *34*(2), 226.

Ansible. (2019). *Why Ansible?* Retrieved January 10, 2019, from https://www.ansible.com/it-automation

Approved IEEE Draft Amendment to IEEE Standard for Information Technology-Telecommunications and Information Exchange Between Systems-Part 15.4: Wireless Medium Access Control (MAC) and Physical Layer (PHY) 2007 Specifications for Low-Rate Wireless Personal Area Networks (LR-WPANS): Amendment to Add Alternate Phy (Amendment of IEEE Std 802.15.4). (2007). *IEEE Approved Std P802.15.4a/D7*. Retrieved from http://ieeexplore.ieee.org/stamp/stamp.jsp?tp=&arnumber=4152704&isnumber=4152703

Araujo, L. S., Shang, X., Lancaster, M. J., de Oliveira, A. J. B., Llamas-Garro, I., Kim, J. M., ... de Rijk, E. (2017). 3-D printed band-pass combline filter. *Microwave and Optical Technology Letters*, *59*(6), 1388–1390. doi:10.1002/mop.30547

Armand, M., & Tarascon, J.-M. (2008). Building better batteries. *Nature*, *451*(7179), 652–657. doi:10.1038/451652a PMID:18256660

Arndt, J., Krause, F., Wunderlich, R., & Heinen, S. (2017). Development of a 6LoWPAN sensor node for IoT based home automation networks. *2017 International Conference on Research and Education in Mechatronics (REM)*, 1-4. 10.1109/REM.2017.8075226

Ashton, K. (2009). That "Internet of Things" Thing. *RFiD Journal, 22*, 97–114.

Aslam, M. (2016). Agricultural productivity current scenario, constraints and future prospects in Pakistan. *Sarhad Journal of Agriculture, 32*(4), 289–303. doi:10.17582/journal.sja/2016.32.4.289.303

AT&T Internet of Things Connectivity Increases Access, Lowers Environmental Impact and Enhances Transportation. (2017). Retrieved from: https://www.qualcomm.com/news/releases/2017/09/11/mobike-att-and-qualcomm-collaborate-mobile-iot-smart-bike-share-technology

Atmel. (2015). *ATmega48A/PA/88A/PA/168A/PA/328/P*. Author.

Atzor, L., Iera, A., & Morabito, G. (2010). The Internet of Things: A survey. *Computer Networks, The International Journal of Computer and Telecommunications Networking*.

AWS. (2019). *Amazon Compute Service Level Agreement.* Retrieved April 10, 2019, from https://aws.amazon.com/compute/sla/

Azari, M. M., Rosas, F., Chen, K. C., & Pollin, S. (2016, December). Joint sum-rate and power gain analysis of an aerial base station. In 2016 IEEE Globecom Workshops (GC Wkshps) (pp. 1-6). IEEE. doi:10.1109/GLOCOMW.2016.7848947

Azfar, S., Nadeem, A., & Basit, A. (2015). Pest detection and control techniques using wireless sensor network: A review. *Journal of Entomology and Zoology Studies, 3*(2), 92–99.

Baccarelli, E., Naranjo, P. G. V., Scarpiniti, M., Shojafar, M., & Abawajy, J. H. (2017). Fog of everything: Energy-efficient networked computing architectures, research challenges, and a case study. *IEEE Access: Practical Innovations, Open Solutions, 5*, 9882–9910. doi:10.1109/ACCESS.2017.2702013

Bae, J.-H., & Lee, H.-K. (2018). *User Health Information Analysis With a Urine and Feces Separable Smart Toilet System.* Special Section on Healthcare Information Technology for the Extreme and Remote Environments.

Bahadori, M., Rumley, S., Nikolova, D., & Bergman, K. (2016). Comprehensive Design Space Exploration of Silicon Photonic Interconnects. *Journal of Lightwave Technology, 34*(12), 2975–2987. doi:10.1109/JLT.2015.2503120

Bahirat, S., & Pasricha, S. (2014). METEOR: Hybrid Photonic Ring-Mesh Network-on-Chip for Multicore Architectures. *ACM Transactions on Embedded Computing Systems, 13*(3s), 1–33. doi:10.1145/2567940

Bai, P., Zhu, G., Liu, Y., Chen, J., Jing, Q., Yang, W., ... Wang, Z. L. (2013). Cylindrical rotating triboelectric nanogenerator. *ACS Nano, 7*(7), 6361–6366. doi:10.1021/nn402491y PMID:23799926

Bakhtiar, L. A., Hosseinzadeh, M., & Reshadi, M. (2017). Reliable communications in optical network-on-chip by use of fault tolerance approaches. *Optik (Stuttgart), 137*, 186–194. doi:10.1016/j.ijleo.2017.03.015

Bandyopadhyay, D., & Sen, J. (2011). Internet of things: Applications and challenges in technology and standardization. *Wireless Personal Communications, 58*(1), 49–69. doi:10.100711277-011-0288-5

Bardram, J., Doryab, A., Jensen, R., Lange, P., Nielsen, K., & Petersen, S. (2011). Phase recognition during surgical procedures using embedded and body-worn sensors. *IEEE International Conference on Pervasive Computing and Communications (PerCom)*, 45–53. 10.1109/PERCOM.2011.5767594

Basak, A., Bhunia, S., Tkacik, T., & Ray, S. (2017). Security Assurance for System-on-Chip Designs with Untrusted IPs. *IEEE Transactions on Information Forensics and Security, 12*(7), 1515–1528. doi:10.1109/TIFS.2017.2658544

Bashir, J., Peter, E., & Sarangi, S. R. (2019). A Survey of On-Chip Optical Interconnects. *ACM Computing Surveys*, *51*(6), 1–34. doi:10.1145/3267934

Bazzazi, A., Manzuri Shalmani, M. T., & Hemmatyar, A. M. A. (2017). Hardware Trojan Detection Based on Logical Testing. *Journal of Electronic Testing: Theory and Applications*, *33*(4), 381–395. doi:10.100710836-017-5670-0

Bello, O., Zeadally, S., & Badra, M. (2017). Network layer inter-operation of Device-to-Device communication technologies in Internet of Things (IoT). *Ad Hoc Networks*, *57*, 52–62. doi:10.1016/j.adhoc.2016.06.010

Ben Achballah, A., Ben Othman, S., & Ben Saoud, S. (2017). Problems and challenges of emerging technology networks−on−chip: A review. *Microprocessors and Microsystems*, *53*, 1–20. doi:10.1016/j.micpro.2017.07.004

Ben Ahmed, A., Meyer, M., Okuyama, Y., & Ben Abdallah, A. (2016). Hybrid Photonic NoC Based on Non-Blocking Photonic Switch and Light-Weight Electronic Router. *Proceedings - 2015 IEEE International Conference on Systems, Man, and Cybernetics, SMC 2015*, 56–61. 10.1109/SMC.2015.23

Ben Ahmed, A., & Ben Abdallah, A. (2015). Hybrid silicon-photonic network-on-chip for future generations of high-performance many-core systems. *The Journal of Supercomputing*, *71*(12), 4446–4475. doi:10.100711227-015-1539-0

Benevolo, C., Dameri, R. P., & D'Auria, B. (2016). Smart mobility in smart city. In *Empowering Organizations* (pp. 13–28). Cham: Springer. doi:10.1007/978-3-319-23784-8_2

Benini, L., & De Micheli, G. (2002). Networks on chips: A new SoC paradigm. *Computer*, *35*(1), 70–78. doi:10.1109/2.976921

Bergman, K., Carloni, L. P., Chan, J., & Hendry, G. (2014). *Photonic Network- on-Chip Design*. Academic Press.

Bertholdo, L., Granville, L., Tarouco, L., Arbiza, L., Carbone, F., & Marotta, M. (2012). Internet of things in healthcare: interoperati-bility and security issues. *IEEE International Conference Communications (ICC, IEEE)*, 6121-6125.

Bertozzi, D., Dimitrakopoulos, G., Flich, J., & Sonntag, S. (2015). The fast evolving landscape of on-chip communication selected future challenges and research avenues. *Design Automation for Embedded Systems*, *19*(1), 59–76. doi:10.100710617-014-9137-6

Bessis, N., & Dobre, C. (2014). *Big Data and Internet of Things: A Roadmap for Smart Environments*. Springer. doi:10.1007/978-3-319-05029-4

Beux, S. L., Li, H., O'Connor, I., Cheshmi, K., Liu, X., Trajkovic, J., & Nicolescu, G. (2014). Chameleon: Channel efficient Optical Network-on-Chip. *Design, Automation & Test in Europe Conference & Exhibition, 2014*, 1–6. doi:10.7873/DATE.2014.317

Bhoj, P., Singhal, S., & Chutani, S. (2001). SLA management in federated environments. *Computer Networks*, *35*(1), 5–24. doi:10.1016/S1389-1286(00)00149-3

Bhunia, S., Abramovici, M., Agrawal, D., Hsiao, M. S., Plusquellic, J., Tehranipoor, M., & Bradley, P. (2013). Protection against hardware trojan attacks: Towards a comprehensive solution. *IEEE Design and Test*, *30*(3), 6–17. doi:10.1109/MDT.2012.2196252

Biberman, A., & Bergman, K. (2012). Optical interconnection networks for high-performance computing systems. *Reports on Progress in Physics*, *75*(4), 046402. doi:10.1088/0034-4885/75/4/046402 PMID:22790508

Biswas, A. K. (2016). Source Authentication Techniques for Network-on-Chip Router Configuration Packets. *ACM Journal on Emerging Technologies in Computing Systems*, *13*(2), 1–31. doi:10.1145/2996194

Biswas, A. K. (2018). Efficient Timing Channel Protection for Hybrid (Packet/Circuit-Switched) Network-on-Chip. *IEEE Transactions on Parallel and Distributed Systems*, *29*(5), 1044–1057. doi:10.1109/TPDS.2017.2783337

Biswas, A. K., Nandy, S. K., & Narayan, R. (2015). Router Attack toward NoC-enabled MPSoC and Monitoring Counter-measures against such Threat. *Circuits, Systems, and Signal Processing, 34*(10), 3241–3290. doi:10.100700034-015-9980-0

Bitra, V. S., Jayapandian, N., & Balachandran, K. (2018, August). Internet of Things Security and Privacy Issues in Healthcare Industry. In *International Conference on Intelligent Data Communication Technologies and Internet of Things* (pp. 967-973). Springer.

Bluestream: Smart Healthcare. (2017). Retrieved from http://www.bluestream.sg/smart-healthcare

Blümm, C., Heller, C., & Weigel, R. (2012). SDR OFDM waveform design for a UGV/UAV communication scenario. *Journal of Signal Processing Systems for Signal, Image, and Video Technology, 69*(1), 11–21. doi:10.100711265-011-0640-8

Bob Yirka, T. X. (n.d.). Echodyne uses metamaterials to make drone sized radar system. Academic Press.

Bockus, W. W., Bowden, R. L., Hunger, R. M., Murray, T. D., & Smiley, R. W. (2010). Compendium of wheat diseases and pests (No. Ed. 3). American Phytopathological Society (APS Press).

Bonomi, F., Milito, R. A., Natarajan, P., & Zhu, J. (2014). *Fog Computing: A Platform for Internet of Things and Analytics*. Springer.

Bontu, C. S., Periyalwar, S., & Pecen, M. (2014). Wireless wide-area networks for internet of things: An air interface protocol for IoT and a simultaneous access channel for uplink IoT communication. *IEEE Vehicular Technology Magazine, 9*(1), 54–63. doi:10.1109/MVT.2013.2295068

Boraten, T., & Kodi, A. (2018). Mitigation of Hardware Trojan based Denial-of-Service attack for secure NoCs. *Journal of Parallel and Distributed Computing, 111*, 24–38. doi:10.1016/j.jpdc.2017.06.014

Bormann. (2001). *Robust Header Compression*. RFC 3095 IETF.

Bormann, C., Castellani, A. P., & Shelby, Z. (2012). Coap: An application protocol for billions of tiny internet nodes. *IEEE Internet Computing, 16*(2), 62–67. doi:10.1109/MIC.2012.29

Bouaziz & Rachedi. (2014). A survey on mobility management protocols in wireless sensor networks based on 6LoWPAN technology. *Computer Communications*.

Bradley, J., Loucks, J., Macaulay, J., & Noronha, A. (2013). *Joseph Internet of Everything (IoE) Value Index: How Much Value Are Private-Sector Firms Capturing from IoE in 2013? Cisco Internet Business Solutions Group (IBSG)*. Cisco Systems, Inc.

BritannicaE. (2019). *Energy*. Retrieved from https://www.britannica.com/science/energy

Brock, D. L. (2001). *The Electronic Product Code (EPC), A Naming Scheme for Physical Objects*. MIT Auto-ID Center, MIT-AU-TOID-WH-002.

Candel, F., Petit, S., Sahuquillo, J., & Duato, J. (2018). Accurately modeling the on-chip and off-chip GPU memory subsystem. *Future Generation Computer Systems, 82*, 510–519. doi:10.1016/j.future.2017.02.012

Casilari, E., Cano-García, J. M., & Campos-Garrido, G. (2010). Modeling of current consumption in 802.15.4/ZigBee sensor motes. *Sensors (Basel), 10*(6), 5443–5468. doi:10.3390100605443 PMID:22219671

Casner & Jacobson. (1999). *Compressing IP/UDP/RTP Headers for Low-Speed Serial Links*. IETF RFC 2508.

Centenaro, M., Vangelista, L., Zanella, A., & Zorzi, M. (2016). Long-range communications in unlicensed bands: The rising stars in the IoT and smart city scenarios. *IEEE Wireless Communications, 23*(5), 60–67. doi:10.1109/MWC.2016.7721743

Cerchecci, M., Luti, F., Mecocci, A., Parrino, S., Peruzzi, G., & Pozzebon, A. (2018). A Low Power IoT Sensor Node Architecture for Waste Management Within Smart Cities Context. *Sensors (Basel)*, *18*(4), 1282. doi:10.339018041282 PMID:29690552

Chandra, S. N., & Haeng-Kon, K. (2016). From Cloud to Fog and IoT-Based Real-Time U-Healthcare Monitoring for Smart Homes and Hospitals. *International Journal of Smart Home*, *10*(2), 187–196. doi:10.14257/ijsh.2016.10.2.18

Chen, M., Valenzuela, S. G., Leung, V. C., & Vasilakos, A. V. (2011). Body area networks: A survey. Mobile Networks and Applications. *ACM/Springer MONET, 16*, 171–193.

Cheng, N., Xu, W., Shi, W., Zhou, Y., Lu, N., Zhou, H., & Shen, X. (2018). Air-ground integrated mobile edge networks: Architecture, challenges, and opportunities. *IEEE Communications Magazine*, *56*(8), 26–32. doi:10.1109/MCOM.2018.1701092

Chen, K., Gu, H., Yang, Y., & Fan, D. (2014). A novel two-layer passive optical interconnection network for on-chip communication. *Journal of Lightwave Technology*, *32*(9), 1770–1776. doi:10.1109/JLT.2014.2311119

Chen, Z., Gu, H., Yang, Y., & Chen, K. (2012). Low Latency and Energy Efficient Optical Network-on-chip Using Wavelength Assignment. *IEEE Photonics Technology Letters*, *24*(24), 1–1. doi:10.1109/LPT.2012.2226939

Chen, Z., Gu, H., Yang, Y., & Fan, D. (2014). A hierarchical optical network-on-chip using central-controlled subnet and wavelength assignment. *Journal of Lightwave Technology*, *32*(5), 930–938. doi:10.1109/JLT.2013.2294863

Chere, N., & Bembe. (2019). Wireless Low Power Area Networks in the Internet of Things: A Glimpse on 6LoWPAN. *International Conference on Electronics, Information, and Communication (ICEIC)*, 1-10. doi: 10.23919/ELINFO-COM.2019.8706392

Chien, E., & Szor, P. (2002). Blended attacks exploits, vulnerabilities and buffer-overflow techniques in computer viruses. *Virus Bulletin Conference*, 1–36.

Chip, F., & Ram, B. (2016). Secure and Dependable NoC-Connected Systems. *IEEE Transactions on Reliability*, *65*(4), 1852–1863. doi:10.1109/TR.2016.2606883

Choi, B. G., Stubbs, M. G., & Park, C. S. (2003). A Ka-band narrow bandpass filter using LTCC technology. *IEEE Microwave and Wireless Components Letters*, *13*(9), 388–389. doi:10.1109/LMWC.2003.817139

Choi, M. K., Park, O. K., Choi, C., Qiao, S., Ghaffari, R., Kim, J., ... Kim, S. J. (2016). Cephalopod-Inspired Miniaturized Suction Cups for Smart Medical Skin. *Advanced Healthcare Materials*, *5*(1), 80–87. doi:10.1002/adhm.201500285 PMID:25989744

Chorost, M. (2016). *The Networked Pill*. MIT Technology Review.

Cianchetti, M. J., Cianchetti, M. J., Kerekes, J. C., Kerekes, J. C., Albonesi, D. H., & Albonesi, D. H. (2009). Phastlane: a rapid transit optical routing network. *International Symposium on Computer Architecture*, *37*(3), 9. 10.1145/1555754.1555809

Cileo, D. G., Sharma, N., & Magarini, M. (2017, August). Coverage, capacity and interference analysis for an aerial base station in different environments. In *2017 International Symposium on Wireless Communication Systems (ISWCS)* (pp. 281-286). IEEE.

Cisco. (n.d.). Retrieved from Internet of Things (IoT): https://www.cisco.com/c/en/us/solutions/internet-of-things/overview.html

ComputerworldUK. (2019). Retrieved from: http://www.computerworlduk.com/news/data/boeing-787s-create-half-terabyte-of-data-per-flight-saysvirgin-atlantic-3433595/

Consulting, T. T. (2019). *Building smart (IoT) solutions with M2M-A Developer Course.* Retrieved from http://consult-timmins.com/building-smart-iot-solutions-with-m2m-a-developer-course-kl/

CytechSmart. (2019). *Smart Home Automation.* Retrieved from http://www.cytechsmart.com/product/sensor_smoke-Sensor.htm

Da Xu, L., He, W., & Li, S. (2014). Internet of things in industries: A survey. *IEEE Transactions on Industrial Informatics, 10*(4), 2233–2243. doi:10.1109/TII.2014.2300753

Dally, W. J., & Towles, B. (2001). *Route packets, not wires: on-chip interconnection networks.* doi:10.1109/dac.2001.935594

Dally, W. J., & Towles, B. (2003). *Principles and Practices of Interconnection Networks.* San Francisco, CA: Morgan Kaufmann Publishers Inc.

Dan, A., Davis, D., Kearney, R., Keller, A., King, R., Kuebler, D., ... Youssef, A. (2004). Web services on demand: WSLA-driven automated management. *IBM Systems Journal, 43*(1), 136–158. doi:10.1147j.431.0136

Datir, S., & Wagh, S. (2014). Monitoring and detection of agricultural disease using wireless sensor network. *International Journal of Computers and Applications, 87*(4).

Deering, S., & Hinden, B. (1988). *Internet Protocol, Version 6 (IPv6) Specification.* IETF RFC 2460.

Degermark, M., Nordgren, B., & Pink, S. (1999). *IP Header Compression, RFC 2507.* IETF.

Depuru, S. S. S. R., Wang, L., & Devabhaktuni, V. (2011). Electricity theft: Overview, issues, prevention and a smart meter based approach to control theft. *Energy Policy, 39*(2), 1007–1015. doi:10.1016/j.enpol.2010.11.037

Dey, N., Ashour, A. S., & Bhatt, C. (2017). *Internet of Things Driven Connected Healthcare. Internet of Things and Big Data Technologies for Next Generation Healthcare.* Springer.

Dhirani, L. L., & Newe, T. (2017). Cloud Computing and Internet of Things Fusion. Academic Press.

Dhirani, L. L., Newe, T., & Nizamani, S. (2018a) Can IoT escape Cloud QoS and Cost Pitfalls. *2018 12th International Conference on Sensing Technology (ICST).*

Dhirani, L. L., Newe, T., & Nizamani, S. (2018b). Federated Hybrid Clouds: Service Level Agreements and Legal Issues. In *Third International Congress on Information and Communication Technology.* Springer.

Dhirani, L. L., Newe, T., & Nizamani, S. (2019). Can IoT escape cloud QoS and cost pitfalls. *Proceedings of the International Conference on Sensing Technology, ICST,* 65–70. 10.1109/ICSensT.2018.8603570

DIGI. (2019). *Customer Stories.* Retrieved from https://www.digi.com/customer-stories

Dizdarević, J., Carpio, F., Jukan, A., & Masip-Bruin, X. (2019). A survey of communication protocols for internet of things and related challenges of fog and cloud computing integration. *ACM Computing Surveys, 51*(6), 116. doi:10.1145/3292674

Domingo, M. C. (2012). An overview of the Internet of Things for people with disabilities. *Journal of Network and Computer Applications, 35*(2), 584–596. doi:10.1016/j.jnca.2011.10.015

Dong, Y., & Itoh, T. (2012). Metamaterial-based antennas. *Proceedings of the IEEE, 100*(7), 2271–2285. doi:10.1109/JPROC.2012.2187631

Drath, R., & Horch, A. (2014). Industrie 4.0: Hit or hype? *IEEE Industrial Electronics Magazine, 8*(2), 56–58. doi:10.1109/MIE.2014.2312079

Dunn, B., Kamath, H., & Tarascon, J.-M. (2011). Electrical energy storage for the grid: a battery of choices. *Science, 334*(6058), 928-935.

Duro, J., Pascual, J. A., Petit, S., Sahuquillo, J., & Gómez, M. E. (2018, June). Modeling and analysis of the performance of exascale photonic networks. *Concurrency and Computation*, 1–12. doi:10.1002/cpe.4773

Ebrahimpouri, M., Quevedo-Teruel, O., & Rajo-Iglesias, E. (2017). Design guidelines for gap waveguide technology based on glide-symmetric holey structures. *IEEE Microwave and Wireless Components Letters, 27*(6), 542–544. doi:10.1109/LMWC.2017.2701308

Elfadel, I. A. M. (2016). *3D Stacked Chips.* doi:10.1007/978-3-319-20481-9

Elhayatmy, G., Dey, N., & Ashour, A. S. (2018). Internet of Things Based Wireless Body. Springer International Publishing AG.

Eltresy, N. A., Elsheakh, D. N., Abdallah, E. A., & Elhennawy, H. M. (2019). RF Energy Harvesting Using Transparent Antenna for IoT Application. *Proceedings of 2019 International Conference on Innovative Trends in Computer Engineering, ITCE 2019*, 287–291. doi:10.1109/ITCE.2019.8646423

Eom, K. H., Kim, M. C., Lee, S., & Lee, C. W. (2012). The vegetable freshness monitoring system using RFID with oxygen and carbon dioxide sensor. *International Journal of Distributed Sensor Networks, 2012*, 1–6. doi:10.1155/2012/472986

Erl, T., Cope, R., & Naserpour, A. (2015). *Cloud computing design patterns.* Prentice-Hall.

Ersoy, C., & Alemdar, H. O. (2010). Wireless sensor networks for healthcare: A survey. Computer Networks. *The International Journal of Computer and Telecommunications Networking, 54*(15), 2688–2710.

Evolution of Cloud to Fog Computing. (2019). Retrieved from: http://rankwatch.com/blog/evolution-of-cloud-to-fog-computing/

ΕΠΙΣΕΥ. (2017). *MELODIC: Multi-cloud Execution-ware for Large-scale Optimized Data-Intensive Computing.* Retrieved August 20, 2018, from https://www.iccs.gr/blog/2017/01/18/melodic-multi-cloud-execution-ware-for-large-scale-optimized-data-intensive-computing/

Fan, F.-R., Lin, L., Zhu, G., Wu, W., Zhang, R., & Wang, Z. L. (2012). Transparent triboelectric nanogenerators and self-powered pressure sensors based on micropatterned plastic films. *Nano Letters, 12*(6), 3109–3114. doi:10.1021/nl300988z PMID:22577731

Fan, Q., & Ansari, N. (2018). Towards traffic load balancing in drone-assisted communications for IoT. *IEEE Internet of Things Journal, 6*(2), 3633–3640. doi:10.1109/JIOT.2018.2889503

Fayez & Haytham. (2009). *Network-on chip theory and practice.* Academic Press.

Fernandes, R., Marcon, C., Cataldo, R., Silveira, J., Sigl, G., & Sepulveda, J. (2016). A security aware routing approach for NoC-based MPSoCs. *Proceedings - SBCCI 2016: 29th Symposium on Integrated Circuits and Systems Design: Chip on the Mountains.* 10.1109/SBCCI.2016.7724054

Fiorin, L., Palermo, G., & Silvano, C. (2008). *A security monitoring service for NoCs.* doi:10.1145/1450135.1450180

Fiorin, L., Silvano, C., & Sami, M. (2007). Security aspects in networks-on-chips: Overview and proposals for secure implementations. *Proceedings - 10th Euromicro Conference on Digital System Design Architectures, Methods and Tools, DSD 2007*, (7945), 539–542. 10.1109/DSD.2007.4341520

Fiorin, L., Palermo, G., Lukovic, S., Catalano, V., & Silvano, C. (2008). Secure memory accesses on networks-on-chip. *IEEE Transactions on Computers, 57*(9), 1216–1229. doi:10.1109/TC.2008.69

Flich, J., Mejia, A., Lopez, P., & Duato, J. (2007). Region-based routing: An efficient routing mechanism to tackle unreliable hardware in network on chips. *Proceedings - NOCS 2007: First International Symposium on Networks-on-Chip*, 183–194. 10.1109/NOCS.2007.39

Foschini, L., Taleb, T., Corradi, A., & Bottazzi, D. (2011). M2M-based metropolitan platform for IMS-enabled road traffic management in IoT. *IEEE Communications Magazine*, *49*(11), 50–57. doi:10.1109/MCOM.2011.6069709

Frederix, I. (2009). Internet of things and radio frequency identification in care taking, facts and privacy challenges. In *Wireless Communication, Vehicular Technology, Information Theory and aerospace and Electronic Systems Technology. IEEE 1st International Conference on Wireless VITAE*, (pp. 319-323). IEEE. 10.1109/WIRELESSVITAE.2009.5172467

Frey, J., & Yu, Q. (2017). A hardened network-on-chip design using runtime hardware Trojan mitigation methods. *Integration, the VLSI Journal*, *56*, 15–31. doi:10.1016/j.vlsi.2016.06.008

Fu, W., Chen, T., & Liu, L. (2014). Energy-efficient hybrid optical-electronic network-on-chip for future many-core processors. *Elektronika ir Elektrotechnika*, *20*(3), 83–86. doi:10.5755/j01.eee.20.3.6682

Gao, T., Zhao, K., Liu, X., & Yang, Y. (2017). Implanting a solid Li-ion battery into a triboelectric nanogenerator for simultaneously scavenging and storing wind energy. *Nano Energy*, *41*, 210–216. doi:10.1016/j.nanoen.2017.09.037

Gartner's hype cycle special report for 2011. (2012). Retrieved from http://www.gartner.com/technology/research/hype-cycles/

Gharibi, M., Boutaba, R., & Waslander, S. L. (2016). Internet of drones. *IEEE Access: Practical Innovations, Open Solutions*, *4*, 1148–1162. doi:10.1109/ACCESS.2016.2537208

Gia, T. N., Jiang, M., Rahmani, A. M., Westerlund, T., Liljeberg, P., & Tenhunen, H. (2015). Fog Computing in Healthcare Internet of Things. *2015 IEEE International Conference on Computer and Information Technology; Ubiquitous Computing and Communications*.

Gia, T. N., Thanigaivelan, N. K., Rahmani, A. M., Westerlund, T., Liljeberg, P., & Tenhunen, H. (2014). *Customizing 6LoWPAN Networks towards Internetof-Things Based Ubiquitous Healthcare Systems*. IEEE.

Gilchrist, A. (2016). *Industry 4.0: the industrial internet of things*. Apress. doi:10.1007/978-1-4842-2047-4

Gomez, C., & Paradells, J. (2010). Wireless home automation networks: A survey of architectures and technologies. *IEEE Communications Magazine*, *48*(6), 92–101. doi:10.1109/MCOM.2010.5473869

Gomez, C., Paradells, J., Bormann, C., & Crowcroft, J. (2017). From 6LoWPAN to 6Lo: Expanding the Universe of IPv6-Supported Technologies for the Internet of Things. *IEEE Communications Magazine*, *55*(12), 148–155. doi:10.1109/MCOM.2017.1600534

Goncalves, R., Carvalho, N. B., Pinho, P., Loss, C., & Salvado, R. (2013). Textile antenna for electromagnetic energy harvesting for GSM900 and DCS1800 bands. IEEE Antennas and Propagation Society, AP-S International Symposium (Digest), 1, 1206–1207. 10.1109/APS.2013.6711263

Gope, P., & Hwang, T. (2016). BSN-Care: A secure IoT-based modern healthcare system using body sensor network. *IEEE Sensors Journal*, *16*(5), 1368–1376. doi:10.1109/JSEN.2015.2502401

Gotra, Varshney, & Singh, Vinay, & Pandey. (2019). Dual-band circular polarisation generation technique with the miniaturisation of a rectangular dielectric resonator antenna. *IET Microwaves, Antennas & Propagation*.

Grammatikakis, M. D., Papadimitriou, K., Petrakis, P., Papagrigoriou, A., Kornaros, G., Christoforakis, I., & Coppola, M. (2014). Security effectiveness and a hardware firewall for MPSoCs. *Proceedings - 16th IEEE International Conference on High Performance Computing and Communications, HPCC 2014, 11th IEEE International Conference on Embedded Software and Systems, ICESS 2014 and 6th International Symposium on Cyberspace Safety and Security*, 1032–1039. 10.1109/HPCC.2014.173

Grammatikakis, M. D., Papadimitriou, K., Petrakis, P., Papagrigoriou, A., Kornaros, G., Christoforakis, I., ... Coppola, M. (2015). Security in MPSoCs: A NoC Firewall and an Evaluation Framework. *IEEE Transactions on Computer-Aided Design of Integrated Circuits and Systems*, *34*(8), 1344–1357. doi:10.1109/TCAD.2015.2448684

Granjal, J., Monteiro, E., & Sa Silva, J. (2015). Security for the internet of things: A survey of existing protocols and open research issues. *IEEE Communications Surveys and Tutorials*, *17*(3), 1294–1312. doi:10.1109/COMST.2015.2388550

Gu, H., Wang, Z., Zhang, B., Yang, Y., & Wang, K. (2017). *Time-Division-Multiplexing – Wavelength- Architecture for ONoC*. Academic Press.

Guan, L., Nilghaz, A., Su, B., Jiang, L., Cheng, W., & Shen, W. (2016). Stretchable-Fiber-Confined Wetting Conductive Liquids as Wearable Human Health Monitors. *Advanced Functional Materials*, *26*(25), 4511–4517. doi:10.1002/adfm.201600443

Gubbi, J., Buyya, R., Marusic, S., & Palaniswami, M. (2013). Internet of Things (IoT): A vision, architectural elements, and future directions. *Future Generation Computer Systems*, *29*(7), 1645–1660. doi:10.1016/j.future.2013.01.010

Gu, H., Chen, K., Yang, Y., Chen, Z., & Zhang, B. (2017). MRONoC: A low latency and energy efficient on chip optical interconnect architecture. *IEEE Photonics Journal*, *9*(1), 1–12. doi:10.1109/JPHOT.2017.2651586

Gui, Q., He, Y., Gao, N., Tao, X., & Wang, Y. (2017). A Skin-Inspired Integrated Sensor for Synchronous Monitoring of Multiparameter Signals. *Advanced Functional Materials*, *27*(36), 1702050. doi:10.1002/adfm.201702050

Guo, B., Zhang, D., Wang, Z., Yu, Z., & Zhou, X. (2013). Opportunistic IoT: Exploring the harmonious interaction between human and the internet of things. *Journal of Network and Computer Applications*, *36*(6), 1531–1539. doi:10.1016/j.jnca.2012.12.028

Guthi, A. (2016). Implementation of an Efficient Noise and Air Pollution Monitoring System Using Internet of Things (IoT). *International Journal of Advanced Research in Computer and Communication Engineering*, *5*(7).

Haberman & Thaler. (2002). *Unicast-Prefix-based IPv6 Multicast Address*. RFC 3306.

Hakiri, A., Berthou, P., Gokhale, A., & Abdellatif, S. (2015, September 16). Publish/subscribe-enabled software defined networking for efficient and scalable IoT communications. *IEEE Communications Magazine*, *53*(9), 48–54. doi:10.1109/MCOM.2015.7263372

Haller, S., Karnouskos, S., & Schroth, C. (2008). The Internet of Things in an Enterprise Context. In *FIS 2008: Future Internet*. Springer.

Ha, M., Lim, S., & Ko, H. (2018). Wearable and flexible sensors for user-interactive health-monitoring devices. *Journal of Materials Chemistry. B, Materials for Biology and Medicine*, *6*(24), 4043–4064. doi:10.1039/C8TB01063C

Hamedani, P. K., Jerger, N. E., & Hessabi, S. (2015). QuT: A low-power optical network-on-chip. *Proceedings - 2014 8th IEEE/ACM International Symposium on Networks-on-Chip, NoCS 2014*, 80–87. 10.1109/NOCS.2014.7008765

Han, C., Jornet, J. M., Fadel, E., & Akyildiz, I. F. (2013). A cross-layer communication module for the Internet of Things. *Computer Networks*, *57*(3), 622–633. doi:10.1016/j.comnet.2012.10.003

Hassanalieragh, M., Page, A., Soyata, T., Sharma, G., Aktas, M., Mateos, G., & Andreescu, S. (2015, June). Health monitoring and management using Internet-of-Things (IoT) sensing with cloud-based processing: Opportunities and challenges. In *2015 IEEE International Conference on Services Computing* (pp. 285-292). IEEE. 10.1109/SCC.2015.47

Hayat, S., Yanmaz, E., & Muzaffar, R. (2016). Survey on unmanned aerial vehicle networks for civil applications: A communications viewpoint. *IEEE Communications Surveys and Tutorials*, *18*(4), 2624–2661. doi:10.1109/COMST.2016.2560343

Healthcare Innovation. (2019). Retrieved from: https://www.hcinnovationgroup.com/cybersecurity/news/13028203/study-87-percent-of-healthcare-organizations-will-adopt-iot-technology-by-2019

Hideo Suzuki, Y. K., Mogi, T., Matsushita, K., Hanada, M., Suzuki, R., & Niijima, N. (2018). *An Updated Watch-over System Using an IoT Device, for Elderly People Living by Themselves. In 3rd International Conferernce on System Reliabilty and Safety*. ICSRS.

Honda, W., Harada, S., Arie, T., Akita, S., & Takei, K. (2014). Wearable, human-interactive, health-monitoring, wireless devices fabricated by macroscale printing techniques. *Advanced Functional Materials*, *24*(22), 3299–3304. doi:10.1002/adfm.201303874

Honggang, Z., Chen, S., & Leyu, Z. (2018). Design and Implementation of Lightweight 6LoWPAN Gateway Based on Contiki. *2018 IEEE International Conference on Signal Processing, Communications and Computing (ICSPCC)*, 1-5. 10.1109/ICSPCC.2018.8567741

Hong, S., Lee, J., Do, K., Lee, M., Kim, J. H., Lee, S., & Kim, D. H. (2017). Stretchable electrode based on laterally combed carbon nanotubes for wearable energy harvesting and storage devices. *Advanced Functional Materials*, *27*(48), 1704353. doi:10.1002/adfm.201704353

Horowitz, M., Labonte, F., Shacham, O., Olukotun, K., Hammond, L., & Batten, C. (2018). *35 Years of Microprocessor Trend Data*. Retrieved from https://www.karlrupp.net/2015/06/40-years-of-microprocessor-trend-data

Hou, H., Xu, Q., Pang, Y., Li, L., Wang, J., Zhang, C., & Sun, C. (2017). Efficient Storing Energy Harvested by Triboelectric Nanogenerators Using a Safe and Durable All-Solid-State Sodium-Ion Battery. *Advancement of Science*, *4*(8), 1700072. PMID:28852625

Howitt, I., & Gutierrez, J. A. (2003). IEEE 802.15.4 low rate - Wireless personal area network coexistence issues. In *Wireless Communications and Networking. WCNC 2003*. IEEE.

HPE. (2017). *Operations bridge*. Retrieved December 30, 2017, from https://saas.hpe.com/en-us/software/operations-manager

Hu, Y., Müller-Gritschneder, D., Sepulveda, M. J., Gogniat, G., & Schlichtmann, U. (2015). Automatic ILP-based firewall insertion for secure application-specific networks-on-chip. *Proceedings - 2015 9th International Workshop on Interconnection Network Architectures: On-Chip, Multi-Chip, INA-OCMC 2015*, 9–12. 10.1109/INA-OCMC.2015.9

Huang, L., Xiao, Y., Liu, J., & Lin, H. (2016). LED intelligent lighting system based on 6LoWPAN. *2016 11th International Conference on Computer Science & Education (ICCSE)*, 529-532. 10.1109/ICCSE.2016.7581636

Hui & Culler. (2007). *Stateless IPv6 Header Compression for Globally Routable Packets in 6LoWPAN Subnetworks*. draft-hui-6lowpan-hc1g-00.

Hui & Thubert. (2011). *Compression Format for IPv6 Datagrams over IEEE 802.15.4-Based Networks*. RFC 6282.

Hui, C. & Chakrabarti. (2009). *6LoWPAN: Incorporating IEEE 802.15.4 into the IP architecture*. Internet Protocol for Smart Object (IPSO) Alliance White Paper.

Huiqin, W., & Yongqiang, D. (2010). An Improved Header Compression Scheme for 6LoWPAN Networks. *2010 Ninth International Conference on Grid and Cloud Computing*, 350-355. 10.1109/GCC.2010.74

Hussain, I., Khan, S. A., Rahimoon, A. Q., Abro, A., Hussain, F. S., & Ali, M. (2019). *Flexible Triboelectric Nanogenerator Based on Paper, PET and Aluminum.* Paper presented at the 2019 2nd International Conference on Computing, Mathematics and Engineering Technologies (iCoMET).

Hussein, A. K. (2015). Applications of nanotechnology in renewable energies—A comprehensive overview and understanding. *Renewable & Sustainable Energy Reviews*, *42*, 460–476. doi:10.1016/j.rser.2014.10.027

Hwang, H. C., Park, J., & Shon, J. G. (2016). Design and implementation of a reliable message transmission system based on MQTT protocol in IoT. *Wireless Personal Communications*, *91*(4), 1765–1777. doi:10.100711277-016-3398-2

Ibrahim, M., Elgamri, A., Babiker, S., & Mohamed, A. (2015). Internet of things based smart environmental monitoring using the Raspberry-Pi computer. *2015 Fifth International Conference on Digital Information Processing and Communications (ICDIPC)*. 10.1109/ICDIPC.2015.7323023

Indrusiak, L. S., Harbin, J., & Sepulveda, M. J. (2017). Side-channel attack resilience through route randomisation in secure real-time Networks-on-Chip. *12th International Symposium on Reconfigurable Communication-Centric Systems-on-Chip, ReCoSoC 2017 - Proceedings*. 10.1109/ReCoSoC.2017.8016142

Infiniti Research. (2018). *Retrieved from Six Innovative Applications of IoT in Healthcare.* Retrieved from Business Wire site: https://www.businesswire.com/news/home/20180828005288/en/Innovative-Applications-IoT-Healthcare-Infiniti-Research

International, W. W. F. (2011). The Energy Report 100% Renewable Energy by 2050. The Energy Report 100% [Gland, Switzerland: World Wide Fund For Nature.]. *Renewable Energy*, ▪▪▪, 2050.

Internet of Things - IERC. (2014). Retrieved from IERC-European Research Cluster on the Internet of Things: http://www.internet-of-things-research.eu/about_iot.htm

Internet of Things in healthcare. (2019). Retrieved from 10 examples of the Internet of Things in healthcare, Econsultancy: https://econsultancy.com/internet-of-things-healthcare/

Islam, S. R., Kwak, D., Hossain, M., & Kwak, K. S. (2015). *Survey, The Internet of Things for Health Care: A Comprehensive.* IEEE.

ISO/IEEE 11073 Committee (ITU-T /Y.2060). (n.d.). Retrieved from ITU-T Recommendations: https://www.itu.int/ITU-T/recommendations/rec.aspx?rec=y.2060

ISO/IEEE. (1996). *IEEE Standard for Medical Device Communication, Overview and Framework.* ISO/IEEE.

Jabbar, S., Ullah, F., Khalid, S., Khan, M., & Han, K. (2017). Semantic interoperability in heterogeneous IoT infrastructure for healthcare. *Wireless Communications and Mobile Computing*, 2017.

Jacobson, Braden, & Borman. (1990). *Compressing TCP/IP headers for low-speed serial links IETF.* Network working group, RFC 1144.

Jaladi, A. R., Khithani, K., Pawar, P., Malvi, K., & Sahoo, G., (2017). Environmental Monitoring Using Wireless Sensor Networks (WSN) based on IoT. *International Research Journal of Engineering and Technology, 4*(1).

Jara, J., Zamora, M. a., & Skarmeta, A. (2010). Intra-mobility for Hospital Wireless Sensor Networks Based on 6LoW-PAN. *Intra-mobility for Hospital Wireless Se 6th International Conference on Wireless and Mobile Communications*. doi:10.1109/ICWMC.2010.54

Jara, Zamora, & Skarmeta. (2010). Intra-mobility for Hospital Wireless Sensor Networks based on 6LoWPAN. 6th IEEE (ICWMC), 389–394.

Jaradat, M., Jarrah, M., Bousselham, A., Jararweh, Y., & Al-Ayyoub, M. (2015). The internet of energy: Smart sensor networks and big data management for smart grid. *Procedia Computer Science, 56*, 592–597. doi:10.1016/j.procs.2015.07.250

Järventausta, P., Repo, S., Rautiainen, A., & Partanen, J. (2010). Smart grid power system control in distributed generation environment. *Annual Reviews in Control, 34*(2), 277–286. doi:10.1016/j.arcontrol.2010.08.005

Jayapandian, N., Rahman, A. M. Z., Koushikaa, M., & Radhikadevi, S. (2016, February). A novel approach to enhance multi level security system using encryption with fingerprint in cloud. In *2016 World Conference on Futuristic Trends in Research and Innovation for Social Welfare (Startup Conclave)* (pp. 1-5). IEEE. 10.1109/STARTUP.2016.7583903

Jayapandian, N., Rahman, A. M. Z., Radhikadevi, S., & Koushikaa, M. (2016, February). Enhanced cloud security framework to confirm data security on asymmetric and symmetric key encryption. In *2016 World Conference on Futuristic Trends in Research and Innovation for Social Welfare (Startup Conclave)* (pp. 1-4). IEEE. 10.1109/STARTUP.2016.7583904

Jayapandian, N. (2019). Business Transaction Privacy and Security Issues in Near Field Communication. In *Network Security and Its Impact on Business Strategy*. IGI Global. doi:10.4018/978-1-5225-8455-1.ch005

Jayapandian, N. (2019). Threats and Security Issues in Smart City Devices. In *Secure Cyber-Physical Systems for Smart Cities*. IGI Global. doi:10.4018/978-1-5225-7189-6.ch009

Jayapandian, N., & Md Zubair Rahman, A. M. J. (2018). Secure Deduplication for Cloud Storage Using Interactive Message-Locked Encryption with Convergent Encryption, To Reduce Storage Space. *Brazilian Archives of Biology and Technology, 61*.

Jayapandian, N., & Rahman, A. M. Z. (2017). Secure and efficient online data storage and sharing over cloud environment using probabilistic with homomorphic encryption. *Cluster Computing, 20*(2), 1561–1573. doi:10.100710586-017-0809-4

Jayapandian, N., Rahman, A. M. Z., Poornima, U., & Padmavathy, P. (2015, November). Efficient online solar energy monitoring and electricity sharing in home using cloud system. In *2015 Online International Conference on Green Engineering and Technologies (IC-GET)* (pp. 1-4). IEEE. 10.1109/GET.2015.7453775

JayashankaraShridevi, R., Ancajas, D. M., Chakraborty, K., & Roy, S. (2017). Security Measures Against a Rogue Network-on-Chip. *Journal of Hardware and Systems Security*, 173–187. doi:10.100741635-017-0008-z

Jiang, Q., Chen, B., Zhang, K., & Yang, Y. (2017). Ag nanoparticle-based triboelectric nanogenerator to scavenge wind energy for a self-charging power unit. *ACS Applied Materials & Interfaces, 9*(50), 43716–43723. doi:10.1021/acsami.7b14618 PMID:29182240

Jisha, R. C., Jyothindranath, A., & Kumary, L. S. (2017, September). Iot based school bus tracking and arrival time prediction. In *2017 International Conference on Advances in Computing, Communications and Informatics (ICACCI)* (pp. 509-514). IEEE. 10.1109/ICACCI.2017.8125890

Joshi, A., Batten, C., Kwon, Y. J., Beamer, S., Shamim, I., Asanović, K., & Stojanović, V. (2009). Silicon-photonic clos networks for global on-chip communication. *Proceedings - 2009 3rd ACM/IEEE International Symposium on Networks-on-Chip, NoCS 2009*, 124–133. 10.1109/NOCS.2009.5071460

Jung, H., Park, M., Yoon, Y.-G., Kim, G.-B., & Joo, S.-K. (2003). Amorphous silicon anode for lithium-ion rechargeable batteries. *Journal of Power Sources, 115*(2), 346–351. doi:10.1016/S0378-7753(02)00707-3

Jun, S. Y., Elibiary, A., Sanz-Izquierdo, B., Winchester, L., Bird, D., & McCleland, A. (2018). 3-D printing of conformal antennas for diversity wrist worn applications. *IEEE Transactions on Components, Packaging, and Manufacturing Technology, 8*(12), 2227–2235. doi:10.1109/TCPMT.2018.2874424

Kanchi, S., Sandilya, S., Bhosale, D., & Pitkar, A. (2013). Overview of LTE-A technology. *IEEE Global High Tech Congress on Electronics.* 10.1109/GHTCE.2013.6767272

Kang, S.-J., Mintz, G. S., Park, D.-W., Lee, S.-W., Kim, Y.-H., Whan Lee, C., ... Park, S.-J. (2011). Mechanisms of in-stent restenosis after drug-eluting stent implantation: Intravascular ultrasound analysis. *Circulation: Cardiovascular Interventions, 4*(1), 9–14. doi:10.1161/CIRCINTERVENTIONS.110.940320 PMID:21266707

Kapoor, H. K., Rao, G. B., Arshi, S., & Trivedi, G. (2013). A security framework for NoC using authenticated encryption and session keys. *Circuits, Systems, and Signal Processing, 32*(6), 2605–2622. doi:10.100700034-013-9568-5

Karjoth, G. (2003). Access control with IBM Tivoli access manager. *ACM Transactions on Information and System Security, 6*(2), 232–257. doi:10.1145/762476.762479

Kaur, K. (2014). Internet of things enabled energy efficient green communication on FPGA. *Proceedings - 2014 6th International Conference on Computational Intelligence and Communication Networks, CICN 2014,* 947-950. 10.1109/CICN.2014.200

Keller, A., & Ludwig, H. (2002). Defining and Monitoring Service Level Agreements for dynamic e-Business. *Proceedings of the 16th System Administration Conference.*

Kelly, S. D. T., Suryadevara, N. K., & Mukhopadhyay, S. C. (2013). Towards the Implementation of IoT for Environmental Condition Monitoring in Homes. *IEEE Sensors Journal, 13*(10), 3846–3853. doi:10.1109/JSEN.2013.2263379

Keramati, M., Modarressi, M., & Rezaei, S. H. S. (2017). Thermal management in 3d networks-on-chip using dynamic link sharing. *Microprocessors and Microsystems, 52,* 1339–1351. doi:10.1016/j.micpro.2017.05.011

Khalid, F., Hasan, S. R., Hasan, O., & Awwad, F. (2018). Runtime hardware Trojan monitors through modeling burst mode communication using formal verification. *Integration, the VLSI Journal, 61,* 1–15. doi:10.1016/j.vlsi.2017.11.003

Khanna, A., Das, B., Pandey, B., Hussain, D. M. A., & Jain, V. (2016). A discussion about upgrading the quick script platform to create natural language based IoT systems. *Indian Journal of Science and Technology, 9*(46). doi:10.17485/ijst/2016/v9i46/106917

Khan, S. A., Gao, M., Zhu, Y., Yan, Z., & Lin, Y. (2017). MWCNTs based flexible and stretchable strain sensors. *Journal of Semiconductors, 38*(5), 053003. doi:10.1088/1674-4926/38/5/053003

Khan, Y., Garg, M., Gui, Q., Schadt, M., Gaikwad, A., Han, D., ... Wilson, W. (2016). Flexible hybrid electronics: Direct interfacing of soft and hard electronics for wearable health monitoring. *Advanced Functional Materials, 26*(47), 8764–8775. doi:10.1002/adfm.201603763

Khawaja, W., Guvenc, I., Matolak, D., Fiebig, U. C., & Schneckenberger, N. (2018). *A survey of air-to-ground propagation channel modeling for unmanned aerial vehicles.* arXiv preprint arXiv:1801.01656

Khawaja, W., Guvenc, I., Matolak, D., Fiebig, U. C., & Schneckenberger, N. (2018). *A survey of air-to-ground propagation channel modeling for unmanned aerial vehicles.* arXiv preprint arXiv:1801.01656.

Khawaja, W., Guvenc, I., & Matolak, D. (2016, December). UWB channel sounding and modeling for UAV air-to-ground propagation channels. In *2016 IEEE Global Communications Conference (GLOBECOM)* (pp. 1-7). IEEE. 10.1109/GLOCOM.2016.7842372

Khush, G. S. (1977). Disease and insect resistance in rice. []. Academic Press.]. *Advances in Agronomy, 29,* 265–341.

Khuwaja, A. A., Chen, Y., Zhao, N., Alouini, M. S., & Dobbins, P. (2018). A survey of channel modeling for UAV communications. *IEEE Communications Surveys and Tutorials, 20*(4), 2804–2821. doi:10.1109/COMST.2018.2856587

Kildal, P.-S., Zaman, A. U., Rajo-Iglesias, E., Alfonso, E., & Valero-Nogueira, A. (2011). Design and experimental verification of ridge gap waveguide in bed of nails for parallel-plate mode suppression. *IET Microwaves, Antennas & Propagation, 5*(3), 262. doi:10.1049/iet-map.2010.0089

Killian, C., Tanougast, C., Monteiro, F., & Dandache, A. (2014). Smart reliable network-on-chip. *IEEE Transactions on Very Large Scale Integration (VLSI) Systems, 22*(2), 242–255. doi:10.1109/TVLSI.2013.2240324

Kim, J. H., Haw, R., & Hong, C. S. (2010). Development of a framework to support network-based mobility of 6LoW-PAN sensor device for mobile healthcare system. *Digest of Technical Papers International Conference on Consumer Electronics (ICCE).* doi:10.1109/ICCE.5418817

Kimani, K., Oduol, V., & Langat, K. (2019). Cyber security challenges for IoT-based smart grid networks. *International Journal of Critical Infrastructure Protection, 25,* 36–49. doi:10.1016/j.ijcip.2019.01.001

Kim, J., Banks, A., Xie, Z., Heo, S. Y., Gutruf, P., Lee, J. W., ... Brown, G. (2015). Miniaturized Flexible Electronic Systems With Wireless Power and Near-Field Communication Capabilities. *Advanced Functional Materials, 25*(30), 4761–4767. doi:10.1002/adfm.201501590

Kim, J., Salvatore, G. A., Araki, H., Chiarelli, A. M., Xie, Z., Banks, A., ... Jang, K.-I. (2016). Battery-free, stretchable optoelectronic systems for wireless optical characterization of the skin. *Science Advances, 2*(8), e1600418. doi:10.1126ciadv.1600418 PMID:27493994

Kim, M.-K., Kim, M.-S., Lee, S., Kim, C., & Kim, Y.-J. (2014). Wearable thermoelectric generator for harvesting human body heat energy. *Smart Materials and Structures, 23*(10), 105002. doi:10.1088/0964-1726/23/10/105002

Kirbas, I., & Bayilmis, C. (2012). A web-based remote monitoring interface for medical healthcare. *Turk J Elec Eng & Comp Sci, 20*(4). doi:10.3906/elk-1011-934

Kodali, R. K., Jain, V., Bose, S., & Boppana, L. (2016). IoT based smart security and home automation system. In *IEEE International Conference on Computing, Communication and Automation (ICCCA)* (pp. 1286-1289). IEEE. 10.1109/CCAA.2016.7813916

Kolberg, D., & Zühlke, D. (2015). Lean automation enabled by industry 4.0 technologies. *IFAC-PapersOnLine, 48*(3), 1870–1875. doi:10.1016/j.ifacol.2015.06.359

Kong, M., Yorkinov, O., Tran, T. H. V., & Shimamoto, S. (2011). Elevation angle-based diversity access employing high altitude platform station and unmanned aerial vehicle (uav) for urban area communications. *GITS, GITI Research Bulletin,* 3-12.

Kooa, D. D., Lea, J. J., Sebastiania, A., & Kimb, J. (2016). An Internet-of-Things (IoT) System Development and Implementation for Bathroom Safety Enhancement. In *International Conference on Sustainable Design, Engineering and Construction.* Elsevier. 10.1016/j.proeng.2016.04.004

Koo, D., Piratla, K., & Matthews, C. J. (2015). Towards sustainable water supply: Schematic development of big data collection using internet of things (IoT). *Procedia Engineering, 118,* 489–497. doi:10.1016/j.proeng.2015.08.465

Koohi, S., & Hessabi, S. (2011). Hierarchical opto-electrical on-chip network for future multiprocessor architectures. *Journal of Systems Architecture, 57*(1), 4–23. doi:10.1016/j.sysarc.2010.07.003

Koohi, S., & Hessabi, S. (2012). Scalable architecture for a contention-free optical network on-chip. *Journal of Parallel and Distributed Computing*, *72*(11), 1493–1506. doi:10.1016/j.jpdc.2012.02.003

Koohi, S., & Hessabi, S. (2014). All-optical wavelength-routed architecture for a power-efficient network on chip. *IEEE Transactions on Computers*, *63*(3), 777–792. doi:10.1109/TC.2012.171

Koohi, S., Yin, Y., Hessabi, S., & Ben Yoo, S. J. (2014). Towards a scalable, low-power all-optical architecture for networks-on-chip. *ACM Transactions on Embedded Computing Systems*, *13*(3s), 1–30. doi:10.1145/2567930

Koop, C. E., Mosher, R., Kun, L., Geiling, J., Grigg, E., Long, S., ... Rosen, J. (2008). Future delivery of health care: Cybercare. *IEEE Engineering in Medicine and Biology Magazine*, *27*(6), 29–38. doi:10.1109/MEMB.2008.929888 PMID:19004693

Kramers, A., Höjer, M., Lövehagen, N., & Wangel, J. (2014). Smart sustainable cities–Exploring ICT solutions for reduced energy use in cities. *Environmental Modelling & Software*, *56*, 52–62. doi:10.1016/j.envsoft.2013.12.019

Ku, M.-L., Li, W., Chen, Y., & Liu, K. R. (2015). Advances in energy harvesting communications: Past, present, and future challenges. *IEEE Communications Surveys and Tutorials*, *18*(2), 1384–1412. doi:10.1109/COMST.2015.2497324

Kumar, A., & Magarini, M. (2016, November). Improved Nyquist pulse shaping filters for generalized frequency division multiplexing. In *2016 8th IEEE Latin-American Conference on Communications (LATINCOM)* (pp. 1-7). IEEE. 10.1109/LATINCOM.2016.7811588

Kumar, P., Ghivela, G. C., & Sengupta, J. (2019). Design and Analysis of Multiple bands Spider Web Shaped Circular Patch Antenna for IoT Application. India International Conference on Power Electronics, IICPE, 2018–Decem, 1–5. 10.1109/IICPE.2018.8709444

Kumar, T., Pandey, B., & Das, T. (2013). Digitally controlled impedance based green design on ultra scale FPGA. In *2013 International Conference on Green Computing, Communication and Conservation of Energy (ICGCE)* (pp. 120-124). IEEE. 10.1109/ICGCE.2013.6823412

Kumar, V., & Tiwari, S. (2012). Routing in IPv6 over Low-Power Wireless Personal Area Networks (6LoWPAN): A Survey. *Journal of Computer Networks and Communications, Hindawi Publishing Corporation*, *2012*, 1–10. doi:10.1155/2012/316839

Kunkun, P., & Xiangong, L. (2014). Reliability evaluation of coal mine internet of things. In *2014 International Conference on Identification, Information and Knowledge in the Internet of Things* (pp. 301-302). IEEE. 10.1109/IIKI.2014.68

Kurian, G., Miller, J. E., Psota, J., Eastep, J., Liu, J., Michel, J., ... Agarwal, A. (2010). ATAC: a 1000-core cache-coherent processor with on-chip optical network. *Proceedings of the 19th International Conference on Parallel Architectures and Compilation Techniques - PACT '10*, 477. 10.1145/1854273.1854332

Kushalnagar, Montenegro, & Schumacher. (2007). *IPv6 over Low-Power Wireless Personal Area Networks (6LoWPANs): overview, assumptions, problem statement, and goals*. IETF RFC 4919.

Kushalnagar, Montenegro, Hui, & Culler. (2007). *Transmission of IPv6 Packets over IEEE 802.15.4 Networks*. IETF RFC 4944.

Kwon, D., Hodkiewicz, M. R., Fan, J., Shibutani, T., & Pecht, M. G. (2016). IoT-based prognostics and systems health management for industrial applications. *IEEE Access: Practical Innovations, Open Solutions*, *4*, 3659–3670. doi:10.1109/ACCESS.2016.2587754

Kyeremateng, N. A., Brousse, T., & Pech, D. (2017). Microsupercapacitors as miniaturized energy-storage components for on-chip electronics. *Nature Nanotechnology*, *12*(1), 7–15. doi:10.1038/nnano.2016.196 PMID:27819693

Lakafosis, V., Rida, A., Vyas, R., Yang, L., Nikolaou, S., & Tentzeris, M. M. (2010). Progress towards the first wireless sensor networks consisting of inkjet-printed, paper-based RFID-enabled sensor tags. *Proceedings of the IEEE*, *98*(9), 1601–1609. doi:10.1109/JPROC.2010.2049622

Lakshay, G., Abhishek, B., & Meetu, G. (2015). Wearable Devices: Google Glass & Smart Watch. *International Journal of Computer Science and Information Technologies*, *6*(2), 1872–1873.

Lamkimel, M., Naja, N., Jamali, A., & Yahyaoui, A. (2018). The Internet of Things: Overview of the essential elements and the new enabling technology 6LoWPAN. *2018 IEEE International Conference on Technology Management, Operations and Decisions (ICTMOD)*, 142-147. 10.1109/ITMC.2018.8691271

Lara, O. D., & Labrador, M. A. (2013). A survey on human activity recognition using wearable sensors. *IEEE Communications Surveys and Tutorials*, *15*(3), 1192–1209. doi:10.1109/SURV.2012.110112.00192

Larcher, D., & Tarascon, J.-M. (2015). Towards greener and more sustainable batteries for electrical energy storage. *Nature Chemistry*, *7*(1), 19–29. doi:10.1038/nchem.2085 PMID:25515886

Lasi, H., Fettke, P., Kemper, H. G., Feld, T., & Hoffmann, M. (2014). Industry 4.0. *Business & Information Systems Engineering*, *6*(4), 239–242. doi:10.100712599-014-0334-4

LaurentPierre. (2016). *IoT Past and Present: The History of IoT, and Where It's Headed Today*. Retrieved from https://www.channelfutures.com/msp-501/iot-past-and-present-the-history-of-iot-and-where-its-headed-today

Le Beux, S, Trajkovic, J., O'Connor, I., Nicolescu, G., Bois, G., & Paulin, P. (2011). Optical Ring Network-on-Chip (ORNoC): Architecture and design methodology. *2011 Design, Automation & Test in Europe*, 1–6. doi:10.1109/DATE.2011.5763134

Le, D., Nguyen, V., & Goh, A. (2009). Matching WSDL and OWL-S Web Services. *IEEE International Conference on Semantic Computing*, 197-202.

Lee, H., & Choi, J. (2017). A polarization reconfigurable textile patch antenna for wearable IoT applications. *2017 International Symposium on Antennas and Propagation, ISAP 2017*, 1–2. doi:10.1109/ISANP.2017.8228882

Lee, J.-H., Kim, J., Kim, T. Y., Al Hossain, M. S., Kim, S.-W., & Kim, J. H. (2016). All-in-one energy harvesting and storage devices. *Journal of Materials Chemistry. A, Materials for Energy and Sustainability*, *4*(21), 7983–7999. doi:10.1039/C6TA01229A

Leskiw, A. (2017). *Understanding Syslog: Servers, Messages & Security*. Retrieved April 30, 2018, from http://www.networkmanagementsoftware.com/what-is-syslog/

Li, G.-B., Wang, S.-H., & Xu, T. (2015). Application of 6LoWPAN in monitoring system for transmission line. *2015 12th International Computer Conference on Wavelet Active Media Technology and Information Processing (ICCWAMTIP)*, 412-415. doi: 10.1109/ICCWAMTIP.2015.7494021

Li, H., & Gu, H. (2010). *A Hierarchical Cluster-based Optical Network-on-Chip*. Academic Press.

Li, J., Ni, L., Chen, J., & Zhou, E. (2017). A novel hardware Trojan detection based on BP neural network. *2016 2nd IEEE International Conference on Computer and Communications, ICCC 2016 - Proceedings*, 2790–2794. 10.1109/CompComm.2016.7925206

Liang, D., & Yao, J. (2018). Application of IPv6 in Coal Mine Safety Production Monitoring. *2018 International Conference on Sensor Networks and Signal Processing (SNSP)*, 45-48. 10.1109/SNSP.2018.00018

Liang, Q., Zhang, Q., Yan, X., Liao, X., Han, L., Yi, F., ... Zhang, Y. (2017). Recyclable and green triboelectric nanogenerator. *Advanced Materials*, *29*(5), 1604961. doi:10.1002/adma.201604961 PMID:27885725

Liao, Y., Deschamps, F., Loures, E. D. F. R., & Ramos, L. F. P. (2017). Past, present and future of Industry 4.0-a systematic literature review and research agenda proposal. *International Journal of Production Research*, *55*(12), 3609–3629. doi:10.1080/00207543.2017.1308576

Li, G., Wu, X., & Lee, D.-W. (2016). A galinstan-based inkjet printing system for highly stretchable electronics with self-healing capability. *Lab on a Chip*, *16*(8), 1366–1373. doi:10.1039/C6LC00046K PMID:26987310

Lin, W., Fan, Z., Zhong, Y., Zi, S., & Xiao, J. (2017). The Research of Long-Chain Wireless Sensor Network Based on 6LoWPAN. *2017 5th International Conference on Enterprise Systems (ES)*, 143-147. 10.1109/ES.2017.30

Lin, L., Wang, S., Xie, Y., Jing, Q., Niu, S., Hu, Y., & Wang, Z. L. (2013). Segmentally structured disk triboelectric nanogenerator for harvesting rotational mechanical energy. *Nano Letters*, *13*(6), 2916–2923. doi:10.1021/nl4013002 PMID:23656350

Lin, M.-C., Gong, M., Lu, B., Wu, Y., Wang, D.-Y., Guan, M., ... Hwang, B.-J. (2015). An ultrafast rechargeable aluminium-ion battery. *Nature*, *520*(7547), 324–328. doi:10.1038/nature14340 PMID:25849777

Liu, X., Zhao, K., Wang, Z. L., & Yang, Y. (2017). Unity convoluted design of solid Li-ion battery and triboelectric nanogenerator for self-powered wearable electronics. *Advanced Energy Materials*, *7*(22), 1701629. doi:10.1002/aenm.201701629

Liu, Z., Qi, D., Hu, G., Wang, H., Jiang, Y., Chen, G., ... Chen, X. (2018). Surface Strain Redistribution on Structured Microfibers to Enhance Sensitivity of Fiber-Shaped Stretchable Strain Sensors. *Advanced Materials*, *30*(5), 1704229. doi:10.1002/adma.201704229 PMID:29226515

Li, X., Gu, H., Chen, K., Song, L., & Hao, Q. (2016). STorus: A new topology for optical network-on-chip. *Optical Switching and Networking*, *22*, 77–85. doi:10.1016/j.osn.2016.04.004

Li, Z., Mohamed, M., Chen, X., Dudley, E., Meng, K. K., Shang, L., ... Sun, Y. (2012). Reliability Modeling and Management of Nanophotonic On-Chip Networks. *IEEE Transactions on Very Large Scale Integration (VLSI). Systems*, *20*(1), 98–111. doi:10.1109/TVLSI.2010.2089072

Li, Z., Mohamed, M., Chen, X., Zhou, H., Mickelson, A., Shang, L., & Vachharajani, M. (2011). Iris: A Hybrid Nanophotonic Network Design for High-Performance and Low-Power on-Chip Communication. *ACM Journal on Emerging Technologies in Computing Systems*, *7*(2), 1–22. doi:10.1145/1970406.1970410

Lizzi, L., Ferrero, F., Monin, P., Danchesi, C., & Boudaud, S. (2016). Design of miniature antennas for IoT applications. *2016 IEEE 6th International Conference on Communications and Electronics*, IEEE ICCE 2016, 234–237. 10.1109/CCE.2016.7562642

Long & Hensley. (1972). Insect pests of sugar cane. *Annual Review of Entomology*, *17*(1), 149–176. doi:10.1016/S0065-2113(08)60221-7

López, O., Rach, M., Migallon, H., Malumbres, M., Bonastre, A., & Serrano, J. (2012). Monitoring pest insect traps by means of low-power image sensor technologies. *Sensors (Basel)*, *12*(11), 15801–15819. doi:10.3390121115801 PMID:23202232

Loss, C., Gonçalves, R., Lopes, C., Pinho, P., & Salvado, R. (2016). Smart coat with a fully-embedded textile antenna for IoT applications. [PubMed]. *Sensors (Switzerland)*, *16*(6), 938. doi:10.339016060938

Lotfi-Kamran, P., Modarressi, M., & Sarbazi-Azad, H. (2016). An Efficient Hybrid-Switched Network-on-Chip for Chip Multiprocessors. *IEEE Transactions on Computers*, *65*(5), 1656–1662. doi:10.1109/TC.2015.2449846

Ludwig, W. (2012). Health-enabling technologies for the elderly--an overview of services based on a literature review. Computer Methods and Programs in Biomedicine.

Lyon, D. H. (2004). A military perspective on small unmanned aerial vehicles. *IEEE Instrumentation & Measurement Magazine, 7*(3), 27–31. doi:10.1109/MIM.2004.1337910

Lyu, Y., & Mishra, P. (2018). *A Survey of Side-Channel Attacks on Caches and Countermeasures.* doi:10.100741635-017-0025-y

Mahajan, U., & Bundel, B. R. (2017). Drones for Normalized Difference Vegetation Index (NDVI), to Estimate Crop Health for Precision Agriculture: A Cheaper Alternative for Spatial Satellite Sensors. In *International Conference on Innovative Research in Agriculture, Food Science, Forestry, Horticulture, Aquaculture, Animal Sciences, Biodiversity, Ecological Sciences and Climate Change (AFHABEC-2016).* Jawaharlal Nehru University.

Mainetti, L., Patrono, L., & Vilei, A. (2011). Evolution of wireless sensor networks towards the Internet of Things: A survey. *SoftCOM 2011, 19th International Conference on Software, Telecommunications and Computer Networks,* 1-6.

Mainetti, L., Patrono, L., & Vilei, A. (2011). Evolution of wireless sensor networks towards the Internet of Things: A survey. *SoftCOM, 19th International Conference on Software, Telecommunications and Computer Networks,* 1-6.

Mal-Sarkar, S., Karam, R., Narasimhan, S., Ghosh, A., Krishna, A., & Bhunia, S. (2016). Design and Validation for FPGA Trust under Hardware Trojan Attacks. *IEEE Transactions on Multi-Scale Computing Systems, 2*(3), 186–198. doi:10.1109/TMSCS.2016.2584052

ManageEngine. (2019). *Homepage.* Retrieved January, 2019, from https://www.manageengine.com

Manavalan, E., & Jayakrishna, K. (2019). A review of Internet of Things (IoT) embedded sustainable supply chain for industry 4.0 requirements. *Computers & Industrial Engineering, 127,* 925–953. doi:10.1016/j.cie.2018.11.030

Mantash, M., Tarot, A. C., Collardey, S., & Mahdjoubi, K. (2011). Wearable monopole zip antenna. *Electronics Letters, 47*(23), 1266. doi:10.1049/el.2011.2784

Mauro Prevostini. (2011). *Wireless Sensor Network for Pest Control, Commission for Technology and innovation CTI.* Retrieved from https://1pdf.net/wireless-sensor-network-for-pest-control-dolphin-engineering_59159fd8f6065d4311b1fb6d

Ma, X., & Luo, W. (2008). The analysis of 6LowPAN technology. *Proceedings of the Pacific-Asia Workshop on Computational Intelligence and Industrial Application (PACIIA '08),* 963–966.

Ma, Y., Liu, N., Li, L., Hu, X., Zou, Z., Wang, J., ... Gao, Y. (2017). A highly flexible and sensitive piezoresistive sensor based on MXene with greatly changed interlayer distances. *Nature Communications, 8*(1), 1207. doi:10.103841467-017-01136-9 PMID:29089488

Mc Gee, K., & Collier, M. (2019). 6LoWPAN Forwarding Techniques for IoT. *2019 IEEE 5th World Forum on Internet of Things (WF-IoT),* 888-893. 10.1109/WF-IoT.2019.8767174

McGuire, S. (2015). *FAO, IFAD, and WFP. The state of food insecurity in the world 2015: meeting the 2015 international hunger targets: taking stock of uneven progress.* Rome: FAO.

Mejia. (2006). An Efficient Fault-Tolerant Routing Methodology for Meshes and Tori. *20th International Parallel and Distributed Processing Symposium,* 10. 10.1109/IPDPS.2006.1639341

Mekala, M. S., & Viswanathan, P. (2017, August). A Survey: Smart agriculture IoT with cloud computing. In *2017 international conference on microelectronic devices, circuits and systems (ICMDCS)* (pp. 1-7). IEEE.

Metis, D. (2015). *D1. 4. METIS Channel Models.* Author.

Meyers, J. P., & Maynard, H. L. (2002). Design considerations for miniaturized PEM fuel cells. *Journal of Power Sources*, *109*(1), 76–88. doi:10.1016/S0378-7753(02)00066-6

Michailow, N., Matthé, M., Gaspar, I. S., Caldevilla, A. N., Mendes, L. L., Festag, A., & Fettweis, G. (2014). Generalized frequency division multiplexing for 5th generation cellular networks. *IEEE Transactions on Communications*, *62*(9), 3045–3061. doi:10.1109/TCOMM.2014.2345566

Microsoft Virtual Academy. (2016). *Homepage*. Retrieved December 15, 2016, from https://mva.microsoft.com

Midgley, P. (2009). The role of smart bike-sharing systems in urban mobility. *Journeys*, *2*(1), 23–31.

Miller, M. (2015). *The internet of things: How smart TVs, smart cars, smart homes, and smart cities are changing the world*. Pearson Education.

Miorandi, D., Sicari, S., Pellegrini, F. D., & Chlamtac, I. (2012). Internet of things: Vision, applications and research challenges. *Ad Hoc Networks*, *10*(7), 1497–1516. doi:10.1016/j.adhoc.2012.02.016

Miotto, R., Wang, F., Wang, S., Jiang, X., & Dudley, J. T. (2017). Deep learning for healthcare: Review, opportunities and challenges. *Briefings in Bioinformatics*, *19*(6), 1236–1246. doi:10.1093/bib/bbx044 PMID:28481991

Miralles, E., Schoenlinner, B., Belenguer, Á., Esteban, H., & Ziegler, V. (2019). A 3-D Printed PCB Integrated TEM Horn Antenna. *Radio Science*, *54*(1), 158–165. doi:10.1029/2018RS006594

Miraz, M. H., Ali, M., Excell, P. S., & Picking, R. (2015). *A Review on Internet of Things (IoT), Internet of Everything (IoE) and Internet of Nano Things (IoNT)*. Conference: Internet Technologies and Applications. ITA.

Mirzaee, M., Noghanian, S., Wiest, L., & Chang, I. (2015). Developing flexible 3D printed antenna using conductive ABS materials. IEEE Antennas and Propagation Society, *AP-S International Symposium (Digest)*, 1308–1309. 10.1109/APS.2015.7305043

Mo, K. H., Ye, Y., Wu, X., Zhang, W., Liu, W., & Xu, J. (2010). A hierarchical hybrid optical-electronic network-on-chip. *Proceedings - IEEE Annual Symposium on VLSI, ISVLSI 2010*, 327–332. 10.1109/ISVLSI.2010.17

Mo-Bike in Europe. (n.d.). Retrieved from: https://news.microsoft.com/en-gb/2017/06/29/mobike-launches-smart-bike-share-service-in-uk-using-microsofts-cloud-service-azure/

Mohapatra, S., & Rekha,, K. S. (2012). Sensor-Cloud: A Hybrid Framework for Remote. *International Journal of Computer Applications, 55*(2).

Monica, M., Yeshika, B., Abhishek, G. S., Sanjay, H. A., & Dasiga, S. (2017, October). IoT based control and automation of smart irrigation system: an automated irrigation system using sensors, GSM, bluetooth and cloud technology. In *2017 International Conference on Recent Innovations in Signal processing and Embedded Systems (RISE)* (pp. 601-607). IEEE. 10.1109/RISE.2017.8378224

Morello, R., De Capua, C., Fulco, G., & Mukhopadhyay, S. C. (2017). A smart power meter to monitor energy flow in smart grids: The role of advanced sensing and IoT in the electric grid of the future. *IEEE Sensors Journal*, *17*(23), 7828–7837. doi:10.1109/JSEN.2017.2760014

Motlagh, N. H., Bagaa, M., & Taleb, T. (2016, December). UAV selection for a UAV-based integrative IoT platform. In *2016 IEEE Global Communications Conference (GLOBECOM)* (pp. 1-6). IEEE.

Motlagh, N. H., Bagaa, M., & Taleb, T. (2017). UAV-based IoT platform: A crowd surveillance use case. *IEEE Communications Magazine*, *55*(2), 128–134. doi:10.1109/MCOM.2017.1600587CM

Moudgil, A. (2015). GTL based Internet of Things enable processor specific RAM design on 65nm FPGA. *Proceedings Elmar - International Symposium Electronics in Marine.* 10.1109/ELMAR.2015.7334514

Moudgil, A., Garg, K., & Pandey, B. (2015). Low voltage complementary metal oxide semiconductor based internet of things enable energy efficient RAM design on 40nm and 65nm FPGA. *International Journal of Smart Home, 9*(9), 37–50. doi:10.14257/ijsh.2015.9.9.05

Mousa, M. E., Abdullah, H. H., & El Din Abo El-Soud, M. (2018). Compact Chipless RFID Tag Based on Fractal Antennas and Multiple Microstrip Open Stub Resonators. Progress in Electromagnetics Research Symposium, 1332–1338. 10.23919/PIERS.2018.8598207

Mozaffari, M., Saad, W., Bennis, M., & Debbah, M. (2016). Efficient deployment of multiple unmanned aerial vehicles for optimal wireless coverage. *IEEE Communications Letters, 20*(8), 1647–1650. doi:10.1109/LCOMM.2016.2578312

Mozaffari, M., Saad, W., Bennis, M., & Debbah, M. (2016). Unmanned aerial vehicle with underlaid device-to-device communications: Performance and tradeoffs. *IEEE Transactions on Wireless Communications, 15*(6), 3949–3963. doi:10.1109/TWC.2016.2531652

Mueller, M., Mathiason, J., & Klein, H. (2007). The Internet and global governance: Principles and norms for a new regime. *Global Governance, 13*(2), 237–254. doi:10.1163/19426720-01302007

Mulligan, G. (2007). The 6LoWPAN architecture. *Proceedings of the 4th Workshop on Embedded Networked Sensors (EmNets '07),* 78–82. 10.1145/1278972.1278992

Musavi, S. H. A., Chowdhry, B. S., Kumar, T., Pandey, B., & Kumar, W. (2015). IoTs Enable Active Contour Modeling Based Energy Efficient and Thermal Aware Object Tracking on FPGA. *Wireless Personal Communications, 85*(2), 529–543. doi:10.100711277-015-2753-z

Mustaqim, M., Khawaja, B. A., Chattha, H. T., Shafique, K., Zafar, M. J., & Jamil, M. (2019). Ultra-wideband antenna for wearable Internet of Things devices and wireless body area network applications. International Journal of Numerical Modelling: Electronic Networks, Devices and Fields, 1–12. doi:10.1002/jnm.2590

Najib, S. M., Hassan, N. B., Shair, N. T., Rahim, N., & Wahab, N. A. (2019). Intelligent Neonatal Monitoring System Based on Android Application using Multi Sensors. *Computer Applications and Industrial Electronics (ICCAIE), International Conference on.* 10.1109/ISCAIE.2019.8743867

Nalini & Ramakrishna. (2018). Smart irrigation system based on soil moisture using iot. *International Research Journal of Engineering and Technology, 5*(6).

Naranjo, P. G. V., Shojafar, M., Mostafaei, H., Pooranian, Z., & Baccarelli, E. (2017). P-SEP: A prolong stable election routing algorithm for energy-limited heterogeneous fog-supported wireless sensor networks. *The Journal of Supercomputing, 73*(2), 733–755. doi:10.100711227-016-1785-9

Nenzi, P., Tripaldi, F., Varlamava, V., Palma, F., & Balucani, M. (2012). On-chip THz 3D antennas. Proceedings - Electronic Components and Technology Conference, 102–108. 10.1109/ECTC.2012.6248813

Niu, S., Wang, S., Lin, L., Liu, Y., Zhou, Y. S., Hu, Y., & Wang, Z. L. (2013). Theoretical study of contact-mode triboelectric nanogenerators as an effective power source. *Energy & Environmental Science, 6*(12), 3576–3583. doi:10.1039/c3ee42571a

Noury, N., Barralon, P., Vuillerme, N., & Fleury, A. (2012). Fusion of multiple sensors sources in a smart home to detect scenarios of activities in ambient assisted living. *International Journal of E-Health and Medical Communications, 3*(3), 29–44. doi:10.4018/jehmc.2012070103

Nuno, R., & da Silva, M. (2010). *Mobility support in Low Power Wireless Personal Area Networks (MLoWPAN).* Coimbra University.

Nurmela, V. (2015). *METIS channel models.* FP7 METIS, Deliverable D 1.

Olaimat, M. M. (2016). Comparison between Rectangular and Circular Patch AntennasArray. *International Journal of Computational Engineering Research*, *6*(9).

Oliver, M. A. (Ed.). (2010). *Geostatistical applications for precision agriculture.* Springer Science & Business Media. doi:10.1007/978-90-481-9133-8

Operations Management, I. T. (2017). *IT Operations Management.* Retrieved December 30, 2017, from https://www.ibm.com/cloud-computing/products/devops/it-operations-management/

Ortín-Obón, M., Suárez-Gracia, D., Villarroya-Gaudó, M., Izu, C., & Viñals-Yúfera, V. (2016). Analysis of network-on-chip topologies for cost-efficient chip multiprocessors. *Microprocessors and Microsystems*, *42*, 24–36. doi:10.1016/j.micpro.2016.01.005

Osibanjo, O., & Nnorom, I. (2007). The challenge of electronic waste (e-waste) management in developing countries. *Waste Management & Research*, *25*(6), 489–501. doi:10.1177/0734242X07082028 PMID:18229743

Osvik, D., Shamir, A., & Tromer, E. (2006). *Cache Attacks and Countermeasures: The Case of AES\nTopics in Cryptology – CT-RSA 2006.* doi:10.1007/11605805_1

Ouyang, H., Tian, J., Sun, G., Zou, Y., Liu, Z., Li, H., ... Fan, Y. (2017). Self-Powered Pulse Sensor for Antidiastole of Cardiovascular Disease. *Advanced Materials*, *29*(40), 1703456. doi:10.1002/adma.201703456 PMID:28863247

Palazzi, V., Alimenti, F., Kalialakis, C., Mezzanotte, P., Georgiadis, A., & Roselli, L. (2017). Highly Integrable Paper-Based Harmonic Transponder for Low-Power and Long-Range IoT Applications. *IEEE Antennas and Wireless Propagation Letters*, *16*, 3196–3199. doi:10.1109/LAWP.2017.2768383

Pan, Y., Kim, J., & Memik, G. (2010). FlexiShare: Channel sharing for an energy-efficient nanophotonic crossbar. *HPCA - 16 2010 The Sixteenth International Symposium on High-Performance Computer Architecture*, 1–12. 10.1109/HPCA.2010.5416626

Pan, Y., Kumar, P., Kim, J., Memik, G., Zhang, Y., & Choudhary, A. (2009). *Firefly : Illuminating Future Network-on-Chip with Nanophotonics Categories and Subject Descriptors.* Academic Press.

Pandey, B., Farulla, G.A., Indaco, M., Iovino, L., Prinetto, P., (2018). Design and Review of Water Management System Using Ethernet, Wi-Fi 802.11n, Modbus, and Other Communication Standards. *Wireless Personal Communications.*

Pang, Z. (2013). *Technologies and Architectures of the Internet-of-Things (IoT) for Health and Well-being* (PhD thesis). Kista Sweden: KTH Royal Institute of Technology.

Panwar, N., Kaushik, S., & Kothari, S. (2011). Role of renewable energy sources in environmental protection: A review. *Renewable & Sustainable Energy Reviews*, *15*(3), 1513–1524. doi:10.1016/j.rser.2010.11.037

Papastefanakis, E., Maitre, B., & Ragot, D. (2015). Security Challenges in ManyCore Embedded Systems based on Networks-on-Chip (NoCs). *Proceedings of the WESS'15: Workshop on Embedded Systems Security - WESS'15*, 1–6. 10.1145/2818362.2818372

Park, D. Y., Joe, D. J., Kim, D. H., Park, H., Han, J. H., Jeong, C. K., ... Lee, K. J. (2017). Self-Powered Real-Time Arterial Pulse Monitoring Using Ultrathin Epidermal Piezoelectric Sensors. *Advanced Materials*, *29*(37), 1702308. doi:10.1002/adma.201702308 PMID:28714239

Paschke, A. (2005). RBSLA A declarative Rule-based Service Level Agreement Language based on RuleML. In *proceeding of International Conference on Computational Intelligence for Modelling, Control and Automation and International Conference on Intelligent Agents, Web Technologies and Internet Commerce (CIMCA-IAWTIC '06)* (vol. 2, pp. 308-314). 10.1109/CIMCA.2005.1631486

Pasricha, S., & Bahirat, S. (2011). OPAL: A multi-layer hybrid photonic NoC for 3D ICs. *Proceedings of the Asia and South Pacific Design Automation Conference, ASP-DAC*, 345–350. 10.1109/ASPDAC.2011.5722211

Pasricha, S., Chittamuru, S. V. R., Thakkar, I. G., & Bhat, V. (2018). Securing Photonic NoC Architectures from Hardware Trojans. *2018 Twelfth IEEE/ACM International Symposium on Networks-on-Chip (NOCS)*, 1–8. 10.1109/NOCS.2018.8512167

Patel, N. (2017). *Internet of things in healthcare: applications, benefits, and challenges*. Retrieved from Peerbits: https://www.peerbits.com/blog/internet-of-things-healthcare-applications-benefits-and-challenges.html

Patel, M., & Wang, J. (2010). Applications, Challenges, and Prospective in Emerging Body Area Networking Technologies. *IEEE Wireless Communications*, *17*(1), 80–88. doi:10.1109/MWC.2010.5416354

Payak, M. M., & Sharma, R. C. (1985). Maize diseases and approaches to their management in India. *International Journal of Pest Management*, *31*(4), 302–310.

Peh, L.-S., & Jerger, N. E. (2017). On-chip networks (2nd ed.). Morgan and Claypool.

Peralta, G., Iglesias-Urkia, M., Barcelo, M., Gomez, R., Moran, A., & Bilbao, J. (2017, May). Fog computing based efficient IoT scheme for the Industry 4.0. In *2017 IEEE International Workshop of Electronics, Control, Measurement, Signals and their Application to Mechatronics (ECMSM)* (pp. 1-6). IEEE. 10.1109/ECMSM.2017.7945879

Perera, C., Zaslavsky, A., Christen, P., & Georgakopoulos, D. (2012, November). Ca4iot: Context awareness for internet of things. In *2012 IEEE International Conference on Green Computing and Communications* (pp. 775-782). IEEE. 10.1109/GreenCom.2012.128

Petrolo, R., Loscri, V., & Mitton, N. (2017). Towards a smart city based on cloud of things, a survey on the smart city vision and paradigms. *Transactions on Emerging Telecommunications Technologies*, *28*(1), e2931. doi:10.1002/ett.2931

Pu, X., Guo, H., Tang, Q., Chen, J., Feng, L., Liu, G., ... Wang, Z. L. (2018). Rotation sensing and gesture control of a robot joint via triboelectric quantization sensor. *Nano Energy*, *54*, 453–460. doi:10.1016/j.nanoen.2018.10.044

Pu, X., Li, L., Song, H., Du, C., Zhao, Z., Jiang, C., ... Wang, Z. L. (2015). A self-charging power unit by integration of a textile triboelectric nanogenerator and a flexible lithium-ion battery for wearable electronics. *Advanced Materials*, *27*(15), 2472–2478. doi:10.1002/adma.201500311 PMID:25736078

Qiu, Y., & Ma, M. (2018). Secure Group Mobility Support for 6LoWPAN Networks. IEEE Internet of Things Journal, *5*(2), 1131-1141. doi:10.1109/JIOT.2018.2805696

Quinn, J.-A., Munoz, F. M., Gonik, B., Frau, L., Cutland, C., Mallett-Moore, T., ... Buttery, J. (2016). Preterm birth: Case definition & guidelines for data collection, analysis, and presentation of immunisation safety data. *Vaccine*, *34*(49), 6047–6056. doi:10.1016/j.vaccine.2016.03.045 PMID:27743648

Raghunathan, V., Schurgers, C., Park, S., & Srivastava, M. B. (2002). Energy-aware wireless microsensor networks. *IEEE Signal Processing Magazine*, *19*(2), 40–50. doi:10.1109/79.985679

Rahmani, A. M., Gia, T. N., Thanigaivelan, N. K., & Granados, J. (2015). Smart e-Health Gateway: Bringing Intelligence to Internet-of-Things Based. *12th Annual IEEE Consumer Communications and Networking Conference (CCNC)*.

Randy, B. (2013). *Cloudscaling*. Retrieved July 8, 2018, from http://cloudscaling.com/blog/cloud-computing/missing-the-point-on-private-public-and-hybrid-cloud-apis/

Rao, R. (2018). *Internet of Things (IoT) Healthcare Benefits*. Retrieved from The IoT Magazine: https://theiotmagazine.com/internet-of-things-iot-healthcare-benefits-2aae663c5c79

Rao, R. N., & Sridhar, B. (2018, January). IoT based smart crop-field monitoring and automation irrigation system. In *2018 2nd International Conference on Inventive Systems and Control (ICISC)* (pp. 478-483). IEEE. 10.1109/ICISC.2018.8399118

Rawat, P., & Bonnin, J.-M. (2010). Designing a header compression mechanism for efficient use of IP tunneling in wireless networks. *Consumer Communications and Networking Conference (CCN C), 7th IEEE*. 10.1109/CCNC.2010.5421788

Reinbrecht, C., Susin, A., Bossuet, L., & Sepúlveda, J. (2016). Gossip NoC - Avoiding timing side-channel attacks through traffic management. *Proceedings of IEEE Computer Society Annual Symposium on VLSI, ISVLSI, 601*–606. 10.1109/ISVLSI.2016.25

Reinbrecht, C., Susin, A., Bossuet, L., Sigl, G., & Sepúlveda, J. (2017). Timing attack on NoC-based systems: Prime+Probe attack and NoC-based protection. *Microprocessors and Microsystems, 52*, 556–565. doi:10.1016/j.micpro.2016.12.010

Rghioui, A., Bouhorma, M., & Benslimane, A. (2013). Analytical study of security aspects in 6LoWPAN networks. *2013 5th International Conference on Information and Communication Technology for the Muslim World (ICT4M)*, 1-5. 10.1109/ICT4M.2013.6518912

Rhoton, J. (2011). *Cloud Computing Explained* (2nd ed.). Recursive Press.

Richter, F., Fehske, A. J., & Fettweis, G. P. (2009, September). Energy efficiency aspects of base station deployment strategies for cellular networks. In *2009 IEEE 70th Vehicular Technology Conference Fall* (pp. 1-5). IEEE. 10.1109/VETECF.2009.5379031

Riel, A., Kreiner, C., Macher, G., & Messnarz, R. (2017). Integrated design for tackling safety and security challenges of smart products and digital manufacturing. *CIRP Annals, 66*(1), 177–180. doi:10.1016/j.cirp.2017.04.037

Rogers, J. A., Someya, T., & Huang, Y. (2010). Materials and mechanics for stretchable electronics. *Science, 327*(5973), 1603-1607.

Rule Based IT Service Management. (2007). *Rule Based IT Service Level Management*. Retrieved May 10, 2018, from http://ruleml.org/reaction/docs/ColloqiumFredericton2007.pdf

Rumley, S., Bahadori, M., Polster, R., Hammond, S. D., Calhoun, D. M., Wen, K., ... Bergman, K. (2017). Optical interconnects for extreme scale computing systems. *Parallel Computing, 64*, 65–80. doi:10.1016/j.parco.2017.02.001

Saeed, A., Ahmadinia, A., & Just, M. (2016). Secure On-Chip Communication Architecture for Reconfigurable Multi-Core Systems. *Journal of Circuits, Systems, and Computers, 25*(08), 1650089. doi:10.1142/S0218126616500894

Salucci, M., Anselmi, N., Goudos, S., & Massa, A. (2019). Fast design of multiband fractal antennas through a system-by-design approach for NB-IoT applications. Eurasip Journal on Wireless Communications and Networking, 2019(1). doi:10.118613638-019-1386-4

Samaila, M. G., Neto, M., Fernandes, D. A. B., Freire, M. M., & Inácio, P. R. M. (2018). Challenges of securing Internet of Things devices: A survey. *Security and Privacy, 1*(2), e20. doi:10.1002py2.20

Samyde, D. (2002). Side channel cryptanalysis. *Computer*, 179–184.

Saravanakumar, B., Thiyagarajan, K., Alluri, N. R., SoYoon, S., Taehyun, K., Lin, Z.-H., & Kim, S.-J. (2015). Fabrication of an eco-friendly composite nanogenerator for self-powered photosensor applications. *Carbon, 84*, 56–65. doi:10.1016/j. carbon.2014.11.041

Sastra, N. P., & Wiharta, D. M. (2016). Environmental monitoring as an IoT application in building smart campus of Universitas Udayana. *2016 International Conference on Smart Green Technology in Electrical and Information Systems (ICSGTEIS)* 10.1109/ICSGTEIS.2016.7885771

Savola, R. M., Abie, H., & Sihvonen, M. (n.d.). Towards metrics-driven adaptive security management in e-health IoT applications. In *Proceedings of the 7th International Conference on Body Area Networks* (pp. 276-281). ICST (Institute for Computer Sciences, Social-Informatics and Telecommunications Engineering). 10.4108/icst.bodynets.2012.250241

Schroff, F., Kalenichenko, D., & Philbin, J. (2015). FaceNet: A unified embedding for face recognition and clustering. *Proceedings of the IEEE Computer Society Conference on Computer Vision and Pattern Recognition, 815–823*. 10.1109/CVPR.2015.7298682

Seliem, M., & Elgazzar, K. (2018). IoTeWay: A Secure Framework Architecture for 6LoWPAN Based IoT Applications. *2018 IEEE Global Conference on Internet of Things (GCIoT)*, 1-5. 10.1109/GCIoT.2018.8620137

Sengupta, A. (2017). Hardware Vulnerabilities and Their Effects on CE Devices: Design for Security Against Trojans. *IEEE Consumer Electronics Magazine, 6*(3), 126–133. doi:10.1109/MCE.2017.2684940

Sepúlveda, J., Flórez, D., & Gogniat, G. (2016). Efficient and flexible NoC-based group communication for secure MPSoCs. *2015 International Conference on ReConFigurable Computing and FPGAs, ReConFig 2015*. 10.1109/Re-ConFig.2015.7393301

Sepulveda, J., Flórez, D., Immler, V., Gogniat, G., & Sigl, G. (2016). Hierarchical group-key management for NoC-based MPSoCs protection. *Journal of Integrated Circuits and Systems, 11*(1), 38–48.

Sepulveda, J., Flórez, D., Immler, V., Gogniat, G., & Sigl, G. (2017). Efficient security zones implementation through hierarchical group key management at NoC-based MPSoCs. *Microprocessors and Microsystems, 50*, 164–174. doi:10.1016/j. micpro.2017.03.002

Sepulveda, J., Pires, R., Gogniat, G., Chau, W. J., & Strum, M. (2012). QoSS Hierarchical NoC-Based Architecture for MPSoC Dynamic Protection. *International Journal of Reconfigurable Computing, 2012*, 1–10. doi:10.1155/2012/578363

Sepúlveda, M. J., Diguet, J. P., Strum, M., & Gogniat, G. (2015). NoC-Based Protection for SoC Time-Driven Attacks. *IEEE Embedded Systems Letters, 7*(1), 7–10. doi:10.1109/LES.2014.2384744

Shacham, A., Bergman, K., & Carloni, L. P. (2008). Photonic networks-on-chip for future generations of chip multiprocessors. *IEEE Transactions on Computers, 57*(9), 1246–1260. doi:10.1109/TC.2008.78

Shah, M. K., & Sharma, L. K. (2018). Study on 6LoWPAN Routing Protocols with SD aspects in IoT. *2018 2nd International Conference on I-SMAC (IoT in Social, Mobile, Analytics and Cloud) (I-SMAC)I-SMAC (IoT in Social, Mobile, Analytics and Cloud) (I-SMAC), 2018 2nd International Conference on*, 60-65. 10.1109/I-SMAC.2018.8653660

Shamsuddin, S. A. K., Khan, S. A., Ali, A., Rahimoon, A. Q., & Jalalzai, P. (2019). Harvesting Energy of Body Motion Through Single Electrode Based Self-Powered Triboelectric Nanogenerator. *Journal Nanoelectronics and Optoelectronics, 14*(11), 1–9. doi:10.1166/jno.2019.2580

Sharma, N., Kumar, A., Magarini, M., Stefano, B., & Jayakody, D. N. K. (2019, April). Impact of CFO on Low Latency-Enabled UAV using "Better than Nyquist" Pulse Shaping in GFDM. In *2019 IEEE 89th Vehicular Technology Conference (VTC)* (pp. 1-6). IEEE.

Sharma, N., Magarini, M., Dossi, L., Reggiani, L., & Nebuloni, R. (2018, January). A study of channel model parameters for aerial base stations at 2.4 GHz in different environments. In 2018 15th IEEE Annual Consumer Communications & Networking Conference (CCNC) (pp. 1-6). IEEE.

Sharma, N., Magarini, M., Reggiani, L., & Alam, M. (2019, April). Channel Characterization at 2.4 GHz for Aerial Base Station. In *2019 10th International Conference on Ambient Systems, Networks and Technologies (ANT)* (pp. 1-8). Elsevier.

Sharma, V., Sharma, N., & Rehmani, M. H. (2019). *Control over Skies: Survivability, Coverage and Mobility Laws for Hierarchical Aerial Base Stations.* arXiv preprint arXiv:1903.03725.

Sharma, N. (2018). *Increasing capacity of wireless networks through aerial base stations.* Milan, Italy: Politecnico di Milano.

Sharma, N., Magarini, M., Jayakody, D. N. K., Sharma, V., & Li, J. (2018). On-demand ultra-dense cloud drone networks: Opportunities, challenges and benefits. *IEEE Communications Magazine, 56*(8), 85–91. doi:10.1109/MCOM.2018.1701001

Sharma, N., Sharma, V., Magarini, M., Pervaiz, H., Alam, M. M., & Moullec, Y. L. (2019). *Cell Coverage Analysis of a Low Altitude Aerial Base Station in Wind Perturbations. In 2019 IEEE GLOBECOM Workshops (GC Wkshps).* IEEE.

Shelby & Bormann. (2009). *6LoWPAN: The Wireless Embedded Internet.* New York: Wiley.

Sheridan, P. L., Solomont, J., Kowall, N., & Hausdorff, J. M. (2003). Influence of executive function on locomotor function: Divided attention increases gait variability in Alzheimer's disease. *Journal of the American Geriatrics Society, 51*(11), 1633–1637. doi:10.1046/j.1532-5415.2003.51516.x PMID:14687395

Shi, Q., Wang, H., Wang, T., & Lee, C. (2016). Self-powered liquid triboelectric microfluidic sensor for pressure sensing and finger motion monitoring applications. *Nano Energy, 30*, 450–459. doi:10.1016/j.nanoen.2016.10.046

Shirbhate, M. D., & Solapure, S. S. (2018). Improving existing 6LoWPAN RPL for content based routing. *2018 Second International Conference on Computing Methodologies and Communication (ICCMC)*, 632-635. 10.1109/IC-CMC.2018.8487866

Sicari, S., Rizzardi, A., Grieco, L. A., & Coen-Porisini, A. (2015). Security, privacy and trust in Internet of things: The road ahead. *Computer Networks, 76*, 146–164. doi:10.1016/j.comnet.2014.11.008

Simsek, M., Aijaz, A., Dohler, M., Sachs, J., & Fettweis, G. (2016). 5G-enabled tactile internet. *IEEE Journal on Selected Areas in Communications, 34*(3), 460–473. doi:10.1109/JSAC.2016.2525398

Simunek, M., Fontán, F. P., & Pechac, P. (2013). The UAV low elevation propagation channel in urban areas: Statistical analysis and time-series generator. *IEEE Transactions on Antennas and Propagation, 61*(7), 3850–3858. doi:10.1109/TAP.2013.2256098

Singh, B., Bhattacharya, S., Chowdhary, C., & Jat, D. (2017). A review on internet of things and its applications in healthcare. *Journal of Chemical and Pharmaceutical Sciences.*

Singh, D. (2015). Thermal aware internet of things enable energy efficient encoder design for security on FPGA. *International Journal of Security and its Applications, 9*(6), 271-278.

Singh, T., & Singh, T. (2016). Hand Held Device for Detection of Pesticides using NDVI. *International Journal of Computer Applications, 154*(9).

Singh, D., Tiwary, U. S., Lee, H., & Chung, W. (2009). Global healthcare monitoring system using 6lowpan networks. *11th International Conference on Advanced Communication Technology*, 113-117.

Sivia, J. S., & Bhatia, S. S. (2015). Design of fractal based microstrip rectangular patch antenna for multiband applications. Souvenir of the 2015 IEEE International Advance Computing Conference, IACC 2015, 1(151302), 712–715. 10.1109/IADCC.2015.7154799

Smith, T. B. (2004). Electricity theft: A comparative analysis. *Energy Policy*, *32*(18), 2067–2076. doi:10.1016/S0301-4215(03)00182-4

Sodhro, A. H., Li, Y., & Shah, M. A. (2016). Energy-efficient adaptive transmission power control for wireless body area networks. *IET Communications*, *10*(1), 81–90. doi:10.1049/iet-com.2015.0368

Sodhro, A. H., Pirbhulal, S., Luo, Z., & de Albuquerque, V. H. C. (2019). Towards an optimal resource management for IoT based Green and sustainable smart cities. *Journal of Cleaner Production*, *220*, 1167–1179. doi:10.1016/j.jclepro.2019.01.188

Son, S.-B., Gao, T., Harvey, S. P., Steirer, K. X., Stokes, A., Norman, A., ... Ban, C. (2018). An artificial interphase enables reversible magnesium chemistry in carbonate electrolytes. *Nature Chemistry*, *10*(5), 532–539. doi:10.103841557-018-0019-6 PMID:29610460

Sreekanth, K., & Niktha, K. (2016). A Study on Health Care in Internet of Things. *International Journal on Recent and Innovation Trends in Computing and Communication*, *4*(2).

Srinivas, S., Harsha, K. S., Sujatha, A., & Kumar, N. (2013). Efficient protection of palms from RPW Larvae using WSN. *IJCSI*, *10*(3), 2.

Srivastavai, N., Chopra, G., Jain, P., & Khatter, B. (2013). Pest Monitor and Control System Using Wireless Sensor Network (with special reference to acoustic device sensor). *International Conference on Electrical and Electronics Engineering*.

Stevenson, R., Sazegar, M., Bily, A., Johnson, M., & Kundtz, N. (2016). Metamaterial surface antenna technology: Commercialization through diffractive metamaterials and liquid crystal display manufacturing. 2016 10th International Congress on Advanced Electromagnetic Materials in Microwaves and Optics, METAMATERIALS 2016, 349–351. 10.1109/MetaMaterials.2016.7746395

Stojkoska, B. L. R., & Trivodaliev, K. V. (2017). A review of Internet of Things for smart home: Challenges and solutions. *Journal of Cleaner Production*, *140*, 1454–1464. doi:10.1016/j.jclepro.2016.10.006

Stoppa, M., & Chiolerio, A. (2014). Wearable electronics and smart textiles: a critical review. *Sensors*, *14*(7), 11957-11992.

Strong, D. R. (2019). Impacts of diffusion policy: Determinants of early smart meter diffusion in the US electric power industry. *Industrial and Corporate Change*. doi:10.1093/icc/dtz011

Sudheesh, P. G., Sharma, N., Magarini, M., & Muthuchidambaranathan, P. (2018). Effect of imperfect CSI on interference alignment in multiple-High Altitude Platforms based communication. *Physical Communication*, *29*, 336–342. doi:10.1016/j.phycom.2017.11.002

Sukanya. (2015). *Internet of things world, Europe*. Retrieved from opentechdiary: https://opentechdiary.wordpress.com/tag/internet-of-things/

Sukayna Mandal. (2016). *Internet of Things (IoT) - Part 4 (Network Protocols and Architecture)*. Retrieved from: https://www.c-sharpcorner.com/UploadFile/f88748/internet-of-thingsiot-part-4-network-protocols-and-arc/

Sulyman, A. I., Oteafy, S. M., & Hassanein, H. S. (2017). Expanding the cellular-IoT umbrella: An architectural approach. *IEEE Wireless Communications*, *24*(3), 66–71. doi:10.1109/MWC.2017.1600433

Suma, N., Samson, S. R., Saranya, S., Shanmugapriya, G., & Subhashri, R. (2017). IOT based smart agriculture monitoring system. *International Journal on Recent and Innovation Trends in Computing and Communication, 5*(2), 177-181.

Sun, S., Rappaport, T. S., Rangan, S., Thomas, T. A., Ghosh, A., Kovacs, I. Z., . . . Jarvelainen, J. (2016, May). Propagation path loss models for 5G urban micro-and macro-cellular scenarios. In *2016 IEEE 83rd Vehicular Technology Conference (VTC Spring)* (pp. 1-6). IEEE.

Surai, S., Kundu, R., Ghosh, R., & Bid, G. (2018). An IoT Based Smart Agriculture System with Soil Moisture Sensor. *Journal of Innovation and Research, 1*(1).

Swain, K. C., & Zaman, Q. U. (2012). Rice crop monitoring with unmanned helicopter remote sensing images. *Remote Snsing of Biomass-Principles and Applications*, 254-272.

Swetina, J., Lu, G., Jacobs, P., Ennesser, F., & Song, J. (2014). Toward a standardized common M2M service layer platform: Introduction to oneM2M. *IEEE Wireless Communications, 21*(3), 20–26. doi:10.1109/MWC.2014.6845045

Systems, O., & Kocher, P. C. (1996). Timing Attacks on Implement at ions of. *Advances*, 104–113.

Szymanski, T. H. (2016). Securing the Industrial-Tactile Internet of Things with Deterministic Silicon Photonics Switches. *IEEE Access: Practical Innovations, Open Solutions, 4*, 8236–8249. doi:10.1109/ACCESS.2016.2613512

Talari, S., Shafie-Khah, M., Siano, P., Loia, V., Tommasetti, A., & Catalão, J. (2017). A review of smart cities based on the internet of things concept. *Energies, 10*(4), 421. doi:10.3390/en10040421

Tanaka, Y., Minet, P., & Watteyne, T. (2019). 6LoWPAN Fragment Forwarding. IEEE Communications Standards Magazine, 3(1), 35-39. doi:10.1109/MCOMSTD.2019.1800029

Tang, W., Meng, B., & Zhang, H. (2013). Investigation of power generation based on stacked triboelectric nanogenerator. *Nano Energy, 2*(6), 1164–1171. doi:10.1016/j.nanoen.2013.04.009

Tang, Y., Zhang, Y., Li, W., Ma, B., & Chen, X. (2015). Rational material design for ultrafast rechargeable lithium-ion batteries. *Chemical Society Reviews, 44*(17), 5926–5940. doi:10.1039/C4CS00442F PMID:25857819

Tan, W., Gu, H., Yang, Y., Wang, K., & Wang, X. (2017). Venus: A Low-Latency, Low-Loss 3-D Hybrid Network-on-Chip for Kilocore Systems. *Journal of Lightwave Technology, 35*(24), 5448–5455. doi:10.1109/JLT.2017.2764956

Tan, X., Yang, M., Zhang, L., Wang, X., & Jiang, Y. (2014). A hybrid optoelectronic networks-on-chip architecture. *Journal of Lightwave Technology, 32*(5), 991–998. doi:10.1109/JLT.2013.2296145

Tan, Y. K. (2013). *Energy harvesting autonomous sensor systems: design, analysis, and practical implementation.* CRC Press.

Tehranipoor, M., & Koushanfar, F. (2010). A survey of hardware trojan taxonomy and detection. *IEEE Design & Test of Computers, 27*(1), 10–25. doi:10.1109/MDT.2010.7

The History of Healthcare Technology and the Evolution of EHR. (2019). Retrieved from vertitechit: https://www.vertitechit.com/history-healthcare-technology/

The Internet of Things. (2005). ITU Internet Reports.

The many faces of IoT in Healthcare. (2014). Retrieved from: http://www.slideshare.net/stockerpartnership/the-many-faces-of-internet-of-things-iot-in-healthcare/11

Theoleyre, F., & Pang, A. C. (Eds.). (2013). *Internet of Things and M2M Communications.* River Publishers.

Touati, F., Mnaouer, A. B., & Tabsih, R. (2013). Towards u-Health: An indoor 6LoWPAN Based Platform for Real-Time Healthcare Monitoring. *Conference: Wireless and Mobile Networking Conference (WMNC), 6th Joint IFIP.*

Trappey, A. J., Trappey, C. V., Govindarajan, U. H., Chuang, A. C., & Sun, J. J. (2017). A review of essential standards and patent landscapes for the Internet of Things: A key enabler for Industry 4.0. *Advanced Engineering Informatics, 33,* 208–229. doi:10.1016/j.aei.2016.11.007

Tripathy, M. R., Ranjan, P., Kumar, A., & Kumar, S. (2015). A compact dual band antenna for IOV applications. *Lecture Notes in Computer Science, 9502,* 315–323. doi:10.1007/978-3-319-27293-1_28

Tsibas, H., Giokas, K., & Koutsouris, D. (2010). "Internet of Things", an RFID - IPv6 Scenario in a Healthcare Environment. In *XII Mediterranean Conference on Medical and Biological Engineering and Computing,* (pp. 808-811). Academic Press.

Tsukada, M., Washio, T., & Motoda, H. (2001). Automatic web-page classification by using machine learning methods. *Asia-Pacific Conference on Web Intelligence Springer,* 303-313. 10.1007/3-540-45490-X_36

Tu, X., Song, C., Huang, T., Chen, Z., & Fu, H. (2019). State of the art and perspectives on silicon photonic switches. *Micromachines, 10*(1), 51. doi:10.3390/mi10010051 PMID:30642100

Ubiquitous Sensor Networks (USN). (2008). ITU-T Technology Watch Briefing Report Series, No. 4.

Ukil, A., Bandyoapdhyay, S., Puri, C., & Pal, A. (2016). IoT healthcare analytics: The importance of anomaly detection. In *2016 IEEE 30th International Conference on Advanced Information Networking and Applications (AINA)* (pp. 994-997). IEEE. 10.1109/AINA.2016.158

Ullah, S., Higgins, H., Braem, B., Latré, B., Blondia, C., Moerman, I., ... Kwak, K. S. (2012). A Comprehensive Survey of Wireless Body Area Networks on PHY, MAC, and Network Layers Solutions. *Journal of Medical Systems, 36*(3), 1065–1094. doi:10.100710916-010-9571-3 PMID:20721685

Usova, M. A., & Velkin, V. I. (2018). Possibility to use renewable energy sources for increasing the reliability of the responsible energy consumers on the enterprise. *2018 17th International Ural Conference on AC Electric Drives (ACED).*

Vantrease, D., Schreiber, R., Monchiero, M., Mclaren, M., Jouppi, N. P., Fiorentino, M., ... Ahn, J. H. (2008). Corona: System implications of emerging nanophotonic technology. *Proceedings - International Symposium on Computer Architecture,* 153–164. 10.1109/ISCA.2008.35

Vasseur, J., & Dunkels, A. (2010). *Interconnecting Smart Objects with IP - The Next Internet.* Morgan Kaufmann.

Vassilaras, S., Gkatzikis, L., Liakopoulos, N., Stiakogiannakis, I. N., Qi, M., Shi, L., & Paschos, G. S. (2017). The algorithmic aspects of network slicing. *IEEE Communications Magazine, 55*(8), 112–119. doi:10.1109/MCOM.2017.1600939

Vattapparamban, E., Güvenç, İ., Yurekli, A. İ., Akkaya, K., & Uluağaç, S. (2016, September). Drones for smart cities: Issues in cybersecurity, privacy, and public safety. In *2016 International Wireless Communications and Mobile Computing Conference (IWCMC)* (pp. 216-221). IEEE. 10.1109/IWCMC.2016.7577060

Verlaine, B., Dubois, Y., Jureta, I., & Faulkner, S. (2010). Towards automated alignment of Web Services to requirements. *2010 First International Workshop on the Web and Requirements Engineering (WeRE),* 5-12. 10.1109/WERE.2010.5623996

Vermesan, O., & Fries, P. (2013). *Internet of Things - Converging Technologies for Smart Environments and Integrated Ecosystems.* River Publishers.

Vineel, S., Chittamuru, R., Thakkar, I. G., Bhat, V., & Pasricha, S. (2018). SOTERIA: Exploiting Process Variations to Enhance Hardware Security with Photonic NoC Architectures. *2018 55th ACM/ESDA/IEEE Design Automation Conference (DAC)*, 1–6. 10.1145/3195970.3196118

Vinoski, S. (2006). Advanced message queuing protocol. *IEEE Internet Computing*, *10*(6), 87–89. doi:10.1109/MIC.2006.116

Vohra, S., & Srivastava, R. (2015). A Survey on Techniques for Securing 6LoWPAN. *2015 Fifth International Conference on Communication Systems and Network Technologies*, 643-647. 10.1109/CSNT.2015.163

Wahlster, W. (2012). From industry 1.0 to industry 4.0: Towards the 4th industrial revolution. *Forum Business Meets Research*.

Wang, Q., Hempstead, M., & Yang, W. (2006). *A realistic power consumption model for wireless sensor network devices*. Paper presented at the 2006 3rd annual IEEE communications society on sensor and ad hoc communications and networks. 10.1109/SAHCN.2006.288433

Wang, J., Li, X., Zi, Y., Wang, S., Li, Z., Zheng, L., ... Wang, Z. L. (2015). A Flexible Fiber-Based Supercapacitor–Triboelectric-Nanogenerator Power System for Wearable Electronics. *Advanced Materials*, *27*(33), 4830–4836. doi:10.1002/adma.201501934 PMID:26175123

Wang, M., Jiang, C., Zhang, S., Song, X., Tang, Y., & Cheng, H.-M. (2018). Reversible calcium alloying enables a practical room-temperature rechargeable calcium-ion battery with a high discharge voltage. *Nature Chemistry*, *10*(6), 667–672. doi:10.103841557-018-0045-4 PMID:29686378

Wang, S., Lin, L., & Wang, Z. L. (2012). Nanoscale triboelectric-effect-enabled energy conversion for sustainably powering portable electronics. *Nano Letters*, *12*(12), 6339–6346. doi:10.1021/nl303573d PMID:23130843

Wang, S., Lin, L., & Wang, Z. L. (2015). Triboelectric nanogenerators as self-powered active sensors. *Nano Energy*, *11*, 436–462. doi:10.1016/j.nanoen.2014.10.034

Wang, S., Lin, Z.-H., Niu, S., Lin, L., Xie, Y., Pradel, K. C., & Wang, Z. L. (2013). Motion charged battery as sustainable flexible-power-unit. *ACS Nano*, *7*(12), 11263–11271. doi:10.1021/nn4050408 PMID:24266595

Wang, S., Niu, S., Yang, J., Lin, L., & Wang, Z. L. (2014). Quantitative measurements of vibration amplitude using a contact-mode freestanding triboelectric nanogenerator. *ACS Nano*, *8*(12), 12004–12013. doi:10.1021/nn5054365 PMID:25386799

Wang, S., Wan, J., Zhang, D., Li, D., & Zhang, C. (2016). Towards smart factory for industry 4.0: A self-organized multi-agent system with big data based feedback and coordination. *Computer Networks*, *101*, 158–168. doi:10.1016/j.comnet.2015.12.017

Wang, S., Xie, Y., Niu, S., Lin, L., & Wang, Z. L. (2014). Freestanding triboelectric-layer-based nanogenerators for harvesting energy from a moving object or human motion in contact and non-contact modes. *Advanced Materials*, *26*(18), 2818–2824. doi:10.1002/adma.201305303 PMID:24449058

Wang, X., Gu, H., Yang, Y., Wang, K., & Hao, Q. (2016). A Highly Scalable Optical Network-on-Chip with Small Network Diameter and Deadlock Freedom. *IEEE Transactions on Very Large Scale Integration (VLSI) Systems*, *24*(12), 3424–3436. doi:10.1109/TVLSI.2016.2561299

Wang, Z. L. (2013). Triboelectric nanogenerators as new energy technology for self-powered systems and as active mechanical and chemical sensors. *ACS Nano*, *7*(11), 9533–9557. doi:10.1021/nn404614z PMID:24079963

Wang, Z. L., Jiang, T., & Xu, L. (2017). Toward the blue energy dream by triboelectric nanogenerator networks. *Nano Energy*, *39*, 9–23. doi:10.1016/j.nanoen.2017.06.035

Wang, Z. L., Zhu, G., Yang, Y., Wang, S., & Pan, C. (2012). Progress in nanogenerators for portable electronics. *Materials Today*, *15*(12), 532–543. doi:10.1016/S1369-7021(13)70011-7

Weissberger, A. (2014). *TiECon 2014 Summary-Part 1: Qualcomm Keynote & IoT Track Overview*. IEEE ComSoc.

Wen, Z., Yeh, M.-H., Guo, H., Wang, J., Zi, Y., Xu, W., ... Hu, C. (2016). Self-powered textile for wearable electronics by hybridizing fiber-shaped nanogenerators, solar cells, and supercapacitors. *Science Advances*, *2*(10), e1600097. doi:10.1126ciadv.1600097 PMID:27819039

Werfelli, H., Tayari, K., Chaoui, M., Lahiani, M., & Ghariani, H. (2016). Design of rectangular microstrip patch antenna. *2nd International Conference on Advanced Technologies for Signal and Image Processing, ATSIP 2016*, 798–803. doi:10.1109/ATSIP.2016.7523197

Werner, S., Navaridas, J., & Lujan, M. (2017). Designing Low-Power, Low-Latency Networks-on-Chip by Optimally Combining Electrical and Optical Links. *Proceedings - International Symposium on High-Performance Computer Architecture*, 265–276. 10.1109/HPCA.2017.23

Werner, S., Navaridas, J., & Lujn, M. (2015). Amon: An Advanced Mesh-like Optical NoC. *Proceedings - 2015 IEEE 23rd Annual Symposium on High-Performance Interconnects, HOTI 2015*, 52–59. doi:10.1109/HOTI.2015.18

Werner, S., Navaridas, J., & An, M. L. (2017). A Survey on Optical Network-on-Chip Architectures. *ACM Computing Surveys*, *50*(6), 1–37. doi:10.1145/3131346

Werner, S., Navaridas, J., & Luján, M. (2016). A Survey on Design Approaches to Circumvent Permanent Faults in Networks-on-Chip. *ACM Computing Surveys*, *48*(4), 1–36. doi:10.1145/2886781

Willink, T. J., Squires, C. C., Colman, G. W., & Muccio, M. T. (2016). Measurement and characterization of low-altitude air-to-ground MIMO channels. *IEEE Transactions on Vehicular Technology*, *65*(4), 2637–2648. doi:10.1109/TVT.2015.2419738

Wollschlaeger, M., Sauter, T., & Jasperneite, J. (2017). The future of industrial communication: Automation networks in the era of the internet of things and industry 4.0. *IEEE Industrial Electronics Magazine*, *11*(1), 17–27. doi:10.1109/MIE.2017.2649104

Wu, M., & Huang, W. (2012). WSN-based Health Care Management Platform for Long-Term Care Institutions. *J. Converg. Inform. Technol.*, *7*(7).

Wu, X., Xu, J., Ye, Y., Wang, Z., Nikdast, M., & Wang, X. (2014). SUOR: Sectioned Undirectional Optical Ring for Chip Multiprocessor. *J. Emerg. Technol. Comput. Syst.*, *10*(4), 29:1–29:25. doi:10.1145/2600072

Wu, Z., Kumar, H., & Davari, A. (2005, March). Performance evaluation of OFDM transmission in UAV wireless communication. In *Proceedings of the Thirty-Seventh Southeastern Symposium on System Theory, 2005. SSST'05.*(pp. 6-10). IEEE.

Xiaojun, Y., Weirui, W., & Jianping, L. (2012). Application mode construction of internet of things (IOT) for facility agriculture in Beijing. *Nongye Gongcheng Xuebao (Beijing)*, *4*, 1–14.

Xie, Y., Wang, S., Niu, S., Lin, L., Jing, Q., Yang, J., ... Wang, Z. L. (2014). Grating-structured freestanding triboelectric-layer nanogenerator for harvesting mechanical energy at 85% total conversion efficiency. *Advanced Materials*, *26*(38), 6599–6607. doi:10.1002/adma.201402428 PMID:25156128

Yahya, M. R. (2018). Review of Photonic and Hybrid On Chip Interconnects for MPSoCs in IoT Paradigm. *2018 21st Saudi Computer Society National Computer Conference (NCC)*, 1–6. 10.1109/NCG.2018.8593055

Yahya, M. R., Wu, N., Ali, Z. A., & Khizar, Y. (2019). Optical Versus Electrical: Performance Evaluation of Network On-Chip Topologies for UWASN Manycore Processors. *Wireless Personal Communications*. doi:10.100711277-019-06630-5

Yahya, M. R., Wu, N., Gaizhen, Y., & Ahmed, T., Yasir, & Zhang, J. (2019). An Algorithmic Framework to Construct Optical Switch via Scaling from N-to-2N Ports for Optical Network on Chip. *IEEE Access: Practical Innovations, Open Solutions*, 1–1. doi:10.1109/ACCESS.2019.2930754

Yan, F., & Gao, J. (2017). Reliable NoC design with low latency and power consumption. *Electronics Letters*, *53*(6), 382–383. doi:10.1049/el.2016.4665

Yang, C., Li, J., Ni, Q., Anpalagan, A., & Guizani, M. (2017). Interference-aware energy efficiency maximization in 5G ultra-dense networks. *IEEE Transactions on Communications*, *65*(2), 728–739. doi:10.1109/TCOMM.2016.2638906

Yang, F., Wang, S., Li, J., Liu, Z., & Sun, Q. (2014). An overview of internet of vehicles. *China Communications*, *11*(10), 1–15. doi:10.1109/CC.2014.6969789

Yang, J., Chen, J., Su, Y., Jing, Q., Li, Z., Yi, F., ... Wang, Z. L. (2015). Eardrum-inspired active sensors for self-powered cardiovascular system characterization and throat-attached anti-interference voice recognition. *Advanced Materials*, *27*(8), 1316–1326. doi:10.1002/adma.201404794 PMID:25640534

Yang, Y., Ding, X., Zhu, J., & Bai, Y. (2010). Assumption of internet of things applied in electric vehicle charging facilities. *Dianli Xitong Zidonghua*, *34*(21), 95–98.

Yang, Y., Zhang, H., Chen, J., Jing, Q., Zhou, Y. S., Wen, X., & Wang, Z. L. (2013). Single-electrode-based sliding triboelectric nanogenerator for self-powered displacement vector sensor system. *ACS Nano*, *7*(8), 7342–7351. doi:10.1021/nn403021m PMID:23883397

Yang, Y., Zhou, Y. S., Zhang, H., Liu, Y., Lee, S., & Wang, Z. L. (2013). A single-electrode based triboelectric nanogenerator as self-powered tracking system. *Advanced Materials*, *25*(45), 6594–6601. doi:10.1002/adma.201302453 PMID:24166972

Yanmaz, E., Kuschnig, R., & Bettstetter, C. (2011, December). Channel measurements over 802.11 a-based UAV-to-ground links. In 2011 IEEE GLOBECOM Workshops (GC Wkshps) (pp. 1280-1284). IEEE.

Yarom, Y., & Falkner, K. (2014). FLUSH+RELOAD: A High Resolution, Low Noise, L3 Cache Side-Channel Attack. *Proceedings of the 23rd USENIX Security Symposium*, 719–732. Retrieved from https://www.usenix.org/conference/usenixsecurity14/technical-sessions/presentation/yarom

Ye, Y., Xu, J., Huang, B., Wu, X., Zhang, W., Wang, X., ... Wang, Z. (2013). 3-D mesh-based optical network-on-chip for multiprocessor system-on-chip. *IEEE Transactions on Computer-Aided Design of Integrated Circuits and Systems*, *32*(4), 584–596. doi:10.1109/TCAD.2012.2228739

Ye, Y., Xu, J., Wu, X., Zhang, W., Liu, W., & Nikdast, M. (2012). A Torus-Based Hierarchical Optical-Electronic Network-on-Chip for Multiprocessor System-on-Chip. *ACM Journal on Emerging Technologies in Computing Systems*, *8*(1), 1–26. doi:10.1145/2093145.2093150

Yi, F., Lin, L., Niu, S., Yang, P. K., Wang, Z., Chen, J., ... Liao, Q. (2015). Stretchable-rubber-based triboelectric nanogenerator and its application as self-powered body motion sensors. *Advanced Functional Materials*, *25*(24), 3688–3696. doi:10.1002/adfm.201500428

Yi, F., Wang, J., Wang, X., Niu, S., Li, S., Liao, Q., ... Wang, Z. L. (2016). Stretchable and waterproof self-charging power system for harvesting energy from diverse deformation and powering wearable electronics. *ACS Nano, 10*(7), 6519–6525. doi:10.1021/acsnano.6b03007 PMID:27351212

Yousaf, H., Zafar, M. I., Anjum, F., & Adil, S. A. (2018). Food security status and its determinants: A case of farmer and non-farmer rural households of the Punjab, Pakistan. *Pakistan Journal of Agricultural Sciences, 55*(1), 217–225. doi:10.21162/PAKJAS/18.6766

Yue, Y., Yang, Z., Liu, N., Liu, W., Zhang, H., Ma, Y., ... Long, F. (2016). A flexible integrated system containing a microsupercapacitor, a photodetector, and a wireless charging coil. *ACS Nano, 10*(12), 11249–11257. doi:10.1021/acsnano.6b06326 PMID:28024378

Zanella, A., Bui, N., Castellani, A., Vangelista, L., & Zorzi, M. (2014). Internet of things for smart cities. *IEEE Internet of Things Journal, 1*(1), 22-32.

Zhang, K. (2019). *Countries adopting a new high-tech approach to aging care.* Retrieved from China Daily: http://www.chinadaily.com.cn/a/201905/21/WS5ce35403a3104842260bcd21.html

Zhang, G., Li, Z., Zhang, B., & Halang, W. A. (2018). Power electronics converters: Past, present and future. *Renewable & Sustainable Energy Reviews, 81*, 2028–2044. doi:10.1016/j.rser.2017.05.290

Zhang, K., Wang, S., & Yang, Y. (2017). A One-Structure-Based Piezo-Tribo-Pyro-Photoelectric Effects Coupled Nanogenerator for Simultaneously Scavenging Mechanical, Thermal, and Solar Energies. *Advanced Energy Materials, 7*(6), 1601852. doi:10.1002/aenm.201601852

Zhang, L., Wang, X., Jiang, Y., Yang, M., Mak, T., & Singh, A. K. (2018). Effectiveness of HT-assisted sinkhole and blackhole denial of service attacks targeting mesh networks-on-chip. *Journal of Systems Architecture, 89*(July), 84–94. doi:10.1016/j.sysarc.2018.07.005

Zhang, N., & Taylor, R. K. (2001). Applications of a field–level geographic information system (fis) in precision agriculture. *Applied Engineering in Agriculture, 17*(6), 885. doi:10.13031/2013.6829

Zhang, S., Speight, D., Paraskevopoulos, A., Fonseca, D., Luxey, C., Whittow, W., & Pinto, J. (2015). On-body measurements of embroidered spiral antenna. *2015 Loughborough Antennas and Propagation Conference*, 1–5. doi:10.1109/LAPC.2015.7366131

Zhang, X. Y., Wong, H., Mo, T., & Cao, Y. F. (2017). Dual-Band Dual-Mode Button Antenna for On-Body and Off-Body Communications. [PubMed]. *IEEE Transactions on Biomedical Circuits and Systems, 11*(4), 933–941. doi:10.1109/TBCAS.2017.2679048

Zhang, X., Du, X., Yin, Y., Li, N.-W., Fan, W., Cao, R., ... Li, C. (2018). Lithium-Ion Batteries: Charged by Triboelectric Nanogenerators with Pulsed Output Based on the Enhanced Cycling Stability. *ACS Applied Materials & Interfaces, 10*(10), 8676–8684. doi:10.1021/acsami.7b18736 PMID:29446611

Zhang, X.-S., Han, M., Kim, B., Bao, J.-F., Brugger, J., & Zhang, H. (2018). All-in-one self-powered flexible microsystems based on triboelectric nanogenerators. *Nano Energy, 47*, 410–426. doi:10.1016/j.nanoen.2018.02.046

Zhao, H., Wang, H., Wu, W., & Wei, J. (2018). Deployment algorithms for uav airborne networks toward on-demand coverage. *IEEE Journal on Selected Areas in Communications, 36*(9), 2015–2031. doi:10.1109/JSAC.2018.2864376

Zhao, J., Han, S., Yang, Y., Fu, R., Ming, Y., Lu, C., ... Chen, W. (2017). Passive and Space-Discriminative Ionic Sensors Based on Durable Nanocomposite Electrodes toward Sign Language Recognition. *ACS Nano, 11*(9), 8590–8599. doi:10.1021/acsnano.7b02767 PMID:28759198

Zhao, K., Yang, Y., Liu, X., & Wang, Z. L. (2017). Triboelectrification-Enabled Self-Charging Lithium-Ion Batteries. *Advanced Energy Materials*, 7(21), 1700103. doi:10.1002/aenm.201700103

Zheng, Q., Shi, B., Li, Z., & Wang, Z. L. (2017). Recent progress on piezoelectric and triboelectric energy harvesters in biomedical systems. *Advancement of Science*, 4(7), 1700029. PMID:28725529

Zhong, J., Zhong, Q., Fan, F., Zhang, Y., Wang, S., Hu, B., ... Zhou, J. (2013). Finger typing driven triboelectric nanogenerator and its use for instantaneously lighting up LEDs. *Nano Energy*, 2(4), 491–497. doi:10.1016/j.nanoen.2012.11.015

Zhou, B., Li, W., Chan, K. W., Cao, Y., Kuang, Y., Liu, X., & Wang, X. (2016). Smart home energy management systems: Concept, configurations, and scheduling strategies. *Renewable & Sustainable Energy Reviews*, 61, 30–40. doi:10.1016/j.rser.2016.03.047

Zhou, Y. S., Liu, Y., Zhu, G., Lin, Z.-H., Pan, C., Jing, Q., & Wang, Z. L. (2013). In situ quantitative study of nanoscale triboelectrification and patterning. *Nano Letters*, 13(6), 2771–2776. doi:10.1021/nl401006x PMID:23627668

Zhu, G., Chen, J., Liu, Y., Bai, P., Zhou, Y. S., Jing, Q., ... Wang, Z. L. (2013). Linear-grating triboelectric generator based on sliding electrification. *Nano Letters*, 13(5), 2282–2289. doi:10.1021/nl4008985 PMID:23577639

Zhu, G., Chen, J., Zhang, T., Jing, Q., & Wang, Z. L. (2014). Radial-arrayed rotary electrification for high performance triboelectric generator. *Nature Communications*, 5(1), 3426. doi:10.1038/ncomms4426 PMID:24594501

Zhu, G., Pan, C., Guo, W., Chen, C.-Y., Zhou, Y., Yu, R., & Wang, Z. L. (2012). Triboelectric-generator-driven pulse electrodeposition for micropatterning. *Nano Letters*, 12(9), 4960–4965. doi:10.1021/nl302560k PMID:22889363

Zi, Y., Niu, S., Wang, J., Wen, Z., Tang, W., & Wang, Z. L. (2015). Standards and figure-of-merits for quantifying the performance of triboelectric nanogenerators. *Nature Communications*, 6(1), 8376. doi:10.1038/ncomms9376 PMID:26406279

About the Contributors

Faisal K. Shaikh is currently working as professor at Department of Telecommunication, Mehran UET, Pakistan. He did his PhD from TU Darmstadt, Germany and Post Doc from University of Umm Al-Qura, Saudi Arabia. He served as Technical Program Committee (TPC) chair and TPC member for several International conferences. His research interests include dependable WSNs, MANETs, VANETs, WBANs and IoT.

Naeem Ahmed Mahoto received Master degree in Computer Engineering from Mehran University of Engineering and Technology, Pakistan and Ph.D in Information and System Engineering from Politecnico di Torino, Italy in 2013. He is currently working as Associate Professor/ Head of Department Software Engineering, Mehran UET Pakistan. His research interests are focused in the field of data mining and bioinformatics. His research activities are also devoted to machine learning, data science, data visualization and educational data mining. He is member of IEEE Computer society and Pakistan Engineering Council (PEC).

* * *

Azrina Abd Aziz is a senior lecturer at the Department of Electrical and Electronic Engineering of Universiti Teknologi PETRONAS (UTP), Malaysia. She is a member of SMART research group at UTP, a member of IEEE and a member of Board of Engineers Malaysia (BEM). Azrina received her Bachelor Degree in Electrical and Electronic Engineering (Hons) from University of Queensland, Australia in 1997 and her MSc. in System Level Integration from the Institute for System Level Integration (ISLI), Scotland in 2003. She then completed her Ph.D. in Electrical and Computer Systems Engineering at Monash University, Melbourne, Australia in 2013. Her recent research interests focus on energy-efficient techniques for topology control in wireless sensor networks (WSNs), wireless body area networks (WBANs) for biomedical applications and medical imaging and also Deep Learning.

Ahsanullah Abro is working as assistant professor in the department of computer science Sukkut IBA University. He got his basic education from Pakistan and PhD degree from UTP Malaysia. He has more than 10 years of teaching experience.

Muhammad Mahtab Alam received M.Sc. degree in electrical engineering from Aalborg University, Denmark, in 2007, and Ph.D. degree from the University of Rennes1 (INRIA Research Center) in 2013, He did his postdoc research in the Qatar Foundation funded project Critical and Rescue Operations using Wearable Wireless Sensor Networks from Qatar Mobility Innovations Center during 2014-2016. In 2016, he has been elected as European Research Area Chair holder in cognitive electronics project and Associate Professor in Thomas Johann Seebeck Department of Electronics, Tallinn University of Technology. In 2018, he has obtained tenure professorship to chair Telia Professorship under the cooperation framework between Telia and Tallinn University of Technology. He has authored and co-authored over 55 research publications. His research interests include self-organized and self-adaptive wireless sensor and body area networks specific to energy efficient communication protocols and accurate energy modeling, Internet-of-things, public safety and critical networks, embedded systems, digital signal processing, and software defined radio. He is a principal investigator of NATO-SPS-G5482 grant as well as Estonian Research Council PUT-Team Grant.

Zain Anwar Ali received B.S. degree in Electronic Engineering from Sir Syed University of Engineering and Technology, Karachi, Pakistan in 2010, Masters in Industrial Control's & Automation from Hamdard University, Karachi, Pakistan in 2012 and Ph.D. in Control Theory and Control Engineering from Nanjing University of Aeronautics and Astronautics, Nanjing, China in 2017. Currently, he is working as Assistant Professor in the Electronic Engineering Department Sir Syed University of Engineering and Technology.

Ahmed Ali has around eight years of diverse experience in academia, industry, and research. In year 2010, he. completed bachelor of engineering (B.E) degree from Mehran university of engineering and technology Jamshoro in electronic engineering. In 2012, he awarded prestigious Higher Education Commission (HEC) Pakistan fully funded HRDI- UET/USTPs scheme scholarship, for MS leading to PhD studies from Hanyang University, South Korea. Presently he is working as assistant professor at Sukkur IBA University.

Adeel Ansari received the PhD degree in Information Technology from the Universiti Teknologi PETRONAS, Malaysia in 2017 and the MPhil. & MBA Degrees in Software Engineering and MIS in 2011 and 2008 from Pakistan Air Force - Karachi Institute of Economics & Technology (PAF-KIET). He did his BSc (Hons) in Computing with a First Class Honors from Staffordshire University, United Kingdom in 2006. He has worked in multinational companies like Siemens, and at PWC. A. F. Ferguson & Co., as Assoc. Consultant. IT. He taught at UTP while doing his PhD. Currently, he is Assistant Professor at the Shaheed Zulfiqar Ali Bhutto Institute of Science and Technology-Karachi, in the Computer Science department. His area of research are software & web development, information systems, algorithm, expert systems, artificial intelligence and data sciences.

Seema Ansari earned her Ph.D. in Telecommunication Engineering at the University of Malaga, Spain in September 2018. Before this she did her MS-CS/Telecommunication from University of Missouri Kansas City, USA and B.E. in Electronics from NED-UET Karachi, Pakistan. Currently, she is the Dean of College of Engineering and Sciences at the Institute of Business Management. Her PhD research includes three publications in JCR Journals with Impact Factor 1.200. She also contributed in international journals & Conferences and book chapters. She contributed chapters in books titled: ''Wireless Sensor Networks and Energy Efficiency: Protocols, Routing and Management'' and ''Handbook of Research on Trends and Future Directions in Big Data and Web Intelligence,'' both published by IGI GLOBAL, USA in Jan. 2011 and 2015 respectively. She is associated with the research group, ETSI

Telecommunication, University of Malaga Spain. Her research area is Underwater Communications, Analysis of MAC strategies for Underwater Acoustic Wireless Sensor Networks. Her ORCID is: 0000-0002-0108-7481, and the link to the ORCID page: https://orcid.org/0000-0002-0108-7481.

Tahniyat Aslam holds M.E Degree in "Telecommunication Engineering" from NED University of Engineering and Technology. She has done B.S in "Telecommunication Engineering" from Sir Syed University of Engineering and Technology. She has worked as a Visiting Teacher in NED University of Engineering and Technology. Currently, she is working as a Junior Lecturer in Electrical Engineering Department at Institute of Business Management. Her area of interest is Antenna and Microwave Systems and Network Security.

Lubna Luxmi Dhirani is currently pursuing her PhD in Hybrid Cloud Computing from the University of Limerick. She has done MSc in Business Information Technology from Southampton Solent University, UK. Lubna has worked as a lecturer for 3 years and taught various IT-based courses at SZABIST, United Arab Emirates Campus and ISRA University, Pakistan. She did her Bachelors in Computer Systems Engineering from Mehran University of Engineering & Technology, Pakistan.

Micheal Drieberg received the B.Eng. degree from Universiti Sains Malaysia, Penang, Malaysia, in 2001, the M.Sc. degree from Universiti Teknologi PETRONAS, Seri Iskandar, Malaysia, in 2005, and the Ph.D. degree from Victoria University, Melbourne, Australia, in 2011, all in electrical and electronics engineering. He is currently a Senior Lecturer with the Department of Electrical and Electronics Engineering, Universiti Teknologi PETRONAS. His research interests include radio resource management, medium access control protocols, energy harvesting communications, and performance analysis for wireless and sensor networks. Dr. Drieberg has published and served as a reviewer for several high impact journals and flagship conferences. He has also made several contributions to the wireless broadband standards group.

Syed Ali Hassan received his Ph.D. in Electrical Engineering from Georgia Institute of Technology, Atlanta, USA in 2011. He received his MS Mathematics from Georgia Tech in 2011 and MS Electrical Engineering from University of Stuttgart, Germany, in 2007. He was awarded BE Electrical Engineering (highest honors) from National University of Sciences and Technology (NUST), Pakistan, in 2004. His broader area of research is signal processing for communications. Currently, he is working as an Associate Professor at the School of Electrical Engineering and Computer Science (SEECS), NUST, where he is heading the IPT research group, which focuses on various aspects of theoretical communications.

Dil Muhammad Akbar Hussain is a professor of Electronics Engineering & Computer Science at the Department of Energy Technology, Aalborg University Denmark. Professor Akbar has a Master degree in Digital Electronics from Govt. College University, Lahore Pakistan and a P-hD degree in Control Engineering from the School of Engineering and Applied Sciences, University of Sussex United Kingdom. He has been serving since 1981 in the industry as well as in the academia in Pakistan, UK, Canada and now for the last 16 years at Aalborg University Denmark.

Saeed Ahmed Khan completed his bachelor of engineering (B.E) degree from Mehran university of engineering and technology Jamshoro in electronic engineering 2006, and master of engineering (M.E) in electronic system engineering in 2011 from Mehran UET Jamshoro. He holds Doctoral degree from university of electronic science and technology of China in 2017. He has more than 10 years' diverse experience in academia, industry, and research. Presently he is working as assistant professor at department of electrical engineering Sukkur IBA University.

Shamsuddin Lakho has done Bachelor of Electrical Engineering from sukkur IBA University in 2016, He is enrolled in Master of Electrical Engineering at Sukkur IBA University. He is also serving as Research Assistant at the Department of Electrical Engineering at Sukkur IBA University.

Jason Levy is a professor of public administration at the University of Hawaii who works with engineers, computer scientists and disaster managers to promote disaster resilience and socio-economic sustainability. Dr. Levy has received more than $3 million in research grants and worked at leading academic centers around the world. He has published over 50 peer reviewed journal publications and serves on the editorial boards of over a dozen academic journals. His research develops timely, interdisciplinary and effective Information and Computer Technologies for managing the unexpected, major and cascading impacts of hazards and disasters that cross policy domains, geographic, political and sectoral boundaries.

Hai Hiung Lo is a lecturer in Universiti Teknologi PETRONAS in the Electrical and Electronic Engineering Department. His research interest is in embedded systems and digital system design.

Maurizio Magarini received the M.Sc. and Ph.D. degrees in electronic engineering from the Politecnico di Milano, Milan, Italy, in 1994 and 1999, respectively. In 1994, he was granted the TELECOM Italia scholarship award for his M.Sc. Thesis. He worked as a Research Associate in the Dipartimento di Elettronica, Informazione e Bioingegneria at the Politecnico di Milano from 1999 to 2001. From 2001 to 2018, he was an Assistant Professor in Politecnico di Milano where, since June 2018, he has been an Associate Professor. From August 2008 to January 2009 he spent a sabbatical leave at Bell Labs, Alcatel-Lucent, Holmdel, NJ. His research interests are in the broad area of communication and information theory. Topics include synchronization, channel estimation, equalization and coding applied to wireless and optical communication systems. His most recent research activities have focused on molecular communications, massive MIMO, study of waveforms for 5G cellular systems, wireless sensor networks for mission critical applications, and wireless networks using unmanned aerial vehicles and high-altitude platforms. He has authored and coauthored more than 100 journal and conference papers. He was the co-recipient of two best-paper awards. Since 2017 he has been an Associate Editor of IEEE Access and of Nano Communication Networks (Elsevier). In 2017 he also served as Guest Editor for IEEE Access Special Section on "Networks of Unmanned Aerial Vehicles: Wireless Communications, Applications, Control and Modelling". He has been involved in several European and National research projects.

Izhar Hussain Memon completed his bachelor of engineering (BE) degree in electrical engineering in 2016 from Sukkur IBA University, He is enrolled in master of engineering (M.E) program at electrical engineering department Sukkur IBA University. He is also working as lecturer at Benazir Bhutto Shaheed University of Technology and skill development Khairpur since 2018.

Rafia Mumtaz received her first degree in software engineering at the Fatima Jinnah Women University, Pakistan. She received her Masters degree in software engineering from the National University of Sciences and Technology (NUST), Pakistan. She successfully completed her Ph.D. in 2010. She was awarded the Endowment Fund Scholarship during her masters studies in 2005. She was awarded a scholarship by NUST in 2006 for her Ph.D. stud- ies abroad. She joined the Astrodynamic Group at Surrey Space Centre, University of Surrey, UK in 2006 and worked on attitude determination of spacecraft. She is an assistant professor at School of Electrical Engineering and Computer Science (SEECS), National University of Sciences and Technology (NUST), Pakistan. Her research interest include remote sensing, Internet of things (IoT), machine learning and GIS. She is the recipient of a total of $103191 of research grants during her research career and has established several national and international collaborations in the domain of IoT and remote sensing. Zahid Anwar received his Ph.D. and M.S. degrees in Computer Sciences in 2008 and 2005 respec- tively from the University of Illinois at Urbana- Champaign. Zahid has worked as a software en- gineer and researcher at IBM, Intel, Motorola, National Center for Super-computing Applications (NCSA), xFlow Research and CERN on various projects related to information security, operating systems design and data analytics. Zahid holds post- doctorate experience from Concordia University. He has worked as a faculty member at the National University of Sciences and Technology and the University of North Carolina at Charlotte. He is currently an Assistant Professor at Fontbonne University. Hirra Anwar received her first degree in Computer and Information Sciences from Pakistan Institute of Engineering and Applied Sciences (PIEAS), Pak- istan. She received her Masters degree in Computer and Communication Security from the National Uni- versity of Sciences and Technology (NUST), Pak- istan. After her masters degree she worked as a researcher at the KTH-Applied Information Security lab at SEECS-NUST. Currently she is an Assistant Professor at School of Electrical Engineering and Computer Science (SEECS), National University of Sciences and Technology (NUST), Pakistan. Her research interests include Internet of things (IoT), Security aspects of IoT, Access control and cloud computing.

Badar Muneer was born in Mirpurkhas Pakistan in 1987. He received the B.S degree in communication systems engineering from Institute of Space Technology, Islamabad, Pakistan, in 2008 and the M.Engg Degree in Telecommunication Engineering from NED University of Engineering and Technology, Karachi, Pakistan, in 2012. He has a Ph.D. degree in Electromagnetism Field and Microwave Technology from University of Science and Technology of China (USTC), Hefei, P.R China. He is currently working as Associate Professor at Department of Telecommunication Engineering, Mehran UET Jamshoro, Pakistan. From 2016 to 2018, he has been associated with Chinese Academy of Science under President's International Fellowship Initiative (PIFI) as postdoctoral fellow. From 20 08 to 2011, he was with a satellite broadcasting company as a satellite engineer. He worked on VSAT, CATV and many modern broadcast equipment. His current research interests are in the area of microwave and millimeter-wave technology, SIW based power dividers and phase shifters and antennas, liquid metal antennas. He is also Senior Member of IEEE USA, faculty adviser of IEEE MTT society and life member of Pakistan Engineering Council.

Jayapandian N. is Currently Working as an Assistant professor at the CHRIST (Deemed to be University), Department of Computer Science and Engineering, Bangalore, India. His research interest includes information security, cloud computing, and grid computing. Dr. Jayapandian is completed PhD (Information & Communication Engineering) from Anna University. He holds a Bachelor of Technology degree in Information Technology from Anna University and Master Degree in Computer Science and Engineering from Anna University. He is published various research article in reputed international journals. He is an active reviewer of reputed international journals. He has participated in numerous national and international conferences and has made a remarkable contribution to cloud data security field and publishing several articles.

Thomas Newe, Senior Lecturer in Computer Engineering in the Department of Electronic & Computer Engineering at The University of Limerick. He holds a B.Eng. in Computer Engineering (1991), a Masters in Engineering in Security Protocol Design (1996) and a PhD in Formal Logics for Security Protocol Verification (2003).He has been a University of Limerick faculty member since 1994. His research interest include: Wireless Sensor Systems and Networks, Security protocol design for Data and the Cloud, Network Security, Security protocol formal verification methods, Cryptography/Encryption algorithms, Embedded system programming, Digital design, Programming languages, Operating systems, Smart cards security protocols, Digital Watermarking and Watermark Benchmarking tools. He has graduated a number of PhD students in the broad area of network security. His students are funded from a variety of sources including: EU, SFI, IRCSET, Internationally and industrially funded.

Shahzad Nizamani, Assistant Professor in the Department of Software Engineering at Mehran University of Engineering & Technology. He did his Bachelors in Software Engineering (2004) and Masters in Information Technology (2006) and PhD in Cloud Computing (2012). His research interests are: Services Oriented Architectures in Cloud Computing, Knowledge Management, Programming Languages, Semantic Technologies and Mobile Computing.

Pablo Otero received the Ingeniero de Telecomunicacion degree from the Polytechnic University of Madrid (UPM), Madrid, Spain, in 1983, and the Ph.D. degree in electrical engineering from the Swiss Federal Institute of Technology (EPFL), Lausanne, Switzerland, in 1998. From 1983 to 1993, he was with the Spanish companies Standard Electrica, E.N. Bazan, and Telefonica, where he was involved in communication and radar systems engineering. In 1993, he joined the University of Seville, Seville, Spain, where he lectured for two years. In 1996, he joined the Laboratory of Electromagnetism and Acoustics, EPFL, where he was a Research Associate, granted by the Spanish Government. In 1998, he joined the University of Malaga, Malaga, Spain, where he is currently an Associate Professor. His research interests include electromagnetic and antenna engineering, underwater communications, and violin acoustics.

Bishwajeet Pandey is a co-founder of Gyancity Research Lab. Gyancity Research Lab organizes three conferences (ICGCET.ORG, RTCSE.ORG, IMCES.TECH) across the globe. He has completed his PhD in CSE from GSSI, Italy. He has worked as Asst. Professor in Department of Research at Chitkara University, Junior Research Fellow (JRF) at South Asian University. He has completed Master of Technology (IIIT Gwalior) in CSE with Specialization in VLSI, Master of Computer Application, R&D Project in CDAC-Noida. He has authored and coauthored over 128 paper available on his Scopus Profile: https://www.scopus.com/authid/detail.uri?authorId=57203239026. He has 1284 Citation according to his Google Scholar Profile: https://scholar.google.co.in/citations?user=UZ_8yAMAAAAJ&hl=en.

Javier Poncela received the M.Sc. degree in telecommunication engineering from the Polytechnic University of Madrid, Spain, in 1994 and the Ph.D. degree from the University of Málaga, Spain. He worked in Alcatel Spacio before joining the University of Málaga at the Communication Engineering Department. He has actively collaborated with multinational companies (Nokia, AT4wireless) on formal modeling and system testing in Bluetooth, UMTS and satellite systems. His actual research interests include methodologies for efficient development of complex communications systems, analysis of end-to-end QoS over heterogeneous networks and systems and models for the evaluation of QoE.

Abdul Qadir Rahimoon has been working with various educational institutions for the past 19 years, he has been affiliated with Sukkur IBA from past 7 years. His research publications has also been published in reputable national and international journals. He got his BS and MS degrees both in Physics from University of Sindh Jamshoro, and PhD degree form Beijing institute of technology china in 2010.

Bhawana Rudra is working as an Assistant Professor at the National Institute of Technology, Karnataka since May 2018. She has worked in various institutions and wrote a text book titled" Flexible Network Architectures Security Principles and Issues. Her interests includes future Internet architectures, Network Protocols, security in routing, Security in Wireless Networks, Loosely coupled protocols and its security, service and composition security, attribute-based authentication, Vector based Identification, Authorization, Confidentiality, Integrity, Availability of the resources. She has published extensively in the areas of security in networks includes Internet of Things, Network Security topic. Dr. Rudra earned Ph.D. degree in Information Technology, March 2015, at Indian institute of Information Technology-Allahabad. She also has a Master degree in Computer Science from SRM University, May 2010. In addition, she earned other degrees from India. She is the reviewer for various Conferences and Journals and is frequently invited to present lectures and tutorials and to participate in panels related to networking and security topics in various parts of India.

Thanmayee S. is working as Assistant Lecturer in the Department of Information Technology, NITK, Karnataka. She has seven years of Teaching experience and one year of Industry experience. Her areas of interest are Internet of Things, Cloud Computing, Big Data, Information Retrieval.

Abu Bakar Sayuti has been teaching at Universiti Teknologi PETRONAS for almost 20 years in courses related to microprocessors, embedded systems and computer programming. He holds a Bachelor of Engineering (Electrical, Electronic & System) from Universiti Kebangsaan Malaysia, and MSc Embedded Systems from University of Manchester Institute of Science and Technology. In his free time, he likes to dable in programming and tinkering with microcontrollers. Once in while he came out with a useful software or two, and a couple of interesting embedded system projects. But his real passion is in sharing his knowledge, however limited it may be, with others.

Patrick Sebastian is currently a Senior Lecturer in the Electrical and Electronic Engineering Department at Universiti Teknologi PETRONAS (UTP). He received his PhD in Parameteric Tracking with Spatial Extraction Across An Array of Cameras from Middlesex University, London. He has interests in the areas of Computer Architectures, Embedded systems, Image Processing and Video Surveillance. Prior to his current appointment, Patrick was a Senior Engineer and a Black Belt Six Sigma at Penang Seagate Industries Malaysia.

Uferah Shafi did MS in Computer Science from Comsats University Islamabad, currently she is doing PhD in Computer Science from School of Electrical Engineering and Computer Science (SEECS)/

NUST Pakistan. Her research areas include Internet of Things, Deep Learning, Computer Vision and Remote Sensing.

Navuday Sharma received his M-Tech in avionics engineering from Institute of Space Science and Technology, Amity University, Uttar Pradesh, India, in 2015 and Ph.D. degree in telecommunication engineering from the Department of Electronics, Information and Bio-engineering (DEIB), Politecnico di Milano, Italy, in 2018. He was also a Research Engineer at Infocomm Lab, School of Computer Science and Robotics, Tomsk Polytechnic University, Russia, from Oct 2017 to June 2018. Currently, he is currently working as a Post-Doctoral Researcher at Thomas Johann Seebeck Department of Electronics, Tallinn University of Technology, Estonia. He has worked on wireless communication with aerial base stations for 5G systems and currently working towards ultra-reliable low latency communication. His other research interests are channel modeling, multi-carrier communication, digital signal processing and internet of things.

Christopher Teh Jun Qian received his degree in Electrical and Electronic Engineering with Honours from Universiti Teknologi PETRONAS in 2018, where he is currently pursuing his MSc degree. He also completed his internship as a research assistant at the University of Applied Sciences Upper Austria in creating an acoustical sensor system to detect applied brakes of train wagons.

Ning Wu was born in Anhui Province, China, in 1956. She received B.S. and M.S. degrees in 1982 and 1985 from University of Science and Technology of China. She is currently a professor and a Ph.D. supervisor in the Department of Electronic Engineering, Nanjing University of Aeronautics and Astronautics. Her research interests include digital system theory and technology, network on chip design, ANN/CNN/Machine Learning based architectures, electronic system integration and ASIC design.

Muhammad Rehan Yahya completed his BS and MS from COMSATS institute of Information technology, Islamabad and UET Taxila, Pakistan respectively. Currently, he is a doctoral student in College of Electronic and Information Engineering, Nanjing University of Aeronautics and Astronautics. His research interests include optical and hybrid Network-on Chip (NOC) architectures, optimization of Network-on Chip, FPGA / ASIC implementations and reconfigurable hardware design.

Syed Ali Raza Zaidi is a University Academic Fellow (Assistant Professor) at the University of Leeds in the area of wireless communication & sensing systems. From 2013-2015, he was associated with the SPCOM research group working on the United States Army Research Lab funded project in the area of Network Science. From 2011-2013, he was associated with the International University of Rabat working as a Lecturer. He was also a visiting research scientist at Qatar Innovations and Mobility Centre from October-December 2013 working on QNRF funded project QSON. He received his Doctoral Degree at the School of Electronic and Electrical Engineering at Leeds and was awarded the G. W. and F. W. Carter Prize for best thesis and best research paper. He has published more than 100 papers in leading IEEE conferences and journals. From 2014-2015, he served as an editor for IEEE Communication Letters. He was also lead guest editor for IET Signal Processing Journal's Special Issue on Signal Processing for Large Scale 5G Wireless Networks. Currently, he is an Associate Technical Editor for IEEE Communication Magazine. Dr. Zaidi is EURASIP Local Liaison for United Kingdom and also General Secretary for IEEE Technical Subcommittee on Backhaul and Fronthaul networks. He is also an active member of EPSRC Peer Review College. His research interests are in the area of design and implementation large scale ad-hoc wireless communication networks for robotics.

Qi Zhu was born in Hefei, Anhui, China in 1968. He received the B. S. and M. S. degrees in physics from Hefei University of Technology in 1989 and 1992, and received Ph. D. degree in airplane from Nanjing University of Aeronautics and Astronautics. In 1998, He joined University of Science and Technology of China (USTC), as an Associate Professor and now he is working for USTC as a Professor. His research interests are in the area of microwave and millimeter-wave technology, electromagnetic theory.

Index

A

Actuator 1, 9, 77
Aerial Base Station 107, 110, 130, 132
Agriculture 16, 71, 108, 134-138, 140, 152-155, 201, 216
AI 94-95, 142
Air-to-Ground Channel 107
Ambient Assisted Living (AAL) 1, 5, 11, 28, 215
Antennas 132, 180, 182-185, 187, 189-192

B

Battery 13, 29, 34-37, 45-50, 68-70, 73-74, 83-86, 88-91, 128, 136, 183, 204-205, 229
Biomechanical energy 29, 42
Biosignals 30, 32, 37, 44

C

Carrier Frequency Offset 111, 129
Cell Coverage 107, 110, 117-119, 121, 132
Cloud computing 2, 6, 9-10, 23, 52-55, 64-66, 153, 177, 194, 197-198, 200, 213, 218, 220, 226, 240
Cloud Federation 52, 54-55
Cloud Operations Management 52

E

Environmental Monitoring 68, 70-73, 92, 174

F

Flexible sensors 45
Food security 134-135, 151, 154
FPGA 94, 101-103, 105-106, 113, 231, 243

G

Generalized Frequency Division Multiplexing 107, 111, 129, 131

H

Hardware Trojan 218-219, 238-240, 242-243, 245
Healthcare monitoring 1, 27, 32, 37, 173, 178
Human skin 29, 33-34
Hybrid Cloud and IoT 52

I

IEEE802.15.4, 155
Industry IoT 193, 198-202, 206-207, 212
Institute of Medicine (IOM) 4
Integrated Chips (IC) 218
International Telecommunication Union 1-3
Internet of Things (IoT) 1-31, 37, 42-44, 49, 52-53, 64-66, 68-73, 91-92, 94, 96-106, 108-109, 129-131, 134-138, 140-141, 145-146, 151-157, 173-178, 180-181, 183-185, 187-191, 193-208, 211-221, 226-227, 233, 237, 240-241, 244-245
IoT applications 1, 7, 19, 23, 52, 64, 70, 91, 100, 106, 178, 180-181, 185, 190-191, 202-203, 212, 218-221, 226-227, 237
IoT Architectures 94
IoT European Research Cluster 1, 3
IPv6 8, 11, 13, 18, 27-28, 73, 94-96, 101-104, 155, 157-158, 160-165, 167-171, 173, 175-177
IPv6 low power personal area networks (6LoWPAN) 6, 8, 11, 13, 25-28, 155, 157-163, 165, 171-179

L

Lifetime 13, 34, 68-70, 73-74, 80-81, 85-86, 88-91, 110, 156-158

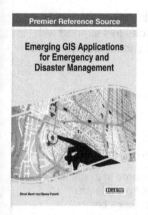
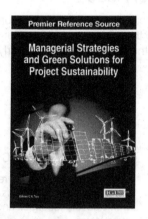